Harriet Jacobs, today perhaps the single most read and studied black American woman of the nineteenth century, has not – until now – been the subject of sustained, scholarly analysis. This anthology presents a far-ranging compendium of literary and cultural scholarship that is sure to become the primary resource for students and teachers of Jacobs's *Incidents in the Life of a Slave Girl*. The contributors include both established Jacobs scholars – such as Jean Fagan Yellin (Jacobs biographer and editor of the annotated edition of *Incidents*), Frances Smith Foster, and Donald B. Gibson – and emerging critics Sandra Gunning, P. Gabrielle Foreman, and Anita Goldman. The essays take on a variety of subjects from *Incidents,* treating representation, gender, resistance, and spirituality from differing angles. The chapters seek to contextualize both the historical figure of Harriet Jacobs and her autobiography as a created work of art; all endeavor to be accessible to a heterogeneous readership.

D1082023

CAMBRIDGE STUDIES IN AMERICAN LITERATURE AND CULTURE

Harriet Jacobs and *Incidents in the Life of a Slave Girl*

Continued on pages following the Index

HARRIET JACOBS AND
INCIDENTS IN THE
LIFE OF A SLAVE GIRL

NEW CRITICAL ESSAYS

Edited by

DEBORAH M. GARFIELD
University of California, Los Angeles

RAFIA ZAFAR
University of Michigan

CAMBRIDGE
UNIVERSITY PRESS

Published by the Press Syndicate of the University of Cambridge
The Pitt Building, Trumpington Street, Cambridge CB2 1RP
40 West 20th Street, New York, NY 10011-4211, USA
10 Stamford Road, Oakleigh, Melbourne 3166, Australia

First published 1996

Printed in the United States of America

Library of Congress Cataloging-in-Publication Data
Harriet Jacobs and incidents in the life of a slave girl : new
critical essays / edited by Deborah M. Garfield, Rafia Zafar.
    p.   cm. – (Cambridge studies in American literature and
                        culture)
          Includes bibliographical references.
      ISBN 0–521–44360–1 (hc). – ISBN 0–521–49779–5 (pb)
    1. Jacobs, Harriet A. (Harriet Ann), 1813–1897. Incidents in the
life of a slave girl.   2. Slaves – United States – Biography – History
and criticism.   3. Women slaves – United States – Biography – History
and criticism.   I. Garfield, Deborah.   II. Zafar, Rafia.
                        III. Series.
                  E444.J17H37   1996
973′.04960–dc20   95–4225
                                                              CIP
A catalog record for this book is available from the British Library.

        ISBN 0–521–44360–1 hardback
        ISBN 0–521–49779–5 paperback

CONTENTS

INTRODUCTION
OVER-EXPOSED, UNDER-EXPOSED

HARRIET JACOBS AND INCIDENTS IN THE LIFE OF A SLAVE GIRL

RAFIA ZAFAR

———

for Nellie Y. McKay

As the coeditor of this volume, my tasks have been fairly specific and predict-
able: I have provided editorial feedback to the contributors, served as a liaison between scholars and press, and written this introductory essay. As a
scholar of African American literature who happens also to be an African
American female, however, the questions associated with my tasks have been
less specific but perhaps more taxing: Where do I stand in relation to this
undertaking? That is to say, has my role in putting together this collection, on
the autobiography of a long-deceased, female, ex-slave, been overdetermined? Fellow scholar Ann duCille noted recently that the rapid increase of
scholarship about black women has "led me to think of myself as a kind of
sacred text. Not me personally, of course, but me black woman object,
Other." What does it mean, she inquired, for "black women academics to
stand in the midst of . . . the traffic jam . . . that black feminist studies has
become?"[1] For to introduce a collection of essays about Harriet Jacobs is not
simply to present a body of scholarly works; it is also to comment upon the
curious resurrection of one particular "black woman object" and her justly
renowned autobiography, *Incidents in the Life of a Slave Girl.*

Such comments may seen strange indeed, especially within the context of
an essay that seeks to situate Harriet Jacobs and her contemporary critics for a
heterogeneous leadership. But there exists a long history of black authorship mid-
wived into national life via a circle of well-intentioned helpmeets – the youngest
scholar of African American letters should be able to recognize an authenticating document when she sees one.[2] That past, like it or not, will necessarily be
reiterated by this current undertaking. To air the quandaries introduced by the

I

existence of our anthology brings us a step past the partnership of Harriet
Jacobs and Lydia Maria Child, an alliance that could only sign at the fissures in
the purported transracial sisterhood of American abolitionism.[3] It may appear
odd to find two women editors, one black, one white, framing the criticism on a
work whose existence long ago played out another association between black
and white women, but it is not without precedent. The secret history of any
number of black women's creative works would tell a similar tale.

Overexposed, underexposed – or not exposed at all: these days it seems
that *Incidents* is on every undergraduate reading list, and that a half-dozen
students in my classes on African American writers have read Jacobs for another class, often in Women's studies. At such times it looks as though Jacobs
is in the process of achieving her "market share," and that the rest will be
history written by lions, if not lionesses. As Jacobs once said in another context, "it is a vast improvement in *my* condition." If the voiced "dream of her
life" was to live with her children in a home of her own, was there another,
unuttered, dream – to have her autobiography placed beside other significant texts of the nineteenth century, to have her life story in its own, literary
home? If one considers how public Jacobs's life and activism became following the appearance of *Incidents,* then believing that she did speculate on a
textual home seems not so farfetched. That *Incidents* may now have such a
permanent home can only recently be said to be the case – courtesy of us late-
twentieth-century critics, with our own agendas, power, and career moves.
The apparent suddenness of Jacobs's entry onto the scene of American literary history can be negated by an examination of the debate swirling around
Jacobs's authenticity (a discussion still capable of generating heat): the argument has been going for some time. Still, for all intents and purposes, it appears that Harriet Jacobs and her autobiography are brand new and permanent members of United States literary history.

Incidents and its authors can be said to be enjoying a kind of overnight success, a vogue not unlike that which sprang up around Zora Neale Hurston
and her works not long ago.[4] I do use the word "vogue" deliberately, for its
connotation of academic fashion speaks to the downside of the university:
Jacobs's recent appearances on campus reading lists reminds me of Genaro
Padilla's remark about how mainstream scholars have discovered other new
voices in literary studies – these writers are not new, he said, they've been "in
the room" the entire time; they were not "silent," they just were "not heard."[5]
The inclusion of Jacobs and *Incidents* within a syllabus on "Classic" American
literature does not by itself indicate a rethinking of the list itself; merely to add
Jacobs, without reimagining the context of that syllabus, exemplifies the
Band-aid approach to literary studies.[6] Excited as I am to see Jacobs's renaissance, I must remind myself that it is just that: a re-birth, not a birth.[7]

Harriet Jacobs was born in Edenton, North Carolina, in 1813, the daughter of
the enslaved Delilah and Daniel Jacobs.[8] As the daughter of slaves, the young

Harriet might have been expected to know hardship early. Instead, as she writes in the opening paragraph of *Incidents,* "I was so fondly shielded that I never dreamed I was a piece of merchandise." She does not know that her life is not her own – nor indeed her parents' – until she is six years old (5). When Jacobs's mother dies, she is sent to live in the household of Margaret Horniblow, the white woman who claimed Molly Horniblow, Jacobs's maternal grandmother, and all of her lineal descendants. Apparently kind and religious, Mrs. Horniblow teaches young Jacobs to read and spell. And yet, while recognizing the girl's intellect, the older woman "did not recognize [Jacobs] as her neighbor" (8), and on her death wills the child to her niece, Matilda Norcom. So the now eleven-year-old girl is given over to the antagonist of her life, her new owner's father, Dr. James Norcom; shortly after that she begins her decades-long freedom struggle. The physician, who holds a number of men, women, and children in his power, desires more from Jacobs than mere physical possession; he wants her complicity in her own sexual degradation. Fortunately, her inner strength – formed in part by the sheer luck of having lived her early childhood in a relatively intact African American family – gives the young woman the courage and strength to resist Norcom's "soul-destroying" concubinage. Her blighted love for a free black man, the torments that Norcom visits on the Horniblow–Jacobs family, the escape that was not an escape, her unceasing efforts on behalf of her children: all are detailed in *Incidents* by Jacobs under a "slave girl's" pseudonym. Remaining anonymous as an author, Jacobs uses instead the character of "Linda Brent" to stand in for both her own self and those of the millions of her oppressed countrywomen.

When Jacobs writes "Reader, be assured this narrative is no fiction," she is well aware that she must begin, before even writing of her birth, by breaking down the walls of prejudice and disbelief between her and her white audience. Rather than embellish her own story, Jacobs says "my descriptions fall far short of the facts" (1). From the time of the first slave who dared tell the story of enslavement, African Americans have faced a hostile, disbelieving audience; but as Robert Stepto has remarked of African American narratives, "it is the reader – not the author or text and certainly not the storyteller in the text – who is unreliable."[9] Jacobs, a woman with a woman's story of sexual oppression and frustrated motherhood, had more reader resistance to overcome than her male counterparts, then and now. As Frances Smith Foster tells us, "Jacobs has more than once been accused of having omitted or distorted details of her own life in order to enhance her personal reputation or to achieve artistic effect"; she had to contend with notions as to how her "victories and values contrast with prevailing theories and opinions of slave life." Jacobs also, at least at the time of the original publication, had to contend with shifting currents in the American political scene. Yellin notes that at the time of its first edition, *Incidents* was received politely, if not appreciatively, but that with the coming of the Civil War the appearance of "another" slave narrative may have "seemed of minor importance."[10] The book, in other words, did not have the impact of Frederick Douglass's first autobiography, *Narrative of the Life of Frederick Douglass* (1845), nor a good-sized fraction of that of Harriet Beecher Stowe's *Uncle Tom's Cabin* (1852), a novel against which Jacobs implicitly framed her story. Jacobs's scrutiny of the particular, sexualized oppression of black slave women may have played a part in its relatively quiet, if benign, reception: as Lydia Maria Child noted in her introduction to the volume, "delicate" ears (4) might have trouble listening to Jacobs's harrowing tale.

Until well into the twentieth century, the reception of *Incidents* attested to the continuing difficulty of Jacobs's, or any black woman writer's, gaining an audience: faced with the "double negative" of black race and female gender, Jacobs, like Wheatley before her and Hurston after her, had to contend with a skeptical readership that said her work could not be "genuine" because of her emphasis on the domestic, her "melodramatic" style, and her unwillingness to depict herself as an avatar of self-reliance.[11] Deborah McDowell rightly identifies much of the problem as lying with "contemporary scholarship on [slave narratives] . . . making the slave a man, according to cultural norms of masculinity."[12] For breaking from this recognized pattern of male slave narrators – Harriet Jacobs is alone among antebellum female writers of book-length secular autobiographies – Jacobs was either decried as inauthentic or dismissed as atypical. One hundred and twelve years were to elapse between the anonymous publication of *Incidents in the Life of a Slave Girl* and the first modern reprint edited by Walter Teller.[13] A century and a quarter would pass before Jacobs's autobiography received a comprehensive, scholarly treatment by Jean Fagan Yellin. The "changing sameness" (McDowell 193) would, at last, shift.

The Modern Language Association, the main organization of literary scholars in the United States academy, publishes an annual record of critical works – in earlier years this compilation appeared in one or more bound volumes; one can now use an electronic compilation. A browse through this online Modern Language Association *Bibliography* provides the outlines, if not the origins, of the sea change leading to Harriet Jacobs's sudden visibility.[14] Despite the appearance of the Teller edition, which followed the late 1960s resurgence of interest in African American writers, the first reference to *Incidents* in the MLA Bibliography does not appear until 1981, or nearly a decade later. (Although a proliferation of references in the *Bibliography* hardly bespeaks canonical status for a work, it does reveal changing trends in scholarship. An examination of citations in a similar compendium for historians of the United States, *America: History and Life*, seemed to demonstrate a similar trajectory: that is, I could find no citations on Jacobs between 1964 and 1980, despite the reissue of Jacobs's autobiography in 1969; between 1980 and 1992, however, the incidence of references rises steadily, from one or two every year in the early to mid-1980s, to a peak of ten citations in 1988 – the year after Yellin's Harvard edition was published – and then four per year in the early 1990s.[15]) Following the MLA's initial notice of Jean Fagan Yellin's first published essay on Jacobs (1981), its listings on Jacobs for the rest of the decade number only a dozen; in 1983 and 1984 no references to Jacobs can be found at all. Yet a number of recent book-length works on African American literature that treated Jacobs in some detail are not included: Joanne M. Braxton's *Black Women Writing Autobiography* (1989), William Andrews's *To Tell a Free Story* (1986), and Hazel Carby's *Reconstructing Womanhood* (1987) are three; at least two essays treating Jacobs, published since September 1990, are also not noted in the bibliography. Sandra Gunning reminds us that this apparent rise to visibility – that is, the steadily increasing references to Jacobs in the *Bibliography* – does not demonstrate that Jacobs was previously "unread" or "unstudied"; black women scholars had been aware of, and discussing, the former slave for some time.[16] The justly influential anthology *But Some of Us Are Brave: Black Women's Studies* (1982) confirmed the work African American women scholars had been performing during the 1970s and earlier.[17] We should not depend on what materials the MLA *Bibliography* includes to estimate scholarly attention, nor should we confuse the so-called center of academic discourse with the sum of intellectual work.

As counterpoint to the unnoted yet published works discussing Jacobs, we should examine the MLA *Bibliography*'s listing of recent dissertations. Again, according to my surveys of the *Bibliography*, no dissertations on Jacobs appeared prior to the 1990s, although I know there were theses completed before then that treated *Incidents* in some detail.[18] Beginning with Harryette Mullen's "Gender and the Subjugated Body" in 1990, dissertations appear to be catalogued in part due to their use of Jacobs as a subject – and thus in the 1990s we find at least ten dissertations reviewing Jacobs in more than a cursory fashion.[19] This increase in such "key words" as "Jacobs, Harriet" or "*Incidents in the Life of a Slave Girl*" since the beginning of this decade merits our contemplation, for, as of 1993, no slowdown of research on Jacobs appears to have occurred; if anything, materials on *Incidents* are proliferating.[20] That the academic "mainstream" has taken up this particular ex-slave narrator as a new subject for analyses that seek to incorporate attention to "race, class, and gender" tells us as much about the "objective" production of knowledge as it does about shifts in academic tastes and agendas. As two critics – one black, one white – have remarked:

> I am hardly alone in suspecting that the [current] overwhelming interest in black women may have at least as much to do with the pluralism and perhaps even the primitivism of this particular postmodern moment as with the stunning quality of black women's accomplishments and the breadth of their contributions to American civilization. . . . In

the midst of the present, multicultural moment, they [black women writers such as Jacobs] have become politically correct, intellectually popular, and commercially precious sites of literary and historical inquiry. (Ann duCille)

[Viewing literature as a] "talking cure" for social ills . . . often exacerbates the impasses it describes and frequently substitutes the critic's own agency for the textual agency supposedly being restored. . . . [What does] it mean for us to recover or recuperate Jacobs' agency when we, as readers, are problematically and unavoidably implicated in the process of its construction? . . . What forms of authority and power do we bring to this text?" (Carla Kaplan)[21]

A caveat then: as much as it is true to assert that *Incidents in the Life of a Slave Girl* has been long overdue for placement within the canon of American literature, it may also be accurate to say that intrinsic worth alone has not brought it to this pinnacle of success. For lack of value could not account for the absence of citations on Jacobs in the pre-1980s MLA *Bibliography*.

Happily, Jacobs's ascent demonstrates more than the slippery terrain of contemporary academia. Her rising fortunes mirror the establishment in the academy of an ever-increasing cohort of scholars, senior and junior, who are themselves black and female. How much coincidence is there, after all, in the rise of articles and books on Phillis Wheatley, Pauline Hopkins, Harriet Jacobs, Zora Neale Hurston, and others, and the appearance of a cohort of African American women in Ivy League and other historically white institutions? How different, and fortunate for the academy, that the career history of a Marion Wilson Starling – whose groundbreaking dissertation, "The Slave's Narrative" (New York University, 1946), did not appear as a book until more than three decades had passed – has been superseded by that of our contributor Frances Smith Foster, whose first book, *Witnessing Slavery* (1979) and most recent, *Written by Herself* (1993), bracket years of productive, *public* scholarship. That black women such as Barbara Christian, Nellie Y. McKay, Hortense Spillers, Mary Helen Washington, and others named herein and elsewhere have reached tenured positions in historically white institutions has much to do with the ever-increasing visibility, if not importance, of Harriet Jacobs and her literary descendants.

Jacobs, a missing person in African American, women's, and nineteenth-century studies for so long, now appears ubiquitous; her autobiography crops up on syllabi in American history, Feminist studies, Africana studies, literature of the United States, and other departmental affiliations. The disappearance and materialization of *Incidents* underscores the arguments against and for African American and Women's studies: if one segregates the study of blacks and females, "mainstream" disciplines will not feel required to include such subjects in their curricula and the status quo will indeed remain the same; if one simply adds such material within the context of a standard course on American literature or history, their specific qualities will dissipate into the utopian American melting pot. Does the apparent pervasiveness of Harriet Jacobs represent the triumph of the "minority" or "underrepresented" studies, the deserved success of a rediscovered classic? Can we fairly say Jacobs is overexposed, or is this current efflorescence confirmation of her long-running underexposure?

As the reader will shortly discover, the new scholarship on Harriet Jacobs answers – and raises – many more questions than I possibly can. From the reverential to the revelatory, the readings of her work collected here span the realm of scholarly thought. This collection proffers a portrait of critical thinking about Harriet Jacobs in the 1990s. Our contributors range from those with established reputations to those on the brink of confirming their place in the academy. The essays seek to contextualize both the historical figure of Harriet Jacobs and her autobiography as a created work of art; all endeavor to be accessible to a heterogeneous readership. Because early scholars often doubted Jacobs's authenticity, citing her autobiography's inability to fit within the parameters of the slave narrative, many of our writers seek to understand and explore that long-running suspicion; because Jacobs's evident emphasis on family and collective action, when opposed to more individualistic conceptions of liberty, can be viewed as anachronistic, a number of our essayists try to examine what effects that perspective had on the gendering of American scholarship. We are fortunate to be able to present such a collectivity of insights as we have gathered: female and male, tenured faculty and doctoral student, African American and European American.

If we find Harriet Jacobs's life story unique in any number of ways, we can also find it so for its being truly a twice-told tale: recounted by Jacobs herself and again by her sibling, who was, like her, an escaped slave and abolitionist speaker. Two of our contributors find this especially pertinent to their analyses: Jacqueline D. Goldsby tackles the ticklish questions of verisimilitude in life writing, especially as they pertain to the study of African American autobiography, and Jacobs's biographer and contemporary editor, Jean Fagan Yellin, re-views Jacobs's "real life" by a close reading of the Jacobs siblings' varying accounts of the sister's bondage, self-imprisonment, and freedom.[22]

Issues of legitimacy and prerogative draw the attention of several of our scholars. In her essay, Frances Smith Foster turns her scrutiny on Jacobs's critics, much as they have interrogated their subject; as nay-sayers from 1861 to the present have questioned the author, so Foster looks for unexamined agendas. The conjunction of the words "sex" and "the black woman" generally predicts another minefield of authenticity, and several scholars attempt to rehabilitate the critical discussion of the African American female and sexuality. P. Gabrielle Foreman uncovers a veritable minefield of quarrels over authenticity, most specifically received critical notions on the black woman's sexuality and oppression. Deborah Garfield analyzes the complex system of signs under which a black woman can be enslaved, by white slaveowners and abolitionists alike. Sandra Gunning's essay breaks down the prurient and judgmental readings of the black woman's body that Jacobs's white audience, past and present, does not want to acknowledge.

No comprehensive examination of *Incidents* can avoid the entwined issues of motherhood, "the domestic sphere," and the folk, especially as those matters bear on the black community. Donald Gibson looks therefore at the competing yet finally complementary ideals of the African American family as limned by Jacobs and Frederick Douglass, her much anthologized antecedent. John Ernest examines the collision between ideologies of patriotic motherhood and the realities of slave parenthood, while Mary Titus demonstrates that to be a slave was not only to be in bondage but, quite literally, to be sickened.

To be a slave was also to engage in oppositional acts, as the last group of our contributors attest. Anne Bradford Warner's essay discusses the African Jonkannau festival, presenting Jacobs as a trickster in a world of bitter humor. Anita Goldman shrewdly perceives Harriet Jacobs as part of a long and prominent line of American civil disobedients. Stephanie Smith's essay demonstrates how Jacobs takes on the masculinist language of American patriarchy to construct her own declaration of independence.

There is no better illustration of the rapidly changing critical landscape in American literary studies than the study, and seemingly instant canonization, of *Incidents in the Life of a Slave Girl*; the essays of our contributors underscore the complexity and breadth of Jacobs scholarship and the larger society it reflects. Harriet Jacobs may have sought and welcomed the editorial aid of Lydia Maria Child, but she also struggled to ensure that she would tell her own story. So do the contributors, from each of their complementary perspectives, seek to honor and situate this nineteenth-century black woman's pioneering autobiography within a critical, historical, and cultural continuum.

"Reader, be assured this narrative is no fiction."

Notes

My thanks go to the following individuals: my friend and contributor, Sandra Gunning, who helped me refine this essay and its title, too; Jean Fagan Yellin, for encouraging words at the right time; the project's first Cambridge editor, Julie Greenblatt, and its current one, the inestimable Susan Chang; guiding spirit Eric Sundquist; my coeditor, Deborah Garfield; P. A. Skantze; and Drs. Joseph P. Lynch, III and Teresa M. Hunt. I would also like to thank my colleagues on the 1993 American Studies Association panel, "Nineteenth Century Activist Women of Letters": our impending meeting lent wings to my fingers, if not my thoughts.

1. Ann duCille, "The Occult of True Black Womanhood: Critical Demeanor and Black Feminist Studies," *SIGNS* 19:3 (Spring 1994): 591, 593.

2. Such "documents written by slaveholders and abolitionists alike" are intended to "authenticate the former slave's account"; see Robert B. Stepto, *From Behind the Veil. A Study of African American Narrative,* 2nd ed. (Urbana: University of Illinois Press, 1991), 3.

3. See Deborah Garfield's epilogue to this volume, "Vexed Alliances: Race and Female Collaboration in the Life of Harriet Jacobs," for an exploration of this dilemma.

4. In 1985 I gave a paper at the New England American Studies Association conference on Hurston's similar "fall and rise." Hurston enjoyed a certain amount of fame, if not notoriety, in her heyday; nevertheless the former Guggenheim fellow died penniless, with her works out of print.

5. Genaro Padilla, Introduction to "Marginality" session, "Autobiography and Self-Representation" Conference, University of California, Irvine, March 3, 1990.

6. My Cambridge colleague Susie Chang reminds me of the "and-Alice-Walker" school of canon-expansion.

7. My friend and colleague P. A. Skantze sketched parallels between Jacobs's sudden "centrality" and recent critical shifts around the seventeenth-century English dramatist Aphra Behn. She noted that scholars tend to underemphasize the significance of *teaching* such writers as Jacobs and Behn, worrying instead about "overexposure" in the critical sense (that is, in the production of scholarly articles). Do classicists worry that their students have read Aristophanes "already"?

8. For biographical information I rely not only on Jacobs's autobiography but also on the research of my esteemed colleague Jean Fagan Yellin. See, for example, her "Chronology," in *Incidents in the Life of a Slave Girl,* ed. Jean Fagan Yellin (Cambridge: Harvard University Press, 1987), 223. All further citations to the text refer to this edition.

   It can be safely said that this anthology could not exist as such without Jean Yellin's literary and historical detective work. By her previous scholarship and current contribution to this project, and by her generous encouragement and support, she has enriched us immeasurably.

9. Robert Stepto, "Distrust of the Reader in Afro-American Narratives," *Reconstructing American Literary History,* ed. Sacvan Bercovitch (Cambridge: Harvard University Press, 1986), 309.

10. Frances Smith Foster, "Resisting *Incidents*," in this volume. In the best sense I hope Professor Foster's essay on this issue will be the last word; my apologies to the reader for having to cover some of the same ground. See also Jean Fagan Yellin's "Introduction" to *Incidents,* xxiii–xxviii.

11. John Blassingame may have been one prominent male scholar who found Jacobs's story unbelievable, but he was not alone in this conviction. Hazel Carby's discussion of Blassingame's initial assessment delivers a solid, convincing counter-argument. See John Blassingame, "Critical Essay on Sources," *The Slave Community: Plantation Life in the Antebellum South,* 2nd ed. (New York: Oxford University Press, 1979), 367–82, and Hazel V. Carby, *Reconstructing Womanhood: The Emergence of the Afro-American Woman Novelist* (New York: Oxford University Press, 1987), esp. 45–6. Despite the work of senior feminist scholars like Carby,

Frances Smith Foster, and Yellin, scholars continue to dispute Jacobs's sole authorship.

12. See Deborah McDowell's "In the First Place: Making Frederick Douglass and the Afro-American Narrative Tradition," for a superb analysis of the "gendering" of African American literary scholarship. In *Critical Essays on Frederick Douglass*, ed. William L. Andrews (Boston: G. K. Hall & Company, 1991), 195.

13. "Linda Brent" [Harriet Jacobs], *Incidents in the Life of a Slave Girl*, ed. Walter Teller (New York: Harcourt, Brace, Jovanovich, 1973).

14. Many thanks to Judy Avery of the Michigan Graduate Library for her assistance with the on-line version of the Modern Language Association Bibliography, which has now become the standard (according to the MLA, the on-line and CD-ROM versions are the most accurate listings available).

15. See the indexes for *America: History and Life* (Santa Barbara, CA: ABC-Clio Press) for 1964–92.

16. Sandra Gunning, personal communication, October 15, 1993.

17. Various courses on black women's literature were offered prior to the 1980s, including, for example, those of Alice Walker (1972), Gloria Hull (1976), and Fahamisha Shariat (1977). See *But Some of Us Are Brave: Black Women's Studies*, ed. Gloria T. Hull, Patricia Bell Scott, and Barbara Smith (Old Westbury, NY: The Feminist Press, 1982), 360–78.

18. The last electronic survey of the MLA Bibliography for this essay took place in September 1994. See, for example, Rafia Zafar, "White Call, Black Response: Adoption, Subversion, and Transformation in American Literature from the Colonial Era to the Age of Abolition," Harvard University, 1989, 157–202. However, apparent absences in the MLA record are doubtless due in part to the vagaries of subject headings: If "Harriet Jacobs" is not listed as a "key word," works discussing *Incidents* will not be easily found.

19. Professor Mullen's book will appear in 1996.

20. A friend at the University of Wisconsin sent me the following information: her current research assistant had found more recent citations on Jacobs than on "Gaskell, Bronte, Eliot, Hardy"; in her course on "Nineteenth Century British and American Social Fiction" (Fall 1993), she found "from a show of hands, Jacobs was more familiar to students than any of the other texts (which happen to be novels) . . . one woman said she's read Jacobs in two other classes." Susan David Bernstein, personal communication, October 29, 1993.

21. duCille, "The Occult," 592, 594; Carla Kaplan, "Narrative Contracts and Emancipatory Readers: *Incidents in the Life of a Slave Girl*," *Yale Journal of Criticism* 6:1 (1993): 104. See also Michael Awkward, "Negotiations of Power: White Critics, Black Texts, and the Self-Referential Impulse," *American Literary History* 2:4 (Winter 1990): 581–4, for an earlier, related exploration of the critical issues surrounding the new interest in black literature.

22. John S. Jacobs, "A True Tale of Slavery," was published in installments in *The Leisure Hour. A Family Journal of Instruction and Recreation* (London), February 7, 14, 21, and 28, 1861.

"I DISGUISED MY HAND"

WRITING VERSIONS OF THE TRUTH IN HARRIET JACOBS'S INCIDENTS IN THE LIFE OF A SLAVE GIRL AND JOHN JACOBS'S "A TRUE TALE OF SLAVERY"

JACQUELINE GOLDSBY

I like a straightforward course, and am always reluctant to resort to subterfuges. So far as my ways have been crooked, I charge them all upon slavery. It was that system of violence and wrong which left me no alternative but to enact a falsehood.

Harriet A. Jacobs as Linda Brent in *Incidents*

I

Linda Brent's stunningly frank admission comes at a crucial moment in *Incidents in the Life of a Slave Girl*.[1] She has settled into a job in New York, having finally escaped from Southern slavery after being sequestered for nearly seven years in her grandmother's garret. Linda has located her daughter Ellen, who is also working in the metropolis, as a servant for the Hobbs family. Anxious to see her child but fearful of being exposed as a fugitive slave, Linda writes her daughter's employer a letter of introduction that masks her Southern history by creating a local, Northern one. In order to obtain leave to visit Ellen, Linda intimates that she is free, having recently relocated from Canada. Although Linda's stated preference for a "straightforward course" implies that this is the first time she has "enact[ed] a falsehood," she has deployed "crooked" ways throughout the narrative up to and including this point. In fact, Linda does not "resort to subterfuges" in this instance alone; she actively engages in them throughout *Incidents* as a political strategy to effect her liberation from bondage and, as she suggests in this passage, as a discursive mode with which to transcribe her experience.

Jacobs's own name provides an example: she adopts the pseudonymous identity of "Linda Brent" to shield herself from public view. And she is not the only one to engage in devious measures. The exchange of correspondence between Linda and her former masters, the Flints, is notable for its duplicitous dealings and forays at forgery. Until his death, Dr. Flint persistently composes missives that aim to manipulate Linda into returning to the South and back into slavery. Indeed, in the world according to *Incidents*, reliable knowledge cannot be gained by way of the "straightforward course" because that path leads only to the hypocrisy of surface representation. "Resort[ing] to subterfuges" is what opens the way to insight. As Jacobs advises her readers,

> If you want to be fully convinced of the abominations of slavery, go on a southern plantation and call yourself a negro trader. Then there will be no concealment; and you will see and hear things that will seem to you impossible among human beings with immortal souls. (*I.* 52)

Here, Jacobs charges that the true nature of slavery can be revealed only through disguise and masquerade. To write a realistic account of the "abominations of slavery," one must rewrite his or her own appearance and fictionalize his or her own identity, otherwise the information one obtains will not be "true." This narrative economy banks on inversion as its principal gesture and funds itself by reconfiguring what, in fact, constitutes "credible" sources. With this approach to describing slavery, *Incidents* proposes that conventional methods of historical investigation are themselves inadequate measures by which to determine what is "authentic" and what is not. Since, according to Jacobs, "truth" can be discovered only if it is left "concealed," rules of documentary evidence may not resolve the dilemma that *Incidents*, as a slave narrative, confronts: how to preserve testimony of an experience that is itself beyond representation.

In this way, the generic lines distinguishing fact and fiction are at once pronounced and difficult to discern in *Incidents*. Predictably, modern readers – twentieth-century historians and literary critics – have debated the efficacy and meaning of Jacobs's "crooked ways" of narration.[2] Intent to recuperate black testimony as substantive evidence in their descriptions and analyses of Southern slaveocracy, various scholars have dismissed Jacobs's narrative as reliable primary source material for two principal reasons. Either they were convinced that *Incidents* was not written by Jacobs herself but by her editor, Lydia Maria Child, or they believed that, because of the literary stylings of the story, Jacobs's life experiences were not true and that she did not even exist. Historian John Blassingame's judgment against *Incidents'* reportorial accuracy sums up these objections most clearly:

In spite of Lydia Maria Child's insistence that she had only revised the manuscript of Harriet Jacobs's [narrative] "mainly for purposes of condensation and orderly arrangement," the work is not credible. In the first place, *Incidents in the Life of a Slave Girl* (1861) is too orderly; too many of the major characters meet providentially after years of separation. Then, too, the story is too melodramatic: miscegenation and cruelty, outraged virtue, unrequited love, and planter licentiousness appear on practically every page. The virtuous Harriet sympathizes with her wretched mistress who has to look on all of the mulattoes fathered by her husband, she refuses to bow to the lascivious demands of her master, bears two children by another white man, and then runs away and hides in a garret in her grandmother's cabin for seven years until she is able to escape to New York. In the meantime, her white lover has acknowledged his paternity of her children, purchased their freedom, and been elected to Congress. In the end, all live happily ever after.[3]

Blassingame's pronouncement influenced subsequent evaluations of *Incidents* for a number of years because of the significance of his own work in the field-at-large. First published in 1972, *The Slave Community* (along with Eugene Genovese's *Roll, Jordan, Roll: The World the Slaves Made*) broke new methodological ground, as it relied almost exclusively upon slave narratives to reconstruct the experience of blacks in antebellum plantation culture. "While other sources are important in any general description of the institution of slavery," Blassingame explained, "they rarely tell us much about how blacks perceived their experiences."[4] Blacks' autobiographies proved their argumentative worth precisely because of their subjective point of view, but Blassingame was careful to recognize that the narratives were not transparent texts. Assuming that the slaves' stories were biased or selective accounts of the witnesses' memories, he also believed that such prejudices could be corrected by comparing the slaves' accounts with one another and using available external sources to cross-check the claims in a given account.[5] In Blassingame's estimation, though, *Incidents* crossed this line of evidentiary propriety. Jacobs's narrative was so subjective and so perceptive that it exceeded Blassingame's requirements for "sample" or "representative" texts; rather, the narrative was itself a representation. However, by omitting *Incidents* from his data set Blassingame endorsed the very problem Jacobs's autobiography raises: what narrative elements or modes produce "credible" texts? At what point does a writer's narrative logic become "too orderly" and, so, not true?

Since any effort to recuperate *Incidents* as a legitimate narrative would have to defend the principle of order in the text, the will to justify the plotted nature of Jacobs's autobiography informs Jean Fagan Yellin's compilation of the narrative published by Harvard University Press in 1987. Now considered to be the definitive edition of the text, Yellin's assemblage of documentary evidence – maps, wills, deeds, newspaper clippings and announcements, photographs, and correspondence – impressively counters arguments that would deny *Incidents'* designation of "authentic" or "true." Yellin's painstaking investigations into archival sources have yielded the references necessary to confirm that Harriet Jacobs did, in fact, exist and that Harriet Jacobs did, indeed, compose *Incidents* "by herself," as stated in the book's subtitle.[6] Not only have these findings rebutted previous skeptics, they have also been a source of narrative satisfaction for Yellin. Compelled by their persuasive weight, Yellin predicts that the reader of the Harvard edition of *Incidents* will, like her, "perhaps be dismayed . . . by parts of the book that are not yet documented."[7]

That Yellin locates the pleasure of reading the text (assuming pleasure would supplant "dismay") in its correspondence to actual, verifiable details from Jacobs's life may be as troublesome an equation as was Blassingame's suggestion that the orderliness of the text belies its claims to truth. Yellin implies that historical veracity makes literary meaning not only plausible but possible. In that formulation, the power of the archive renders the text accessible and literate and thus confirms its narrative value. The canonical stature of the Harvard edition of *Incidents* rests upon Yellin's effort to set Jacobs's story before the public as being incontrovertibly "true," to narrow (if not forge closed altogether) the gaps between fact and fiction by subjecting the text to rigorous archival verification.

Far from bridging interdisciplinary boundaries, however, this ethic allows history to subsume the narrative imperatives of literature. It presumes an economy of value that defines "credibility" and "authenticity" similarly when, in fact, literature happens and works precisely because of its contestation of those very terms. Thus, where Yellin locates and defines the textual authority of *Incidents* by its correspondence to factual history, literary critic William L. Andrews associates it with the narrative's manipulation of historical facts. Andrews's literary historiography, *To Tell a Free Story: The First Century of Afro-American Autobiography, 1760–1865*, classifies *Incidents* as an "experimental" slave narrative, arguing that Jacobs's text was composed at the cultural moment during the nineteenth century when (ex-)slave narrators approached their life stories in a radically new way. As a "liminal autobiographer," Jacobs sought to map out the impasse slaves faced when writing: how to make their narratives "authentic" for a white audience that could – more than ever after the 1850s – expect (if not demand) specific, racialized conventions from them. These authors struggled to balance the competing claims placed upon them between sincerity and authority or, as Andrews conceptualizes it, to reconcile the relationships between "literary priorities and freedom of expression over facts of experience."[8]

Thus, when Andrews considers the question of *Incidents'* authenticity, what matters most is the status of Jacobs's authorship. Whether or not she actually wrote her narrative alone needs verification, for that point opens these matters to historical debate: Why did Jacobs employ certain narrative strategies to write her story? What commentary do those devices offer regarding her immediate cultural milieu? These questions guide the task of authentication as an enterprise within literary criticism because the burden of proof weighs upon the notion of authorial intentionality and the indeterminacy of meaning. That is to say, a text's value for literary analysis depends on the ways in which it engages and resists the closure implied by historical documentation.

As historians, both Blassingame's and Yellin's insistence on obtaining unimpeachable facts assumes that the narrative power of *Incidents* rests upon whether or not those facts can be externally referenced, while it is in the prevalence of internal ambiguities that the literary meaning of the narrative finds its charge.[9] But there lies precisely the quarrel over *Incidents'* authenticity: what and where are the limits to reading history into literature and vice versa? Following a self-declared "crooked" path in the composition of her autobiography, Harriet Jacobs trespasses across disciplinary boundaries, and the critical reception accorded to her book suggests that the narrative strategies available to and employed by black writers during the antebellum period are themselves a function and evidence of history; or, put another way, history marks and is marked by the writing of narrative itself.

Incidents is still further marked by another narrative whose history has barely been considered by either historians or literary critics: the autobiography written by Harriet Jacobs's brother, John S. Jacobs.[10] The scant attention paid to "A True Tale of Slavery" is remarkable, because the fortuitous coincidence of having extant records of the Jacobses' lives would, presumably, reap evidentiary rewards to researchers. One would think that "A True Tale of Slavery" could be used as a contemporary source to verify Harriet Jacobs's *Incidents*; however, it cannot. "A True Tale of Slavery" fails to fulfill this ideal expectation because it does not exactly corroborate Harriet Jacobs's vision of specific people or her version of certain events in *Incidents*. Depictions of their father and grandmother, statements about John Jacobs's literacy levels, accounts of their reunion and, most critically, information about Harriet Jacobs's escape are so dissimilar that the reader must ask which narrative is the "true tale," and what becomes of the notion of referentiality if we cannot determine which story stands as the "actual" base for comparison?

Do the inconsistencies between *Incidents* and "A True Tale of Slavery" indicate yet another occasion where Harriet Jacobs "resort[s] to subterfuge"? After all, as "Linda Brent" Harriet Jacobs had this to say about narrative collaborations with her brother:

> I missed the company and kind attentions of my brother William, who had gone to Washington with his master, Mr. Sands. We received several letters from him, written without any allusion to me, but expressed

in such a manner that I knew he did not forget me. I disguised my hand, and wrote to him in the same manner. (*I*, 133)

Harriet Jacobs suggests here that writing in disguise and writing as a form of disguise describe the operative mode of communication between herself and her brother.[11] In this essay, I would like to consider whether *Incidents* and "A True Tale of Slavery" address one another – and the reader – in a similar way. That is to say, I want to examine what the discrepancies between *Incidents* and "A True Tale of Slavery" suggest, within the texts themselves, about the function of writing. Specifically, I am interested in knowing whether the lack of correspondence between Harriet's and John Jacobs's narratives can be read as commentary against the formal restrictions placed upon black testimony within the abolitionist movement and, if so, how that "allusion" (to use Harriet Jacobs's term) impacts upon the debates concerning *Incidents'* claim to be a "true" text.

II

The abolitionist movement was an influential arbiter in the definition and public perception of "truth" as it was articulated by black slaves. At its inception in 1833, the American Anti-Slavery Society staffed seventy whites on its roster of lecturers, and it was not until six years later that the group finally let its charges speak for themselves. At that point the Society's leader, Theodore Dwight Weld, nominated the group's first black speakers to join its ranks.[12] The gamble paid off as huge audiences came to antislavery meetings to hear the chilling and compelling stories of recently escaped fugitives. These face-to-face encounters with blacks proved highly effective in converting the white public to the cause for black freedom. In a letter to fellow political traveler Gerrit Smith, Weld predicted that black lecturers "would do more to kill prejudice . . . than all our operations up to now" and, Weld continued, "a colored man who is eloquent in all parts of the North [would] draw larger audiences than of [sic] white."[13] Historians August Meier and Elliott Rudwick confirm the outcome Weld imagined:

> Audiences flocked to hear these speakers describe the whippings administered by overseers, the separation from loved ones sold down the river, and the often hectic efforts to get beyond the reach of slave-catchers and bloodhounds. In the most personal terms they told exactly what slavery meant to them, and, speaking of what they had seen and experienced, they were deeply convincing.[14]

Oftentimes, however, white audiences were not fully persuaded by the direct testimony offered by blacks, and they subjected the speakers to rigorous cross-examinations following the presentations. For example, in the second edition of his narrative published in 1845, fugitive slave Lewis Clarke added an appendix listing the thirty-five questions he was asked most frequently during discussion periods with white audiences.[15] To ensure the (ex-)slave's credibility and to maintain the New England Anti-Slavery Society's reputation, William Lloyd Garrison advocated the use of a questionnaire to screen out imposters' stories.[16] As critic John Sekora argues, this instrument was used to evaluate potential black lecturers and to structure both the live lecture and its eventual written version, for the typical procedure called for the slaves' narratives to be published *after* their oral presentation on the abolitionist lecture circuit.[17] According to John Blassingame, antislavery societies printed less than 20 percent of the slave testimonies that were collected and presented in lecture form because the expediency factor was too large to ignore: "In contrast to the small number of people who might read a slave's story," Blassingame points out, "one long lecture tour would enable a fugitive to tell his story to thousands."[18]

Pressured to recite their histories in monitored accordance with the standards of proof imposed by their white political patrons and audiences, slave narrators could not, in a sense, speak freely. And yet it was the oral presentation of their testimony that conferred their value as "true" texts. To be able to witness black narrators testify in their immediate presence, to be able to assess the stories' credibility by way of queries meant to fill in perceived gaps, to catch and expose supposed contradictions, or to amplify points of interest and intrigue must have satisfied white listeners in ways that reading a printed version of the speech did not. For example, the "Boston correspondent" for the *National Anti-Slavery Standard* reported to the paper's readers that Harriet Jacobs's *Incidents* possessed "vivid dramatic power as a narrative" and predicted that the book "should have a wide circulation." But the reviewer also bristled at "a few sentences, in which the moral is rather oppressively displayed," expressing his wish that Lydia Maria Child had "felt herself authorized to expunge" Jacobs's forthright assertions. The correspondent would have preferred to take Jacobs's testimony in a form wherein he could determine for himself the moral meaning to be inferred from the narrative: "they are the strongest witnesses who leave the summing up to the judge, and the verdict to the jury," the journalist advised.[19] The role of writing became lost and, at the same time, made all the more important as a repository of black-authored truth precisely because of its repression in abolitionist discourse as a "second" or lesser text of sorts.[20]

Within this context the publication of Harriet Jacobs's *Incidents* takes on a new meaning. Consider Jacobs's remark to her confidante, antislavery activist Amy Post:

> I had determined to let others think of me as they pleased but *my lips should be sealed and no one had the right to question me* for this reason when I first came North I avoided Antislavery people as much as pos-

sible because I felt that I could not be honest and tell the whole truth. (my emphasis)[21]

No doubt Jacobs was reticent to approach the "Antislavery people" because she felt ashamed about the indecorous details of her experience as a slave: she had fled North Carolina to protect herself from the sexual wrath of her master and to secure the freedom of her children, born out of wedlock and fathered by a white Congressman. Jacobs's worry about the reception of her story demonstrates an awareness of the demands placed upon blacks who would speak publicly against slavery. She wants to tell her story "honestly" and "truthfully," but is determined not to be second-guessed as to the integrity of her experience, even if it is beyond the pale of chaste civility. However, committing herself to silence – that is, choosing not to present her case as a speech – could have lost Jacobs the ability to contribute to the cause of freedom. Writing about her life as a slave presented another venue, a different option. Through print, she could exercise the modicum of discretion and authority she feared would be denied to her should she offer her narrative as abolitionist protocol would have, accept, and prefer it – in the form of oral testimony.[22]

Jacobs's apparent resistance to this routine is not surprising, given her close proximity to abolitionist political culture. By the date of her letter to Post (1852), Jacobs was working in Cornwall, New York, as a nurse-housemaid to the family of Nathaniel and Cornelia Willis. This was three years after her stay in Rochester, New York, where she had worked in the Anti-Slavery Office and Reading Room established by her brother. For much of 1849, Jacobs managed the facility while John Jacobs traveled throughout western New York state on lecture tours for the American Anti-Slavery Society.[23] In this position, Jacobs undoubtedly had access to the newspapers and other publications disseminated by the abolitionist movement; just downstairs from the Jacobses' library were the headquarters of Frederick Douglass's *North Star*.[24] Jacobs was also aware of her brother's growing reputation as a gifted activist; the *National Anti-Slavery Standard* rated his oratorical skills as second only to the brilliant Douglass and, as Jacobs told Amy Post, "they [abolitionists] do not know me[;] they have heard of me as John Jacobs' sister."[25] It seems plausible to suggest that, given the concerns she expresses to Amy Post and her active presence in the antislavery politics and communications networks, Harriet Jacobs knew how slave narratives were formulated and presented to the public. The question then becomes, what meaning is to be had in the apparent fact that Jacobs wrote and published her narrative before she presented it in person?[26]

Logistical answers to this question are not hard to surmise. First of all, the constraints of Jacobs's job could easily have prevented her from promoting the book aggressively. Nathaniel Willis, head of the household in which she was employed, was an apologist for slavery. Jacobs composed *Incidents* at night because she did not want to incite Willis's disapproval, nor did she want to cause dissension between the journalist–editor and his wife, who evinced her antislavery sentiments through her efforts to protect Jacobs from capture.[27] If the worry that her writing might cause her to lose her job was not enough, there were the demands of the position itself: Jacobs's duties as housemaid and nanny to the Willis children consumed much of the time she would have spent on a tour for the book.[28] Then again, compared to their male counterparts, fewer female fugitives appeared and spoke at abolitionists' lecture series.[29] And further, Jacobs herself felt stymied by a gnawing fear of failure. She fretted over her inability to withstand open scrutiny from the sophisticates she imagined would people her audience. In another letter to Amy Post, Jacobs relates her insecurities:

> To get this time [free hours during which to write] I should have to explain myself, and no one here except Louisa [Jacobs's daughter] knows that I have ever written anything to be put in print. I have not the courage to meet the criticism and ridicule of educated people.[30]

Any or all of these reasons could explain why Jacobs apparently did not deliver *Incidents* in the lecture format prior to its publication. This order of presentation is important because it calls attention to the procedure of authorship governing the production of black narrative within abolitionist discourse. Dispensing with the preferred convention of speech – or orality – as the proper and primary source of black testimony, *Incidents* foregrounds the idea of textuality – or the fact and function of writing – as the means to represent black testimony.[31] *Incidents'* manuscript status thus calls attention to the ways in which abolitionists linked the idea of narrative form to the notion of authenticity, because the autobiography's claim to be a "true" statement does not depend on a sequence in which oral recital happens first. Nor is *Incidents'* claim to "truth" contingent upon the idea of surveyed "facticity" – of measuring up to standards of credibility promulgated by abolitionists in the form of diagnostic questionnaires or demoralizing interrogations conducted by skeptics and sympathizers alike. Indeed, what is significant in and significant about *Incidents* are the ways in which Harriet Jacobs's narrative, when read together with John Jacobs's "A True Tale of Slavery," reveals how abolitionist protocol compromised the relation between truth, black speech, and black script.

III

John S. Jacobs's "A True Tale of Slavery" appeared in the London-based weekly, *The Leisure Hour*, in February 1861.[32] Out of offices located at 164 Paternoster Row and Picadilly Lane in London, England, a Dr. Maculay headed the editorial operations of the magazine on behalf of the Religious

Tract Society, an ecumenical publishing cooperative founded in 1799. During its years of distribution (1852 to 1905), the magazine maintained a secular outlook, billing itself as a "Family Journal of Instruction and Recreation." At its peak in 1860, the *Leisure Hour* reached a fairly large audience; just one year before "A True Tale of Slavery" appeared in its pages the journal circulated to at least 100,000 readers in and about the London area.[33] Priced to sell at a penny, the magazine's subscribers came primarily from the lower to middle classes. Additional support came from Sunday schools, which distributed the magazine at weekly class sessions throughout the metropolitan region.[34]

John Jacobs's autobiography was indexed under the special category of "tales and narratives" – suspense-tinged stories whose plots unfolded over the course of consecutive issues. Why Jacobs chose to publish "A True Tale of Slavery" in *The Leisure Hour* instead of in a well-known abolitionist organ such as the British Foreign Anti-Slavery Society's *Antislavery Reporter* or one of the movement's premier publications in America, the *Liberator* or the *National Anti-Slavery Standard*, is not known.[35] However, a letter to Isaac Post offers evidence that can be used to speculate as to Jacobs's motives.

Dated June 5, 1861, four months after his narrative appeared in *The Leisure Hour*, Jacobs's letter reveals his growing irritation with abolition politics in England. "Yesterday I read the view of one man who believed it best to let the old slaves work out the freedom of their children, and when they have died off, then let the children be free, and there would be an end to the evil," Jacobs complains to Post. He continues:

> This reminded me of the story of the poorhouse, which I will not repeat. Last night I heard our tried and true friend, George Thompson, who tried to convince the people of this country of the grave mistake they had made in not encouraging the cultivation of cotton in their colonies, and to explain the true cause of the slaveholders seceding from the Union. I am sorry to say, that with all the blood and guilt on the slaveholders' souls, there are Englishmen here that dare express sympathy for them.[36]

Perhaps Jacobs placed his narrative in *The Leisure Hour* because the magazine's popular appeal and its sizable audience could counter what he perceived to be a widespread campaign of disinformation about American slavery. Seven chapters long, "A True Tale of Slavery" provided instructive copy for the journal's audience. Punctuated by graphic descriptions of the emotional and physical cruelty suffered by slaves and highlighted by the clever execution of his escape out of bondage, the narrative also demanded moral reflection of the sort Jacobs believed was missing from British antislavery rhetoric. Its denouncements of the rights-denying prohibitions of chattel slavery no doubt reminded *The Leisure Hour*'s white working and middle class male readers that, as subjects of "wage slavery," they too had lost authority in the brave new world of the Industrial Revolution. On this and other points, John Jacobs's narrative deserves a reading of its own. In this essay, however, I want to consider the titular claim of "A True Tale of Slavery" in relation to the meaning of "truth" as expounded by Harriet Jacobs in *Incidents*, because what would seem to be a logical strategy to implement – using one text to corroborate the other – fails in such a highly conspicuous way.

IV

An admittedly "short statement"[37] of John Jacobs's experience of slavery, "A True Tale of Slavery" contrasts sharply with *Incidents* in both form and content. As a serialized narrative with a limited run, Jacobs's story presses *The Leisure Hour*'s column space to these stipulated limits. Each installment is prefaced by subheads that announce a declared focus for Jacobs's recollections but instead signal how far astray he wanders into detailed discussions of incidental characters and events. These digressions divert the reader's attention and, at times, distract Jacobs himself: "return to my subject," he urges; "make my story short," he observes. Reading "A True Tale" one comes to appreciate both the exposition of detail that the book-length *Incidents* affords Harriet Jacobs and the narrative concision resulting from Lydia Maria Child's editorial influence on the book.

Nevertheless, "A True Tale" presents an eloquent and forceful case for the "darkest of fates" (ATT, 85) befalling male slaves – their disenfranchisement from the privileges of patrimony. The symbol of this deprivation comes in the figure of John Jacobs's father, who, the son writes, "made impressions on my mind in childhood that can never be forgotten" (ATT, 85):

> To be a man and not a man – a father without authority – a husband and no protector. . . . Such was the condition of my father and such is the condition of every slave in the United States: he owns nothing, he can claim nothing. His wife is not his: his children are not his; they can be taken away from him, and sold at any minute, as far away from each other as the human flesh monger may see fit to carry them. Slaves are recognized as property by the law, and can own nothing except by the consent of their masters. (ATT, 85)

In *Incidents*, Linda Brent's inability to choose her sexual partners and to defend herself against Dr. Flint's harassing advances bespeaks how "consent," as a term of bondage, applies to her. In her case, "consent" concerns possession insofar as she can (or cannot) act as the sole arbiter of her sexuality. Or, as Harriet Jacobs movingly states this point:

> to be an object of interest to a man who is not married, and is not her master, is agreeable to the pride and feelings of a slave, if her miserable situation has left her any pride or sentiment. It seems less degrading to

give one's self, than to submit to compulsion. There is something akin
to freedom in having a lover who has no control over you, except that
which he gains by kindness and attachment. (*I*, 54–5)

For John Jacobs, "consent" has to do with property rights per se, because
slaves are categorically denied the right to possess themselves and their kin.
As he posits it in "A True Tale," if black men are to become free and wholly
human – that is, truly masculine – under the rule of the law, they must reclaim these relations as part of an order of objectification that sanctifies patriarchal authority. As John Jacobs demands, "according to the American declaration of independence, it is a self-evident truth that all men are created by
their Maker free and equal, and endowed with certain inalienable rights –
life, liberty, and the pursuit of happiness. Where are the coloured man's
rights to-day in America?" (ATT, 140).

That "A True Tale" centers upon this meditation about male prerogative
to power clearly distinguishes John Jacobs's narrative from his sister's con-
templations about the morally vexed obligations of female sexuality and maternity.[38] It is precisely this gendered focus, however, that links the texts together. This becomes clear when we consider John Jacobs's philosophy of
natural rights. "I cannot agree with that statesman who said, 'What the law
makes property, is property'," Jacobs contends:

> What is law but the will of the people – a mirror to reflect the nation's
> character? . . . No law, unless there be one that can change my nature,
> can make property of me. Freedom is as natural for man as the air he
> breathes, and he who robs him of his freedom is also guilty of murder;
> for he has robbed him of his natural existence. (ATT, 140)

As a "mirror" that "reflect[s] the nation's character," civil law is a social construction, a representation of cultural ideals whose form depends upon that
which appears before it. Here, Jacobs construes civil law to be a form of narrative, or fiction. Even further, he suggests that civil law (or fiction) contradicts the eternal, life-giving, organic principles of its opposite, natural law, or
truth. However, Jacobs implicitly recognizes that civil law (or fiction) has material consequences: natural law may presume a condition of existence –
"freedom is as natural for man as the air he breathes," Jacobs argues – but
civil law mandates a state of being that is compelling in itself: slavery. In other
words, civil law (or fiction) can be "real" and yet not be natural or "true."

Although John Jacobs's understanding of truth and realism emerges from
his male-identified preoccupation with property rights and his stated desire
for patriarchal authority, this distinction offers an interesting – and, I believe,
appropriate – way to examine the debates concerning the authenticity of
Harriet Jacobs's *Incidents*. It is no small coincidence that "A True Tale" appeared contemporaneously with *Incidents* (both appeared in print in February
1861). Nor is it unremarkable that each narrative received critical attention in

the other's place of publication: *Incidents* was reviewed in the London-based *Anti-Slavery Advocate* in May of 1861 and was published in England in August of that year under the title, *The Deeper Wrong: Or, Incidents in the Life of a Slave Girl*.[39] "A True Tale" was highlighted in Richard D. Webb's column in the New York-based *National Anti-Slavery Standard*. Writing to his American compatriots, the Irishman Webb announced:

> Indeed, the anti-slavery education of the British people goes on with rapidly increasing celerity and effectiveness. The most popular of our periodicals swarm with illustrations, moral, ethical, religious and narrative, of the character and tendency of slavery. . . . It is only the other day I met in four consecutive numbers of the 'Leisure Hour,' a weekly periodical of vast circulation, the narrative of an escaped slave, who turns out to be the brother of my estimable friend 'Linda,' whose narrative is one of the most interesting and affecting in the whole compass of anti-slavery literature.[40]

That Webb joins and collapses any sequential relation between the *Incidents* and "A True Tale" reminds us of the insistence upon order in black testimony on the abolitionist lecture circuit – with oral speech occurring first and printed texts appearing later, and of John Jacobs's hypothesis regarding civil and natural law, because the narratives' simultaneous appearance invokes his trope of the mirror. On the one hand, the image of the looking glass obliges us not to take either text as a reflective or mimetic statement of the other, since that symbol (as Jacobs understands it) would imply that the autobiographies are "fictional" and so not exactly "true." On the other hand, because the two narratives present conflicting accounts of crucial events and personages in the Jacobs family history, whatever biological or "natural" link would bind the siblings' biographical accounts together is compromised as well. Indeed, what "truth" does the reader come to know about the Jacobses' lives and on what grounds are we then meant to judge the veracity of *Incidents* when we cannot ascertain what "really" occurs in either account?

V

John Jacobs recalls his father as a morose, moody, and conflict-ridden man whose "violent temper" (ATT, 85) siphoned off into a "pent up agony" (ATT, 86). This uneven blend of emotions became unbearable to Daniel Jacobs once he was sold to another master who prohibited him from saving his earnings as a carpenter. Spiraling down into a "state of mental dejection" (ATT, 86), Daniel Jacobs died a broken man in his son's eyes. To his daughter, the elder Jacobs was a figure of towering strength whose stature protected her from the harsh realities of slavery. "I was so fondly shielded that I never dreamed I was a piece of merchandise, trusted to [my parents] for safe keeping, and liable to be demanded of them at any moment," Harriet Jacobs rem-iniscences (*I*, 5). In their remembrances of their father, the children sing Blake-like songs of experience and innocence – the one lamenting the social death of Daniel Jacobs's worldly authority, the other praising the relative scope of the father's will to power.[41]

The siblings remember their grandmother differently, too. Whereas John describes Molly Horniblow as "meek" (85) in comparison to his father, Har-riet remembers her as a "very spirited woman" (I, 11):

> Although my grandmother was all in all to me, I feared her as well as loved her. I had been accustomed to look up to her with a respect bordering upon awe. I was very young, and felt shamefaced about telling her such impure things, especially as I knew her to be very strict on such subjects. Moreover, she was a woman of a high spirit. She was usually very quiet in her demeanor; but if her indignation was once roused, it was not very easily quelled. I had been told that she once chased a white gentleman with a loaded pistol, because he insulted one of her daughters. (*I*, 28–29)

Self-sufficient and self-supporting, "Aunt Martha" (as she is called in *Incidents*) enjoys the respect of both blacks and whites in the town, and her stock of moral principles forms the standard against which Linda Brent evaluates how far she falls in her efforts to escape slavery.[42]

How do we explain the discrepancies in the characterizations of the Jacobses' elders? Perhaps Molly Horniblow and Daniel Jacobs appear as they do in "A True Tale" and *Incidents* because John and Harriet – as a son and a daughter, as a man and a woman, as a frustrated patriarch and a striving (but besieged) mother – identified with them as gender-appropriate role models and rendered them in their worlds accordingly.[43] However, there is more to their differences of opinion, and the surplus for explanation derives from the Jacobses' deployment of writing in their accounts of their grandmother's sale.

According to John Jacobs, when his mistress died, he, his sister, their grandmother, and other slaves were auctioned as a part of the estate inven-tory. As in *Incidents*, "A True Tale" laments the fact that Molly Horniblow's "grey hairs and many years' hard service in the public-house [i.e., hotel] did not save her from the auctioneer's hammer" (ATT, 86). However, a "tried and trusty friend" (ATT, 86) of Molly's, a white man, assists in her plan to silence the rap of the trading gavel. Over time, the unnamed ally has stored Molly's savings for her and, at this critical juncture, he uses the sum to place a successful bid on her and her son, Mark. The friend then consigns Mark over to Molly, reuniting the mother and child. Enabling her to confirm "that [Mark] was her property by right of purchase" (ATT, 86), the transaction also illustrates the perversion of black familial relations under slavery. "It may seem strange that my grandmother should hold her son a slave; but the law required it," John Jacobs explains.

She was obliged to give security that she would never be any expense to the town or state before she could come in possession of her freedom. Her property in him was sufficient to satisfy the law; he could be sold at any minute to pay her debts, though it was not likely this would ever be the case. (ATT, 86)

In *Incidents,* this episode also explores how the logic of capital and property rights works against the grandmother's self-interest, but with significant shifts in details and emphasis. To begin with, "a maiden lady" (*I,* 11), the sister of the deceased mistress, buys Martha at the auction and does so with her own fifty dollars. The gender switch effected here is remarkable; more important, though, are Harriet's and John Jacobs's descriptions of the flow of money, because their representations of currency in this event convert the dollars used to buy the grandmother into a form of narrative capital itself.

In *Incidents,* Martha dutifully collects her earnings from her baking business to purchase her children out of slavery. When, at one point, her mistress approaches Martha for a loan, Martha agrees to help. The two agree that the mistress will repay Martha promptly since the loan exhausts the latter's resources. However, the mistress dies before she can satisfy the debt. Appointed executor of the estate, Dr. Flint refuses to honor his mother-in-law's verbal contract with Martha, pleading that the deceased's accounts are bankrupt. Though the mistress' death and the subsequent auction of her belongings leads to sale of the grandmother in both *Incidents* and "A True Tale," John Jacobs does not mention the debt between Molly Horniblow and her owner as a significant factor in this event. On the other side of this token, "Aunt Martha" has no secret savings with which to negotiate her freedom; in *Incidents,* the grandmother is completely dependent upon the "maiden lady" to win the bidding contest and to transfer the deed of ownership back to her. In the words of John, the grandmother is financially solvent at the moment of the sale; in the words of Harriet, the grandmother is without reserves of any sort – she is broke. How can the reader assess the relative value of money in this exchange when we cannot even determine whether it exists or not?

This is why it matters in *Incidents* that the mistress uses Martha's $300 to buy a silver candelabra. Transformed into a family heirloom, the money relates back to Southern rules of propriety and property, for the souvenir of bourgeois culture recalls the unfree labor blacks expended to obtain it. That Dr. Flint decides, on the one hand, to keep the candelabra to fulfill its function as a commodified form of memory and, on the other hand, to sell Martha as a way of forgetting the mistress's promise and to realize Martha's value as a commodity object herself is an ironic equation that *Incidents* asserts quite forcefully on its own. However, when this episode is paired with its analogue in "A True Tale," the two versions confound each other's claims. Was the "tried and trusty friend" who acted on the grandmother's behalf male or female, a relative of the deceased mistress or not? Did Molly Horniblow / Aunt

Martha loan her savings to her mistress? Did Dr. Norcom / Flint renege on his mother-in-law's alleged debt and promise? What, finally, do these differences in detail make? If we rely upon both Jacobses' narratives as source material, the addition or subtraction of these points of information confirms nothing. This leaves the reader unable to specify which version is more credible because it is impossible to know what "really" happened in connection with the grandmother's sale. Thus, individually, *Incidents* and "A True Tale" have the sum effect of rendering this episode illegible: It is precisely because the Jacobses' testimonies have been transcribed and are in conflict with one another that the event cannot be read.

Dating the historical moment at which John Jacobs learns to read tests the issue of order, sources, and credibility with regard to *Incidents* yet again. In "A True Tale" John Jacobs tells us that, at age ten, he was owned by an unnamed relative of Dr. Norcom who then turned managerial control of the boy over to the physician. Jacobs was removed to the Norcom household, where he was placed to labor in the doctor's shop. Jacobs reports that, prior to this move, his father had tutored him in mental pursuits: "[He] had endeavored to bestow upon both of us [John and Harriet] some rays of intellectual light, which the tyrant could not rob us of," Jacobs recalls (ATT, 86). However, once he comes under Norcom's watch, Jacobs loses his intellectual way because the doctor sets John and Harriet on separate paths of education:

> [Norcom] too well knew the value of knowledge, and the danger of communicating it to human "property," to allow it to be disseminated among his slaves; and he therefore instructed his sons, who had charge of me, to see that I did not learn to write. Soon after this, my sister was taken into his house, but no interdict against the acquisition of knowledge, such as he imposed upon me, could avail in her case. (ATT, 86)

In his mind, John Jacobs was kept from being and becoming literate – an "interdict" was "imposed upon [him]" – whereas his sister was, presumably, allowed to develop her skills in what he imagines to be a properly male realm of power and freedom. Only after he escapes from slavery does John Jacobs become literate; he enlists for a three-and-a-half-year whaling expedition in order to have uncontested space and time to teach himself to read and write. By returning to nature, Jacobs aims to become a citizen of culture: aboard the *Francis Henrietta* Jacobs enjoys the security to "raise [himself] above the level of the beast, where slavery had left [him], and fit [himself] for the society of man" (ATT, 126).

If Norcom's "interdict" enhanced Harriet Jacobs's educational development, being literate subjects Linda Brent to the violence of "male society." As they are represented in *Incidents*, Dr. Flint's sexual transgressions and abuses against Linda are literally graphic because they assume linguistic forms: his "restless, craving, vicious nature" finds textual release in "stinging, scorching words; words that scathed her ear and brain like fire" (*I,* 18). Because Flint's wife suspects her husband's fidelity, she watches him "with unceasing vigilance," and the doctor "manifest[s] in signs" what he cannot "say in words" (*I,* 31), especially when he realizes that Linda Brent can read.[44]

As Linda Brent, Harriet Jacobs maintains that her brother William was made privy to these exchanges; that is to say, in *Incidents,* John Jacobs knows how to read. Assigned to work as Flint's medical assistant (and not as a laboring hand in the shop), William "had taught himself to read and spell" to the point where his sister "was proud of [her] brother; and the old doctor suspected as much" (*I,* 61). Wanting to spoil Linda's joy and William's achievement, Flint intervenes to belittle them both; he uses the boy as a courier to send his lurid entreaties to Linda. "One day, when I had not seen [Flint] for several weeks, I heard his steps approaching the door," Jacobs recalls in *Incidents*:

> I dreaded the encounter, and hid myself. He inquired for me, of course; but I was nowhere to be found. He went to his office, and despatched William with a note. The color mounted in my brother's face when he gave it to me; and he said, "Don't you hate me, Linda, for bringing you these things?" I told him I could not blame him; he was a slave, and obliged to obey his master's will. (*I,* 61)

Obviously, William comprehends the contents of what he brings to Linda; his face becomes flushed with anger and his plea for forgiveness indicates that he knows the nature of Flint's malicious intentions toward them both. However, whether John Jacobs himself could have been capable of this level of insight is not at all clear, given his own assessment of his literacy skills in "A True Tale."

John Jacobs states that Dr. Norcom forbade him from learning to write, but he does not specify that the prohibition included reading. The exemption is significant for two reasons and has tremendous implications for an evaluation of Harriet Jacobs's contention in this instance. First, if we assume that John already had some reading skills (thanks to his father's instruction), then his sister's claim that he was implicated in Flint's scheme to harass her gains credence. In that scenario, the brother's role becomes plausible; if John / William could read, then Norcom / Flint could have used him in that debasing way. The second set of circumstances poses a problem, though. If we assume that John Jacobs was unable to interpret those "stinging, scorching words" or to decipher those cryptically coded "signs" authored by Flint, then Harriet Jacobs's version of this incident was indeed her own invention. The question then becomes, for what purpose?

Assuming the validity of the *Incidents* version, William's role in the note exchange becomes clear. More than a mere messenger or a problematic participant, the boy becomes a witness to the illicit proceedings. That he is able to read doubles as testimony supporting Linda's accusation of Dr. Flint's assaults. However, with John Jacobs's ability to read cast in doubt, it remains Harriet Jacobs's exclusive claim that her brother was drafted into Flint's conspiracy against her; in "A True Tale" John Jacobs neither explicitly states nor subtly suggests that such a plan was in effect and that he was an active (though unwilling) agent in it. Indeed, his one reference to his sister's sexual travails all but denies that she even suffered in that way. Linda Brent's tortuous battles with Flint, and her subsequent affair with and pregnancies by Mr. Sands, register a zero sum effect when John Jacobs flatly relates Harriet's situation: "Some six or eight years have passed since I was sold, and she has become the mother of two children" (ATT, 86).

One could reasonably assume that John Jacobs deliberately censored discussion of his sister's ordeals, but, in fact, that would be rather odd. It could not be that he felt compelled to honor social codes of decorum; he does not exercise similar discretion in the final chapter of "A True Tale," where he describes the whipping of a pregnant slave with unflinching precision. Is his denial then born of ignorance – does he not know the intimate details of Harriet Jacobs's struggles with the white men of Edenton? If he does not, is it because he could not read and so was unable to decipher Flint's notes to Linda Brent? If John Jacobs could not and did not read these messages, however, then we cannot readily assume that the exchange between Flint and Linda Brent occurred. At this point, John Jacobs's metaphoric mirror cracks; the idea of one narrative servicing the other as a template does not work, because there are one too many narrative forms to deal with as the model base. As with their respective versions of their grandmother's sale, we cannot determine what is "true" in this instance because the "reality" of it is concealed by written script.

VI

Given these discrepancies between the Jacobses' narratives, the reader cannot unquestioningly rely upon one text to confirm the claims of the other. It would seem that we have to look to other external sources to verify the authenticity of both or, in the extreme, that we have to forget that one or the other narrative exists. That the reader cannot escape the consequence of the coincidence of the publication of *Incidents* and "A True Tale" turns the most poignant moment in both texts into unmitigated irony: the occasion of John and Harriet Jacobs's reunion after their escapes from slavery.

When John Jacobs first encounters his sister in New York he is shocked into a paroxysm of anguish and grief:

At first she did not look natural to me; but how should she look natural, after having been shut out from the light of heaven for six years and eleven months! I did not wish to know what her sufferings were while living in her place of concealment. The change that it had made in her was enough to make one's soul cry out against this curse of curses, that has so long trampled humanity in the dust. (ATT, 127)

In her hand, Harriet Jacobs's recollection of their meeting rises, Lazarus-like, with a conviction born of faith renewed:

One bright morning, as I stood at the window, tossing baby in my arms, my attention was attracted by a young man in sailor's dress, who was closely observing every house as he passed. Could it be my brother William? It *must* be he – and yet, how changed! I placed the baby safely, flew down the stairs, opened the front door, beckoned to the sailor, and in less than a minute I was clasped in my brother's arms. How much we had to tell each other! How we laughed, and how we cried, over each other's adventures! I took him to Brooklyn, and again saw him with Ellen, the dear child whom he had loved and tended so carefully, while I was shut up in my miserable den. He staid [*sic*] in New York a week. His old feelings of affection for me and Ellen were as lively as ever. There are no bonds so strong as those which are formed by suffering together. (*I*, 170)

The constrasts between these passages seem innocent because they are so blatantly incongruous; at the same time, the discrepancies consciously dare the reader not to interpret them as meaningful in and of themselves. John solemnly reports that Harriet looks "unnatural" to his eye, that the changes wrought by her ordeal made him want to "cry out against this curse of curses." Harriet rejoices that her brother is a new man: "Could it be my brother? It *must* be he – and yet, how changed!" she exclaims. John intimates that they passed their first hours together in silence – "I did not wish to know what her sufferings were, while living in her place of concealment," he acknowledges somewhat sheepishly. Harriet remembers their party to be full of talk: "How we laughed, and how we cried, over each other's adventures!" The sight of his sister's haggard demeanor enrages John; the thought of their "suffering" inspires Harriet to feel even deeper affection for her sibling.

If read separately, as the single account of their reunion, the reader could fairly assume that, in either *Incidents* or "A True Tale," Harriet and John Jacobs see each other perfectly; if read together, as dual experiences of the same moment, the reader will recognize that Harriet and John Jacobs do not see each other at all. At this point – the point at which, understandably, neither of them wants to confront the pain of their past – the reader is once again reminded of John Jacobs's distinction between civil and natural law and the figure of the mirror. An organically based integrity preserves Harriet and John Jacobs's relation to one another: they are biological relatives; they are racial kin – in a word, they are family (which was no small claim to preserve under slavery). That "natural" bond has been sundered by the differences civil law ascribes to them on the basis of their race and gender. What slavery means for black women and for black men is not, as *Incidents* and "A True Tale" attest, one and the same thing. Because the conditions of servitude experienced by each do not exactly coincide, the nature of John and Harriet Jacobs's pain is different and their expressions of its manifestations can be – and are, as these passages show – different, too.[45] Thus, "A True Tale" does not – and, furthermore, cannot – reflect back the image and meaning of suffering *Incidents* portrays here, and vice versa. By that same logic, the Jacobses' accounts of their reunion contradict one another so forthrightly not simply because of differences founded on body-based identity, experience, and perception. Rather, the discrepancies emerge strategically, as a challenge to the discursive constructs that would impose a particular idea of order and representation upon their narratives. Trying to figure out whose is the "true" story becomes a lost cause precisely because, between *Incidents* and "A True Tale," truth no longer bridges a causal relation to reality.

VII

If Angelina Grimké was correct, what was most intriguing about black slave narratives, what made them seem "real" to white audiences, were the details of the fugitives' escape. Writing in 1838, Grimké explained to her comrade Theodore Dwight Weld:

> We rejoiced to hear of the fugitives' escape from bondage, tho' some of the pleasure was abridged by the caution to keep these things close. . . . Yes – publish his tale of woe, such narratives are greatly needed, let it come burning from his own lips in England and publish it here; it must do good. Names, dates and facts will give additional credibility to it. Many and many a tale of romantic horror can the slaves tell.[46]

According to Grimké's taste, the line separating politics from entertainment runs a narrow course. Finding "pleasure" in the climactic moment of the slaves' escapes, she is also transported by the "romantic horror" of the fugitives' tales. The "credible" portions of the presentations – "names, dates and facts" – Grimké suggests, have a medicinal effect; she concedes that they "must do good." But the reader of *Incidents* and "A True Tale" does not – and cannot – achieve the peak experience Grimké longs for and reluctantly renounces. Consistently frustrated that the Jacobs texts fail to coincide at certain, crucial points, the reader has to consider whether the Jacobses' narratives "abridge" this experience in order to heed the "caution to keep these things closed," or whether the texts function to open up the abolitionists' outlook on black testimony for critical examination.[47]

It should not be surprising, then, that *Incidents* and "A True Tale" relay information about Harriet Jacobs's escape from slavery by way of pleasure-denying contradictions. As a single woman, Harriet Jacobs risks her integrity to protect herself from physical harm; as a single mother she jeopardizes her own life to secure the freedom of her children. Whether the task requires yielding to the white gentleman Sands's affection for her or sequestering herself in her grandmother's attic for seven years, Jacobs confronts these dangers, fully cognizant of their implications: "I knew what I did," she declares, "and I did it with deliberate calculation" (*I*, 54). And so, thinking woman that she presents herself to be, Jacobs plots the letters between Linda Brent and the Flints to be part of a *concerted* campaign devised by Linda and which are exchanged *over a period of time*. Indeed, Linda Brent believes the correspondence between her and her masters to be a "competition in cunning" (*I*, 128), and she wages it not only to "keep up [a] delusion, [which] made me and my friends feel less anxious" (*I*, 132), but also to taunt her nemesis Flint. Observing the doctor pursue the false leads she creates to mask her actual whereabouts from her post in the garret, Linda reflects upon her strategy: "It was a satisfaction to have miles of land and water between us, even for a little while [when Flint traveled north to search for her]; and it was a still greater satisfaction to know that he believed me to be in the Free States" (*I*, 116).

Although John Jacobs vouches for his sister's most extraordinary claim – that she hid in her grandmother's garret for almost seven years – he also contends that what prompts Harriet to leave her "strange place of concealment" (ATT, 110) is news of *his* successful escape from his owner (and the father of Harriet's children), Mr. Sawyer. Inspired by her brother's example and fearful that retaliation will follow from her own master, Harriet, according to John, sends a letter to Dr. Norcom asking him to sell her to her grandmother. She arranges to have the letter routed from New York, in order to continue the charade that she has already escaped to the North. Responding on behalf of his father, Caspar Norcom rejects Harriet's proposal and, John reports, "resort[s] to a cunningly devised artifice" (ATT, 127) to dupe his sister into returning to Edenton. With kindly turned phrases the younger Norcom tries to lure Harriet back into bondage by feigning goodwill and interest in reuniting her with her family.[48]

These and other elements in John Jacobs's recounting of his sister's escape do not find exact correlates in *Incidents*. For instance, by the time Linda Brent receives what John Jacobs claims is Caspar Norcom's letter in *Incidents*, she has moved beyond Flint's reach to New York and found work in the Bruce household. Indeed, this letter marks the final, not the first, correspondence between Linda and the Flint family. Nor do the texts' character references confirm one another. Missing from "A True Tale" is the brave Samaritan Peter who, in *Incidents*, risks his life to arrange Linda Brent's passage to New York. Partially present, though, is Caspar Norcom: *Incidents* charges that his father forged the letter in the son's name on behalf of Linda Brent's actual legal owner, Emily Flint. What do these missed representations mean?

In "A True Tale," Harriet Jacobs's project of writing fictitious letters was short-lived and was a plan their Uncle Mark – not Harriet – thought would be a useful ploy to stage her departure from Edenton. Once in New York, the Harriet Jacobs of "A True Tale" remains a character in need, a woman who cannot (as she does in *Incidents*) manage to rally her inner strengths and her own allies to act on her behalf.[49] According to John Jacobs, his sister no sooner makes her way North than Dr. Norcom's daughter decides to force her and her children back to North Carolina. A frightened and distraught Harriet pleads with her brother for assistance and he complies, leading them to safe shelter in Boston. When Harriet's employer, Mrs. Willis, learns of John's intention to seek final refuge abroad, she confronts him about his plans and convinces him to let Harriet remain in the United States under her benevolent guard. "'John, I know that the [Fugitive Slave] law is an absolute one, and that the prosecutors are deaf to the claims of justice and humanity,'" the matron begins, "'but I have resolved that Harriet shall not be taken out of my house. This I will promise you as a lady'" (ATT, 127).

By accepting the mistress' pledge of protection, it may seem that John Jacobs relinquishes his claim to his sister. On the contrary, at this meeting John Jacobs replaces their felled father and becomes the patriarch who assigns his sister / daughter's welfare to the socially influential white matriarch. His agreement constitutes a transfer of power from him to her. However, the mistress' request for an audience with John to negotiate her proposal – an encounter at which Harriet is present but remains silent throughout – not only dramatizes the restoration of John Jacobs's masculinity, but also displays the construct of racial power inherent in the audience relations between black slave narrators and white abolitionists.[50]

Positioning himself and his text as the references of appeal (the mistress asks permission to keep the silent Harriet, the declarative tone of the narrative directs the reader to accept the account as accurate), John Jacobs and "A True Tale" all but appropriate *Incidents'* status as the primary source of information about Harriet Jacobs's escape. John Jacobs reconsiders, reorganizes, and reinterprets the details of his sister's act with the effect of reproducing the dynamics fueling the consumption of black slave narratives by white abolitionist audiences. For *Incidents* and "A True Tale" more than fulfill Angelina Grimké's desire for "unabridged" recitations of fugitives' experiences in slavery; their respective versions of Harriet's escape disclose too much, the differences between their texts effectively jeopardizing either narrative's claim to credibility. In both *Incidents* and "A True Tale" the adaptations of Harriet Jacobs's escape suggest that the tenets upon which abolitionists asserted slave testimony to be "true" were no less problematic than the discrepancies between the Jacobses' narratives are conspicuous.

Writing about his sister's escape does not necessarily mean that John Jacobs is writing against it. To charge him with appropriating Harriet Jacobs's narrative presumes that her text is the original source and, as I have argued thus far, that relationship – of copy to original, secondary to primary source, oral to printed testimony, reality to truth – is effectively debunked when *Incidents* and "A True Tale" are read together.[51] More specifically, John and Harriet's respective versions of incidents common to their lives link the narratives together and, at the same time, separate out what one text "really" or "truthfully" means in relation to the other. The grammatical construction of John Jacobs's report of Harriet Jacobs's escape diagrams the logic of this relationship.

The use of the quotation mark in narrative raises the issue of citation. This, in turn, raises the issue of sources, which, because it is so basic, suggests how indebted the forms of black narrative were to the abolitionists' definitions of what constituted the truth.[52]

In "A True Tale" John Jacobs sets the "facts" about his sister's escape between quotes. He records, the marks imply, what she says: He writes, she speaks. However, as I have demonstrated, the citation of Harriet Jacobs's testimony in "A True Tale" contradicts her written account in *Incidents*; indeed, both the details and the tone with which Harriet Jacobs describes her bid for freedom in print construct an altogether different self from the one presented in her brother's story. The Harriet of "A True Tale" is a passive, diminutive figure who submits to the decision-making prowess of men. She is a foil to *Incidents*' Linda Brent, who is a persistent and shrewd tactician whose courageous resolve to act is remarkable precisely because she is a woman. Which narrative depicts the "real" Harriet Jacobs? Which account of her life and escape is more "true"?

There are no definitive answers to these questions, precisely because *Incidents* and "A True Tale" dissemble the very ideas of order and causation. For example, as references to and about one another, *Incidents* and "A True Tale" contravene the notion of originality in both senses of that term. We cannot tell which narrative should be read "first," nor can we discern which one gives rise to the inconsistencies that clearly characterize them both. If we cannot establish which narrative is the "primary" text, by what means and measures do we categorize what is a "secondary" or "contemporary" source in relation to it? Put another way: in the representation of her escape from slavery, what came first, John's quotation or Harriet's written account? Because neither narrative form can definitively assure a causal relation between what is "true" and what is "real" about the event, it is impossible to know which version of Harriet Jacobs's testimony proves what case. Her brother's hearsay report is, as far as we know, no more (or no less) accurate than is the version written by Harriet Jacobs herself. The narrative formats of *Incidents* and "A True Tale" thus reprise the abolitionist movement's protocol of having black slaves speak before they write, for the texts prompt us to reconsider just where the order of truth in one's voice lies.

VIII

Although there is no ready way to ascertain the definitive "truth" of what occurred to either John or Harriet Jacobs in terms of how each of them represents their own (and each other's) experience, this is not to say that *Incidents* and "A True Tale" are not "reliable" historical records. Nor is it to say that the Jacobs narratives make the idea of truth a relative concept. Rather, between *Incidents* and "A True Tale," truth becomes a function and trope of representation, each narrative promoting versions of Harriet Jacobs's self that simultaneously present and re-present her life as a matter for textual interpretation. Indeed, to the extent that we cannot use one story as a "reality check" for the other, what we come to know about Harriet Jacobs's life as a slave girl does not strictly depend on the literal, point-by-point correspondence between her narrative and her brother's, but on the gaps produced by their respective perceptions of what "really" happened to them both.

In this way, *Incidents* both anticipates and historicizes the debates that have been and continue to be formative in the development of African American literature and its attendant critical paradigms. The charge that black fiction must necessarily engage history (which is itself supposed to be a transparent and nonnarrative entity) to render the literal, authentic "truth" of black existence and experience is the directive that *Incidents* challenges thoroughly. When considered in relation to John Jacobs's "A True Tale" and the distinction made between oral and written discourse as approved modes of black testimony in abolitionist politics, *Incidents* proposes that truth can, as fact, assume symbolic forms, and requires that received ideas about what counts as "authentic" narrative be reconceived in nonracial terms. In such a reading, *Incidents* can be seen to retract its own claims to autobiography, its factual differences with "A True Tale" bracketing the "auto" and "bio," leaving us to contend with the "graphy" or, simply, the writing itself.

Notes

1. Linda Brent [Harriet A. Jacobs], *Incidents in the Life of a Slave Girl: Written by Herself,* ed. Jean Fagan Yellin (Cambridge, MA: Harvard University Press, 1987). Hereafter cited as *Incidents*. Individual references from the text will be noted parenthetically in the essay as "*I*," followed by the page number.

2. In "Texts and Contexts of Harriet Jacobs' *Incidents in the Life of a Slave Girl Written by Herself,*" Jean Fagan Yellin identifies and briefly summarizes the positions scholars have adopted on this point over the years. See Yellin in *The Slave's Narrative*, ed. Charles T. Davis and Henry Louis Gates, Jr. (New York: Oxford University Press, 1985), p. 278, n. 2.

3. John W. Blassingame, "Critical Essay on Sources," in *The Slave Community: Planta-tion Life in the Antebellum South*, rev. ed. (New York: Oxford University Press, 1979), 373.

4. Blassingame, *Slave Community*, 367.

5. Blassingame outlines his criteria in the following: "Critical Essay on Sources" in *The Slave Community*, esp. 368–72; the introductory essay to *Slave Testimony: Two Centuries of Letters, Speeches, Interviews, and Autobiographies* (Baton Rouge: Louisiana State University Press, 1977); and "Using the Testimony of Ex-Slaves: Ap-proaches and Problems," *Journal of Southern History* 60 (Nov. 1975): 473–92.

6. Prior to the publication of the Harvard edition of *Incidents*, Yellin reported the results of her research to the scholarly community in the following essays: "Writ-ten by Herself: Harriet Jacobs' Slave Narrative," *American Literature* 53:3 (Nov. 1981): 479–86; "'Texts and Contexts of Harriet Jacobs' *Incidents in the Life of a Slave Girl Written by Herself*," in Davis and Gates, *The Slave's Narrative*; and "Profile: Har-riet Ann Jacobs," *Legacy* 5:2 (1988): 55–60. In addition to Yellin's work, Dorothy Sterling's publication of excerpts from Harriet Jacobs's correspondence was an essential contribution to the documentary defense of *Incidents*. See Dorothy Ster-ling, *We Are Your Sisters: Black Women in the Nineteenth Century* (New York: Norton, 1984).

7. "Preface," viii. Yellin admits that she once harbored doubts about the trust-worthiness of Jacobs's autobiography. Yellin initially assumed *Incidents* was a "false slave narrative," relying on "received opinion" that the text was not histori-cally authentic ("Preface," vii).

8. Specifically, Andrews argues that Congress's adoption of the Fugitive Slave Law in 1850 and the Supreme Court's decision in the Dred Scott case of 1857 nation-alized the political marginality of Southern slaves. Black narrators responded to these arbitrary re-definitions of their social status by crafting life stories that cri-tiqued such legislative rulings and judicial decisions as fictitious constructions that could, as such, be questioned and rewritten in the text of their narratives. See Andrews, *To Tell a Free Story* (Urbana: University of Illinois Press, 1988), 169–79, as well as "The Novelization of Voice in Early African-American Narrative," *PMLA* 105:1 (Jan. 1990): 23–34.

9. I am well aware that a "new historicist" would argue against the distinction I have drawn thus far and make the case that history is itself a narrative whose claims to certainty are no more assured than is any given interpretation of a literary text. I would not disagree with that position; in fact, I am sympathetic to it. It is worth remembering, though, that *Incidents* emerged as a subject of (and for) histo-riographical debate prior to the ascension of new historicism as an interpretative framework for literary study.

10. I want to thank P. Gabrielle Foreman not only for reminding me to read John Jacobs's narrative, but for providing me with my first copy of the text as well.

11. In a letter to Amy Post, Jacobs described the comfort she experienced confiding in and commiserating with John: "Often I have gone to my poor brother with my gurived [grieved?] and mortified spirits," she confessed. "He would mingle his tears with mine while he would advise me to do what was right." As recent scholar-ship persuasively suggests, strong sentiment such as this proved to be a powerful

inducement for writers in nineteenth-century America. See Jacobs's letter to Post, dated 1852, in *Incidents*, 232.

12. August Meier and Elliot Rudwick, "The Role of Blacks in the Abolitionist Movement," in *Blacks in the Abolitionist Movement*, ed. John H. Bracey, Jr., et al. (Belmont, CA: Wadsworth Publishing Co., 1971), 115. It is worth noting that the recruitment of blacks as lecturers coincides with the American Anti-Slavery Society's loss of financial support from two of its principal backers, Lewis and Arthur Tappan. These New York merchants suffered monetary setbacks in the Panic of 1837, and the brothers' weakened financial status reduced the organization's ability to continue its pamphlet campaign and to maintain its bureau of white speakers. In short, the turn to black lecturers may have been as much a matter of expediency as the reflection of a shift in moral or political outlook. See the following: Ronald G. Walters, *The Antislavery Appeal: American Abolitionism after 1830* (Baltimore: Johns Hopkins University Press, 1976), 4–5; Leonard L. Richards, *Gentlemen of Property and Standing: Anti-Abolition Mobs in Jacksonian America* (NY: Oxford University Press, 1970), 157–9; Gilbert H. Barnes, *The Antislavery Impulse, 1830–1844* (1933; rpt. New York: Harcourt, Brace, & World, 1964), 145; Bertram Wyatt-Brown, *Lewis Tappan and the Evangelical War Against Slavery* (Cleveland: Case Western Reserve University, 1969), 174–5; and Letter from Elizur Wright, Jr., to Theodore Dwight Weld, dated Nov. 4, 1836, in *The Letters of Theodore Dwight Weld, Angelina Grimké Weld, and Sarah Grimké*, ed. Gilbert H. Barnes and Dwight L. Dumond (New York: Appleton, 1934), Vol. 1, 346.

13. Letter from Weld to Smith, dated New York, Oct. 23, 1839, in Barnes and Dumond, *Letters*, Vol. 2, 811.

14. Meier and Rudwick, "The Role of Blacks," 121; see also Larry Gara, "The Professional Fugitive in the Abolition Movement," *Wisconsin Magazine of History* 48:3 (Summer 1965): 196–204.

15. Marion Wilson Starling, "The Slave Narrative: Its Place in American Literary History" (Ph.D. dissertation, New York University, 1946), 331–2.

16. John Sekora, "Black Message / White Envelope: Genre, Authenticity, and Authority in the Antebellum Slave Narrative," *Callaloo* 10 (Summer 1987): 488, 496–7, 501–2. Theodore Dwight Weld also encouraged the use of such a device, emphasizing that accurate "facts and testimony are troops, weapons, and victory, all in one." See Weld's letter to Gerrit Smith, dated Fort Lee, New Jersey, Oct. 23, 1839, in Barnes and Dumond, *Letters*, Vol. 2, 807–9.

17. In addition to Sekora's account of this practice, see the following: John Blassingame, "Introduction," *Slave Testimony: Two Centuries of Letters, Speeches, Interviews, and Autobiographies* (Baton Rouge: Louisiana State University Press, 1977), xxii, xxvii; C. Peter Ripley, *The Black Abolitionist Papers* (Chapel Hill and London: University of North Carolina Press, 1991), Vol. 3, 28–32; Robert B. Stepto, *From Behind the Veil: A Study of Afro-American Narrative* (Urbana: University of Illinois Press, 1979), 9; and Henry Louis Gates, Jr., "Introduction," *The Classic Slave Narratives* (New York: New American Library, 1987), xi, and "The Language of Slavery" (with Charles T. Davis) in Davis and Gates, *The Slave's Narrative*, xvi.

18. Blassingame, *Slave Testimony*, xxix. Meier and Rudwick make this same point, in "Role of Blacks," pp. 121–2. In *Black Protest: Issues and Tactics* (Westport, CT:

Greenwood Press, 1974), Robert C. Dick suggests that there was a further division of blacks' labor on the abolitionist touring circuit. Some speakers were "narrators" while others were "lecturers," and these designations did not mean one and the same thing. "Narrators" (229) recited the chronology of their experience as slaves. "Lecturers" analyzed slavery and its attendant issues in the abstract as a matter of political principle and theory. Frederick Douglass's hard-fought struggle to enter into the ranks of the latter is well known and led, in part, to his break from William Lloyd Garrison in the late 1840s. For more on this distinction, see Dick, chapter 6.

19. "Our Boston Correspondent," *National Anti-Slavery Standard*, Feb. 16, 1861, 3. For a harrowing description of the scrutiny black lecturers had to face, see Charles Lenox Redmond's letter to Austin Willey dated Oct. 27, 1839, in *Witness for Freedom: African-American Voices on Race, Slavery, and Emancipation*, ed. C. Peter Ripley et al. (Chapel Hill: University of North Carolina Press, 1993), 72.

20. It is only fair to state that the lecture format or oral presentations could introduce abolitionist ideology to people who were unable to read printed narratives. James Walvin also observes that, in British society, the lecture was a "conventional political custom" as well as an "art which both entertained and entranced, often converted and excited" listeners. Donald Scott makes a similar point about the lyceum movement and the culture of public speaking in antebellum America. See Walvin, "The Propaganda of Anti-Slavery," in *Slavery and British Society, 1776–1846*, ed. James Walvin (Baton Rouge: Louisiana State University Press, 1982), 51–2, and Scott, "Print and the Public Lecture System, 1840–1860," in *Printing and Society in Early America*, ed. William L. Joyce et al. (Worcester, MA: American Antiquarian Society, 1982), 278–99.

21. Jacobs to Amy Post [1852?] in *Incidents*, 232.

22. To be sure, writing entailed its own risks and Jacobs was well aware of them, too. Setting forth the "cruel wrongs" done to her via print unnerved her no less than doing so in a public lecture; Jacobs understandably preferred to "whisper . . . [them] into the ear of a very dear friend." See Jacobs's letter to Amy Post, dated June 21, [1857] in *Incidents*, 242. Writing also set her in competition with other antislavery authors, most notably Harriet Beecher Stowe. Jacobs frankly states her irritation with Stowe's rebuffs of her and Stowe's less than charitable attempt to incorporate Jacobs's narrative as part of the *Key to Uncle Tom's Cabin*. See the following letters in *Incidents*: Jacobs to Post, [1852?], 232; Jacobs to Post, dated Feb. 14, [1853], 233–4; Jacobs to Post, dated April 4, [1853], 234–5; Jacobs to Post, dated Oct. 9, [1853], 236. Despite these conflicts, the prospect of being a published author seemed to intrigue and excite Jacobs. Her correspondence also expresses her fascination (and frustrations) with the process of shaping her narrative into, specifically, book form. See the following for statements of Jacobs's writerly ambitions: Jacobs to Post in Sterling, *We Are Your Sisters*, dated June 25, 1853, p. 78; Jacobs to Post in Sterling, dated Jan. 11, 1854, 80; Jacobs to Post in *Incidents*, dated March 1854, 237–8; and Jacobs to Post in *Incidents*, dated June 21, 1857, 243.

23. Ripley, *Black Abolitionist Papers*, Vol. I, 493, n. 4. Harriet Jacobs also mentions the enterprise in *Incidents*, p. 189. Yellin confirms this point in her "Introduction," xvi.

24. Yellin, "Introduction," xvi, and "Profile," 57. Also see Harriet Jacobs's letter to

Amy Post, dated March [1857] in *Incidents*, 240; there she mentions reading the *Liberator* and the *National Anti-Slavery Standard* to keep tabs on the Posts' activities.

25. Ripley, *Black Abolitionist Papers*, Vol. I, 493, n. 4; Jacobs to Post in *Incidents*, [1852?], 232.

26. I have arrived at this conclusion based on the chronology presented by Yellin in the Harvard edition of *Incidents*. Harriet Jacobs began work on the manuscript in 1853 and completed it in 1858. After several failed negotiations with publishers in the United States and in England, Jacobs contracted for the book to be privately printed in America, in 1861. Jacobs traveled to Philadelphia in February of that year, when and where she sold fifty copies of the narrative to (presumably) abolitionists and their supporters. On these points, see Yellin, "Introduction" and "Chronology" in *Incidents*, xxiv–xxv and 224–5, respectively. There is, to my knowledge, no published documentation currently available to prove that Jacobs did – or did not – read or otherwise orally present her story at the Philadelphia meeting or at any other public gathering. Even if she did, and even though it would be useful to know the itinerary Jacobs followed and how extensive were her efforts to publicize and sell *Incidents*, my point is this: the book was published first and her appearance(s) followed.

27. Yellin, "Introduction," xvii; Harriet Jacobs to Amy Post [1852?], in *Incidents*, p. 232.

28. Yellin, "Introduction," xx; Harriet Jacobs to Amy Post [1854] in *Incidents*, 237–8 and Jacobs to Amy Post [1857] in *Incidents*, 243.

29. See Shirley J. Yee's *Black Women Abolitionists: A Study in Activism, 1828–1860* (Knoxville: University of Tennessee Press, 1992), 113–17, for a useful explanation for the particular constraints faced by black women on the abolitionist lecture circuit.

30. Jacobs to Post, dated 1854, cited in Yellin, "Written by Herself," 485.

31. Strictly speaking, *Incidents* did not appear first; in 1853 Jacobs published two articles about slavery in the New York *Tribune*, "Letter from a Fugitive Slave. Slaves Sold Under Peculiar Circumstances" (June 21, 1853), and "Cruelty to Slaves" (July 25, 1853).

32. "A True Tale" was published in four installments that month: Feb. 7, 14, 21, and 28 of 1861.

   In her memoir, *Recollection of Fifty Years* (London: John Murray, 1910), Isabella Fyvie Mayo (who wrote under the nom de plume "Edward Garrett"), identifies members of *The Leisure Hour*'s staff. Their biographies and activities should be traced in order to determine how and why John Jacobs placed his narrative in this publication. Mayo, who submitted freelance verse to the magazine, lists her contacts as follows: William Stevens, coeditor of the journal beginning in 1862, and Dr. [Zachary?] Maculay (whose first name she never provides), who was recommended to her by Charles Gordon, manager of the Partridge Publishing house, also located on Paternoster Row in London.

33. Alvar Ellegård, "Readership of the Periodical Press in Victorian England" (Göteborg, 1957); see 37 and table 16, 35. In his survey of English periodicals in print during the later years of the Victorian era (1860 to 1870), Ellegard rates *The Leisure Hour*'s educational standard as somewhere between "low to fair." Typically sixteen pages in length, *The Leisure Hour* featured articles that sought to introduce its readers to a wide range of popular topics in a straightforward prose style. To-

gether with eye-catching pen-and-ink illustrations on the cover (an innovation during the period) and occasional light verse, *The Leisure Hour* did not exceed the expectations its title implied. See the editors' statement of purpose, "A Word with Our Readers," in the inaugural issue of the magazine (Jan. 1, 1852), 8–10; William Jones, *The Jubilee Memorial of the Religious Tract Society: Containing a Record of Its Origins, Proceedings, and Results*, A.D. 1799 to A.D. 1849 (London: Religious Tract Society, 1850), esp. chap. 12; and Roger H. Martin, *Evangelicals United: Ecumenical Stirrings in Pre-Victorian Britain, 1795–1830* (Metuchen, NJ: Scarecrow Press, 1983), esp. chap. 8.

34. Ellegård, "Readership," 37.

35. Howard Temperley's analysis of the political stature of the British Foreign Anti-Slavery Society (BFASS) at this time may shed some light on Jacobs's decision. In *British Anti-Slavery, 1833–1870* (London: Longman, 1972), Temperley chronicles the declining fortunes of the organization in the 1850s. Its membership had declined and, most critically, fiscal support from sympathetic philanthropists had withered. These developments forced the BFASS to curtail its publishing activities. The *Antislavery Reporter* cut back its publication schedule from bimonthly to monthly during these years (in 1868 the paper appeared quarterly), and its size shrank from quarto to octavo. By 1860, the *Reporter's* circulation had plummeted to 700, of which only 80 copies sold. In terms of market strength, then, *The Leisure Hour* would have been a more strategic medium to carry John Jacobs's message. On these points, see Temperley, 228–30. On the Religious Tract Society's marketing strategies, see Jones, *Jubilee Memorial*, 118–21.

36. John Jacobs to Isaac Post, June 5, 1861, in Ripley, *Black Abolitionist Papers*, Vol. 3, 491.

37. John S. Jacobs, "A True Tale of Slavery," *The Leisure Hour*, Feb. 28, 1861, 139. Hereafter cited as "A True Tale." Individual references will be noted in the essay as ATT, followed by the page number.

38. The standard-bearing interpretations read *Incidents* as a critique of the racially coded tenets of antebellum domestic ideology and the "cult of true womanhood." Hazel V. Carby and Jean Fagan Yellin's analyses remain the most forceful arguments establishing this point of view. See Carby, *Reconstructing Womanhood: The Emergence of the Afro-American Woman Novelist* (New York: Oxford University Press, 1987), esp. 47–61, and Yellin's "Preface" and "Introduction" to *Incidents*, the essay "Texts and Contexts," and *Women and Sisters: The Antislavery Feminists in American Culture* (New Haven: Yale University Press, 1989), esp. 87–96.

39. Yellin, 255 n. 28; and Yellin, "Introduction" to *Incidents*, xxiv.

40. Webb, "Our European Correspondent," *National Anti-Slavery Standard*, Aug. 17, 1861, 3. Apparently, Webb actually met Harriet Jacobs: "When I looked on her kind, good-natured face, I little knew what a heroine of freedom stood before me," Webb reminisces. Note, though, how Webb's admission also indicates that he cannot reconcile Jacobs's personal appearance (her "oral" self, so to speak) with her self-representation in print.

41. As Rafia Zafar reminded me, John Jacobs's characterization of his father illustrates the theory behind Orlando Patterson's *Slavery and Social Death: A Comparative Study* (Cambridge, MA: Harvard University Press, 1982). The son's desire to recover the father's forbidden authority reveals an unstated premise of Patterson's

argument as well. If "natal alienation" – or the practice of denying slaves the right
to claim and live in accordance with blood-based kinship ties – makes slaves "socially dead," the concept implicitly avows the primacy of heterosexuality as a root
principle of social life and, by extension, of freedom. To argue that slavery is degrading because of "the loss of ties in birth in both ascending and descending generations" (7) suggests that reproduction would resurrect the slave into the order of
humanity; to make this point without specifying whether configurations besides
heterosexuality could restore or comprise these ties limits our view of how community – indeed, the very notions of kinship and society themselves – can be constructed. See Patterson, chap. 2.

42. For an intriguing discussion of the ideological role Aunt Martha plays in *Incidents*,
see Bruce Mills, "Lydia Maria Child and the Endings to Harriet Jacobs's *Incidents
in the Life of a Slave Girl*," *American Literature* 64:2 (June 1992): 255–72.

43. For discussions of gender differences in slave narratives, see Frances Smith Foster,
"'In Respect to Females': Differences in the Portrayals of Women by Male and
Female Narrators," *Black American Literature Forum* 15:2 (1981): 66–70; Mary Helen
Washington, "Meditation on History: The Slave Narrative of Linda Brent," in
Invented Lives: Narratives of Black Women, 1860–1960 (New York: Doubleday, 1987);
and Joanne M. Braxton, "Harriet Jacobs' *Incidents in the Life of a Slave Girl*: Re-
definition of the Slave Narrative Genre," *Massachusetts Review* 27:2 (Summer 1986):
379–87.

44. The following statement embodies how Jacobs merges the act of physical abuse
with the signs of discourse: "He [Dr. Flint] clinched my arm with a volley of
oaths" (*I*, 81). See P. Gabrielle Foreman's "The Spoken and the Silenced in *Incidents in the Life of a Slave Girl* and *Our Nig*," *Callaloo* 13:2 (Spring 1990): 317–18, for
persuasive exposition of this point.

45. See Franny Nudleman's "Harriet Jacobs and the Politics of Sentimental Suffering," *English Literary History*, 59:4 (Winter 1992): 939–64, for a provocative and useful exploration of the relation between suffering, claims of "truth," and forms of
representation within abolitionist discourse.

46. Letter from Grimké to Weld, dated Jan. 21, 1838, in Barnes and Dumond, Vol. 2,
523.

47. Precedent for this interrogation was founded by Frederick Douglass. In his 1845
Narrative, he explicitly denounced the disclosure of the fugitives' escape strategies
and routes to abolitionist audiences, a stand he inscribed into the formal structure
of both the 1845 *Narrative* and *My Bondage and My Freedom* (1855). Douglass accomplishes this in two ways: first, by positing other experiences as being equally liberating as his literal escape; and second, by carefully plotting toward the moment of
departure and refusing to describe it in great detail. See Andrews, *To Tell a Free
Story*, 128–129 and 136–7, for a succinct analysis of this point.

48. John Jacobs discusses this exchange of the letters in his own correspondence to
Sydney Howard Gray, dated June 4, 1846, in *Incidents*, 228–9.

49. Notably, Linda Brent's reliance upon women to assist in her struggles against the
Flints is all but negated in her brother's account. John Jacobs seems to prize the idea
of freedom as a flight from community, while Harriet Jacobs valorizes it as an
entrance into social relations and obligations. For discussions of this difference as a
marker of *Incidents'* proto-feminist outlook, see Yellin, Carby, Andrews, and Braxton.

50. For an important discussion of this point, see Karen Sanchez-Eppler, "Bodily Bonds: The Intersecting Rhetorics of Feminism and Abolition," *Representations* 24 (Fall 1988): 28–59. Also see Sekora; Nudleman; Yellin, *Women and Sisters*; and Andrews, *To Tell a Free Story*, esp. 105–8.

51. For a challenging meditation of this point vis-à-vis gender and sexuality, see Judith Butler's "Imitation and Gender Insubordination," in *Inside / Out: Lesbian Theories, Gay Theories*, ed. Diana Fuss (New York: Routledge, 1991).

52. See Andrew Levy's "Dialect and Convention: Harriet A. Jacobs's *Incidents in the Life of a Slave Girl*," *Nineteenth Century Literature* 45:2 (Sept. 1990): 206–19, for a parallel argument on this point.

Bibliography

Andrews, William L. *To Tell a Free Story: The First Century of Afro-American Autobiography, 1760–1865*. Urbana: University of Illinois Press, 1985.

"The Novelization of Voice in Early African American Narrative." *PMLA* 105:1 (Jan. 1990): 23–34.

Barnes, Gilbert H. *The Antislavery Impulse, 1830–1844*. 1933. Reprint, New York: Harcourt, Brace & World, 1964.

, and Dwight L. Dumond. *The Letters of Theodore Dwight Weld, Angelina Grimké Weld, and Sarah Grimké*. 2 vols. New York: Appleton, 1934.

Blassingame, John W. *The Slave Community: Plantation Life in the Antebellum South*. Revised Edition. New York: Oxford University Press, 1979.

, ed. *Slave Testimony: Two Centuries of Letters, Speeches, Interviews and Autobiographies*. Baton Rouge: Louisiana State University Press, 1977.

"Using the Testimony of Ex-Slaves: Approaches and Problems." *Journal of Southern History* 60 (Nov. 1975): 473–92.

Braxton, Joanne M. "Harriet Jacobs' *Incidents in the Life of a Slave Girl*: Re-definition of the Slave Narrative Genre." *Massachusetts Review* 27:2 (Summer 1986): 379–87.

Brent, Linda. [Jacobs, Harriet A.] *Incidents in the Life of a Slave Girl: Written by Herself*, ed. Jean Fagan Yellin. Cambridge: Harvard University Press, 1987.

Butler, Judith. "Imitation and Gender Insubordination." In *Inside / Out: Lesbian Theories, Gay Theories*, ed. Diana Fuss. New York: Routledge, 1991.

Carby, Hazel V. *Reconstructing Womanhood: The Emergence of the Afro-American Woman Novelist*. New York: Oxford University Press, 1987.

Davis, Charles T., and Henry Louis Gates, Jr. *The Slave's Narrative*. New York: Oxford University Press, 1985.

Dick, Robert C. *Black Protest: Issues and Tactics*. Westport, CT: Greenwood Press, 1974.

Ellegård, Alvar. "The Readership of the Periodical Press in Victorian England." *Göteburgs hogskolas arsskrift* 63:3 Göteborg: Acta Universitatis Göthobeurgensis, 1957.

Foreman, P. Gabrielle. "The Spoken and the Silenced in *Incidents in the Life of a Slave Girl* and *Our Nig*." *Callaloo* 13:2 (Spring 1990): 313–324.

Gara, Larry. "The Professional Fugitive in the Abolition Movement." *Wisconsin Magazine of History* 48:3 (Summer 1965): 196–204.

Gates, Henry Louis, Jr., ed. "Introduction." *The Classic Slave Narratives*. New York: New American Library, 1987.

Jacobs, John S. "A True Tale of Slavery." *The Leisure Hour* (London, February 1861).
  Letter to Isaac Post. June 5, 1861. In *The Black Abolitionist Papers*, Vol. 3, ed. C. Peter
  Ripley. Chapel Hill and London: University of North Carolina Press, 1991.

Jones, William. *The Jubilee Memorial of the Religious Tract Society: Continuing a Record of Its
  Origins, Proceedings, and Results*, A.D. 1749 to A.D. 1849. London: Religious Tract
  Society, 1850.

Levy, Andrew. "Dialect and Convention: Harriet A. Jacobs's *Incidents in the Life of a
  Slave Girl*." *Nineteenth Century Literature* 45:2 (Sept. 1990): 206–19.

Litwack, Leon F. "The Emancipation of the Negro Abolitionist." In *Blacks in the Abolitionist Movement*, ed. John H. Bracey, Jr., et al. Belmont, CA: Wadsworth Publishing Co., 1971.

Martin, Roger H. *Evangelicals United: Ecumenical Stirrings in Pre-Victorian Britain, 1795–
  1830*. Metuchen, NJ: Scarecrow Press, 1983.

Mayo, Isabella Fyvie [Edward Garrett]. *Recollection of Fifty Years*. London: John Murray, 1910.

Meier, August, and Elliot Rudwick. "The Role of Blacks in the Abolitionist Movement." In *Blacks in the Abolitionist Movement*, ed. John H. Bracey, Jr., et al. Belmont,
  CA: Wadsworth Publishing Co., 1971.

Nudleman, Franny. "Harriet Jacobs and the Politics of Sentimental Suffering." *English Literary History* 59:4 (Winter 1992): 939–64.

Olney, James. "'I Was Born': Slave Narratives, Their Status as Autobiography and as
  Literature." *Callaloo* 7:1 (Winter 1989): 46–73.

Patterson, Orlando. *Slavery and Social Death: A Comparative Study*. Cambridge, MA: Harvard University Press, 1982.

Richards, Leonard L. *Gentlemen of Property and Standing: Anti-Abolition Mobs in Jacksonian
  America*. New York: Oxford University Press, 1970.

Ripley, C. Peter, ed. *The Black Abolitionist Papers* 5 vols. Chapel Hill and London: University of North Carolina Press, 1991.

, et al. *Witness for Freedom: African-American Voices on Race, Slavery, and Emancipation*.
  Chapel Hill: University of North Carolina Press, 1993.

Scott, Donald M. "Print and the Public Lecture System, 1840–1860." In *Printing and
  Society in Early America*, ed. William L. Joyce et al. Worcester, MA: American Antiquarian Society, 1983.

Sekora, John. "Black Message / White Envelope: Genre, Authenticity, and Authority
  in the Antebellum Slave Narrative." *Callaloo* 10:3 (Summer 1987): 482–515.

Starling, Marion Wilson. "The Slave Narrative: Its Place in American Literary History." Ph.D. Dissertation. New York University, 1946.

Stepto, Robert B. *From Behind the Veil: A Study of Afro-American Narrative*. Urbana: University of Illinois Press, 1979.

Sterling, Dorothy. *We Are Your Sisters: Black Women in the Nineteenth Century*. New York:
  Norton, 1984.

Temperley, Howard. *British Antislavery, 1833–1870*. London: Longman, 1972.

Walters, Ronald G. *The Antislavery Appeal: American Abolitionism after 1830*. Baltimore:
  Johns Hopkins University Press, 1976.

Walvin, James. "The Propaganda of Anti-Slavery." In *Slavery and British Society, 1776–
  1846*, ed. James Walvin. Baton Rouge: Louisiana State University Press, 1982.

Wyatt-Brown, Bertram. *Lewis Tappan and the Evangelical War against Slavery*. Cleveland: Press of Case Western Reserve University, 1969.

Yee, Shirley J. *Black Women Abolitionists: A Study in Activism, 1828–1860*. Knoxville: University of Tennessee Press, 1992.

Yellin, Jean Fagan. "Written by Herself: Harriet Jacobs' Slave Narrative." *American Literature* 53:3 (Nov. 1981): 479–86.

——— "Texts and Contexts of Harriet Jacobs' *Incidents in the Life of a Slave Girl: Written by Herself*." In *The Slave's Narrative*, ed. Charles T. Davis and Henry Louis Gates, Jr. New York: Oxford University Press, 1985.

——— "Introduction" and "Preface." *Incidents in the Life of a Slave Girl: Written by Herself*, ed. Jean Fagan Yellin. Cambridge: Harvard University Press, 1987.

——— "Profile: Harriet Ann Jacobs." *Legacy* 5:2 (Fall 1988): 55–60.

——— *Women and Sisters: The Antislavery Feminists in American Culture*. New Haven: Yale University Press, 1989.

THROUGH HER BROTHER'S EYES

INCIDENTS AND "A TRUE TALE"

JEAN FAGAN YELLIN

———

When I first read John S. Jacobs's slave narrative, "A True Tale of Slavery," I thought it an exciting corroborative text. Engaged in the double task of establishing Harriet Jacobs's *Incidents in the Life of a Slave Girl* as an African American text and as an autobiography, I welcomed her brother's narrative because it corroborates some of the most outrageous claims made by Jacobs's alter ego Linda Brent – including her assertion that she hid in Grandmother's house, within earshot of her vindictive master, for almost seven years. Further, I thought John S. Jacobs's narrative important because it gives additional detailed information about Jacobs's life. "A True Tale" includes the first initial of proper names, for example, so tentative identifications of various individuals could be corroborated. Further, it gives information that *Incidents* omits – for instance, it carefully explains Grandmother's ownership of her oldest son, and it clearly describes the architecture of the "loophole of retreat."[1]

But I also valued "A True Tale" for other reasons. I had already realized that Harriet Jacobs chose a unique subject for her book. Although Frederick Douglass had described the brutalities inflicted upon his Aunt Hester, and William Wells Brown had recorded Patsey's suffering, only Harriet Jacobs wrote an antebellum slave narrative in which the sexual oppression of slave women and their struggle against this oppression is central.[2] In addition, I had known that Harriet Jacobs created two interlocking texts: her public writing – the pseudonymous slave narrative *Incidents* – and her private letters to her friend Amy Post that discuss the inception, composition, and publication of her book. Now, encountering "A True Tale," I saw that this narrative by Jacobs's brother constitutes an additional textual layer. "A True Tale" not

44

only reiterates some of the events and clarifies the identities of people and places in *Incidents,* it also offers a different perspective – that of a male narrator – on the people, places, and events Harriet Jacobs wrote about. For the reader of *Incidents,* John S. Jacobs's "A True Tale" can be used as a lens affording a male angle of vision on Harriet Jacobs's book, the most female-centered of the narratives. Although "A True Tale" and *Incidents* share much of their subject matter, the stories that Harriet Jacobs and John S. Jacobs tell are not the same.

Before turning to these texts, however, it is important to learn more about the author of "A True Tale" than is divulged in *Incidents.* John S. Jacobs's life was very different from that of his sister. Although she had no public presence until she wrote her book, he was an experienced movement speaker long before he became a slave narrator. By 1846, when Harriet Jacobs returned from her first trip to England, he was already an activist, serving as an intermediary between the black community and the Garrisonian abolitionists and as corresponding secretary of the New England Freedom Association, a Boston-based African American group. When his sister's North Carolina owners attempted to harass and intimidate her after she fled to New York, John S. kept the Garrisonians informed. Particularly active on behalf of fugitive slaves, in 1846 John S. was described by a fellow abolitionist as "zealous" in his failed effort to rescue an escaped New Orleans slave who was captured in Boston: "For one whole dark night (after vainly seeking for help in his chosen plan of rescue,) he was watching on the islands in the harbor, hoping to secure freedom to his brother." For the next several years, he was deeply involved with the Garrisonians, attending meetings, signing protests against the Mexican War, and donating money for the Irish starving in the potato famine.[3]

By 1848, John S. had been hired to work as an Agent of the Massachusetts Anti-Slavery Society. Undertaking a four-and-a-half-month antislavery lecture tour, he traveled with Jonathan Walker, the white Massachusetts sea captain who, after being captured in Florida for aiding fugitive slaves, was jailed, fined, pilloried, and branded with the letters "S S" (slave stealer) as punishment. John S's published reports of his lecturing experiences suggest his full-blown platform style. In one letter indicting the hypocrisy of pro-slavery churches, he condemned their faith as "a baby-stealing, woman-shipping, man-murdering and war-making religion."[4]

Finding his provocative manner effective with audiences, John S. next arranged a lecture tour of his own. One listener, who praised his "devotion to the cause, and his integrity of character," commented that he spoke "with fluency and depth of interest scarcely excelled by any of his predecessors – even by *Douglass* himself."[5] That summer, when John S. participated in the Garrisonians' "100 conventions," a reporter noted that in his remarks John S.

humorously incorporated comments on his escape from his master, *Incidents'*
Mr. Sands:

> The moderator [was kept] on the grin by his witty allusions to the love
> he used to bear his old master, a North Carolina lawyer, and a member
> of Congress, and by his playful remarks on the manner in which he
> escaped from bondage. His massa, while doting upon a newly married
> wife, whom he became acquainted with at Washington, and with
> whom he came North to be joined to, was sufficiently in love to be a
> little *blind* in one eye, while the mulatto's suavity of manner pulled the
> wool over the other. Thus he escaped."[6]

Rehired as an agent, in 1849 John S. undertook a joint speaking tour with
Frederick Douglass. Commenting on the proslavery racist opposition they
encountered, Douglass praised John S.'s "calm but feeling manner" and
spoke of the "deep impression" his speeches made on their audiences.[7] Lecturing alone later that spring, John S. reported crowds that were smaller and
less sympathetic. Discouraged, he wrote to Douglass: "At no time during my
laboring in the cause as a lecturer, have I found so few friends, as on the present occasion."[8]

Characteristically, when faced with opposition, John S. counterattacked.
Hissed and threatened at one meeting after he had condemned President
Zachary Taylor as a slaveholder, John S. lashed back at his hostile audience:

> Have I asked you for gold and silver, or have I asked you to take your
> feet off the necks of three millions of your countrymen, whom you have
> so long oppressed? For this you threatened to stone me, where is your
> sympathy? Is it with the oppressed or the oppressors? Dare you call
> yourselves friends to your country, who have elected to the highest of-
> fice in the gift of the nation, a man in whom you could see nothing but
> blood, rapine, and robbery?[9]

His work on the lecture platform won John S. recognition among the anti-
slavery faithful. At the Fifteenth Annual Meeting of the American Anti-
Slavery Society, where he entered into debate with the likes of Wendell Phillips, Edmund Quincy, and William Lloyd Garrison, his efforts, as well as
those of the other organizers and speakers at the One Hundred Conventions,
were praised.[10] Reporting on John S.'s rhetorical use of his personal experiences in slavery, one newspaper noted that, endorsing the Garrisonian politics of disunion, he condemned "the *social* union between Northern men and
Southern slave-holders" by referring directly to a man whom Harriet Jacobs
obliquely mentions in *Incidents*: "a Mr. Skinner of North Carolina, whom he
well knew as the holder of near one hundred slaves. He has, said Mr. J., a
relative in this city, (Rev. Dr. Skinner,) whom he frequently visits, and is received and welcomed there, though the enslaver of so many of his equal

brethren. How many such instances are to be found in every Northern community!"[11]

In the spring of 1849, Harriet Jacobs moved to Rochester to be near her brother. That March, he assumed proprietorship of the Rochester Antislavery Office and Reading Room, housed one floor above Frederick Douglass's newspaper offices on Buffalo Street. Advertising in *North Star* that the library "has been newly stocked with the latest and best works on slavery and other moral questions," John S. lists a series of current titles, including his colleague Jonathan Walker's *The Branded Hand*, Theodore Parker's sermons, and Richard Hildreth's treatise *Despotism in America*. Although Harriet Jacobs worked hard to make the Antislavery Office a success, by summer, John S. had given it up. In late autumn, he tried his hand as a restaurateur, opening "a spacious oyster saloon" on State Street. But this venture, too, failed.[12]

Early in 1850, after passage of the new Fugitive Slave Law, John S. decided to go west to seek his fortune in the California goldfields, and Harriet Jacobs returned to New York City and to her job with the Willis family. She later recalled that, at this time, her brother expressed "bitterness of spirit and stern hostility to our oppressors." John S. made public his righteous anger at the repressive law in an impassioned appeal at a meeting protesting the seizure of James Hamlet, the first New York victim of the new Fugitive Slave Law. His oratorical skills were impressive:

> My colored brethren, if you have not swords, I say to you, sell your garments and buy one. . . . They said that they cannot take us back to the South; but I say, under the present law they can; and now I say unto you, let them only take your dead bodies. . . . I would, my friends, advise you to show a front to our tyrants, and arm yourselves; aye, and I would advise the women to have their knives too. But I don't advise you to trample on the laws of this State, but I advise you to trample on this bill, and I further advise you to let us go on immediately, and act like men.[13]

He did not, however, limit himself to arousing the crowd but, calling on his organizational skills, proposed that they organize "a registry" of fugitives to help each other avoid being seized under the provisions of the new law. Then, disgusted by American racism and slavery, he left for California and later set sail for Australia, searching for gold.

Like so many others, however, he failed to strike it rich. In 1858, when Harriet Jacobs made her second trip to the British Isles in an effort to sell her book manuscript, John S. was working as a seaman, sailing out of London. After the Civil War broke out, he voiced his skepticism about America's antislavery commitment in a letter to American abolitionists:

> You that have believed in the promise, and obeyed His word, are be-
> ginning to see the moving of His hand to execute judgment and bestow
> mercy. Those who have long sown chains and fetters will reap blood
> and carnage. Their troubles have begun; God only knows where they
> will end.[14]

Because he could not be sure that the war would become a war of liberation,
he wrote, he had not yet decided to return home:

> I do not think of leaving London at present. I shall wait to see what
> course the North intends to pursue. If the American flag is to be
> planted on the altar of freedom, then I am ready to be offered on that
> altar, if I am wanted; if it must wave over the slave, with his chains and
> fetters clanking, let me breathe the free air of another land, and die a
> man and not a chattel.[15]

John S. Jacobs published "A True Tale of Slavery" in the popular London
magazine *The Leisure Hour: A Family Journal of Instruction and Recreation* in four
installments in February, 1861, only weeks after his sister had finally managed
to bring out *Incidents* in Boston.[16] Reading his male-authored narrative and
her female-authored book affords us an extraordinary perspective on the
gendering of texts, on the ways in which texts are informed by the conventions concerning male and female at a particular place and time. In "A True
Tale," we hear the practiced male voice of John S., who sounds the notes of
anger, militancy, and humor that the nineteenth century assigned to men. "A
True Tale" contrasts dramatically with *Incidents* not only in its voice, but also
in the audience it targets and in its announced purpose.[17] Where Harriet
Jacobs's Linda Brent explains to her American readers that she is writing "to
arouse the women of the North to a realizing sense of the conditions of two
millions of women at the South," John S. challenges his British readers (of
unspecified gender), announcing that he will "defy the world to prove false"
his testimony about slavery and asserting that he has written to punish his
oppressors: "If possible, let us make those whom we have left behind [in the
United States] feel that the ground they till is cursed with slavery, the air they
breathe poisoned with its venom breath, and that which made life dear to
them is lost and gone."[18]

In terms of the stories they tell and the stories they do not tell, both Harriet
and John S. address the conventions of nineteenth-century gender. Further,
both reveal that these gender conventions are status-specific and race-
specific, and that, in their specificity, they function to condemn black people
held as slaves.[19] As *Incidents* dramatizes the exclusion of a female slave from
the nineteenth-century category of True Womanhood because her status
prevented her from the requisite piety, purity, and domesticity required of
females, so "A True Tale" reveals that a male slave was excluded from

nineteenth-century True Manhood because his status prevented him from assuming for mother, sister, wife, and children the responsibility required of males.[20]

Exploring these notions of gender, it is instructive to compare the treatment of family members in these narratives. If *Incidents* can be read as Harriet Jacobs's *homage* to Grandmother, whose life presents an alternative model of Womanhood – and it can – then "A True Tale" is John S.'s *homage* to his father, whose life presents an alternative model of manhood. His father, he confides, "made impressions on my mind in childhood that can never be forgotten." Of his father, John S. eloquently writes:

> To be a man, and not to be a man – a father without authority – a husband and no protector – is the darkest of fates. Such was the condition of my father, and such is the condition of every slave throughout the United States: he owns nothing, he can claim nothing. His wife is not his: his children are not his; they can be taken from him, and sold at any minute, as far away from each other as the human fleshmonger may see fit to carry them. Slaves are recognised as property by the law, and can own nothing except by the consent of their masters. A slave's wife or daughter may be insulted before his eyes with impunity. He himself may be called on to torture them, and dare not refuse. To raise his hand in their defence is death by the law. He must bear all things and resist nothing. . . . My father taught me to hate slavery, but forgot to teach me how to conceal my hatred. I could frequently perceive the pent-up agony of his soul, although he tried hard to conceal it in his own breast. The knowledge that he was a slave himself, and that his children were also slaves, embittered his life, but made him love us the more.[21]

Perhaps it is because of this male perspective that it is in John S.'s brief narrative, and not in Harriet Jacobs's full-length book, that their father's death is explained. The son writes that following the marriage of his young mistress, his father became the property of her new husband:

> Being, as he was then considered, the best house-carpenter in or near the town, he was not put to field-work, although the privilege of working out, and paying his owner monthly, which he once enjoyed, was now denied him. This added another link to his galling chain – sent another arrow to his bleeding heart. My father, who had an intensely acute feeling of the wrongs of slavery, sank into a state of mental dejection, which, combined with bodily illness, occasioned his death when I was eleven years of age. He left us the only legacy that a slave father can leave his child, his whips and chains. These he had taught us to hate, and we resolved to seek for liberty, though we travelled through the gates of death to find it.[22]

Like Harriet Jacobs's Linda, John S. comments on the love of freedom that he and his sister share, which he attributes to their father's example. Linda writes that their father "had more of the feelings of a freeman than is common among slaves," and she recalls that he once reprimanded her little brother for ignoring him and obeying his mistress.[23] But unlike "A True Tale," which assigns this youthful hatred of slavery solely to their father's influence, *Incidents* presents a range of characters, both male and female – including family members like Uncle Benjamin and Grandmother, and neighbors like Peter and Aunt Aggie – all of whom demonstrate their hatred of slavery.

The gendering of these texts is further demonstrated in their treatment of the situation of women in slavery. Although John S. includes an acknowledgment of the importance of "my dear old grandmother," and although he voices the pain of a slave mother, it is his sister who repeatedly describes the torture of slave mothers. She writes of rape, concubinage, and insanity; of the death of a young slave girl who has just delivered a "nearly white" baby while her mother mourns and her mistress mocks her; of a mother fearing to name her master as father of her child; of the torture and sale of a woman who *has* named her master; of a woman locked away from her nursing baby; of a wetnurse who, ordered stripped and whipped for "some trifling offense," commits suicide; of a slave mother's fears for her children on hiring-day; of a mother's suffering when her children are sold away from her and of her torment when her last child is sold; of a woman's grief when her son is tortured and murdered; of an old woman abandoned and "left to be sold to any body who would give twenty dollars for her."[24]

Although these gendered perspectives clearly distinguish "A True Tale" from *Incidents*, its unusual structure testifies to its connections with Harriet Jacobs's book. John S.'s text consists of seven chapters. By the end of Chapter Five, its narrator has completed the story of his successful escape from slavery. Instead of following this with the expected concluding chapter, however, he then turns to his sister's experiences in Chapter Six. Here the narrator presents her escape, her reunion with him in the North, and her manumission. Only after completing this second fugitive slave story does the narrator append the usual final chapter, complete with anecdotes illustrating the brutality of chattel slavery and general comments on the South's peculiar institution.[25]

Surprised by the insertion of Harriet Jacobs's story in Chapter Six, I reexamined John S.'s earlier treatment of her in this text. She does not appear to be the object of any special interest. In Chapter One, John S. notes his sister's existence, commenting only that when young, she was put into Dr. Norcom's household, and that "no interdict against the acquisition of knowledge, such as he had imposed upon me, could avail in her case."[26] In Chapter Two, he discusses a number of family events that she, too, describes in her narrative, usually at greater length: the sale of John S., Uncle Mark, and Grandmother;

Grandmother's manumission; the escape efforts of Uncle Joseph, and his meeting in New York with Uncle Mark. John S. then includes a dozen sentences about his sister. Prefacing these with the words, "But to return to my subject" – a transition suggesting that not he, but she, is the focus of his narrative – he summarizes her current situation:

> I left my sister in the doctor's family. Some six or eight years have passed since I was sold, and she has become the mother of two children. After the birth of her second child, she was sent to live on his plantation, where she remained for two or three months, and then ran away. As soon as she was gone, my aunt, the two children, and myself, were sent to gaol. . . .
>
> The old doctor no doubt thought that this would be the means of bringing my sister back; but you will see by-and-by that she did not leave with the intention of returning. She had not yet been called to make her back bare for the lash; but she had gone to live on the doctor's plantation, where she daily expected it. Her mental sufferings were more than she could longer bear. With her it was, in the language of one of our fathers, "liberty or death."[27]

This passage in Chapter Two comprises John S.'s entire treatment of Harriet Jacobs's experiences at the hands of Dr. Norcom, the "Dr. Flint" of *Incidents*. He ignores her completely in Chapter Three, briefly describes her hiding place in Chapter Four, and mentions her only once in Chapter Five. Then, in Chapter Six, he focuses on the story of her escape and manumission.

Neither "A True Tale" nor *Incidents* claims that Harriet Jacobs was the victim of physical abuse by a jealous master, as was Aunt Hester, whose torture is described in Douglass's *Narrative*, or Patsey, whose ordeal is described by Brown. But whereas *Incidents* details Linda's sexual history, "A True Tale" does not even refer to Norcom's sexual harassment of Jacobs or to his threat of concubineage. John S. does not mention his sister's desperate decision to become Sawyer's mistress; he does not mention her determination, after giving birth to a little girl, that her daughter must be saved from the sexual bondage of women in slavery; he does not mention her hopes that the children's father will free them; he does not mention that she was punished by being sent out to the plantation after rejecting, for a second time, her master's demand that she submit to concubinage; he does not mention her desperate plan to run away in order to tempt her master to sell the children to their father, who, she thinks, will free them. Although he devotes an entire chapter to his sister, John S.'s telling of her story leaves her story virtually untold. Reading "A True Tale," we hear neither the guilty recital of a woman's sexual history nor the heroic tale of a mother's struggle to free her children that we find in *Incidents*. Even though he entirely omits the history of Harriet Jacobs's sexual experiences, John S. does report the existence of her children, her punishment by Norcom, her determination to be free, her years in hiding, her escape from Edenton, and the Norcoms' determination to catch her. He reports, that is, the *results* of Jacobs's sexual experiences.

These omissions and inclusions are significant. By including in Chapter Two the results of her sexual experiences, and especially by devoting Chapter Six to her escape and manumission, John S. suggests that his sister's story is somehow extremely important. Yet his decision to erase her sexual history makes it difficult for his reader to understand why Norcom "so closely pursued" Harriet that she could not escape Edenton. It is difficult to understand why she remained in her "strange place of concealment six years and eleven months before she could get away!" And it is difficult to appreciate her fierce determination to save her daughter from a life in slavery.[28]

Harriet Jacobs herself attests to the importance of the information that John S. erases. In *Incidents*, describing her initial encounter in the North with an antislavery sympathizer, she writes that she revealed her sexual history to him because she thought it enormously significant:

> I frankly told him some of the most important events of my life. It was painful for me to do it, but I would not deceive him. If he was desirous of being my friend, I thought he ought to know how far I was worthy of it.[29]

In erasing this sexual history, "A True Tale" reveals how fully gendered its text is, and how fully gendered the text of *Incidents in the Life of a Slave Girl* really is. Without Linda Brent's sexual history, without the story of the besieged desperate girl, the "fallen woman," and the fierce mother, what story is left to tell?

The differences between these texts is not limited to their treatment of Harriet Jacobs's story. Like many slave narratives, "A True Tale" charts the developing integrity of its outraged narrator. Here – as in his abolitionist speeches – John S. early presents himself as a male trickster who outwits his master.[30] Writing about being jailed after his sister's escape, he states that he had the run of the place because he was friends not only with the jailer, but (challenging the taboos against any suggestion of interracial sex) he was also friends with the jailer's daughter! Further, he claims that while in prison he conspired with a slavetrader to convince Dr. Norcom to sell him, and that he outwitted Norcom in face-to-face conversation about his sister's whereabouts. He again shows himself as a trickster when he notes that he neglected to mention to Sawyer how long he would be willing to serve him. John S. asserts, however, that he outgrew this role. Commenting that slavery forced him to learn to lie, he explains that he became disgusted by deceit and by the easy prevarications of the slaveholding Congressmen he met while serving his master in Washington. Finally, he writes, he decided to run away when he realized that while he remained in slavery he would be unable to help his sister. Ultimately, John S. presents himself as an honorable man oppressed by a corrupt society.

Readers of *Incidents* realize that this is precisely the claim that Harriet Jacobs's Linda Brent does not make. Writing to Amy Post in 1852, Jacobs offers her inability to make this claim as the reason she is reluctant to compose her slave narrative: "Dear Amy if it was the life of a Heroine with no degradation associated with it." As I have pointed out elsewhere, Harriet Jacobs's solution to the problem of writing about a life that had a great deal of "degradation associated with it" was to construct, in Linda Brent, a new kind of female protagonist. Much of the tension in *Incidents* results from this narrator's conflict between her pleasure in her role as the liberator of her children and her shame in reciting her sexual history. Nevertheless, she resolutely takes responsibility for all of her actions, both those she judges good and those she judges bad, simultaneously declaring that "the condition of a slave confuses all principles of morality, and, in fact, renders the practice of them impossible." But nowhere does she permit herself to affirm that she is a wholly honorable individual.[31]

To the reader of *Incidents*, both John S.'s self-presentation as a good man caught in a cruel system and his decision to tell a censored version of his sister's story raise a series of questions. Does he ignore her sexual harassment and exploitation because, as her brother, he feels hurt and embarrassed by her abuse? This is certainly possible, although other male slave narrators, including Douglass, Henry Bibb, and the Clarke brothers, earlier had managed to write of the terrible sexual experiences of women in their families.[32]

Or does John S. erase his sister's sexual history because, if he revealed it, he could not adequately explain his relationship to his master, the father of her children? After all, it was Samuel Tredwell Sawyer, a man functionally his brother-in-law, whom he accompanied on a honeymoon with a young white bride. If John S. were to clarify his complex roles – as Sawyer's slave, as the brother of Sawyer's slave mistress, and as the uncle of the slave son and daughter of his master – would he not expose himself to the accusation that he had played a role antithetical to nineteenth-century manhood, that he was not the protector but the betrayer of his sister and her children? If he revealed his complex roles, could John S. maintain the respect of his reader when, after describing how he won his freedom, he includes a passage on reconciliation, a staple of many slave narratives? At the end of Chapter Five, after asserting that he has forgiven Dr. Norcom, *Incidents'* cruel Dr. Flint, he writes the following sentence: "The lawyer [his master, Sawyer / "Sands"] I have quite a friendly feeling for, and would be pleased to meet him as a countryman and a brother, but not as a master."[33] If he had not erased his sister's sexual history, might not his British readers, unfamiliar with the pressures he faced, interpret this statement as a betrayal of his sister and her children?

Or does the logic follow another path altogether: If John S. were to clarify his complex roles, would he not reveal his sister's sexual history and thereby seem to betray his brotherly role by denying any claims she might have to True Womanhood? Given the power structures embedded in the discourses of gender and in the system of chattel slavery, is it possible for him to present her as worthy of protection? Is it possible for him to present himself as her worthy protector?

Jacobs's Linda ends her book quietly, in a manner appropriate to a nineteenth-century woman. Commenting that she has not yet managed to establish a home for herself and her children, and that it has been "painful" to remember her years in slavery, she writes that she has found solace in her memories of Grandmother.[34] In contrast, John S., although he says he has forgiven each of his masters, concludes "A True Tale" with a nineteenth-century jeremiad:

> When I have thought of all that would pain the eye, sicken the heart, and make us turn our backs to the scene and weep, I then think of the oppressed struggling with their oppressors, and have a scene more horrible still. But I must drop this subject; I do not like to think of the past, nor look to the future, of wrongs like these."[35]

Overwhelmed by a vision terrible beyond words, he retreats into silence.

Re-reading *Incidents* in light of "A True Tale," I find striking the gendering of both these texts, from their contrasting tones to their carefully selected content, from their targeted audiences to the stated intentions of their authors. Both narratives expose the structures of race and status implicit in contemporary categories of gender. In *Incidents*, Harriet Jacobs reveals that the roles that define womanhood in her America – the innocent girl, the devoted wife, the nurturing mother – are first denied to women held in slavery, then used to condemn slave women who do not play them. Similarly, in "A True Tale," John S. shows that the roles that characterize nineteenth-century American manhood – the upright honest boy, the protective brother, father, and husband – are forbidden to slave men, and then used to damn them. To the reader of *Incidents*, however, "A True Tale" has an importance beyond its corroborative and informational value, and even beyond its value as a dramatization of attitudes concerning slavery and gender. Reading John S.'s narrative, seeing what is underscored and what is erased, enables us to understand more clearly the ways in which Harriet Jacobs shaped and crafted her story, to see more fully the enormity of her accomplishment. Frederick Douglass's brutalized Aunt Hester and William Wells Brown's pathetic Patsey never wrote their lives. Amazingly, John S. Jacobs's sister did.

Notes

1. "A True Tale of Slavery," *The Leisure Hour: A Family Journal of Instruction and Recreation* (London), February 7, 14, 21, and 28, 1861; Harriet Jacobs, *Incidents in the Life of a Slave Girl: Written by Herself* (1861), ed. Jean Fagan Yellin (Cambridge, MA: Harvard University Press, 1987). I am grateful to Donald Gibson for his helpful comments on an early version of this essay.
2. Frederick Douglass, *Narrative of the Life of an American Slave: Written by Himself* (1845), ed. B. Quarles (Cambridge: Harvard University Press, 1960); William Wells Brown, *Narrative of William Wells Brown, a Fugitive Slave . . .* (1847), in *Puttin' On Ole Massa*, ed. G. Osofsky (New York: Harper, 1969).

3. For John S. Jacobs's letter informing New York Garrisonian Sydney Howard Gay about his sister, see John S. Jacobs to Sydney Howard Gay, June 4, 1846, Columbia University Library; for his letter about an Edenton freedman perhaps returning South, see John S. Jacobs to Sydney Howard Gay, Boston, September 7, 1845, Columbia University Library; for other references to his activism, see *Liberator*, December 12, 1845; *Liberator*, June 5, 1846; *Liberator*, December 3, 1847; "Jonathan Walker and John S. Jacobs," *North Star*, March 31, 1848; *Black Abolitionist Papers (BAP)* 05:0605. For more on this attempted rescue, see *Address of the Committee Appointed by a Public Meeting Held in Faneuil Hall, September 24, 1846, for the Purpose of Considering the Recent Case of Kidnapping from Our Soil and of Taking Measures to Prevent the Recurrence of Similar Outrages* (Boston, 1846), cited in Quarles, *Black Abolitionists*, 154.

4. *North Star*, March 3, 1848; also see *Liberator* March 31, 1848.

5. *National Anti-Slavery Standard*, January 8, 1848.

6. "Refuge of Oppression: Correspondence from the Boston *Daily Atlas*: Anti-Sabbath Convention," *Liberator*, August 18, 1848, p. 129.

7. "Editorial Correspondence," *North Star*, March 9, 1849.

8. John S. Jacobs to Frederick Douglass, *North Star*, April 20, 1849.

9. *North Star*, May 4, 1849.

10. *Liberator*, June 1, 1849, p. 86. At this meeting, John S. took a straight Garrisonian line, opposing political abolitionism. Reports of the meeting signal his status among the abolitionists. Not only was he a member of the Rochester contingent (Amy Post and Frederick Douglass were among them), but he was one of a group of agents that included antislavery notables Parker Pillsbury, Lucy Stone, William Wells Brown, and Stephen S. and Abby Kelley Foster. Also see *National Anti-Slavery Standard*, May 17, 1849.

11. *Incidents*, 246, n. 7; 276, n. 3; *Liberator*, May 18, 1849, p. 79.

12. *North Star*, March 23–July 27, 1849; William C. Nell to Amy Post, June 30, 1849, Isaac and Amy Post Family Papers, University of Rochester Library (hereafter cited as IAPFP). In August, John S. was one of the vice-presidents of the meeting celebrating West Indian independence at Auburn; see *North Star*, August 10, 1849; "Oysters! Oysters!" *North Star*, November 2, 1849; also see Louisa M. Jacobs to "Dear Uncle," Clinton, November 5, 1849, IAPFP. In December 1849, the abolitionist leader Anne Warren Weston was inquiring about John S. Jacobs's whereabouts, evidently with an eye to hiring him for the Boston Bazaar. Nell writes, "They know his worth and so do the Western New York antislavery friends." William C. Nell to Amy Post, December 12, 1849, IAPFP.

13. *Incidents in the Life of a Slave Girl*, p. 191; *National Anti-Slavery Standard*, October 10, 1850; for one individual's praise of his performance, see Sarah L. Willis to Amy Post, October 20, 1850, IAPFP.

14. John S. Jacobs to Isaac Post, June 5, 1861, London, "A Colored American in England," *The Anti-Slavery Advocate* (London), Sept 2, 1861, p. 460, rpt. in *Black Abolitionist Papers*, I: *The British Isles, 1830–1865*, ed. C. Peter Ripley (Chapel Hill: University of North Carolina Press, 1985), 491.

15. Ibid.

16. At this time, there is no information whatever concerning the composition and publication of "A True Tale." Harriet Jacobs's narrative, retitled *The Deeper*

Wrong, or Incidents in the Life of a Slave Girl, Written by Herself, was published in London by W. Tweedie in September, 1862.

17. *The Leisure Hour* was not addressed to an antislavery audience. Between 1860 and 1862, John S. Jacobs's "A True Tale" was the only slave narrative appearing in its pages. Although in those years, under the editorship of James MaCauley, the magazine ran a series called "American Sketches," it did not feature items on the slavery controversy. In 1862, it ran "Eustache, the Faithful Negro," set in Santo Domingo. *The Leisure Hour* did not illustrate "A True Tale," but in 1860 it had illustrated a fictional piece called "The Captain's Story: or, Adventures in Jamaica Thirty Years Ago."

18. "A True Tale," 86.

19. On the gendering of the narratives, see, for example, Frances Smith Foster, "In Respect to Females: Differences in the Portrayals of Women by Male and Female Narrators," *Black American Literature Forum* 15 (1981): 66–70. On the question of gender definitions as weapons, see, for example, Hazel Carby, *Reconstructing Womanhood* (New York: Oxford University Press, 1987), and my *Women and Sisters* (New Haven: Yale University Press, 1989).

20. For analyses of codes of gender in nineteenth-century United States, see, for example, Barbara Welter, "The Cult of True Womanhood," *Dimity Convictions: The American Woman in the Nineteenth Century,* ed. Barbara Welter (Columbus: Ohio State University Press, 1975).

21. "A True Tale," 85–6.

22. "A True Tale," 86.

23. *Incidents,* 9.

24. *Incidents,* 56, 51, 13–24, 35, 13 and 123, 13, 122, 16, 16, 70, 48, 151, 16. It is, however, John S. Jacobs, and not his sister, who reports the flogging of a woman; see "A True Tale," 140.

25. Although a great many slave narratives incorporate disparate materials, John S.'s extended digression about his sister is highly unusual. For a brief discussion of the pattern of the slave narrative, see my *Intricate Knot* (New York: New York University Press, 1972), 126–7.

26. "A True Tale," 86.

27. "A True Tale," 110.

28. "A True Tale," 110.

29. *Incidents,* 160.

30. For the trickster figure in African American literature, see William Andrews, *To Tell a Free Story* (Urbana: University of Illinois Press, 1986); for an early discussion of this folkloristic figure, see G. Osofsky, "Introduction," *Puttin' On Ole Massa.*

31. Harriet Jacobs to Amy Post [October? 1852?] in *Incidents,* pp. 231–3; "Introduction," *Incidents,* xxx–xxxiii; *Incidents,* p. 55.

32. See *Narrative of the Life and Adventures of Henry Bibb, an American Slave, Written by Himself* (New York: the Author, 1849); and *Narratives of the Sufferings of Lewis and Milton Clarke . . . Dictated by Themselves,* ed. Joseph C. Lovejoy (Boston: B. Marsh, 1846).

33. "A True Tale," 126.

34. *Incidents,* 201.

35. "A True Tale," 141.

RESISTING INCIDENTS

FRANCES SMITH FOSTER

Particular communicative contexts seem inevitably to trigger resistance. When a writer or narrator is different in race, gender, or class from the implied or actual reader, questions about authority and authenticity multiply. As Susan Lanser points out in *The Narrative Act*, a writer's or a narrator's social identity is never totally irrelevant, but readers automatically assume that the "unmarked" narrator is a literate white male.[1] When the title page, the book jacket, or any other source marks one as not white, not a man, or not to the manor born, different sets of cultural assumptions "determined by the ideological system and the norms of social dominance in a given society" (Lanser, 166) come into play. When the topic or the general development of the text coincides thematically with the readers' assumptions about the writer's or narrator's social identity, status becomes particularly significant to the discursive context. "Social identity and textual behavior," Lanser concludes, "combine to provide the reader with a basis for determining the narrator's mimetic authority" (Lanser, 169).

Lanser uses gender as her primary focus, but her thesis applies as well to other writers whose race or class places them outside the courts of power and privilege. Any attempt by an individual who is not white, male, and at least middle class to be acknowledged as part of the literary or intellectual community is inevitably challenged, even by readers who share their racial, social, or gender status. When a readership is invited into communicative contexts with writers of a race, gender, or class that it assumes to be equal or inferior to its own, questions about authority and authenticity take on an intensity and texture that obscure other aspects of the discourse. Readers tend to assume that cultural landscapes not dominated by written texts are inferior and individuals native to such cultures can hardly be expected to represent the best thoughts of the best minds or to create things of beauty that are joys to behold. When, as they often do, such writers do not replicate that with which readers are already familiar, claims and challenges to authorial prerogatives and to the authenticity of their depictions may become contentious. More readers try to compete with the writers, to rearrange the writers' words, details, and intentions to make them more compatible with the readers' own experiences and expectations. Oppositional intensity varies by time, place, and circumstance, but African Americans inevitably encounter a significant number of obstinate readers. From the publication of *Poems on Various Subjects, Religious and Moral,* the earliest extant volume by an African American, to the present time, the mimetic details, social relevance, and political implications of their texts have been particularly challenged.

Although resistance may be absolutely the right way to read a particular text or a particular author, the fact that literary productions of African American writers, particularly of those who were or had been slaves, are habitually greeted with resistance is provoking and problematic. Consider the case of Phillis Wheatley, the author of the earliest extant volume of poetry by an African American. In order to convince readers to accept Wheatley as the author of *Poems on Various Subjects, Religious and Moral,* before the book was published (1773), it was deemed necessary to include various authenticating documents, including her picture, a biographical sketch from her master that explains how she came to acquire literacy, and an affidavit from eighteen of "the most respectable characters in Boston,"[2] who had examined her and determined that Wheatley was indeed capable of writing the poems.

Once her authorship was established, Wheatley became a celebrity, but the significance of her contributions, even her identification as a poet, were not unequivocally granted. Phillis Wheatley wrote *Poems on Various Subjects, Religious and Moral* (emphasis mine), but eighteenth-century readers, especially, were inclined to read her words as those of a former pagan who could testify to acquired piety but could contribute nothing original about theology or morality. Thomas Jefferson spoke for many when he stated, "Religion, indeed, has produced a Phyllis Whately [*sic*]; but it could not produce a poet." In order to bar Wheatley from poetic society, Jefferson had to ignore the consensus of Western aesthetics that *utile* and *dulce* were essential literary components and that *utile,* especially in the New England colonies, had always meant that the writings serve a religious and moral purpose. To demonstrate that religion may have inspired Wheatley to write but that her writing about religion precluded her acceptability as a poet, Jefferson defined not religion or morality but romantic love as the "peculiar oestrum of the poet." Romantic love, Jefferson then pontificated, could kindle the senses of blacks but not their imaginations.[3]

Whether Phillis Wheatley was surprised by her readers' reactions is a matter of conjecture, but that misreadings and misinterpretations of her work and worth continue to this day should shock more people than it does. Today, Phillis Wheatley is lauded as the first African American and the second woman in colonial America to publish a volume of poetry. Her works are included in virtually every anthology that purports to be "inclusive." Her debts to Greek and Roman mythology, to evangelical Methodist rhetoric, and to neoclassicism are frequently cited as evidence that, when given the opportunity, she – and by implication other blacks – could and did learn as well as or better than whites. But until recently, most readers considered her to be of "the mockingbird school," able to imitate but not to interpret or debate. Until recently, few scholars would entertain the notion that Phillis Wheatley made original contributions to eighteenth-century theology, to the rhetoric of the U.S. Revolution, and to the discourse on race and gender.

The standard interpretation of "On Being Brought from Africa to America," the most anthologized of Phillis Wheatley's poems, demonstrates this. The poem is an eight-line monologue addressed to Christians by an African convert. It has three distinct parts with three increasingly authoritative tones. The poem begins as a hymn of gratitude for the divine mercy that brought the speaker from a "benighted land" to one where she learned to seek and to know spiritual redemption. In line five the narrator switches from grateful testimony and reproves those who believe that the "sable" skins of Africans signify diabolical natures. The last two lines are didactic and ominous: "Remember, *Christians, Negroes,* black as *Cain,* / May be refin'd, and join th' angelic train" (emphasis hers). In this poem, a newly enlightened member does not simply recite catechism but argues theology and warns the entire congregation against presumptions of exclusivity by declaring that the gift of salvation makes all converts joint heirs in Christ. Despite, or perhaps because of, the simple diction and the authority manifest in the tonal changes, readers have historically misinterpreted the text. They have emphasized the first lines and read the poem as Wheatley's disavowal of her African heritage and as evidence of her "pious sentimentalizing about Truth, Salvation, Mercy, and Goodness"[4] while ignoring the changes in tone and focus that begin with line five and saying nothing of the audacity of the last two lines, which claim divine authority to testify for racial equality. Although summaries or interpretations that take into account only part of the text subvert literary convention and violate basic tenets of exposition, it seems easier for readers to ignore half of a poem than to acknowledge that an African slave girl barely out of her teens would be audacious enough not only to write poetry, but also to use it to instruct and to chastise her readers.

For African American women writers, the resistance to the authority of blacks or of slaves was compounded by gender prejudices. Even if the authorship were acknowledged and their accounts were verified, their writings were still perceived through a veil of sexism that obscured their individuality and revealed only the shadowy contours their readers expected to see. As African American women proved their imaginativeness with romantic prose and poetry and their political acumen with logical and incisive analyses, nineteenth-century audiences struggled desperately against the belief that black women could be intelligent and eloquent. The nineteenth-century author and orator Frances Ellen Watkins Harper provides another example of the lengths to which some audiences would go to deny what they saw and heard. By all accounts she was very ladylike in appearance and few contemporary reporters failed to note her "slender and graceful" form and her "soft musical voice" when recounting her public presentations. Harper's writings have often been summarized as sentimental, moral, and chaste. Some of them were. But Frances Harper was also a militant evangelist for equality. She worked with the Underground Railroad, staged sit-ins on public transportation, and supported John Brown's Harper's Ferry attack. During Reconstruction, Frances Harper went around the South lecturing on political and social change. Hers was not a pitiful plea for acceptance. "We are all bound up together in one great bundle of humanity, and society cannot trample on the weakest and feeblest of its members without receiving the curse in its own soul," she argued. Her writings and her speeches explained why the fate of the country rested in its solution to the economic problems of poor whites and blacks, the suffrage demands of women of all races, and a variety of other major issues. For a black woman to speak publicly and aggressively on political, economic, and social issues was so alien to traditional expectation that many simply could not believe their ears or eyes. In a letter to a friend, Harper writes, "I don't know but that you would laugh if you were to hear some of the remarks which my lectures call forth: 'She is a man,' again, 'She is not colored, she is painted.'"[5]

Other African Americans learned from the experiences of writers such as Wheatley and Harper. African Americans who wrote for publication in the eighteenth and nineteenth centuries knew as well as, if not better than, other writers that successful communication required appropriate attention to content and context. They knew that some readers would be unable or unwilling to concede that they legitimately could or would act, think, and write in ways contrary to the ideas with which those readers approach that text. African Americans quickly understood that in order to employ the power of the pen, they had not only to seize it but to wield it with courage, skill, and cunning. Unable to trust their readers to respond to their texts as peers, they developed literary strategies to compensate.

It is beyond the scope of this paper to entertain all the manifestations of resistance or to speculate about their motivations. This discussion will focus upon examples of reader and writer resistance as demonstrated in Harriet Jacobs's *Linda; Or, Incidents in the Life of a Slave Girl*. The case of this author and this text has its own unique aspects, but it is a good representation of the more general situation. Resistance to Jacobs's *Incidents*, like that to Wheatley's *Poems on Various Subjects*, to Harper's lectures, and to other African American writers, stems in large measure not from the text or its author's manifest ability but from the readers' response to both. Resistance to *Incidents* is rooted in a usually unspoken, perhaps unconscious, recognition that the book exposes as fabrications many of the truths which we hold to be self-evident and that the writer expects us to reconsider both the grounds for our perceptions of reality and the limitations of our abilities to accept competing versions.

Resistance characterized both Jacobs's life and the genesis and the renaissance of her autobiography. Both her biographers and her autobiography demonstrate that she was born into a family that refused to accept others' definitions of who they were and how they ought to live. Jacobs's self-esteem was strong enough that she could reject her master's edict that she consider herself his property and submit to his will in both thought and deed. When her resources dwindled and the confrontations seemed unending, she chose confinement in a nine-by-seven-foot attic for more than six years rather than live as her master commanded her. Eventually she did flee to the North. Harriet Jacobs was regularly asked to contribute her story to the antislavery effort, but she withstood those pleas for almost twelve years before she agreed to testify. It was only after the Compromise of 1850 created the Fugitive Slave Law, which made it possible for slave owners to claim individuals as their private property even in states where slavery was illegal, that Jacobs agreed to publicize some of her most personal experiences.

Hers was a particularly difficult decision because Harriet Jacobs valued her privacy and believed that "no one had a right to question" her.[6] She was proud of her triumphs and her achievements, but she did not consider hers to be "the life of a Heroine with no degradation associated with it" (Jacobs, 232). Although she could justify her actions in her own mind, Jacobs was reluctant to explain them to strangers and unwilling to accept their pity or censure. When she finally decided to reveal some of her personal history, however, Jacobs resolved to "give a true and just account . . . in a Christian spirit" (Jacobs, 242), but not to pander to her audience. As a former slave, she knew that stereotypes about people of her race and class encouraged her audience to expect a certain kind of testimony, yet Jacobs refused to divulge the kinds of things that she thought "the world might believe that a Slave Woman was too willing to pour out" (Jacobs, 242). She decided to use her position as one of a very few antislavery writers who could relate from personal experience incidents in the life of a slave girl to introduce a different perspective on slavery and slave women. Like other antislavery writers, she did not deny the prevalence of rape and seduction. In fact, her text appears to be unprecedented in its use of sexual liaisons and misadventures as a prime example of the perils of slave womanhood. But hers was a story of a slave woman who refused to be victimized. Harriet Jacobs used her own experiences to create a book that would correct and enlist support against prevailing social myths and political ideologies.

Another reason for her original resistance to writing her narrative was that Harriet Jacobs knew that writing a well-crafted autobiography required more time and talent than she had. During an era in which the majority of Americans could barely write their names, Jacobs enjoyed reading, corresponding, and conversing with a coterie of intellectuals, artists, and social activists, and she had enough literary sophistication to know that literacy was but one requirement for authorship. She was well acquainted with many of the attitudes and assumptions of the Anglo-American literary establishment, for not only did she read widely, but she lived in the household of Nathaniel Willis, the editor and writer whose home was a rendezvous for New York literati. She knew also the conventions of abolitionist and African American literature. Jacobs had worked for a year in her brother's Rochester antislavery reading room. Since it was located over the offices of Frederick Douglass, she may have heard the history of the resistance that Douglass had encountered, especially from his most ardent abolitionist friends, when he decided to tell his story his way. Because Jacobs was a live-in domestic worker, stealing the time and marshalling the energy to develop her own writing skills to the level that she judged adequate for her intentions were more complicated for her than for many others. As a fugitive slave, she also knew that friends or employers, who were willing to adhere to the "Don't ask, don't tell" philosophy in her case, might not be supportive if she went public about her status. And if Jacobs had not known about professional jealousy and competition, she soon learned that she had to fight to protect her story and to establish her right to determine what should be told and how to tell it. In the process of getting her story told, she had to defy such opportunists as Harriet Beecher Stowe, who wanted to appropriate her narrative in order to enhance Stowe's own authority.

Harriet Jacobs had ample reason to know the perils that African American writers, especially women, faced, and it would have been very strange indeed had she not carefully considered the rhetorical and narrative strategies that they had used as she outlined her own story. When she stated in the preface that "I want to add my testimony to that of abler pens to convince the people of the Free States what Slavery really is" (Jacobs, 1–2), the words "convince" and "really" were undoubtedly chosen with care. She knew she could not trust her readers to understand or to accept what she would relate. She also knew that there was no literary model to fit her task and her temperament. Nonetheless, Harriet Jacobs chose to record her history as she had lived it, to confront her readers with an alternative truth, and to demand that they not only acknowledge it but act upon it. To that end, Harriet Jacobs created a new literary form, one that challenged her audiences' social and aesthetic assumptions even as it delighted and reaffirmed them.

Jacobs's narrative records the struggle of a young girl to resist the sexual advances of a man who was thirty-five years older, better educated, and socially superior. Obviously its story of a young virgin's attempts to defend her chastity against the wiles and assaults of an older, more experienced, and socially privileged male makes it clear kin to Fielding's *Pamela* and other such seduction stories. However, Linda never confuses a threatened loss of chastity with a loss of self-worth or reason for living. Harriet Jacobs colors the plot even further by painting the man – Flint – as driven by more than lust or moral turpitude and the girl – Linda – as resisting from motives only partially shaded by fear of social censure or pregnancy. Perhaps she had learned from fireside stories of Brer Rabbit or from observations within the slave quarters, perhaps it was just common sense, but Linda understood that physical superiority or social status is not necessarily the deciding factor in any contest.

With *Incidents in the Life of a Slave Girl* Harriet Jacobs reconstructs the standard seduction pattern of urbane seducer versus naive maiden. Jacobs expands the peasant or proletariat categories to include the slaves in the United States. Moreover, she makes it clear that the impoverished are not the only oppressed and that slaves are not the only victims. Mrs. Flint is driven to distraction by her husband's infidelity, and the narrator informs us that the seventh is not the only commandment violated in such situations, that young white boys follow the grown men's examples, and so do some white women. Jacobs asserts that slave girls are not the only ones to be prematurely robbed of their innocence. The daughters of slaveholders, she warns, overhear the quarrels between their parents, learn about sexual oppression from slave girls, and sometimes "exercise the same authority over the men slaves" (Jacobs, 52). While she writes to encourage Northern women to resist slavery, Harriet Jacobs does not allow them to distance themselves too thoroughly. She reminds her readers that they sometimes marry and ofttimes are kin to slaveholders. She explains how the Fugitive Slave Law represents an attack upon the freedom of Northerners. And in noting that Linda technically belonged to Dr. Flint's daughter, who was not able either as a child or as an adult to claim or to direct her inheritance, Jacobs suggests a larger definition of "slave girl." Linda is the heroine who struggles against evil, but Harriet Jacobs identifies other women and men, white and black, Northern and Southern, who are similarly victimized or are potential victims.

Once Harriet Jacobs had completed the narrative of her life in bondage and her struggle for freedom, she spent several years trying to find a publisher. Although publishers, especially those of antislavery leanings, were generally eager to print slave narratives, Jacobs's account was so original and so striking that they required more than the usual endorsements by others. Two prominent friends, one a white woman and the other a black man, had written letters of recommendation to be published along with Jacobs's text. But as Jacobs reported in a letter to a friend, the publishers wanted "a Satellite of so great magnitude" as Harriet Beecher Stowe, Nathaniel Willis, or Lydia Maria Child before they would issue her account (Yellin, xxii). With the help of William C. Nell, another African American writer and activist, Jacobs contacted Lydia Maria Child, who agreed to serve as her editor. With Child's support, the firm of Thayer and Eldridge contracted to print two thousand copies. In 1861, nearly a decade after she had decided to write the book, Harriet Jacobs's narrative was finally published. It appeared as the anonymous testimony of "A Slave Girl: Written by Herself." Child was identified as its editor. The publication immediately stirred controversies that have waxed and waned but continue to this day. Despite the testimonies of Jacobs's contemporaries and the meticulous evidence of present-day scholars, a good many readers continue to resist identifying the book as an autobiography by a former slave woman named Harriet Jacobs.

Some antebellum reader caution is understandable. Slave narratives were written to help destroy an institution, swaddled in myth and mystery, and deeply rooted in U.S. culture. Slave narrators, like other purposeful writers, were particularly careful to select incidents and language for maximum persuasive value. Readers of such texts had the privilege and probably the obligation to consider carefully the arguments and the motivations of those whom they read. Especially when faced with direct statements of intention, readers, then as now, should not be expected to squelch their inclinations to contest the validity or the relevance of surprising revelations. Not surprisingly, even the most sympathetic readers wanted then, as they do now, to have certain expectations met and some assumptions confirmed. Moreover, in the mid-1850s, resistance to women writers was decreasing but still pervasive, and Harriet Jacobs presented more than the usual challenge to literary tradition. She was one of those strange, modern, and frightening women who dared to take pen to paper about politics and moral values, to urge resistance to laws and social mores. And, finally, questions of authority and authenticity were not then, as they are not now, intrinsically inappropriate or unimportant to the study of any literature and especially not to the study of autobiographical writings. Such scholars as Albert E. Stone have demonstrated that autobiography is a "mode of storytelling" and that any given autobiography is "simultaneously historical record and literary artifact, psychological case history and spiritual confession, didactic essay and ideological testament."[7]

The modifications in genre that Jacobs made probably did not bother antebellum readers as much as they seem to bother twentieth-century ones, but they certainly must have noticed them. Since she was obviously not an educated white male, the resistance that other writers routinely inspire was certainly augmented by her daring to tamper with traditional literary forms.

Jacobs obviously borrowed from the novel of seduction, the criminal confessional, the American jeremiad, the slave narrative, and other popular forms. The melodramatic and feminist elements in *Incidents in the Life of a Slave Girl* were fairly common in antislavery novels. Harriet Beecher Stowe's *Uncle Tom's Cabin* was the most famous, but neither the first nor the last to enlist melodrama in the antislavery cause. Harriet Jacobs began her book at about the same time that William Wells Brown was writing *Clotel* and Harriet E. Wilson was writing *Our Nig*, but by the time *Incidents* was published in 1861, these two writers and others had already introduced the heroic African American woman protagonist. Brown had already demonstrated that an African American female slave might be morally superior to the white man who claimed both social superiority and physical ownership. But Harriet Jacobs claimed more social prestige than did Harriet E. Wilson and Linda is less compromising or compromised than Clotel. Jacobs wrote not to secure money to save her sickly son but to convince readers to heal their ailing society. Dr. Flint's offer of a cottage in the woods and an almost-marriage is comparable to what Brown's heroine accepts, but Linda is not in the least tempted, and the relationship between Linda and Congressman Sands may be read as a deliberately empowered version of the Clotel and Horatio affair. The struggle between Linda and the father of her children, like that between her and Dr. Flint, is a true contest. Sands, like Flint, had "power and law on his side," but, Linda says, "I had a determined will. There is might in each" (Jacobs, 85).

The changes that Harriet Jacobs wrought in the slave narrative genre were even more remarkable. When she agreed to write her personal narrative, Jacobs set out to wrestle with the "serpent of Slavery" and to expose and detoxify its "many and poisonous fangs" (Jacobs, 62). To accomplish this, she incorporated the basic elements of the slave narrative genre, but modified them to fit the experiences of those who did not resist by fleeing the site of conflict. The antebellum slave narrative featured a protagonist best described as a heroic male fugitive. The usual pattern of the narrative was to demonstrate examples of the cruelty and degradation inherent in the institution of slavery, then to chronicle an individual's discovery that the concept and the condition of slavery were neither inevitable or irrevocable. Following that revelation, the typical slave narrator secretly plotted his escape and, at the opportune time, struck out alone but resolved to follow the North Star to freedom. Slave narratives generally ended when, upon arrival in the free territory, the former slave assumed a new name, obtained a job, married, and began a new happy-ever-after life.

In contrast, Jacobs's female fugitive refuses to abandon her loved ones and spends the first several years of her escape hiding in places provided by family and friends. When her grandmother accidentally jeopardizes the security of her retreat, Linda has to flee to the North. Even then she does not run alone.

Instead, she leaves the South on a ship in the company of another fugitive woman, her friend Fanny. Jacobs does not report a name change, and Linda does not marry. And although she does set about the task of creating a new life for herself and for her children, that task is complicated by failing health and persistent pursuit from those who claim her as their property. Jacobs's narrative makes it clear that racial discrimination and the Fugitive Slave Law ensured that the North was not the Promised Land. The passages in which Jacobs chronicles the abuses of slaves are common to antebellum slave narratives, but her personal testimony of will power and peer protection proving stronger than physical might and legal right are unique. She weaves incidents that she experienced or witnessed into a narrative that was common to the "two millions of women at the South, still in bondage, suffering what [she] suffered, and most of them far worse" (Jacobs, 1).

In appropriating the elements of various genres into one more suitable for her intents, Harriet Jacobs was following a convention that African American writers had been using for at least a century before her, and it was this tradition of improvisation and invention that also provided her with the techniques that she could adapt to meet her particular circumstances. Some of these African American rhetorical devices have been described quite aptly by others as "sass,"[8] "signifying,"[9] or "discourse of distrust."[10] I say more about the discourse of distrust later; the focus of this discussion is upon specific ways in which *Incidents* resists and is resisted. Like flies or mosquitoes, many of these incidents of resistance would be obvious but insignificant were they not so numerous, did they not unexpectedly appear in inappropriate places, and did their persistent buzzing not distract our attention from more productive occupations.

One example that gains importance when considered in relation to myriad other small instances is the way in which twentieth-century readers have insisted upon renaming Jacobs's book. In 1861 the work was published and reviewed as *Linda: Or, Incidents in the Life of a Slave Girl* and it was as "Linda" that Harriet Jacobs come to be known by the reading public. She signed autographs, letters, and other publications with that name. Today, however, readers know the text only by its subtitle, *Incidents in the Life of a Slave Girl*, and it is by its subtitle that the book is now reprinted, discussed, and claimed as "a classic slave narrative," "one of the major autobiographies in the Afro-American tradition," or simply as a "classic" of African American literature.[11] Although not unprecedented nor without merit, this renaming is a little odd. Referring to the book as *Incidents in the Life of a Slave Girl* subordinates the individual protagonist to the general type, as its author intended. Rather than use her experiences as representative of others, however, too many scholars and critics have used the experiences of others to invalidate those that Jacobs recounted. Their interest revolves almost exclusively around Harriet Jacobs as both author and subject and around how her victories and her values contrast with prevailing theories and opinions of slave life. Since the author / narrator is of such interest, it is particularly noteworthy that the work is not known by the narrator's name and that Jacobs's authorship is continually questioned. To cite racial prejudice would be an inadequate explanation for this because slave narratives do tend to be known by the names of their authors. Nor is gender bias a satisfactory conclusion, for the formal and functional similarities of Jacobs's narrative to those of nineteenth-century sentimental fiction is consistently mentioned. Still, unlike *Pamela*, *Clotel*, *Ramona*, and others, *"Linda"* is not the name by which Jacobs's tale is known. Harriet Stowe's book is linked in content and context to Harriet Jacobs's and has undergone a similar transformation. Despite the fact that Eliza's escape, Eva's death, and Topsy's devilment all eclipse Uncle Tom's crucifixion, we do not normally refer to Stowe's work by its more appropriate subtitle, *Life Among the Lowly*. We accept *Uncle Tom's Cabin*.

Complicating Jacobs's situation is the fact that even while the narrative no longer carries the title "Linda" and while the authenticity of Jacobs's recitations is questioned, it is with Linda or Harriet that readers are most concerned. Given the extraordinary character of most slave narrators and the uniqueness of many of the incidents they relate, one is not overly surprised when their narratives are treated as documentaries and their self-depictions are taken as fact. But even in the case of one so unique as Frederick Douglass, readers tend to accept their personal narratives as representative of at least one particular kind or group of slaves. In the *Narrative of the Life of Frederick Douglass, an American Slave*, the climactic scene is one in which the slave boy physically resists punishment by his white boss. Douglass introduces the fight between him and Covey as if it were representative by saying, "You have seen how a man was made a slave; you shall see how a slave was made a man."[12] Readers have accepted this unusual rite of passage as archetypal even though almost no other narrator admits to such an experience. Douglass's narrative is considered a "master narrative," a model against which all others should be measured, while in fact, though not unheard of, scenes of physical combat between blacks and whites are rare in the genre.[13] With Harriet Jacobs, however, the concerns and consensus are different. Since it is a common belief that slave women were routinely raped and that slaves generally did not know their ancestry or other details of their personal histories, Jacobs's family pride and self-confidence are considered aberrations. Moreover, Harriet Jacobs has more than once been accused of having omitted or distorted details of her own life in order to enhance her personal reputation or to achieve artistic effect. Historian Elizabeth Fox-Genovese, for example, has declared that Jacobs's "pivotal authentication of self probably rested upon a great factual lie, for it stretches the limits of all credulity that Linda Brent actually eluded her master's sexual advances."[14]

Another and more worrisome form of resistance has been the skepticism and concern about authorship that has become more pronounced in the twentieth century. That the book was first published anonymously and its editor was herself a prominent figure would provide some excuse were it not in such contrast to the reception of other anonymously published books, including Richard Hildreth's *Archy Moore; or The White Slave*, Mattie Griffiths's *Autobiography of a Female Slave*, and James Weldon Johnson's *Autobiography of an Ex-Colored Man*. That she consulted with and sometimes accepted the advice of her editor should pose no more serious concerns about authorship for Jacobs's text than it does for D. H. Lawrence's *Sons and Lovers*, certain poems signed by T. S. Eliot, or virtually any book authored by Thomas Wolfe.[15] Neither the decision to publish the book anonymously, the reputation of Lydia Maria Child, nor the generic modifications and innovations such as changing names and creating dialogue in an autobiography account sufficiently for the resistance that *Incidents* continues to encounter.

Arguments presented in recent studies of women's and of African American narrative strategies help clarify the reasons for such reader resistance while offering insight into specific techniques by which writers have combated it. Jeanne Kammer's discussion of the diaphoric imagination and the aesthetic of silence suggests two.[16] Like many of the women poets that Kammer discusses, Jacobs adopts an oratorical model and "depends on the capacity of the voice, not only to invest the words with a persuasive *timbre*, but to sustain the performance over a long enough time to move the listener to the desired conclusions" (Kammer, 159). Harriet Jacobs was writing prose of fact rather than poetry; therefore, she could substitute incidents for images, but she too produces "new meaning by the juxtaposition alone of two (or more) images, each term concrete, their joining unexplained" (Kammer, 157). She too elevates the speaker into a focus of interest in the text. She presents that speaker as "the only available guide through its ambiguities, and the source of its human appeal" (Kammer, 159).

Jacobs's text also provides an opportunity for "the broader look at the historical and literary contexts" that Robyn R. Warhol intends her discussion of the "engaging narrator" to stimulate.[17] Warhol's examination is limited to a pattern of narrative intervention used by three novelists of Jacobs's time, but its similarities to this nonfiction text are several and significant. Like Stowe, Gaskell, and Eliot, Jacobs wrote "to inspire belief in the situations their [texts] describe" and "to move actual readers to sympathize with real-life slaves, workers, or ordinary middle-class people" (Warhol, 811). Each writer uses her narrator as a "surrogate" working "to engage 'you' through the substance and, failing that, the stance of their narrative interventions and addresses to 'you'" (Warhol, 813). Such an "engaging narrator" intrudes into the text, and although neither she nor her reader is a participant in the narrative itself, the narrator engages the reader in dialogue and sometimes implies "imperfections in the narratee's ability to comprehend, or sympathize with, the contents of the text, even while expressing confidence that the narratee will rise to the challenge" (Warhol, 814).

Both Kammer and Warhol focus their discussions on texts by white women, but they agree that diaphor, oratory, and narrative engagement are employed, with some variation, by other writers. Race and class are two very salient variables for Harriet Jacobs. That she was African American and a former slave was vital to her message and to her mission. Yet, in emphasizing both of these factors, she was stirring up attitudes that she preferred to ignore. Like other African Americans and former slaves, Harriet Jacobs did not subscribe to the racial and literary stereotypes that formed the collective consciousness of her white readers. There may be exceptions that prove the rule but, as Raymond Hedin explains, "Black writers have never relished the need to take into account the racial assumptions of white readers, but their minority status and their unavoidable awareness of those assumptions have made it all but inevitable that they do so. The notion of black inferiority has become the 'countertext' of black writing."[18] "One constant among the variables," Hedin notes, is "a distinctive continuing tradition of narrative strategy deriving from black writers' continuing awareness that a significant part of their audience, whatever its proportions – or at the very least a significant part of the larger culture they find themselves in – clings to reservations about the full humanity of blacks" (Hedin, 36). The result is "an implicitly argumentative tradition" that manifests in the fact that African American writers "felt [an often vehement] need to confront and alter the white reader's possible racial biases" (Hedin, 37).

Hedin's "implicitly argumentative tradition" is quite similar to what Robert B. Stepto calls a "discourse of distrust," for both approaches are derived from the same speech acts regularly used by blacks in conversation with whites. In a discourse of distrust, Stepto tells us, "distrust is not so much a subject as a basis for specific narrative plottings and rhetorical strategies . . . the texts are fully 'about' the communicative propects of Afro-Americans writing for American readers, black and white, given the race rituals which color reading and / or listening" (Stepto, 305). Such writers often try to initiate "creative communication" by getting readers "told" or "told off" in such a way that they do not stop reading but do begin to "hear" the writer. In Jacobs's text the telling off begins with the title and the prefatory material. That aspect of "authority," with its implicit claims to accuracy and reliability, is then supplemented by the characterizations and the reconstructed relations among the characters.

The spines of the original editions of Harriet Jacobs's book are imprinted only with the word "Linda." The title pages carry only the subtitle, *Incidents in the Life of a Slave Girl: Written by Herself.*[19] Together the title and subtitle offer a balance of the exemplar and the example. Without the proper name, the subtitle emphasizes the generic and general over the personal and individual.

The subtitle in concert with the title also challenges more explicitly the usual hierarchy of race, class, and gender. "Written by Herself" invests authority in the author / narrator's participant / observer status while simultaneously subordinating that of the readers. *Incidents in the Life* also implies that the narrator is not simply reporting her life history, but she is selecting from a multitude of possibilities those events that she chooses to share. *A Slave Girl* establishes this narrative as one common to or representative of a class. "Girl" is a term rarely applied to slaves in literature; thus, it disrupts the expected discourse by resisting more common epithets such as "pickaninny" or "young slave." There may even be a subtle suggestion about the intelligence of African Americans, since there were even fewer girls than there were women being published at that time. But with "Linda," the subtitle more readily establishes this as a female slave's narrative whose authority is not easily disputed since it is *her* life of which she writes. The unnamed author writes as a mediator, a first-person narrator now more experienced but still sympathetic, who looks back upon her girlhood and selects those experiences that she deems most appropriate for her audience and her literary intentions. Reading the words "Written by Herself" that follow the subtitle and the words "Published for the author" that come at the bottom of that page, a reader confronts not only the exercise of literary prerogative, of claiming authorial responsibility for the text's selection and arrangement, but also an assumption of self-worth, of meaning and interest in her personal experiences that exceed the specific or personal.

The title page carries two epigrams that are compelling when read in light of what Karlyn Kohrs Campbell has termed "'feminine' rhetoric."[20] Such writing, Campbell asserts, is

> usually grounded in personal experience. In most instances, personal experience is tested against the pronouncements of male authorities (who can be used for making accusations and indictments that would be impermissible from a woman) . . . [It] may appeal to biblical authority . . . The tone tends to be personal and somewhat tentative, rather than objective or authoritative . . . tends to plead, to appeal to the sentiments of the audience, to "court" the audience by being "seductive." . . . [to invite] female audiences to act, to draw their own conclusions and make their own decisions, in contrast to a traditionally "Masculine" style that approaches the audience as inferiors to be told what is right or to be led.

What Campbell terms "feminine rhetoric" is comparable to the "discourse of distrust" and certain other rhetorical strategies developed by African Americans. It too strives to thwart the resisting reader's urge to compete with the author for authority and to enlist the reader instead as a collaborator. But for Jacobs, as for other African Americans, not all the strategies of "feminine rhetoric" would work for her purposes. Though she was a woman writing primarily to other women, she was also a black woman writing to white women. Racism exacerbates distrust. Racial stereotypes would make certain conventions, such as the seductive speaker, the tentative tone, and the laissez-faire lecturer, work against her. But the use of quoted authority to state the more accusatory or unflattering conclusions had great potential. And, those "feminine" literary conventions that Jacobs does adopt are adapted to project images more in line with her purposes as a writer and her status as a black woman.

Consider, for example, the ways in which Jacobs employs verification, the process of using quotations from others to state the more accusatory or un-flattering conclusions. As Campbell notes, women writers frequently used references from scripture to validate their claims and they often cited the words of others, especially the pronouncements of men, to state directly the accusations or indictments that the women writers were implying. Jacobs includes two quotations on her title page. The first declares that "Northerners know nothing at all about SLAVERY . . . They have no conception of the depth of *degradation* involved . . . if they had, they would never cease their efforts until so horrible a system was overthrown."[21] This quotation is unmistakably patronizing if not actually accusatory or indicting. However, Harriet Jacobs does not attribute these words to a man, but cites, instead, an anonymous "woman of North Carolina." Sophisticated readers of abolitionist literature would recognize these words as those quoted by Angelina E. Grimké in her *Appeal to the Christian Women of the South* in 1836. Such a scholarly reference would enhance the author's claim to learnedness. But in 1861, it is doubtful that many readers would have recognized the source of this quote. Jacobs's decision not to identify the speaker with any more accuracy than that of gender and geography allows a more powerful use of verification even as it demonstrates elements of "sass" and "signifying." Given the assumed inferiority of blacks to whites, this modification would be acceptable to most of her readers. They would assume that a black woman's appeal to authority by citing a white woman was comparable to a white woman's seeking verification from a white man and, given the racism of that time, they would undoubtedly assume that the anonymous woman was in fact white. But, the woman's race is not stated, and although there are at least two Southern white women in *Incidents* who surreptitiously work against slavery, none is as outspokenly antislavery as the black women in Jacobs's narrative or the Northern white women who wrote the authenticating statements that frame Jacobs's narrative. The only women from North Carolina in Harriet Jacobs's text who exhibit the spirit and audacity of the woman quoted on her title page are black. Since Harriet Jacobs was a "woman of North Carolina" and her book is designed to effect the kind of awareness and action referred to in the quotation, it is quite likely that readers, especially those who were African

American, might assume that Jacobs is quoting another slave woman or herself. Such a reading would be subtly empowering.

Jacobs's second quotation is Biblical. It too functions as verification, to increase her authority. The words are those of Isaiah 32:6: "Rise up, ye women that are at ease! Hear my voice, ye careless daughters! Give ear unto my speech." The relationship between this command and the theme of *Incidents* is fairly obvious. But the quotation does more than refer to a precedent for women becoming politically active. This quotation comes from the section of Isaiah that warns directly against alliances with Egypt, a word synonymous in the antebellum United States with "slavery." And in this chapter, Isaiah's prophecy is actually a warning. The women "that are at ease," the "careless daughters" who fail to rise up and support the rights of the poor and the oppressed, will find themselves enslaved. Again, Jacobs has revised the "feminine" rhetorical convention, for this citation is more demanding and declarative than it is seductive or suggestive.

The author's preface follows the title page. As is expected in the discourse of distrust, Jacobs's first words "tell off" the reader in ways that she or he must "hear." "Reader, be assured this narrative is no fiction." This statement is neither apology nor request. It is a polite command, soothingly stated but nonetheless an imperative. The next sentence neither explains nor defends: "I am aware that some of my adventures may seem incredible; but they are, nevertheless, strictly true." Instead of elaborating upon her claim to authenticity in the preface, Jacobs requires an even higher level of trust, for she advises her readers that she has not told all that she knows. "I have not exaggerated the wrongs inflicted by Slavery" she writes, "on the contrary, my descriptions fall far short of the facts." With these words, the author claims superior knowledge and plainly privileges her own interpretation over any contrary ideas that the reader may have as to the text's authenticity.

At the conclusion of her narrative, Jacobs's struggle has gained her a conditional freedom. "We are as free from the power of slave holders," she argues, "as are the white people of the north." But she continues, "that, according to my ideas, is not saying a great deal. . . . The dream of my life is not yet realized" (Jacobs, 201). Ironically, her authorial efforts, as creative and effective as they are, have not achieved an unmitigated success either.

The situation with *Incidents in the Life of a Slave Girl* is an extreme example of that faced by "other" writers. Especially with African American women, reader resistance seems neverending. However, I am convinced that Harriet Jacobs, like many others, anticipated a hostile and incredulous reception to her narrative. And using techniques from her multiple cultures, she created a transcultural[22] text that begged, borrowed, stole, and devised the techniques that would allow her maximum freedom to tell her story in her own way and to her own ends. Jacobs may well have underestimated the persistence of resistance, but she did in fact create a brilliantly innovative autobiography.

That the incidents of resistance were not quelled may say more about the perspicaciousness of her readers than about imperfections in the text itself.

Notes

This essay is a substantially revised version of an earlier publication in *The (Other) American Traditions*, ed. Joyce Warren (New Brunswick: Rutgers University Press, 1992).

1. Susan Lanser, *The Narrative Act: Point of View in Prose Fiction* (Princeton: Princeton University Press, 1981). Subsequent references are found in the text.

2. Phillis Wheatley, *Poems on Various Subjects, Religious and Moral*, in *The Poems of Phillis Wheatley*, ed. Julian D. Mason, Jr. (Chapel Hill: University of North Carolina Press, 1989), 48. Subsequent references to Wheatley's poems and letters are from this source and noted in the text.

3. Thomas Jefferson, *The Writings of Thomas Jefferson*, ed. Albert Ellery Bergh (Washington, D.C., 1907), Vol. 2, 196; quoted in Mason, *The Poems of Phillis Wheatley*, 30, n. 10.

4. Richard Barksdale and Keneth Kinnamon, *Black American Writers* (New York: Macmillan, 1972), 39–40.

5. Frances E. W. Harper, "Almost Constantly Either Traveling or Speaking," in *A Brighter Coming Day: A Frances Ellen Watkins Harper Reader*, ed. Frances Smith Foster (New York: Feminist Press, 1990), 126–7.

6. Letter from Harriet Jacobs to Amy Post in 1852. Quoted in *Incidents in the Life of a Slave Girl: Written by Herself*, ed. Jean Fagan Yellin (Cambridge, MA: Harvard University Press, 1987), p. 232. Unless otherwise noted, all quotations from Jacobs's letters and from her book are from this source and noted in the text.

7. Albert E. Stone, "Introduction: American Autobiographies as Individual Stories and Cultural Narratives," in *The American Autobiography: A Collection of Critical Essays*, ed. Albert E. Stone (Englewood Cliffs, NJ: Prentice Hall, 1981), 1–2.

8. Joanne M. Braxton defines "sass" as "a mode of verbal discourse and as a weapon of self defense." Sass and "the outraged mother" are key to her discussion of *Incidents*. Joanne M. Braxton, *Black Women Writing Autobiography: A Tradition within a Tradition* (Philadelphia: Temple University Press, 1989), 10.

9. The most famous discussion of "signifying" is from that of Henry Louis Gates, Jr., in *The Signifying Monkey: A Theory of Afro-American Literary Criticism* (New York: Oxford University Press, 1988). Gates is building upon the work of several people, but two are particularly helpful: Claudia Mitchell-Kernan, "Signifying as a Form of Verbal Art" in *Mother Wit from the Laughing Barrel: Readings in the Interpretation of Afro-American Folklore*, ed. Alan Dundes (Englewood Cliffs, NJ: Prentice Hall, 1973), 310–28, and Geneva Smitherman, *Talkin and Testifyin: The Language of Black America* (Boston: Houghton Mifflin, 1977).

10. Robert B. Stepto. "Distrust of the Reader in Afro-American Narratives," in *Reconstructing American Literary History*, ed. Sacvan Bercovitch (Cambridge, MA: Harvard University Press, 1986), 305. Subsequent references are from this source and found in the text.

11. Here I am quoting from Henry Louis Gates, Jr., *The Classic Slave Narratives* (New York: New American Library, 1987), xvi. I, too, find it easier to go along with the

tide than to swim against it. In this discussion, I too will refer to the text as "*Incidents in the Life of a Slave Girl.*"

12. *Narrative of the Life of Frederick Douglass, an American Slave* (1845; rpt. New York: Doubleday, 1963), 68.

13. Another example is that of Elizabeth Keckley in *Behind the Scenes* (1867; rpt., New York: Oxford University Press, 1988), whose graphic accounts of a series of incidents in which she physically resisted beatings despite the inherent sensationalism of the gender differences has excited virtually no comment.

14. *Within the Plantation Household* (Chapel Hill: University of North Carolina Press, 1988), 392.

15. Scholars have long acknowledged that these writers, like many others, relied heavily upon the advice and sometimes the revisions of their friends and editors. This has not been a major impediment to their reputations as writers or to the acceptance of their work as serious contributions.

16. Jeanne Kammer, "The Art of Silence and the Forms of Women's Poetry," in *Shakespeare's Sisters: Feminist Essays on Women Poets*, ed. Sandra M. Gilbert and Susan Gubar (Bloomington: Indiana University Press, 1979), 153–164. Subsequent references are from this edition and found in the text.

17. Robyn R. Warhol, "Towards a Theory of the Engaging Narrator: Earnest Interventions in Gaskell, Stowe, and Eliot," *PMLA* 101:5 (October 1988): 811–17. Subsequent references are in the text.

18. Raymond Hedin, "The Structuring of Emotion in Black American Fiction," *Novel* 10 (Fall 1982): 36. Subsequent references to Hedin's argument are from this source and noted in the text.

19. Here I am assuming that if the presentation of the book was not orchestrated by Jacobs, it certainly met her approval. Although it is possible that the cover and the title page were her publisher's or her editor's design, Jean Fagan Yellin's documentation of the relationship between Jacobs and Child suggests that Jacobs was actively concerned with every aspect of the production of her text. Moreover, since the original publisher went bankrupt and Jacobs purchased the plates, she had the opportunity to change the design had it been contrary to her intentions.

20. Karlyn Kohrs Campbell, "Style and Content in the Rhetoric of Early Afro-American Feminists," *Quarterly Journal of Speech* 72 (1986): 434–45. Subsequent references are from this source and found in the text.

21. I am grateful to Elizabeth Spelman for recognizing this quotation as having been published by Angelina Grimké. While it may correct my earlier theory that Jacobs was quoting herself, the fact that I originally read it that way supports the overall concept. Attributing the quote to an anonymous woman of North Carolina in a text where the most assertive and "real" women are black allows and encourages readers to make such assumptions.

22. Here I am adapting definitions that Masao Miyoshi posits in his discussion of transnational and multinational corporations. The distinction, he argues, is "problematic" and frequently the terms may be used interchangeably. The differences are "in the degrees of alienation from the countries of origin." Multinational corporations belong to one nation and operate in several. Transnational corporations, on the other hand, are not tied to their nations of origin but are more self-

contained and self-serving. Although there may be obvious incompatibilities be-tween the discussion of multicultural and multinational businesses and discourse, Miyoshi's discussion stimulated my own thinking in this matter. See his "A Bor-derless World? From Colonialism to Transnationalism and the Decline of the Nation-State," *Critical Inquiry* 19 (Summer 1993): 726–51.

MANIFEST IN SIGNS

THE POLITICS OF SEX AND REPRESENTATION
IN INCIDENTS IN THE LIFE OF A SLAVE GIRL

P. GABRIELLE FOREMAN

Untruth becomes truth through belief,
and disbelief untruths the truth.

Patricia Williams

Tell all the Truth but tell it slant –
success in Circuit lies
Too bright for our infirm Delight
The Truth's superb surprise . . .

Emily Dickinson

I

Harriet Jacobs's *Incidents in the Life of a Slave Girl* (1861) has been dismissed, and resuscitated, precisely on the basis of its value as "truth,"[1] even though it is widely accepted today that "the 'unreliability' of autobiography is an inescapable condition, not a rhetorical option."[2] Although there are explicit markers of the distance between "truth" and its representation in the text, contemporary critics overwhelmingly accept the transparency between the life of Harriet Jacobs and her narrative self-construct "Linda Brent."[3] Jean Fagan Yellin, perhaps Jacobs's most important critic, maintains that "you can trust her. She's not ever wrong. She may be wrong on incidentals like the birth order of her mistress's children – after all she was a woman in her forties trying to remember what happened to her as a teenager – but she's never wrong in substance."[4] The coordinates (right / "wrong," "substance" / incidentals, "trust"[worthy] / liar) are inscribed in *Incidents*'s reception, even though the maxim Sidonie Smith articulates is accepted when contemporary critics deal with autobiography generally. Indeed, today, as we are more and more engrossed in the politics of aesthetics and representation, "truthfulness," as Smith affirms, "becomes a much more complex and problematic phenomenon" that does not emphasize "the truth . . . in its factual or moral dimensions."[5] Rather than emphasize *auto*, the assumed transparent self, or *bio*, the life, "there is a new concern with *graphia*, 'the careful teasing out of warring forces of signification within the text itself.'"[6] Still, Jacobs's text often remains mired in implicit demands for referentiality, if not of her *auto*, then of her *bio* – demands that we interpret the principal script as if she had not loaded it with narrative explosions, with subversive scriptmines, so to speak. It is as if the black female, even today, must not only "tell the truth" but embody it, or collapse it into the very stereotypes the black sentimental heroine was, on one level, devised to refute.[7]

"Truth," however, was a sign-cluster that was highly valued in abolitionist rhetoric. Black authors and speakers were valued precisely because their bodies stood in its rhetorical stead and displaced Southern apologist versions of "slavery as it is." Nineteenth-century "truth," for the slave narrators' audience, was most threatened by exaggeration of the social evils of slavery, by, in other words, rhetorical excess.[8] "Delicacy" and "modesty," virtues valorized in women's, and even in African American male's narratives,[9] allowed for and even demanded that narrators systematically come short of the "truth," that they maneuver in the field of what I call the undertell. Tracing the signs of the undertell complicates Jacobs's traditional script and offers an alternative reading: that Dr. Norcom did rape Jacobs, rather than that Linda triumphed over Dr. Flint, not only in her material escape, but in her sexual one. However, the following analysis is not meant to substitute one argument for the other. Rather, I mean to call into question the politics of transparency that often frame our consideration of *Incidents* and our approach to black sentimental writing, and I would like to offer less determinate, if more tortuous, readings of the relation between coded silences and "truth," between signs and literal script.

Jacobs signals throughout *Incidents* that the surface script – that Linda had an affair with the white bachelor Mr. Sands in order to fend off the sexual threat of her master Dr. Flint – is undertold. She constantly reiterates that "the degradation, the wrongs, the vices that grow out of slavery are more than I can describe. They are greater than you would willingly believe" (28). This admonition echoes her preface, where she tells her readers that the events related in *Incidents* are "strictly true. I have not exaggerated the wrongs inflicted by Slavery; on the contrary, my descriptions fall far short of the facts" (1). The acknowledged tension between the "strict truth," which nonetheless "falls far short of the facts," and a mistrust for an audience she feels will not accept the "facts" reverberates throughout the narrative and informs her rhetorical strategies.

Or perhaps Jacobs measures the changing mores and expectations of the mid-nineteenth century and expects her readers on some level to comprehend her coded narrative strategies. The cult of sincerity that had dominated the previous two decades faded in importance in the fifties, the decade during which Jacobs composed *Incidents*. Karen Halttunen argues that the "sentimental typology of conduct" – the valorization of transparency of character – was fast being replaced with laws of polite social performance.[10] She notes that "the most important law of polite social geography was that no one shatter the magic of the genteel performance by acknowledging back regions that alone made the performance possible."[11] Jacobs may well have understood her implicit contract with her readers, and could expect her white bourgeois female audience to play its part – to perceive, but to be "delicate" enough never to admit to the comprehension of the sexually determined black "back regions" of her textual performance.[12] Jacobs might well have known that rules of decorum, in that era of shifting truth expectations, were as compelling as those of disclosure. By de-emphasizing Jacobs's mediation of truth and the politics of sexual revelation and discursive autonomy, we allow Lydia Maria Child's introductory claim that Child presents the "veil withdrawn," the back regions exposed, to act as the guiding con-text, and so we continue to accept Jacobs as a narrator who has internalized, or at least deferred to, unmediated tenets of true womanhood.

Yet Jacobs herself is much more resourcefully artful than such an account would have us believe. She measures her audience's interpretative capacities, so well laid out by Child's explanation of why she, a prominent white abolitionist, might be associated with so "indelicate" a text. Child presents the "veil withdrawn . . . for the sake of my sisters in bondage, who are suffering wrongs so foul that our ears are too delicate to listen to them" (4). As Valerie Smith notes, Child places herself and her imagined readers in the slave victim's stead; she substitutes "our," or rather white, ears in the grammatical place that should call for black reactions or bodies.[13]

Importantly, "ear," as the orifice penetrated by words, acts to degenderize sexual exploitation and break down oppositions of male / female abuse.[14] In Jacobs's narrative, slave men, as well as women, are sexually terrorized by white people of either sex. In language that comes just shy of explicitly exposing the homosexual abuse to which male narrators rarely, if ever, admit,[15] Jacobs writes of Luke, the slave of a dissipated and sick young master:

> As [the master] lay there on his bed, a mere degraded wreck of manhood, he took into his head the strangest freaks of despotism; and if Luke hesitated to submit to his orders, the constable was immediately

sent for. Some of these freaks were of a nature too filthy to be repeated. I left poor Luke still chained to the bedside of this cruel and disgusting wretch. (192)

Jacobs also asserts early on that "from others than the master persecution also comes in such cases" (13), and exposes white women with the "veil withdrawn." Karen Sánchez-Eppler notes that it is the "whispering" Mrs. Flint who realizes her demand to have Linda sleep in her room, who leans suggestively over her slave's body at night (22). Young mistresses too, Jacobs notes,

> hear their parents quarreling about some female slave. Their curiosity is excited . . . and they hear talk as should never meet youthful ears, or any other ears. They know that the women slaves are subject to their father's authority in all things; and in some cases they exercise the same authority over men slaves. (52)

Again in this passage, sexualized language attracts varied agents. The white woman here is both sexual aggressor and subject of Jacobs's narrative control: she is stripped of her usually protected status as true woman and, "curiosity" excited, ears exposed, she is sexualized. In these incidents, Jacobs undertells both slave's abuse and white guilt.

II

Jacobs encodes her descriptions of varied types and agents of sexual abuse to preserve her own authority as she simultaneously evokes sympathy from her readers. Yet she carefully avoids complete discursive victimization.[16] In other words, rather than Jacobs representing herself as a sentimental victim so she can speak, such a location generically denies her speech. The delimited arena of interracial "victimization" is characterized by lack of explicit expression, at least by the "victims." The nineteenth-century white woman only pointed (at a black man), and the legal apparatus need not be brought to bear on him – it was silenced – before he was sold, shot, or lynched. Conversely, Southern recognition of the sexual abuse of slave or freed African American women was as alien in concept as in fact.[17]

What, then, legitimized speech-rights for slaves? Houston Baker claims that the male slave "*publicly* sells his voice in order to secure *private* ownship of his voice-person,"[18] and so shifts concepts of desire and privatization from a gendered (public / private) to an economically dominated terrain. Jacobs, however, already free, cannot justify her ultimately public publishing venture into the male and public realm to secure ownership of her person. Nor can she invoke the accepted model of the era in which women writers legitimize their trade by emphasizing explicit ties to an overriding and valorized motherhood. Louisa Picquet (1861) unveils her sexual past only as a last attempt to purchase her mother out of slavery; Harriet Wilson (1859) in effect writes in order to "buy" her son. In contrast, like their mother, Jacobs's children are free, despite her circumlocutions;[19] her free grandmother has recently died. She never claims that she is attempting to buy, through this work, a "home of her own" (201). Nor does she make claim to another popular justification for women writers' indelicate jaunt into the public sphere – destitution. Rather, she asks her abolitionist friend Amy Post to mention in the appendix to *Incidents* that "I lived at service all the while that I was striving to get the Book out . . . [as] I would [not] like to have people think that I was living an Idle life – and had got this book out merely to make money" (242). How, if Jacobs refuses to invoke received legitimizing strategies, does one account for her economy of voice and possession? Indeed, Jacobs's model does not refer to economies of self-possession; rather, it is predicated upon the politics of desire and textual autonomy. She sells her voice in order to secure and express private ownership – not of her body – but of its discursive embodiments, her voice and text themselves.

The right to speak freely, to articulate one's rights, was clearly and constitutionally denied to African Americans in Jacobs's antebellum South. Nor should this fact be taken lightly because of our familiarity with it. Denied access to unrestricted speech, Jacobs maneuvers with the sphere of more sanctioned speech. Her writing often gives the impression, as Valerie Smith contends, "that the [sentimental] form only allows Jacobs to talk about her sexual experiences when they are the result of victimization."[20] Yet, the very appellation "victim" exonerates one from guilt, and so from compulsion toward speech. Those whom society recognizes as "true" victims cannot confess – they instead identify those at fault – for society does not assign the victim blame. Jacobs's depiction of slave sexual exploitation is complicated both by race and by a victim's – and victimization's – relationship to confession. Jacobs subscribes to certain taxonomies which grant her the right to confess. Thus, Jacobs expresses agency where male slave narrators most often depict complete female victimization. Indeed, to be a sexual actor, to choose Sands, allows her to appropriate speech rights.[21]

The calculus of speech, sex, and confession had already made its mark in the literary history of race, rights, and the most popular of all early slave narratives, the criminal "confession."[22] But, the criminal genre's often explicit titillation was ultimately resolved in outrage and punishment – the subgenre itself was predicated upon the suppression of the connected rights of black speech and criminal justice. Jacobs's confession, in contrast, with its emphasis on a rapacious master, could easily collapse for her readers into the arousal of imagined sadistic pornography. Yet Jacobs carefully contains her writing, refusing to describe Linda's more private moments with Mr. Sands, and so distinguishes the more acceptable titillation and resolution of confession and absolution from the pornographic excitement that would be labeled unacceptably illicit in Victorian America. Confession, then, is the currency with which she purchases the sanitized, and so legitimate, attention of her readers. Her much quoted "Pity me and pardon me, O virtuous reader" (55) acts to relieve the titillated audience from its excited state; in a sense, this passage acts to absolve them as much as it seeks to absolve Linda. Through confession, then, Jacobs converts religious invocation into both narrative and political agency.[23] Indeed, through being a sexual actor, by understanding and choosing it knowingly, she attempts to assert the rights of African American female speech and being. It is not only Jacobs's victimization but also her sexual agency, then, that generates much of *Incidents*'s narrative energy.

Jacobs delineates the relationship between master, slave, "sex," and criminalized speech, although she is rarely explicit. Instead she locates her astute analysis in the realm of the undertell. Silence and unreadable speech, she reiterates again and again, stand in fungible relation to security from sale. In the first few weeks after Linda has been willed to young Emily Flint, Jacobs writes that Dr. Flint hands a slave mother and her "husband" over to a trader: "You *promised* to treat me well," the mother says. "To which [Flint] replied, 'You have let your tongue run too far; damn you!' She had forgotten that it was a crime for a slave to tell who was the father of her child" (13). As Jacobs continually does when describing Linda's experience as Flint's sexual "victim," she switches to the plural and notes, "[s]ometimes he had stormy, terrific ways, that made his *victims* tremble" (27, emphasis mine).[24] This harassment, we can deduce, was actualized, for Jacobs later notes that:

> The secrets of slavery are concealed like those of the Inquisition. My master was, to my knowledge, the father of eleven slaves. But did the mothers dare to tell who was the father of their children? Did the other slaves dare to allude to it, except in whispers among themselves? No indeed! They knew too well the terrible consequences. (35)

Did these women form whispering communities of support analogous to white bourgeois culture where women provided each other with advice, solace, and aid?[25] Or did these slaves come to understand that such sharing constituted punishable speech? The formula of Silence or Sale renders the subject closed to the inquiries of the supportive and / or enraged husband, family, and green-eyed mistress alike. Jacobs's text, the sales she depicts, her reticence toward her grandmother, strongly suggest that at least some slave women quickly learned that they could whisper only if they were not the subject; they were required to suture over their violation with silence, to reinforce, perversely, their own objectification. The shared whisperings "among themselves" then exclude the assaulted object, whose confirmation of her abuse might actualize the constant threat of sale and endanger others' security as well; her required silence, though it does not ensure her own safety from rape or sale, makes her responsible for maintaining the "security" of her community.

Yet might not the signs of a "favorite" slave's pregnancy, or the child itself, constitute punishable speech? Can her silence perform what is demanded of it? Can it nullify bodily speech? The slave mother flings back Flint's commitment – "you *promised* to treat me well" – and he acknowledges their agreement but accuses her of breaching it, replying, "'you have let your tongue run too far; damn you!'" Jacobs's following comment – "she had forgotten that it was a crime . . . to tell" – concretizes the language of contract she represents in the passage. Jacobs transfers the juridical consequences of breaking contracts to a figure of speech, speech that in this nonactionable situation between slave and master nonetheless carries the punitive forces of punishment. What is clear, however, is that silence – the slave mother's agreed-upon item of exchange – is neither delimited by speech nor defined by its absence. Rather, it is the *issue* who is at issue, for the slave mother and husband "were both black and the child was very fair" (13). Her tongue, in other words, did not have to produce the telling text. No one has to *say* anything, for the child's color speaks for itself. Jacobs describes the slave mother as drawn (seduced, coerced, threatened, raped?) into an agreement in which even her agreed-upon part was never tenable. Not only are slave–master contracts always nonbinding and duplicitous, they will also turn a slave's speech *and* silence against her.

One might argue, then, that because Jacobs knew "too well the terrible consequences" (35), that "as soon as a new fancy took him, his victims were sold far off to get rid of them, especially if they had children" (55); because she had seen this, she began her affair with Sawyer (Sands). She explains that "of a man who was not my master I could ask to have my children well supported; and in this case, I felt confident I should obtain the boon and that they would be made free" (55). These lines directly precede the most oft-quoted "sentimental" lines in *Incidents*: "With all these thoughts revolving in my mind, and seeing no other way of escaping the doom I so much dreaded, I made a headlong plunge. Pity me, and pardon me, O virtuous reader!" (55). What is consistently read as a concession to or internalization of true womanhood can be read in this context as masked and mocking irony, a tone one cannot help but notice throughout the narrative. "Doom's" antecedent is most pointedly not the threat of sex, the trope of "doom" in a sentimental lexicon, but the threat of sale. And Jacobs's maneuvering works, for she turns words that most often figure in narratives as broken promises ("I will never sell you," Flint bellows after Sands's offers) into an unreserved threat that nullifies the loss she fears – not of virtue, but of family.

Although Jacobs would have us take her at her "word" and believe that her master never "succeeded" in his ultimate assault, I argue that it is equally valid to suggest that Norcom did rape his much-desired slave girl. Whatever one's textual interpretations, the word is a terrain Jacobs has much complicated with hidden and competing valences. The entire passage describing Linda's "plunge" is muddled with signs of undertell. Indeed, Jacobs ends the paragraph in which she introduces Sands by contending that

> a master may treat you as rudely as he pleases, and *you dare not speak*; moreover, the wrong does not seem so great with an unmarried man, as with one who has a wife to be made unhappy. There may be sophistry in all this; but the condition of a slave confuses all principles of morality, and, in fact, renders the practice of them impossible. (55, emphasis mine)

The imperative to remain silent surfaces yet again. Though the immediate referent for Jacobs's "sophistry" is her justification for Linda's relationship with Sands, there is reason to interpret her words in "all this" more broadly.

Throughout the text, the author elides the obvious question of Flint's "restraint," of why, if he could treat Linda "as rudely as he please[d]," he chose not to. Jacobs describes Flint's language as ranging from the affectional to the authoritative, but never do his tactics shift from the discursively sexual to the physically sexual.[26] I have argued elsewhere that as Jacobs translates her life into discourse, she transcribes the *events* of her life to that level. He whispers foul words, writes obscene notes, yet never does Jacobs present erotic foul play. She first presents Flint as a personal threat by recounting

> my master, whose restless, craving, vicious nature roved about day and night, seeking whom to devour, had just left me, with stinging, scorching *words; words* that scathed ear and brain like fire. O, how I despised him! I thought how glad I should be, if some day when he walked the earth, it would open and swallow him up and disencumber the world of a plague. (18, emphasis mine)

This passage displays the imbalance of Flint's actions and Linda's reactions; the passion in her language does not seem to have a direct correlation with what Jacobs claims Flint "says." Jacobs transfers Linda's (unacknowledged) violated body to the body of the word. By both serving for and providing the trope for physical abuse, words act to describe her violation and to absorb it.[27] If one argues that neither Jacobs's experience, temperament, nor text genuflects at the feet of true womanhood, Linda's reactions to Flint's verbal abuse throughout the text beg for another explanation.

There is much in *Incidents* to support an interpretation that Jacobs may be pregnant with Norcom's child when she begins her relationship with Sawyer.[28] Ostensibly referring only to the threat of an isolated cottage that Dr. Flint is building for Linda's *future* concubinage, Jacobs writes that

> the crisis of my fate now came so near that I was desperate. I shuddered to think of being the mother of children that should be owned by my old tyrant. I knew that as soon as a new fancy took him, his victims were sold far off to get rid of them; especially if they had children. I had seen several women sold with his babies at the breast. He never allowed his offspring by slaves to remain long in sight of himself and his wife. Of a man who was not my master I could ask to have my children well supported; and in this case, I felt confident I should obtain the boon and . . . that they would be made free. (55)

Linda takes the plunge because of Flint's immanent sexual threat. Yet Jacobs has presented Linda as eluding her master shrewdly on every preceding occasion. It seems just as likely, then, that the elisions are textual ones, that her analogy of other "victims" fully obtains, and that her crisis is an impending pregnancy. The space between her statement – "I shuddered to think of being the mother of children that should be owned by my old tyrant," a concern she expressed earlier when considering her free black suitor – differs importantly from all that follows from the next sentence – "I knew that as soon as a new fancy took him his victims were sold" (55). The first emphasizes Flint's purely legal claim; the second, with its inclusive victimization, implies sexual possession as well. It is this scenario that Jacobs's grandmother and Mrs. Flint are all too ready to believe. Hazel Carby suggests that "from [Linda's] experience she knew that Dr. Flint sold his offspring from slave women and hoped that if her children were fathered by Sands he could buy them and secure their future."[29] Carby's language reflects the ruptures in Jacobs's own; if Flint sold "*his* offspring from slave women" and Linda's "children were fathered by Sands," then Jacobs presents no reason for Flint to sell them.[30] Indeed, both the narrator's and her latter day critics' language imply what neither of them say: for this slave mother's strategy to work, Sands's role as father must be contested. Jacobs diffuses "the crisis of [her] fate" as best she can by complicating paternity. By anticipating and so framing bodily speech, she overturns a most basic tenet of slave law; she empowers a slave woman to identify the father of her child, and makes her naming important indeed.

Jacobs understands the multiple codes of silence and self-preservation on the plantation and their appurtenances in the North. Linda learns that there is no radical geographical rupture in the first few moments after her arrival. She confides in her first host, a black minister she "would not deceive" (160), and he responds by warning: "don't answer everybody so openly. It might give some heartless people a pretext for treating you with contempt" (160). His words, Jacobs writes, "made an indelible impression upon me" (161), an impression, I would argue, the author transfers indelibly onto *Incidents*. Jacobs's own letters to Amy Post express her perception that de facto laws of silence in the South become rules of disclosure in the North. She writes,

> I had determined to let others think as they pleased but my lips should be sealed and no one had a right to question me for this reason when I first came North I avoided the Antislavery people as much as possible because I felt that I could not be honest and tell the whole truth.[31]

"Some heartless people" in this lexicon is an expansive term. As Jacobs learns in the South upon the death of what Child calls Linda's "kind, considerate friend," the mistress who teaches her to read and write and then wills Jacobs to her niece and so to Dr. Norcom, those who can be trusted aren't easily emotionally and politically classifiable. Resisting the simple ("sentimental") dichotomies of "good" and "bad," Jacobs now separates bodily threat, the fear of actual repossession, from the politics of trust and speech, and relocates the relationship of truth to silence to the realm of Northern power relations invoked by the stinging word "contempt." William Andrews's commentary on James Pennington transfers easily:

> as a black autobiographer among suspicious whites, [Jacobs] was not morally obliged to deal truthfully with [her] audience if that meant putting [herself] in jeopardy. On such autobiographical occasions self interest takes priority over truth by claiming it, appropriating it, to its own needs. In an ultimate sense . . . one could lie and still be true – to oneself. Under such conditions willed autobiographical concealments and / or deceptions might be the truest form of self-expression.[32]

Jacobs replots received relations between slave truth and freedom. While in the South the female slave's agency of lips and tongue was muzzled; now North, she seals her lips, the double entendre only too evident, by her own accord.[33] However, this is no mimetic adaptation of Northern Victorian mores, discursive and sexual. What Jacobs appropriates in denying others free rein to question her is her own rights of choice. She envisions discursive property rights – the license and comfort that make it possible "to be free to *say* so" (174), as Pennington does, by appropriating them into her own protective economy. Thus, she dismisses the legal (and extralegal) economies that bind her and her children to interpretations which grant their bodies to the Master and the master text: "I could not possibly regard myself as a piece of property," she writes; "I knew the law would decide that I was his property, and would probably give his daughter a claim to my children; but I regarded such laws as the regulations of robbers, who had no rights that I was bound to respect" (187). If, as Patricia Williams argues, slavery is a structure that denies black generative independence,[34] then what Jacobs affirms, in her private overturning of Dred Scott and in her strong claims to nondisclosure, is the generative independence in a discursive realm that is denied her by slavery in a biological one.

Jacobs's relish in relating Brent's letter-writing maneuvers from her grand-mother's garret bolsters a reading of the author as trickster or artful narrator. As Andrews argues, confessing to morally compromising behavior in slavery "is a traditional rhetorical strategy of antebellum Black autobiography."[35] He goes on to suggest that "each [author] takes steps to preserve his bond with the reader by repudiating that behavior and requesting the reader's sympathy for the slave in his tragic moral dilemma. Still, he seems to savor the sufficiency of his invention, performance and manipulation."[36] Although Jacobs disavows the sexual past of slavery, she "clearly delights" in her letter writing,[37] and she does so without ever disowning these activities. Further, though Andrews's analysis does apply to Jacobs, male authors distance them-selves from their trickster past by insisting that it is the circumstances of slav-ery which engendered their behavior; and their geographical and behavioral change is often symbolized by a change in name itself.[38] That the audience knows their new names – William Wells Brown, Frederick Douglass – signi-fies that they can gauge black narrators' interior subjectivity unmediated by the distance of manipulative representation: "My character, yes, was forced to be duplicitous; but me, your narrator, transformed by freedom, you can trust," they seem to say; "[n]ow that I own myself, my name, I share them freely with you."[39] In contrast, Jacobs's symbolic relation to her narrator's trajectory of undertell and coded dissimulation stands in opposition to the regained candor of the male narrator. Whereas the men transform from trickster to true-name-trusted author, the narrator of *Incidents* veils herself in more opaque layers of representation: she becomes the fictive character, Linda Brent.

Jacobs collapses the rhetorical opposition between North and South (that in *Narrative of the Life* Douglass so consciously constructs) and so further com-plicates her narrator's status as "truthsayer."[40] She envisions her Northern situation as analogous to her life in the South. Working as a domestic in Nathaniel Willis's home, Jacobs engages in a competition in cunning that echoes that chapter in her narrator's Southern struggle with Dr. Flint. From her letters we know that Jacobs sees Willis as a creative obstacle. She finds herself working in the eighteen-room manor of a famous newspaper editor with proslavery sentiments who is concerned less with social welfare than with social status. In his day, Willis was often criticized for his "dandyism in dress";[41] he can be easily characterized as Halttunen's midcentury confi-dence man: a man of few values, conscious of his less than qualifying social beginnings, who dupes society by his attire, charm, and newly made money to marry into status and leisure.[42]

Willis, who supported a select group of women journalists, could not be trusted by those too close to home. While he wrote in the best of circumstances,[43] the other authors in his life, his sister "Fanny Fern" and nurse Harriet Jacobs, often wrote at night and published anonymously, in large part because of him. Like Fern, Jacobs received no encouragement from Willis: he "is too proslavery he would tell me that it was very wrong [to write a book] and that I was trying to do harm or perhaps he was sorry for me to undertake it while I was in his family" (232). By writing secretly, Jacobs matches her cunning against a new but familiar type: in Willis the licentious Southern master is replaced by the Northern confidence man, a "modern industrial version of the trickster."[44] Jacobs keeps her job by playing her own trickster – the faithful servant – and plays her role well enough to convince Willis's most thorough biographer that her "attachment to the interests of the family during the whole period of her service was a beautiful instance of the fidelity and affection which sometimes, but not often, distinguish the relation of master and servant,"[45] well enough for her "master" and Mrs. Willis, unsolicited, to secure her official freedom, and for her to have her narrative published without their knowledge or help. The closing passage in *Incidents* reflects Jacobs's artful constructions:

> I still long for a hearthstone of my own, however humble. I wish it for my children's sake far more than for my own. But God so orders circumstances as to keep me with my friend Mrs. Bruce. Love, duty, gratitude, also bind me to her side. It is a privilege to serve her who pities my oppressed people, and who has bestowed the inestimable boon of freedom on me and my children. (201)

Jacobs cloaks her own domestic desire with the justification of motherhood and then quickly reduces it to the "privileges" of service. Yet her language almost seethes, as the careful usage of "bind me to her side" recalls Luke's being "chained to the bedside" of his abusive master; it thus disrupts the Northern economy of genteel servitude invoked by both Willis's biographer's and her own sentimental language. Linda's barely checked anger at being "*sold* at last " (200) to the Bruces also serves as a referent that disrupts a closing passage dripping not with sentimentality but with irony. Jacobs's sentimental subversion demonstrates that she recognizes the costs of a system in which parties suppress the "indelicate" issue of division of labor and property exchange.[46]

III

Jacobs's depiction of her grandmother further complicates her role as artful narrator. Valerie Smith contends that from her garret Brent is a voyeur "who sees but remains herself unseen."[47] Karen Sánchez-Eppler extends the dy-

namics of the gaze further when she notes that "the peephole [Brent] bore in
the wall of her grandmother's attic does not provide her with a view of the
house's interior, (she cannot watch her grandmother care for her children;
instead she watches the street)."[48] What the latter observation suggests is
Jacobs's glaring emphasis on her grandmother's exteriority. Just as Jacobs
"remains unseen," so she shields Molly Horniblow, protecting her, in turn,
from the sexual unveilings to which she herself is discursively subjected. By
casting her gaze outside, Jacobs refuses to compromise the integrity of her
grandmother's home; consequently, the older woman's privacy – and private
life as well – remains intact.

Jacobs's emphasis on Aunt Martha's exteriority is necessary so she can
offer her grandmother as her own balancing substitution. Pious and domestic, Aunt Martha counsels contentment, submissiveness, and purity; she is,
indeed, the only Southern representative of true womanhood Jacobs offers.[49]
As Hazel Carby has noted, the grandmother possesses the tenets of true
womanhood to an almost formulaic degree. Even if, as Carby contends, in
her feistier moments she lacks submissiveness,[50] she consistently counsels it,
insisting that her granddaughter should not run away. Jacobs writes early on,

> Most earnestly did she strive to make us feel that it was the will of God:
> that He had seen fit to place us under such circumstances; and though
> it seemed hard, we ought to pray for contentment. It was a beautiful
> faith, coming from a mother who could not call her children her own.
> But I, and Benjamin, her youngest boy, condemned it. (17)

Jacobs's seemingly approving depiction ("most earnestly," "beautiful") only
strengthens the passage's tensions, its undercutting parodic bitterness, and
the ultimate rejection of her grandmother's piety she expresses by its end.
Jacobs calls into question the tenets of motherhood – domestic contentment
and submission to God's will – by illustrating the delimited maternal power
true womanhood ostensibly brings. By expressing the link between mother
and child through the trope of "one's own," she appeals to bourgeois sentiment: a mother's claim to "her own children" and to legal negations of
nineteenth-century maternal ownership that she and her white female
readers share: ultimately, neither free nor slave women have rights of "ownership" to their children.

Jacobs's condemnation also sets her in opposition to her grandmother's
status as the defender of motherhood. When asked to weigh Linda's rights to
freedom against the responsibility of motherhood, Aunt Martha insists that
the latter admits no mitigating circumstances; she denies even temporary
abeyance of Linda's responsibilities for her family's later good. When Linda
expresses her serious intent to run, her grandmother advises her instead to

> stand by your own children, and suffer with them till death. Nobody

respects a mother who forsakes her children; and if you leave them, you
will never have a happy moment. If you go, you will make me miserable the short time I have to live. . . . Try to bear a little longer. (91)[51]

Aunt Martha locates Linda in sole relation to motherhood: as both good
mother and good "daughter." According to her grandmother, Linda's responsibilities cancel out any personal interest in her "own" liberatory agency.
Aunt Martha's totalizing position anticipates the logic of those who support
contemporary concepts of motherhood, which insist on its primacy above
and beyond the "health of the mother," just as her methods of emotional
manipulation also anticipate those who advance the child as always already
primary. The very person who nurtures and protects her, counsels Linda that
the rights to her body are again subsumed, this time by motherhood's overriding interests.

Aunt Martha is practically reified as Protector of True Womanhood in the
climactic passage of revelation. Pregnant, Jacobs writes, "I secretly mourned
over the sorrow I was bringing on my grandmother, who had so tried to
shield me from harm. I knew . . . that it was a source of pride to her that I had
not degraded myself, like most of the slaves. I wanted to confess to her that I
was no longer worthy of her love; but I could not utter the dreaded words"
(56). The tensions between Aunt Martha's acknowledgment of her granddaughter's victimization that Jacobs expresses in "shield from harm," and the
projected participation and blame contained in "degraded myself like most
of the slaves," read loudly in this passage, if only because Jacobs presents
"most of the [harassed female] slaves" as unwilling victims throughout the
rest of the narrative. The tension escalates shortly thereafter:

> I went to my grandmother. My lips moved to make confession, but the
> words stuck in my throat. . . . I think she saw something unusual was
> the matter with me. The mother of slaves is very watchful. She knows
> that there is no security for her children. After they have entered their
> teens she lives in daily expectation of trouble. . . . Presently, in came
> my mistress, like a mad woman, and accused me concerning her hus-
> band. My grandmother, whose suspicions had been previously awak-
> ened, believed what she said. She exclaimed, "O Linda! has it come to
> this? I had rather see you dead than to see you as you now are. You are
> a disgrace to your dead mother." She tore from my fingers my mother's
> wedding ring and her silver thimble. "Go away!" she exclaimed, "and
> never come to my house, again." Her reproaches fell so hot and heavy,
> that they left me no chance to answer. (56–7)

Jacobs's aborted voicings ("the words stuck in my throat" and "they left me
no chance to answer") leave intact the narrative myth that she is pregnant
with Dr. Flint's child. Her silence also allows Aunt Martha's interpretation of
"what she [Mrs. Flint] said" (Jacobs pointedly does not reproduce Mrs.

Flint's words), accusations of Linda and Dr. Flint's supposed affair we can only deduce, to engage in another sort of myth-making. In this passage, which contains what must be one of the most dismaying nonsequiturs in the slave narrative genre, Aunt Martha's concern, fear, and protection – all of which presuppose her understanding of abusive sexual and power relations under slavery – transform into her condemnation and blame. Her new position suppresses that which has previously informed almost all of her actions.

Fully transformed into the defending and deafening trope of true womanhood, Aunt Martha is the relegator of its most recognizable signs. She divests Linda of the loud symbols of true womanhood's construction: her mother's wedding ring and silver thimble. Aunt Martha's home had previously provided safety in contradistinction to that negated homespace in slavery (even Stowe doesn't allow Chloe and Tom to regulate their comfortable cabin from intrusions of various sorts). Using Mrs. Flint's words, however, Aunt Martha erects walls that turn a zone of safety into an exclusively bourgeois space, "my house," whose only inhabitants are the purity and domesticity that are, according to Jacobs, almost impossible to realize under slavery.[52]

Jacobs sanitizes her construct Aunt Martha in order to offer a balance to her readers; Aunt Martha is made to embody the model true woman from which Jacobs herself falls short; in some sense Jacobs advances grandmother, mother, and daughter as aspects of a Gestalten self – with Aunt Martha standing as the covering unit, what Houston Baker might call the phaneric mask.[53] Smith-Rosenberg notes that gender roles and the "biological realities of frequent pregnancies, childbirth and nursing" in part accounted for "the roles of daughter and mother [that] shaded imperceptibly and ineluctably into each other."[54] Indeed, the politics of flexible identities that Jacobs offers, symbolized by generational parameters between her mother and grandmother, are further blurred in the presentation of *Incidents'* most definitive edition. As Jacqueline Goldsby maintains, the large framing portrait found on both the side and the frontispiece of Yellin's widely circulated paperback reveals a white-haired, white-skinned elderly woman seated in an elaborately carved wooden chair. Her body is almost protected by a dark wrap tied over her shoulders and breasts, by the sturdy chair arm, and by her hands crossed demurely in her ample lap; she looks directly at her readers; she has, her direct gaze tells us, nothing to hide. Who, in the narrative we are about to encounter, could this photo represent but Jacobs's grandmother?[55] The seeming replacement of Linda Brent by Aunt Martha supplants the cover etching of the previous edition of *Incidents* (1973), where we are confronted instead with a young black woman of Linda's age – hair shorn, eyes averted, satchel in hand, her clothes clinging lightly to her. There is little tension between this earlier illustration and the Linda represented in the pages of *Incidents*. Even though the frontispiece on Yellin's edition is the only extant photo she could find, Yellin inadvertently follows Lydia Maria Child's framing lead; the photo balances Child's editorial decision to close with "tender memories of my good old grandmother" (201) instead of ending with John Brown, as Jacobs wished. Rather than bolster Jacobs's condemnation and revision of true womanhood, the photo offers its iconographic triumph as the opening image of *Incidents in the Life of a Slave Girl*.

However, Jacobs's text itself continually disrupts the substitution she, too, seems to offer. Again the black female body cannot elide the information Jacobs neglects to provide. Although she presents Aunt Martha as the embodiment of courageous and respectable motherhood, Jacobs cannot successfully cleave maternity from the sexual moment of conception. Aunt Martha's role is as angelic nurturer, the mother forced to wean her daughter (Jacobs's mother) in order to nurse her mistress's (Mrs. Flint), holding no grudge. Yet her body itself presents textually unrepresented questions. The slave nurse, Sánchez-Eppler notes, is "comestible, literally consumed by her owners and their offspring. The ability to nurse, like the ability to bear children and to provide sexual gratification, manifests the particular utility of the female slave: a utility resulting not simply from the labor performed by her body, but rather from the body itself."[56] The textual labor Aunt Martha performs in *Incidents*, then, is disrupted by her body's birthings, its issues. In a heated volley between Flint and Aunt Martha, she, "almost choking with grief . . . replies 'It was not I that drove Linda away. My grandchildren are gone; and of my nine children only one is left. God help me!'" (145). Jacobs's, or Aunt Martha's, very appeal to the sentiment of motherhood poses obvious questions. How, after all, were all these children begotten? What indelicate questions must we ask here?

Jacobs's grandmother bears children, like most nineteenth-century women, for more than fifteen years, and so both her cultural and biological mothering overlaps with her daughter's.[57] Of her grandmother's youngest son, Jacobs notes: "there was so little difference in our ages that he seemed more like my brother than my uncle" (6). She goes on that "he was a bright, handsome lad, nearly white" (6), whose "white face [later] did him a kindly service"; slave catchers "had no suspicion that it belonged to a slave" (24). Though Jacobs maintains that he inherited the complexion of his grandmother's white father, she is hardly convincing. For the absence of his father, whom Jacobs, so close to her uncle's age, might have known, speaks louder than her reassurances do. If Molly Horniblow's partner(s) had been sold, wouldn't Jacobs have presented this in *Incidents*? The most obvious reason, at least, for Jacobs's failure to mention any legitimizing husband(s) or father(s) would be that there were no such person(s).

Jacobs's representation of her grandmother's road to freedom raises similar questions. Despite her mistress's wish that Molly Horniblow be left free, the mistress' brother-in-law, Dr. Norcom / Flint, puts her up for sale. Jacobs writes of the community's outrage, that

no one bid for her. At last, a feeble voice said, "Fifty dollars." It came
from a maiden lady, seventy years old, the sister of my grandmother's
deceased mistress. . . . She knew how faithfully she had served her
owners, and how cruelly she had been defrauded of her rights; and she
resolved to protect her. . . . She gave the old servant her freedom. (11–12)

What Jacobs declines to include here is that Hannah Pritchard, the maiden
lady, who possessed no property of her own and, according to Jacobs, had
lived in her sister's household for forty years, also purchased Molly Horniblow's son Mark for four hundred dollars – not a paltry sum.[58] Nor does
Jacobs mention the role of Congressman Alfred Gatlin, whom the author's
brother credits with purchasing both the grandmother and her son with
money Molly Horniblow had entrusted to him.[59] Jacobs doesn't include that
it is Gatlin, too, who buys Molly a seven-room house the year of her emancipation for which he paid $364.50, and which he sold to her three years later
"for many good Causes and reasons and also in Consideration of one Dollar"
(Yellin, 263).[60] To comment that Molly Horniblow's relationship with Congressman Gatlin was sexual would be conjecture. Thirty-one years old the
year he contributed to her freedom, he was nineteen years her junior and
about ten years Mark's senior. Nonetheless, Jacobs's complete omission can
be read to signal that his presence would in some way significantly undermine
her construction of Aunt Martha as untainted True Woman, a construction
her friend and the *maiden lady*'s role only helps to affirm.

Had Jacobs's grandmother suffered similar circumstances to those of her
granddaughter, the climactic passage of revelation, its heavy signifiers glaring, would become completely destabilized. The consummate artful narrator, Jacobs constructs a bipartite melange, a complex character construct
that simultaneously embodies, reinvents, and condemns aspects of true womanhood. By offering Aunt Martha both in Linda's stead and as an alter-self
she rejects, Jacobs presents violent back regions that only genteel readers
would fail to note; she delicately transplants true womanhood – hers, her
grandmother's, slave women's – in radically different dark soil.

What marks this text, I would maintain, is not the central question of "is
Linda, or until when is Linda, pure?" Rather, it is how ingeniously Jacobs
constructs fields of warring signification and obscured indeterminacy. Yet,
despite her scriptmines, her multiple sites of undertell, the narrator forcefully
maintains that Linda's triumph over Flint is sexual – that he never succeeds
in seducing his slave girl (53–4). One could argue that Jacobs distinguishes
rape from seduction, that she never gave into the latter, and rejects the cult of
purity by redefining it. She constructs another set of values; to give in, to consent, might be to lose purity, while to be forced does not affect her "purity" at
all. Yellin notes that the narrator "indicates that she had distinguished between virginity and integrity even when very young: 'I wanted to keep myself

pure; and, under the most adverse circumstances, I tried hard to preserve my self-respect'" (Yellin, 258). One might also argue that Jacobs avoided confessing to Norcom's actual violence because the audience expected what she and others present as the inevitable violation of slave girls: "there are somethings that I might have made plainer I know . . . I have left nothing out," she admits, "but what I thought – the world might believe that a Slave Woman was too willing to pour out – that she might gain their sympathies" (Yellin, 242). Yet, ultimately, her multiple and overlaid voicings illustrate Sidonie Smith's theory that a woman narrator "may even create several, sometimes competing stories about versions of herself as her subjectivity is displaced by one or multiple representations."[61] Although I contend that reconsidering Jacobs's subtexts calls for a possible reconstitution of her plot – that Norcom might well have "succeeded" and that she inscribes this in *Incidents* – in no way do I wish to be understood to ascribe to a reductive notion that might logically extend to labeling Jacobs a "liar." The binary characterization that she is telling the truth, the whole truth, or that she is lying, would beg all the questions I mean to raise here. This essay does not attempt to substitute one reading (Jacobs's triumph over Norcom) for another (that Norcom really raped her). I resist accepting, or offering, any critical exegesis as a definitive one. Yet I do mean to call into question the politics of transparency that often lead critics to accept Jacobs's principal script, her sexual "triumph," and that act to quiet down a subtext which constitutes her signifying narrative success.

Notes

I take the chapter title from Jacobs's description of Dr. Flint: "What he could not find opportunity to say in words," she writes, "he manifested in signs." *Incidents in the Life of a Slave Girl*, ed. Jean Fagan Yellin (Cambridge: Harvard University Press, 1987), 31. All subsequent references to *Incidents* will be found within the body of the text. Thanks to Barbara Christian, Jacqueline Goldsby, Karen Sánchez-Eppler, Laura Wexler, and Richard Yarborough for their generous feedback on various drafts of this essay.

1. *Incidents in the Life of a Slave Girl* had long been thought to have been composed by Lydia Maria Child, its editor (see Jean Fagan Yellin's introduction for more details). Many twentieth-century black writers, anthologists, and historians denigrated and dismissed it as well. Among them are Sterling Brown, Arthur Davis, Ulysses Lee, Arna Bontemps, and John Blassingame. See Yellin's "Text and Contexts of Harriet Jacobs's *Incidents in the Life of a Slave Girl: Written by Herself*," in Charles T. Davis and Henry Louis Gates, Jr., eds., *The Slave's Narrative* (New York: Oxford University Press, 1985), and Blassingame's *The Slave Community: Plantation Life in the Antebellum South* (New York: Oxford University Press, 1979), p. 373.

2. Sidonie Smith affirms the notion of unreliability as she quotes Francis R. Hart, *The Poetics of Women's Autobiography: Marginality and the Fictions of Self-Representation* (Bloomington: Indiana University Press, 1987), 46.

3. Jean Fagan Yellin, Mary Helen Washington, Linda Mackethan, and William Andrews, to name a few, all basically accept a one-to-one correlation between

Jacobs's life and her representation of it. Yet Andrews argues that slave narrators' "actual life stories frequently dispute, sometimes directly but more often covertly, the positivistic epistemology, dualistic morality, and diachronic framework in which antebellum America liked to evaluate autobiography as either history or falsehood," *To Tell a Free Story: The First Century of Afro-American Autobiography, 1760–1865* (Urbana: University of Illinois Press, 1986), 6.

4. Mary Helen Washington, ed., *Invented Lives: Narratives of Black Women* (New York: Doubleday, 1987), 9.

5. Sidonie Smith, as quoted in James Olney, *Autobiography: Essays Theoretical and Critical* (Princeton: Princeton University Press, 1980), 5.

6. Sidonie Smith, in James Olney, 20.

7. See Barbara Christian's *Black Women Novelists: The Development of a Tradition* (Westport, CT: Greenwood Press, 1980), and Arlene Elder's *The "Hindered Hand"* (Westport, CT: Greenwood Press, 1978) for an in-depth discussion of counter-stereotypes.

8. Lundsford Lane, for example, writes that he chooses "to come short of giving the full picture" rather than to "overstate," Andrews, *To Tell a Free Story*, 115. Northup also states that the point of his narrative is "to repeat the story of my life, without exaggeration," Solomon Northup, *Twelve Years a Slave* (Baton Rouge: Louisiana State University Press, 1968), 3. Garrison says of Douglass's *Narrative of the Life*: "I am confident that it is essentially true in all of its statements; that nothing has been set down in malice, nothing exaggerated, nothing drawn from the imagination; that it comes short of the reality, rather than overstates a single fact in regard to SLAVERY AS IT IS," *Narrative of the Life of Frederick Douglass, an American Slave*, ed. Houston A. Baker (New York: Penguin, 1985), 38.

9. Edmund Quincy, a white Garrisonian, noted of William Wells Brown's narrative, that it was told with greater "propriety and delicacy" than was Douglass's. See Andrews, *To Tell a Free Story*, p. 108.

10. See Karen Halttunen, *Confidence Men and Painted Women: A Study of Middle-Class Culture in America, 1830–1870* (New Haven: Yale University Press, 1982), 40, 52; and also Carroll Smith-Rosenberg, *Disorderly Conduct: Visions of Gender in Victorian America* (New York: Oxford University Press, 1985), 26.

11. Halttunen, *Confidence Men and Painted Women*, 107.

12. The parlor, Halttunen asserts, mediated between the public and the private. Her "back regions" refer to the indelicate preparations of bourgeois parlor performances – dinners, parties, and the intricate rules of formal visits. Preparations include personal grooming and servant relations. Anything, one might add, which would connect labor to the art of the performance. Black back regions is a pregnant metaphor which resonates temporally (back when), geographically (back South). Such resonances would always be overdetermined sexually. Indeed, one metaphor for white and black female difference was medically construed as located in the back regions or buttocks (see Sander L. Gilman, "Black Bodies, White Bodies: Toward an Iconography of Female Sexuality in Late Nineteenth Century Art, Medicine, and Literature," *Critical Inquiry* 12 [Autumn 1985]: 204–42.) Jacobs may well assume a bourgeois reception. Such a contract of delicacy is well illustrated in Jacobs's relationship with Mrs. Willis, who never inquires as to the circumstances of Jacobs's children's conception, yet is assumed to know. Jacobs

writes of this to Amy Post: "I had never opened my lips to Mrs Willis concerning my Children – in the Charitableness of her own heart she sympathized with me and never asked their origin   my suffering she knew," *Incidents*, 235.

13. Valerie Smith, "'Loopholes of Retreat': Architecture and Ideology in Harriet Jacobs' *Incidents in the Life of a Slave Girl*," *Reading Black, Reading Feminist* ed. Henry Louis Gates, Jr. (New York: Penguin, 1990), 222.

14. In nineteenth-century iconographics and physiognomy, ears were constructed, as were genitalia, as organs that exposed pathological essence, particularly of prostitutes and sexual women. See Sander Gilman, "Black Bodies, White Bodies," 224.

15. Frances Foster notes parenthetically that "rare indeed is any reference to sexual abuse of slave men by white women, and homosexuality [or homosexual abuse] is never mentioned" in narratives authored by men, "'In respect to Females . . . ': Differences in the Portrayals of Women by Male and Female Narrators," *Black American Literature Forum* 15 (Summer 1981): 67. Similarly, Mary Helen Washington maintains that "in the male slave narrative . . . sexuality is nearly always avoided, and when it does surface it is to report the sexual abuse of female slaves. The male slave narrator was under no compulsion to discuss his own sexuality nor that of other men," *Invented Lives*, p. xxiii.

16. Hazel Carby, Mary Helen Washington, and others argue, I think rightly, that male depictions of black women as victims deny these women agency in other parts of their lives, and limit women's expressive agency. See Carby, *Reconstructing Womanhood: The Emergence of the Afro-American Woman Novelist* (New York: Oxford University Press, 1987); Washington, *Invented Lives*.

17. See Angela Davis's now classic essays "Rape, Racism and the Myth of the Black Rapist," and "The Legacy of Slavery: Standards for a New Womanhood," in *Women, Race, and Class* (New York: Vintage Books, 1981). In antebellum Missouri, if a white man forced himself on a slave he did not own, he could be charged with "trespassing." The concept of master / slave rape was inconceivable since someone who owned property could not be a trespasser on it. These relations reveal themselves in recent scholarship as well. In *The American Law of Slavery*, a legal history informed by Marxist methodology, when rape is mentioned white men are never the culprit. And though the antebellum social system sometimes recognized that black on black rape could occur, the legal apparatus of the South refused to give such standards judicial consideration. In other words, black women were not legally rapeable. See Melton A. McLaurin, *Celia, A Slave* (Athens: The University of Georgia Press, 1991), p. 93, and Mark Tushnet, *The American Law of Slavery, 1810–1860: Considerations of Humanity and Interest* (Princeton: Princeton University Press, 1981).

18. Houston A. Baker, Jr., *Blues, Ideology, and Afro-American Literatures: A Vernacular Theory* (Chicago: University of Chicago Press, 1984), p. 50.

19. Sawyer draws up the children's bills of sales in Jacobs's grandmother's name; they are no longer, then, legally under his power.

20. Valerie Smith, "Form and Ideology in Three Slave Narratives," *Self Discovery and Authority in Afro-American Narrative* (Cambridge: Harvard University Press, 1987), 222.

21. As Foucault has made clear, "from the Christian penance to the present day, sex

was a privileged theme of confession." See Foucault, *The History of Sexuality*, Vol. 1 (New York: Vintage, 1980).

22. See John Sekora, "Black Message / White Envelope: Genre, Authenticity, and Authority in the Antebellum Slave Narrative," *Callaloo* 10 (Summer 1987): 489.

23. Hazel Carby, *Reconstructing Womanhood*, argues explicitly what Mary Helen Washington maintains, that Jacobs is "informed not by the cult of domesticity or domestic feminism but by politicial feminism; *Incidents* is an attempt to move women to political action." *Invented Lives* (New York: Doubleday, 1987), p. xxxii.

24. Jacobs's move from her singular oppression to an expression of it through use of a representative plural is developed more fully in Foreman's "The Spoken and the Silenced in *Incidents in the Life of a Slave Girl* and *Our Nig*," *Callaloo* 13 (Spring 1990): 313–24.

25. See Smith-Rosenberg, chapters 1 and 2 in *Disorderly Conduct*, and especially Nina Auerbach in *Communities of Women: An Idea in Fiction* (Cambridge, MA: Harvard University Press, 1978), chapter 1.

26. Flint's tactics do include the physical. Richard Yarborough suggests that this physical abuse might be a loophole metaphor for a shift to physical sexual abuse as well.

27. Jacobs's transference from the sexual to the rhetorical is developed more fully in Foreman's "The Spoken and the Silenced," 317–18.

28. Timing supports this possibility. She begins her affair when she is fifteen (54); born in 1813, Jacobs then dates 1828 or 1829 as the year she begins her affair with Sawyer. Joseph Jacobs is born *c.* 1829. It is also in 1828 and 1829 that Mrs. Norcom's suspicions get particularly heated. See *Incidents*, p. 35, and Yellin's attendant note 5, p. 266.

29. Carby, *Reconstructing Womanhood*, p. 58.

30. Even though Flint needs no reason in order to sell off Jacobs's, or others', children, Jacobs stresses throughout the narrative that he sells the children he fathers. She does not mention his sales of random children, and emphasizes, as Douglass does in both his 1845 and 1855 narrative, that masters often sell children that remind them – and their wives – of their own philandering.

31. In the same letter Jacobs writes "I never would consent to give my past life to any one for I would not do it with out giving the whole truth." The tensions between the two statements, among self-protection and possession and layers of consent between an artful narrator and her "trusted" friend Post, and between Jacobs and an untrustworthy public, aptly demonstrate seemingly unreconcilable "warring forces of signification" and truth; *Incidents*, 232.

32. In *To Tell a Free Story*, p. 164 (my substitution); Andrews, here, doesn't apply his brilliant analysis of the male trickster narrator to Jacobs. Instead, his reading, too, suggests a transparent relation between Jacobs and her tale.

33. Jacobs's silence on any personal sexual interest or involvement echoes her construction of her grandmother as a nonsexual being. Though in her twenties when she escapes to the North, not only does this narrative not end "in the usual way, with marriage," never does she even intimate another romantic "lover" after her free suitor moves from Edenton.

34. Patricia Williams, *The Alchemy of Race and Rights* (Cambridge, MA: Harvard University Press, 1991), p. 163.

35. Andrews, *To Tell a Free Story*, p. 165.

36. Andrews, *To Tell a Free Story*, pp. 165–6.
37. Valerie Smith, "Loopholes of Retreat," p. 215.
38. Andrews develops this fully in *To Tell A Free Story*, p. 148.
39. For a full discussion, see Andrews, *To Tell a Free Story*, chapter 4.
40. The black or oriental woman as soothsayer has a vivid iconographic history. Recent examples include the cover painting on bell hook's *Yearning* (see Foreman, *Women's Review of Books*, September 1991) and Whoopie Goldberg's Oscar-winning portrayal of a medium in *Ghost*. Goldberg literally becomes transparent and, in an amazing scene where her body is taken over by Patrick Swayze's and iconographically erased, made invisible. In image power, at least, many find Goldberg's role as truthsayer / soothsayer in *Ghost* comfortable, for she becomes the second black woman to earn an Oscar – not as a maid this time, but as American truth / sooth.
41. His treatment of his destitute sister Sara Payson Willis, later Fanny Fern, reveals this. She fictionalizes her scathing critique of her brother in the novel *Ruth Hall* (1854). Complementary biographers, minimizing when even mentioning N. P. Willis's relation with his sister, admit that he had "a continued preoccupation with wanting to be liked by all with whom he associated," – that is, by all with social standing, his lack of which he was acutely aware. Cortland Auser, *Nathaniel P. Willis* (New York: Twayne Publishers, 1969), p. 20. In *Ruth Hall* Sara Willis suggests that he marries Cornelia Grinnell, niece and adopted daughter of the wealthy Hon. Joseph Grinnell, for money. It was with her inheritance that they built their eighteen-room home on the Hudson, Idlewild (Henry Beers, *American Men of Letters: N. P. Willis* [New York: Houghton Mifflin, 1885], p. 337). Jacobs's belief that he was proslavery, or at least in no way antislavery, is confirmed by his paper's (*The Home Journal*) stated policy: "it is entirely neutral in politics, free from all sectionalism and sectarianism" (quoted from Auser, p. 128). Not until after the South seceded did he take a public stance (p. 128).
42. His autobiographer, Auser, notes that Willis wished to "exemplify himself as the epitome of the fashionable gentleman," *Nathaniel P. Willis*, p. 24. His first wife, Mary Stace Willis of England, was also well off; her father provided his daughter and son-and-law with £300 per annum – about half of their yearly income.
43. Beers writes that "From early spring till after Christmas the family at Idlewild kept open house, almost always having company staying with them. . . . The place had become celebrated through Willis's descriptions of it in 'Home Journal.' . . . Willis's habit was to breakfast in his own room and write till noon. Sometimes he would take a stroll . . . before dinner. After dinner we would write letters or do scissors work before the afternoon ride. The evening was spent with his guests, or, if the family were alone, he would write again and come down to a nine o'clock dinner," *American Men of Letters*, p. 330. Contrast this with Jacobs's description of Idlewild of 1854. "My friends . . . were here . . . and saw from my daily duties that it was hard for me to find much time to write   as yet I have not written a single page by daylight Mrs. Willis dont know from my lips that I am writing. . . . I told her in the Autumn that I would give her Louisa services through the winter if she would allow me my winter evenings to myself but with the care of the little baby and the big Babies and at the household calls I have but a little time to think or write," *Incidents*, pp. 237–8. At this point, the Willises had four children (the last child to survive was born in 1857), to whom Jacobs was nurse.

44. Haltunnen, *Confidence Men and Painted Women*, p. 24.

45. Beers, *American Men of Letters*, p. 285.

46. Linda's "benefactress" says to her when she returns home free: "you wrote to me as if you thought you were going to be transferred from one owner to another. But I did not buy you for your services. I should have done just the same, if you had been going to sail for California tomorrow. I should, at least, have the satisfaction of knowing that you left me a free woman" (*Incidents*, p. 200). Without impugning Cornelia Willis's motives, their exchange can be read to signal that her sincere effusion works to silence Jacobs's feelings of outrage at the broader issues of commodity exchange and power relations.

47. Valerie Smith, "Loopholes of Retreat," p. 215. Barbara Christian notes that the word "voyeur" reflects a kind of choice that may not be appropriate in Jacobs's case: the slave woman *must* remain unseen. However, by boring through "the interstices," she chooses to remain sighted, to have a view of the outside world.

48. Karen Sánchez-Eppler, "Harriet Jacobs: Righting Slavery and Writing Sex," *Touching Liberty: Abolition, Feminism and the Politics of the Body* (Berkeley: University of California Press, 1993, 87–8).

49. Jacobs offers her mother too, posthumously. Aunt Nancy, in contrast, is not submissive. Jacobs writes, "when my friends tried to discourage me from running away, she always encouraged me. When they thought I better return and ask my master's pardon . . . she sent me word never to yield" (p. 144). Mrs. Flint is true womanhood's opposite. The white woman who harbors Linda is much "too" radical: she hides the runaway, in conspiracy with her cook, without her husband's knowledge, much less his permission. Jacobs's grandmother, without a husband, can be the assertive head of her household without conflicting with dominant notions of true womanhood.

50. Carby, *Reconstructing Womanhood*, p. 57.

51. Aunt Martha later moves from an idealogical embracing of true motherhood to personal considerations of her own burdens of caring for the children, asking "Linda, do you want to kill your old grandmother? Do you mean to leave your little, helpless children? I am old now, and cannot do for your babies as I once did for you" (p. 91).

52. Jacobs invokes the concept of an expandable family throughout *Incidents*, as she consistently refers to Mrs. Flint as Aunt Martha's foster daughter (see pp. 85, 145–6) in direct opposition to white families, who deny more definite ties. Aunt Martha sides with her white "daughter" over her black grandchild.

53. Baker explains this term, which he borrows from Hugh Cott, this way: "Rather than concealing or disguising in the manner of the *cryptic* mask (a colorful mastery of codes), the phaneric mask is meant to advertise. It distinguishes rather than conceals." Houston A. Baker, Jr. "Caliban's Triple Play," *"Race," Writing, and Difference*, ed. Henry Louis Gates, Jr. (Chicago: University of Chicago Press, 1986), p. 390.

54. Smith-Rosenberg, *Visions of Gender*, p. 60.

55. Jacqueline Goldsby, "'Screens,' 'Snares,' and 'Loopholes': The Problematics of Literacy and Reading the S(t)ex(t) in Harriet Jacobs's *Incidents in the Life of a Slave Girl*." Unpublished typescript.

56. Sánchez-Eppler, "Righting Slavery," p. 91.

57. Yellin's research confirms this. She notes that her eldest, Betty, was probably born in 1794, her youngest, Joe, in 1808 (Yellin, p. 268). Yet, these years include only the five children who survived. Four, then, Yellin notes, probably died early or in childbirth. Carroll Smith-Rosenberg notes that "the clean lines that distinguish the generations in twentieth-century families . . . were inconceivable in most eighteenth- and nineteenth-century homes. The ages of biological siblings could span the twenty-odd years of their mother's reproductive life, easily permitting . . . mothers and daughters to be pregnant and give birth together," *Disorderly Conduct*, p. 22.

58. See Yellin's note 6, p. 262. Yellin does not comment on Jacobs's truncated representation of Mark's freedom. Although she presents her readers with Joseph Jacobs's conflicting version, she quickly redirects our attention to the issue of Molly Horniblow holding her son as a slave, rather than addressing the significance of these absences and competing renditions.

59. See John Jacobs, "A True Tale of Slavery," in *The Leisure Hour* (London; February 1861), p. 86.

60. Yellin suggests that the money Horniblow had saved might not have been sufficient to buy herself, her son, and their home and that she borrowed the balance from Gatlin. See p. 264, n. 13.

61. Sidonie Smith, *The Poetics of Women's Autobiography*, p. 46.

EARWITNESS

FEMALE ABOLITIONISM, SEXUALITY, AND
INCIDENTS IN THE LIFE OF A SLAVE GIRL

DEBORAH M. GARFIELD

I. The Ravishing of the Ear: Oral Agency, Seduction, and the Female Abolitionist

At the first convention of the American Anti-Slavery Society in 1833, members called for the mobilization of free blacks and ex-slaves as professional "agents" who would bear oral witness to the wrongs of captivity. Writing to Theodore Weld in 1838, the abolitionist Angelina Grimké champions these roving lecturers by exalting the dynamic between the listener's ear and the speaker's ignited voice: The slave's "narratives" must "come burning from his own lips. . . . Many and many a tale of romantic horrors can the slaves tell."[1] In her pun at Pennsylvania Hall, Grimké endorses hearing as an almost mystical transportation into the *space* of political reform – the "here" of the Hall itself: "*Here* it – *hear* it. . . . Every man and woman present may do something . . . by opening our mouths for the dumb and pleading the cause of those who are ready to perish."[2] The outrage of abolitionists like Grimké consistently took the form of meticulous rhetorical suasion. But she and other cohorts understood that an impassioned speech might, by ravishing the senses, open consciousness to reason.

If Grimké often relied on what might seem the conventionally "feminine" Radcliffean allure of such oral testimonies, John Collins, a correspondent to William Lloyd Garrison, also intuited the talismanic aura that an audience, seized by slavery's "romantic horror," might *hear* in an agent's lectures. "The public," he notes, "have itching ears to hear a colored man speak, and particularly *a slave*. Multitudes will flock to hear one of his class speak."[3] Indispensable as the written slave autobiography became, it remained the austere, but privative, form of the oratory that was its lively original.[4] As if writing were slightly at odds not just with speech, but also with the character generating it, the editor of Josiah Henson's 1849 autobiography lamented that the published work "loses the attraction derived from . . . the natural eloquence of a man who tells a story in which he is deeply interested."[5]

A similar insight into charismatic telling prompted a reporter for the *Salem Register* to respond that Douglass's cogent arguments, stoked by his voice, "created the most indescribable of sensations in the minds of those unaccustomed to hear *freemen* of color speak in public." He provided "living, speaking and *startling* proof of the folly . . . of slavery."[6] Again the argumentative compact between ear and speech requires those "indescribable . . . sensations," the "startling" ineffability, which ripens into revelation. Numerous former slaves – including Douglass, Henry Bibb, William Wells Brown, Henry "Box" Brown, the Clarkes, Josiah Henson, and Moses Grandy – who initiated their writing careers as circuit-speakers, were proof of the centripetal tug of oratory, for they resumed lecturing after the narratives were published. Speech enabled narrative; narrative then facilitated a return to the "living, speaking" Logos parenting it.[7] Although, as John Sekora adeptly argues, the black orators' spontaneity was cramped and orchestrated by white mentors' questionnaires and interviews, and by the pragmatics of audience response, the political utterance retained for many an etiological pedigree.[8]

Although the male agent's speech was frequently cherished as the word made flesh,[9] it was in that momentous *embodiment* of language – its "romance," "horror," and rush of "sensations" – that the perils for the female lecturer resided. The word, indeed, proved more fearfully incarnated for women orators narrating the sexual biographia of slavery than for Douglass, recording the sadistic lashing of Aunt Hester, or for Garrison, in his diatribes against the South as a regional brothel. The assumption lingered, in response to speakers as diverse as the African American Maria W. Stewart and white antislavery feminists like the controversial Grimké sisters, Lydia Child, and Abby Kelley, that the ear wooed in the service of abolitionist conversion could also be hopelessly defiled. One of the recurring criticisms of the Grimkés was that their lectures on slavery's sexual crimes wounded the fragile ears of their middle-class female auditors. The Congregationalist Church of Massachusetts in 1837 roundly scorned the "promiscuous conversation of females" for examining issues "'which ought not to be mentioned.'"[10] This accusation in particular rankled Sarah Grimké, the more religious of the two Quakers, for it was issued not by the popular presses, but from within the august enclaves of New England's clergy; and Angelina, too often demoted to "Devilina," now seemed clipped of her wings by men of God. Through the canny, if slippery, rubric of "conversation," the ministers indicted speaker and audience alike for a rendezvous in lyceum prurience.

Even in John Greenleaf Whittier's versified retort to the ministers' "Pastoral Letter," there is a somewhat hybrid suggestion that the Grimkés' lectures merged lofty religious precedent with a high-pitched Gothic fervor. The Congregationalists, he claims, "scorn the thrilling tale / Of Carolina's high-souled sisters."[11] In the double signification of "thrill," implied in Collins's "itching ears," and in the work of Angelina Grimké, Whittier, and their Northern and Southern antagonists, evangelical and sexual excitement seemed perilously fused. Were the female orators, skeptics wondered, prophetic Deborahs of the present, tunneling to the conscience through the ears? Or were they, in a vocal sublimation, celebrity seducers luring the audience into the complicit role of eavesdroppers on deep-South blandishments? The Reverend Samuel May, usually an unruffled advocate of the Garrisonians, found himself "not a little disturbed in my sense of propriety" by the traveling female speakers;[12] and the indictment found a historical scaffolding in what certain ministers remembered as the Puritans' judgmental ire at the flamboyant disrobings of colonial Quaker matriarchs. The Reverend Leonard Bacon was said to have likened Angelina to the "Quaker woman" once walking "through the streets of Salem, *naked as she was born* – But that Miss Grimké [was not] known to make such an exhibition of herself *yet*."[13] A charged or sexually explicit lecture, no matter how scrupulously reasoned, was too frequently refigured by detractors into the visual metaphor of striptease, as if the female voice, confounding sound and flesh, were the exposed body itself.

Urban tabloids made salaciously explicit what May and Bacon left oblique: that speaking of and listening to the forbidden descriptions of rape and seduction were tantamount to a desire for the slave's body: "The Misses Grimké have made speeches . . . but have not found husbands yet. We suspect that they would prefer white children to black under certain circumstances, after all."[14] The women's lectures were therefore construed as a rhetorical display of the racial "amalgamation" which even Elijah Lovejoy, canvassing for the slave, shunned as the "polluted intercourse between the whites and the blacks."[15] This lingering correspondence between speech and miscegenation[16] unsettled writers like Caroline Healey Dall, who refused to transcribe the vernacular of the fugitive slave originally articulating the plot behind her story "The Inalienable Love."[17] No stranger to her culture's biases in reading across racial and gender lines, she claimed that if she "were to use the English tongue with the nervous strength he did . . . all the women in the land would tear the pages out of the fair volume." Dall comprehends that only the mediations of a sentimental discourse would cushion her readers from slavery's naked "villainies" and, in turn, their ears from the "nervous strength" (87) of a black man's speech. The meeting between the fugitive's muscular colloquialisms and the white reader's modesty might well seem a tawdry amalgamation, a crisis partly averted through the female reader's ironically *masculine* assault upon the pages of the "fair" text in order to ward off incursions against her own fairness.

Such incursions were too often seen as emanating not simply from the male fugitive's raw colloquialism, but from the female slave's candor. Southerner James A. Thome, invariably more concerned with slavery's dismemberment of white morality than of black bodies, warned the Anti-Slavery Society against what he saw as the lurid doubling of white and black sexuality even in the muffled gossip between slave girls and their white companions. "As they [the miss and slave girl] come in contact through the day," Thome explains, "the courtesan feats of the over night are whispered into the ear of the unsuspecting [white] girl and poison her youthful mind."[18] Acting in the male patriarch's stead, the victimized slave girl is said to poison the white miss's ear, thus replaying, through the seduction of her playmate's hearing, the rape in the slave-cabin. The well-meaning Thome injudiciously reformulates the white innocent's fall. It is one not just into an illicit sexuality, but also into a dual miscegenation, as the miss hears of the mating of black girl and white man and as her untutored ear opens itself to the black female's supposed verbal agency. For Thome the captive's revelations to her white friend skew both spatial boundaries, between the mansion and slave quarters, and temporal logic, between childish days and lascivious nights. Deflecting the blame from her defiler, Thome therefore features the slave adolescent as the plotter against a deictic and feminine order.

As the hounded slave girl is misconstrued as male seducer to her fair friend, so also is the apprehensive stir over the blurring of races complicated by one over the "unnatural" admixture of male and female, by the oxymoronic contemplation of a particularly female "agency." When the Grimkés began to lecture to "mixed audiences" – men and women – they asked Theodore Weld and the New York Executive Committee to specify whether they were in fact antislavery "agents" and thus subject to the committee's codes of conduct. Weld's response points suggestively not so much to his own biases, but to the collective jitters he discerned as the committee mused on the American listeners' musings on womanly "agency." After consulting with the official members, Weld unmoored the role of female speakers by informing them that they could inhabit only a precarious island between agency and submission. Their purpose was "a sort of *cooperative* relation," but not one involving "*authority* on the one hand and a *representative* agency on the other." The committee fostered doubts about their speaking to "promiscuous assemblies."[19] Weld was tactful enough to locate the "promiscuous" urges in the listeners, not in female speakers. But his judgment, often more radical and permissive, was now practically keyed to an audience's prejudices. The committee's reticence about "agency" echoes the Congregationalists' apprehension that when a female reformer assumes the "tone of man," the "vine" assumes "the independence . . . of the elm, [and] will not only cease to bear fruit, but fall in shame and dishonor into the dust."[20] To preside as public "agents" before "mixed" auditors made women abolitionists at once the dominant speakers for whom erotic and rhetorical powers were intermingled – their audience the passive vessels of untoward persuasions – *and* the dust-bound harbingers of national sterility. As male proxies, vamps or barren vines, the women forfeited through public utterance nothing less than their childbearing capacity, for the image in which the dizzying array of stereotypes cohered was one of a withered maternity, of America's moribund white destiny.

Although free black women speakers, because of the urgency of articulating African American liberation, were allowed a more expansive survey of the slave's dilemma,[21] they too discovered their vocal presentation bound in a connubial or courtly configuration. As Shirley Yee explains, black leaders prohibited women from assuming "a position of authority in gatherings where men" of either race convened.[22] Such taboos forced orators like the candid Maria Stewart to bid a chilly valediction to the agents' circuit, while a consensus about Frances Harper's feminine propriety often inoculated her against derisive censorship and appeared to sculpt her into the compliant form of "beloved" or "wife," with the male listener as a version of suitor or audience-spouse. William Still commented on Harper's status as a "gentle . . . heroine" in "charming her audiences."[23] Activating a rhetorical model of courtship or marriage between an orator and her audience, Still's choice of "heroine" pertains both to the political savvy of Harper's "eloquent" rhetoric and to a more submerged and white sentimental distinction between "light" and "dark" heroines that was operative even on the black circuit. In an 1856 speech in Elkhorn, Indiana, Mary Ann Shadd Cary was lauded less for her message than for her tranquil voice's "modest . . . keeping with the popular notions of the 'sphere of women.'"[24]

As witnessed in the more chivalric approbation of Frances Harper and Mary Shadd, the only alternative to the sullying apothegms applied to the female orator, black or white, appeared to be an uneasy detente between passivity and agency. In *What Answer?*, the 1869 novel by the white abolitionist speaker Anna Dickinson, the tautology of an inactive and uncarnal feminine agency is shrewdly addressed.[25] Here, a virgin's "voice" in a commencement polemic against slavery both "astound[s]" and woos a traditional hero, who expects from so prim a countenance a more corsetted recitation. Yet the heroine Francesca is no scarlet *improvisatrice*. Unlike the testimony of Anne Hutchinson in Hawthorne's 1830 sketch,[26] in which the female's exegesis temporarily blunts the Puritans' "sharpened intellects" (20), Francesca's speech "thrill[s]" without psychologically unmanning the listener or figuratively disrobing its female orator.[27] Instead, Francesca narrates plantation crimes as a haunting interplay between her own wounded ear and the audible shrieks of slavery. A female Assizes summoning "this monster to the bar of God's justice" (42), Francesca at least begins her recitation with Hutchinson's prosecutorial rigor, but the slaves' groans ultimately wrench from her a helplessly feminine "cry" to God. This assent to gendered identity should remind us of Harper's demure, womanly salve for the black male audience who acquiesced to her rhetoric but jeered Stewart's authority. Passive captive to the captives' anguished pleas, Francesca unconsciously mutes her chastening vocality into a meek reverberation in the echo-chamber of the slave's despair. She

> thrilled out, "I look backward into the dim, distant past. . . . I turn to the present, but I hear naught save the mother's broken-hearted shriek, the infant's wail, the groan wrung from the strong man in agony; and I look forward into the future, but the night grows darker, the shadows deeper . . . and involuntarily I cry out, 'How long, O God, how long?'" (42)[28]

The distant mental gaze of "looking backward" across the shadowy continuum between "past" and "present" narrows suddenly into an empathic hearing that wrenches from her the naked cry once discerned only from manacled others. Francesca's speech is an auditory rendition of what the gifted abolitionist writer Elizabeth Margaret Chandler called the art of "Mental Metempsychosis,"[29] an emotive and at times corporeal form of negative capability in which the free woman endeavored to suffer, through a heightened *imitatio*, the slave's afflictions – the meditator's stigma against the slave's marginality punitively literalized into her own stigmata. There was, however, a conspicuous inequality between those bodies. Francesca's identification with the slave exudes a reticence to take on the violation, even through euphemism, of chattel flesh. Sharing the "shriek[s]" of mother, infant, or oppressed "strong man" is one ordeal; sharing the defiled black female body quite another. Francesca's oratory supplants the more explicit image of the desecrated slave body with the metonymical groans of the "present." The slave woman's cries emanate from the severed, but rhetorically safe, bond between mother and child, not from the primal scene of rape or conception.[30]

Though traditional male listeners brand Francesca's address "bad taste" (43), her frantic question now enters the hero Surrey's doting ear and sweeps him into the cycle of sentiment precisely because her words are immunized against the dual prohibitions of masculine authority and black sexuality.[31] Despite its manic verve, Francesca's speech excites "sensations" within its auditor, without permitting them to coil into a forbidden corporeality. Instead, love and political conversion, not the infatuated auditor's libido, win the day, and *thrill* (92), for all the connotations it accumulated in Puritan and abolitionist lexicons, is here cleansed of its "promiscuous" taint. The hero instantaneously feels his passion and contains it within the armor of a courtly stereotype. "Filled with an insane desire to seize her . . . like a knight of old," he finally desires to carry her "to some spot where he could seat her and kneel at her feet" (43). Surrey's "fire" and heretical "desire to seize" cool into the more poised counterpart of rescue and genuflection to an immobilized object. San-

itized romance, not seductive ambush, Francesca's rhetoric seems the curative model for the sometimes berated speeches of Dickinson herself, lectures
here transmogrified into a species of oratorical wish-fulfillment. The heroine's speech entices Surrey because, never engaging the slave woman's debased body or an appropriative "masculine" gusto, it paradoxically enters
the hero's ear without exposing or penetrating it.

The distinction between permissible entrance into the ear and invasive
"agency" is a subtle one; yet it defines the paradox confronting white and
black abolitionist alike. The rhetorical intimacy between Dickinson's
Francesca and her "voice"-struck acolyte seems particularly relevant to antebellum women speakers of both races. Their aim was to attract the public
through a "living" word provoking dark "sensations," but with the untainted
bravura of this refined fictional advocate, who engenders neither lecherous
itch nor antifeminist disgust in her sympathetic auditor. The challenge for the
female abolitionist, in short, was to be an "agent" without appearing to be
one.

II. Eloquent Gesticulations: Jacobs's American Sign-Speak

Given the sexual and racial bias behind this cultural paradox, how does the
woman tell and not tell, smite her auditors with scenes of violation but maintain at least the apparent innocence of their ears and her own vocal propriety? Whereas Harriet Beecher Stowe surrenders her claims to a transparent
discourse through her admission that a true representation of slavery "would
be a work which could not be read,"[32] Abby Kelley evades the contradiction.
She argues for an oral performance that bypasses the American language expressing sexual atrocity, and the lash that symbolizes it, for a more atavistic
sign-system. The lash's cuts, Kelley speculates, cannot be translated even into
a mangled English. After enduring the psychosomatic stripes of her own
"metempsychosis," she claims that "when my flesh quivers beneath the lash
. . . the English language is not adequate." We must regress to the primitive's
"significant signs" and "eloquent gesticulations."[33]

Kelley's call for a resumption of sign language cannot help but remind us
of Freud's more modern hypotheses about Dora's "hysteria" – that the parts
of the body enact the trauma scrambled in the civilized transference of an-
alyst and patient. But Kelley's plea for a primitive's signing raises as many
conundrums as it dispels. The woman's tribal gesticulations would certainly
dramatize to the racist American mind an "enthusiasm" too reflexively attached to dubious abolitionist histrionics, like Garrison's notorious torching
of copies of the *Constitution*; and the woman's recourse to "barbaric" signs
might image that fearful symbiosis with the black body for which detractors
reviled her.

At first we might imagine, in reading Harriet Jacobs's correspondence to abolitionist Amy Post about the writing of *Incidents in the Life of a Slave Girl* (1861),[34] that there is no suitable means through which to balance the needs of the innocent ear and the woman's political voice. The slave-author is, even while writing her narrative, ill at ease with her own precarious status as its representative woman.[35] The act of writing *Incidents* would prove less burdensome "if it was the life of a Heroine with no degradation associated with it"; but this species of heroine Jacobs is not. Her admitted sexual relations with the white man Samuel Sawyer, and the children she cherished as the product of that encounter, imperil her role as her book's maternal icon, so long a welcome fixture of sentimental decor. Jacobs was undoubtedly aware of the middle-class fear of abolitionism, what Child tactically debunked as the abolitionists' ruse to "introduce the negroes into our parlours."[36] Because of her liaison with a white lawyer, Jacobs might seem disqualified both as sentimental "Heroine" *and* as racial amalgamator, her voice the impure body articulated. Such factors might well account for Jean Fagan Yellin's conclusion, in her arduous sleuthing, that Jacobs probably never became a lecturing "agent," even on the British abolitionist circuit. In addition, as slave-author, Jacobs finds herself at odds with the more natural category of "Woman": "Woman can whisper – her cruel wrongs into the ear of a very dear friend – much easier than she can record them for the world to read" (242).

As Jacobs's stress on her own sexual compromise suggests, to narrate her experience she must, to a certain degree, exile herself from it, substituting for the self's dense particularity the abstract persona of "Heroine" or "Woman," avatars that don't truly describe her. This authorial displacement from Heroism and Womanhood is played out privately in her letters' self-reflexive allusions to an epistolary inadequacy. In apologies to Post for her "Hasty scrawl" (236), the "nothing" of her "poor scrawls" (239), her "unconnected scrawl" (242), Jacobs frets that the female voice too readily fragments into what might prove a humiliated and unpolished public inscription. Threatening respectively to rush, extinguish, and deform confessional intimacy, the letters to a stalwart white ally become, for the less literate slave writer, unsightly prostheses for the truer feminine exchange between talking and hearing. "I wish," Jacobs bemoans to Post, "that I could sit by you and talk insted [sic] of writing but that pleasure is denied and I am thankful for this" (235). If Jacobs appears "thankful" that the missed "pleasure" of spilling tears through speech forces the author into spilling polemical ink, she also senses that the pen distorts the writer's image and "unconnect[s]" her from lived identity. Jacobs's pen *scrawls* and apologizes, its writer understandably consenting to one too many genuflections about her literary embarrassments.

With a similar self-consciousness Jacobs's navigation in her letter to Post from "I" to the more enlarged representativeness of "Woman" or "Heroine" forms a discursive pattern throughout the text itself, as she swerves from private to public in order to deflect sexual blame. Thus, as Gabrielle Foreman observes, the term "poor slave girl" or "miserable slave mother" frequently substitutes for subjective particularity.[37] Representativeness not only discloses the lot of the slave community through Brent's example; it also acts as a guise concealing the details of the individual life from a scandalized audience.[38] Displaced from "Heroine" and "Woman," the author often stands peculiarly outside even the more explicit role of "slave woman," for she must manipulate its very comprehensiveness as a generalized mask for her own transgressive female "I." That the letter's reference to sexual "degradation"[39] so quickly lapses into an expression of Jacobs's hesitance in writing about it suggests that *Incidents* itself, primarily addressed to slavery's ills, is also about its own troubled rhetorical birth.[40]

In her "Introduction" to the work, Child seconds the apprehension. Despite her willingness to confront miscegenation in her own "Tragic Mulatto" stories,[41] Child gets snagged in Stowe's paradox, the tautology of a mute telling and an understanding of the bond between writer and reader as a potentially promiscuous female "conversation." Her tropes, at once visual and aural, careening nervously between writing and speech, express the confusion. Child's desire to remove, through printed revelation, "the veil" from slavery's atrocities converts, as Valerie Smith notes, into a preoccupation for Child's own female coterie,[42] explicitly for "our . . . too delicate" (4) ears. In Child's attempt to urge a solidarity amongst women, a collective female body, she actually suggests a divided sisterhood in which the slave must starkly impose her sexual ordeals on a white counterpart's bashful listening. Thome's reversal of victim and villain is here rearticulated. In a tragic usurpation, the black female target, not the lewd patriarch, becomes the satanic tempter whose candid whispers risk blighting the white auditor's purity.

The conflation of speech and visual exposure, or a preemptory unveiling, hints at Child's unconscious assent to the apprehensions of those who derided the woman's oratory as exhibitionism or masculine invasion. The rubric of *delicacy* here embraces both the reader, with her "delicate" ears, and the teller, with her "delicate subjects" (4). Indeed, Child herself, while militating against polite deafness, actually enacts her audience's skittishness. She presides like a blushing impresaria over Jacobs's textual performance and ultimately remains silent in elaborating even the minor particulars of its subject. Although she gathers Jacobs under the aura of her good name, sexual assault remains one of slavery's abstract "wrongs," that oft-invoked "peculiar phase" which is here peculiarly deferred for the black voice to reveal. Preparing to present "the veil withdrawn" (4), Child clings tenaciously to it, as though she, and not the veil, will withdraw. If sentimental discourse is, as Jane Tompkins argues, particularly adept at eroding the boundary between reader and character, at eliciting from the reader the protagonist's tears (130–5),[43] then reading about sexual victimization in a sentimental idiom might itself prove a contamination. Like Jacobs, Child implies that Linda Brent's mission with Dr. Flint – to flee ravishment, to maintain innocence – is the reader's agenda as well.

Given the cultural context in which she worked, Jacobs's authorial coup lies partially in unraveling Stowe's paradox of an untold articulation, complicating Kelley's call for a sign language dispatching signification back to gesticulation, and exploiting and redefining Child's concern with the maiming of her white readers' ears. Jacobs actually invests in a cunning manipulation of the very sign-systems of nineteenth-century American abolitionism – especially the paradigm of an apparently "promiscuous" speech and the ear it enters – in order to open her text to whispered revelation.[44] In *Incidents* speech and hearing represent sexually resonant events through which Jacobs intimates to her reticent audience – preferring its bitter truths spooned in euphemisms – violations that cannot be explicitly uttered. This dynamic between speaking and hearing emerges most obviously as much of the sexual abuse of Linda is displaced into language.[45] Since the word takes on the carnal will of the male seducer, the face-offs between Linda and her owner are rarely experienced in the flesh. Instead, the blows of Flint, especially, are more frequently deflected into verbal insults – lewd hectoring that corrupts Linda's ears as, according to Child, those of her readers might be by her narrative – or into descriptions of the lacerating import of Flint's linguistic abuses.[46] The Doctor's taunts are "foul" and "unclean" (27) – "stinging, scorching words; words that scathed ear and brain like fire" (18) – and Brent must "stand and listen" before them as passively as the victim suffers her rapist's will. The relationship between male seducer and female object is partially encoded as that between unclean speaker and besmirched listener.[47] Informing her readers while safeguarding their "delicate" ears, Jacobs somewhat prefigures the defensive agility of Francesca's chaste allusions to the auditory synecdoches of maternal and infant cries.

But Jacobs is no simple schoolgirl entrancing a smitten hero while escaping pollution. Although allowing the trope of the ear and a despoiling speech to substitute for the sexual act, and thus honoring her audience's inviolability, Jacobs also deploys a series of variations on this dialectic in order to invade the ear she would ostensibly shield. The uneasy pact between speaking and hearing becomes the discursive ploy through which she attempts to reverse the roles of master and slave in her text, as well as the corresponding hierarchy of coddled reader and writer-victim.[48] Through Flint's threats and Linda's pained reaction to them, Jacobs makes Brent the original and more tormented persona for Child's delicate auditor.[49] She is both the young slave who receives Flint's verbal advances in person and the delicate reader commanded, as part of a linguistic sexuality, to scrutinize and recite his obscene notes.[50] Flint thus tries to impose upon her an erotic reciprocity in which she is both seduced object of his spoken and written crudity and the would-be seducer told to utter his epistolary come-ons back to him. While these scenes bind fragile reader and slave-author in an appalled female consciousness, they deftly spotlight the schism between the bourgeois woman preoccupied with her own fragile reception of slavery's defilements and the slave whose actual vulnerability is translated into aural apprehension. "You," Jacobs reminds her readers, "never shuddered at the *sound* of his footsteps, and trembled within *hearing* of his voice" (55; emphasis mine). Jacobs is a fallen but wiser precursor to Francesca. She works artfully both to placate and to expose the "delicate" reader for whom speech is apparently but a discursive veil.[51]

III. Writing in Tongues: Exposure and Regeneration

It is this implicit sense of exposure that the affinity between hearing and sexuality activates in the reader when she least anticipates it. From the book's second epigraph, from Isaiah 32:9, Jacobs enlists the trope of the ear to invert the power relations between black and white implicit in Child's "Introduction," its latent assumption that the white mentor remains veiled while her black sister lifts the curtain both from slavery's monstrosity and from her own body. "Rise up," Jacobs quotes, "ye women that are at ease! Hear my voice, ye careless daughters! Give ear unto my speech." But the audience schooled in its theology cannot dismiss the lines arriving one verse later as a more incendiary reverberation: "Tremble, ye women that are at ease; be troubled, ye careless ones: strip you, and make you bare, and gird *sackcloth* upon *your* loins" (Isa. 32:11). In the memory of this invisible command, the discerning white reader should find herself in her black sister's place, in the humiliated nakedness of confession; and Jacobs, seizing the agency of a discourse in which she is supposedly the logical victim, adroitly unwrites Child's protection of her readership. In the epigraph's mute addendum about bared bodies, the code of black sexuality is subtly revised, the categories of vulnerable black teller and decorous white listener undermined. Instead of catering to the infamous characterization of the black woman as the explosive sign of sexuality – wench, concubine, breeder – Jacobs reverses the terms of sexual politics as she links white women with the shame so routinely attributed to the unclad slave in bed, under the lash and on the block. She consequently asserts a partial mastery over female slavery's sexual onus rather than permit it to master her.[52] If Jacobs is a seductress, then the term retains the connotations of rhetorical control while erasing the cultural brand of the slave woman's erotic predispositions.

The comprehension of listening as a sexual event visited upon the ruling as well as the enslaved class is intensified in the text itself, when hearing becomes the entrée into a particularly white female sexual desire. In adolescence, white girls

hear their parents quarreling about some female slave. Their curiosity is excited . . . and they hear such talk [from their father's concubines] as should never meet youthful ears. . . . They know that the women slaves are subject to their father's authority in all things; and in some cases they exercise the same authority over the men slaves.

While the slaveholding father seeks vengeance against the "offending black man," the "daughter . . . [has] given him free papers, and sent him out of the state" (52). With this rivetting identification of listening and an awakened white female eros, the young miss bypasses her slave double's unchosen vulnerability in order to assert an apparently torrid free will. To listen, for the white woman auditor, is to be triply sexed: by the allure of her father's empowering license; by her mother's outrage at a "female slave" rival and the Oedipal dynamics of how to oust that adversary; and by disclosures from the miss's "corrupted" (52) black attendants. For Jacobs, as for Thome, the white girl is viewed as a casualty of slavery's sexual pathology. Yet in a seeming afterthought, Jacobs suggests a more compounded threat to the plantation hierarchy: the white girl's subversive usurpation of sexual, and perhaps generative, authority from her duped father; the possibility of racial amalgamation, as the miss takes the male slave as a sexual prize; and the appropriation of her father's economic impetus, as she liberates this human property and delivers him from the state. The unsettling of gender and race is hearing's twinned catastrophes. As listening quickens into sexual activity, the white female abdicates her membership in the cult of compliant Womanhood. Moreover, if we chart the passage's suggestions, it is the so-called offending *male* slave – the "most brutalized" (52) symbol of unabashed sexuality for this culture – who here occupies the passive female role to the young mistress's emergent sexual helmsmanship. Jacobs warns the very keepers of the code, her readers, that slaves are not the only women who "mate."

While Jacobs projects herself out of the book as the offended listener, then, she also tugs the self-protective reader into its very midst. Master Flint is one in a matrix of characters through whom Jacobs inveighs against the violence of protected hearing. Warning her readers about the perils of their own closed ears, she renders their need to remain deaf to the slave woman's revelations merely a genteel extension of the patriarch's bans against revelatory speech. The account of the torture and sale of a slave who, Brent guesses, broke his silence about Flint's fathering of his wife's child literalizes Linda's fear of the master's decrees against speaking. Flint sells the couple in order to banish its talk, at which time he reminds the wife that "You have let your tongue run too far, damn you!" (13). With his prohibitions against the slaves' disclosures, Flint impels the slave community to gossip about the reasons for the husband's prolonged punishment. Flint's edicts thus divert shame to the female victim. By brutally reinforcing the couple's silence, Flint casts the abused slave as the guilty object of communal gossip – *tongues running* furiously about her sexuality – not simply of his own recalcitrant proscriptions. The cautious reader should find in this depiction of the silencing patriarch an unexpected, if more sinister, alter-ego, for the female reader who would tie Jacobs's tongue as surely as he bullies his slaves into muteness about his philandering. Moreover, a reticence to promote the slave's speech enmeshes that same reader in the Master's murderous impulses: "Dr. Flint swore he would kill me, if I was not silent as the grave" (28).

Jacobs turns the Northern woman's auditory decorum into the partial cause of the South's crimes, as the author entangles delicacy and evil as cannily as she conflates Dixie womanhood and sadism in her mention of her Mistress's languishing delight, from the porch, in the whipping of a slave. Jacobs argues that Northern readers "surely would refuse to do for the master, on your own soil, the mean and cruel work which trained bloodhounds and the lowest class of whites do for him at the south" (28). Jacobs identifies her audience with both the hounds' bestiality and the demeaned class that is, after all, portrayed as little more than human hounds itself. She smudges the neat topographical grid that she will later question more manifestly with polemical diatribes against the Fugitive Slave Law – staples of abolitionist writing. Of equal import here, however, is how female "delicacy" is instructively detached from solipsistic decorum and reemerges as a generous moral attentiveness and self-criticism. The reader's decency should result in her appraisal of her own thoughtless complicity with those villains she once deemed exclusively Southern: the slave master, lowbrow posse, a hound foaming in the chase.

The feat of baring the ears of a woman who prefers them covered – the variations rung on the theme of vulnerable listener and emboldened speaker – finds a stunning expression in Jacobs's description of her confession to her jealous mistress. Mrs. Flint interrogates Linda after discovering that Flint has moved his daughter to his bedroom under the pretext of having the slave care for her there:

> ". . . tell me all that has passed between your master and you."
>
> I did as she ordered. As I went on with my account her color changed frequently, she wept, and sometimes groaned. She spoke in tones so sad, that I was touched by her grief . . . but I was soon convinced that her emotions arose from anger and wounded pride. . . . She pitied herself as a martyr; but she was incapable of feeling for the condition of shame and misery in which her unfortunate, helpless slave was placed. (33)

This scene prepares us for the luminous transparency of confession and builds toward an expected *simpatico* between mistress and slave. Yet that confession, whether in the voice of Linda or in Jacobs's narrative summary, is withheld,[53] as if disclosure must be rerouted from the dangerous trajectory of its subject. Linda's explanation is replaced by a swift declaration of her com-

pliance with her mistress's edict – "I did as she ordered" – and the recitation
of Flint's offenses usurped by its emotional repercussions of groans and sobs
on listener and speaker. The dynamics of heterosexual aggression are tact-
fully deflected into the less shocking nuances of female discourse.

The dialectic between Linda and her mistress, however, does more than
appease Child's fretful reader. Linda and her mistress enact a rite of blurred
identities in this inquisition, as Linda, recounting the doctor's advances and
maledictions, becomes *Master*-speaker to Mrs. Flint's revamped part of *slave*-
auditor. In her emerging awareness that Mrs. Flint's tears are spent not for
the slave girl but for herself, Linda may well intend such a speech, with what
must be its exhaustive inventories, as merited revenge. This time the mistress,
not Linda, is the besieged auditor of compromising insults. As the confession
unfolds, Linda delivers, in obedience to her mistress's very "orders," an account of Flint's "foul" words. We have no way of knowing through what insulating euphemisms Linda expresses Flint's lechery. Yet just as he harasses
Linda in his bedroom, so Linda's speech convulses Mrs. Flint in hers – and
elicits from her the "groans," "anger," and tears once attributed to the slave
girl plagued by Flint's insults. Linda thus momentarily confers upon herself
the stinging verbal mastery of the doctor and appears to tar his wife with his
verbal brush. Like Linda, throughout "obliged to stand and listen to such
language," Mrs. Flint is now the relatively passive recipient of Linda's recitation of the doctor's infidelities. Her "color," observes Jacobs, "changed frequently" (33). The rites of Chandler's mental exchange are not superfluous
here. Linda's confession *imposes* upon Mrs. Flint a "metempsychosis" which
maneuvers the latter into a seeming, though unconscious, unwanted, and benighted, symbiosis with the slave's role of hounded object.

This nocturnal reversal of captivity, while momentarily empowering
Linda, does little to assuage her own imprisonment or to effect the salvation
Chandler envisioned for the white soulmate of "metempsychosis." Preempt-
ing Linda's account of her own vulnerability, Mrs. Flint rescripts herself as
the martyr of the drama and Linda as co-conspirator in debauchery. The
mistress herself thus becomes an unsavory type within the text of Child's
"delicate" reader, who might eclipse a concern for the slave's sufferings with
that for her own embattled image. Indeed, the fact that Mrs. Flint does not
halt the confession after her own inklings of marital doubt fester into hope-
lessness might make us question the motives for her capitulation to Linda's
detailed rehearsal of Flint's treachery. Cowered by a disclosure of her husband's connubial sins, the duped spouse also arrays them as the background
for a histrionic pose as mythic wife–victim – a scenario of more magnified
precedent than that of a Carolinian housefrau bereft of an aging spouse's attentions.[54]

In this instance, Jacobs might contend, reader and wife are bound in a
frivolous melodrama of blighted womanhood. Mrs. Flint's self-ignited stature
as grandiose sufferer is not unlike the theatrical self-indulgence of sentimental

cult-reader. The deification afforded by purified "Womanhood," with its feat of guarding the ear's sanctity, frees the auditor from the claustrophobic powerlessness of nineteenth-century domesticity into the more sublime apotheosis of "household goddess" and consequently allows her to withhold her ears from the slave who should amplify her political ire. Moreover, the revelations meant to prove Linda's innocence and to seal an empathic pact against the Master merely *replay* the moments of Flint's violations – as if there is something so enduring in the master–slave dialectic that roles can be mystically exchanged in narrative but never permanently escaped. Nor do such exercises confer upon Linda, as proxy-master, lasting power over Flint. Linda will, of course, play despot to Flint's outraged "ear" when she taunts him with her pregnancy by Sands. But such victories are somewhat ephemeral. The confession to Mrs. Flint consequently underscores the impotence of wife and potential concubine in the thrall of the Master's dominance: "the power was still all in his own hands" (33), an admission which seems a sour pastiche of the famous spiritual, as it jettisons reprobate for heavenly Master. In elaborating Flint's crimes, Linda's speech actually mimics and therefore reinforces the patriarchal configuration her words were meant to disperse. At the close of the chapter, the hints of this nocturnal reversal are gone. Like the members of a spectral square dance, its figures have eased pneumatically back into place.

The narrative remains dense with expressions of its own censored crime, though one locked safely within the fences of womanly discourse. The connection between speech, hearing, and seduction is refined in the following scene between the mistress and Linda, one in which the former inquisition, with its hints of impersonation and role-reversal, are clarified with an epiphanic force. The chamber of the book's most vivid sexual enactment is not the master's bedroom, but the mistress's, for seduction must be transported from the locus of male sexuality to that of female jealousy, lest the reader's honor be affronted:

> She now took me to sleep in a room adjoining her own. There I was an object of her especial care, though not of her especial comfort. . . . Sometimes I woke up, and found her bending over me. At other times she whispered in my ear, as though it was her husband who was speaking to me, and listened to hear what I would answer. If she startled me, on such occasions, she would glide stealthily away; and the next morning she would tell me I had been talking in my sleep, and ask who I was talking to. At last, I began to be fearful for my life. (34)

This phantom encounter makes the sexual displacements manifest and intimidates Linda, who partially triumphed in the preceding paragraphs. Surrogate for the humbled slave in the first scene, Mrs. Flint is a stand-in for her husband in the next one.[55] In the transfer from male to female bedroom, in the mock-intercourse of the mistress's "bending over" the slave's body, in Mrs. Flint's whispers into Linda's ears, in her replacement of "comfort" with the eagle-eyed "care" displayed by her husband, even in the modulation of the Doctor's philandering into the less venial intrusions of wifely "jealous[y]" (34), the author has managed both to replicate the sexual act and to block her reader from its reality. When Jacobs describes Mrs. Flint's slithering departure from her victim's bed as *stealthy*, she attributes to the mistress the common adjective given to stage and Gothic villains – not villainesses – and to Flint, the premier reptile, himself. Mrs. Flint would pretend a trespass into the secretum of Linda's dreams and thus play auditor to the forbidden revelations of sleep-talk. Prying, speaking: these are two of the book's characteristic sexual endeavors. Here, as moves in the same erotic gambit, they mime an intrusive eavesdropping on the libido's articulations.

Sexual mastery and whispering in this nocturnal haunting approach an eerie identification. Given the affinity between sexual pursuit and verbal effrontery in *Incidents*, whispering is not, as Jacobs wishes it were in her letter to Post, a confidence uttered to a dear friend. In the muffled expletives of Dr. Flint or the wife who whispers his whispers, it represents pursuit or rape itself – those violations which Child instructed Jacobs to sequester in Chapter Nine so that the reticent reader could evade them. Moreover, the listener's transition from a fear of her defiler's abrasive words to one for her life is hardly farfetched. Speech, listening, and murder in this text are disguised strands in the same circuit of experience.

Mrs. Flint's imitations are still grounded in her husband's physical and discursive presence. As with Jacobs's repetition of Flint's words, to assume the Master's language and the posture of sexual authority is not to be his heir but to play the unwitting dummy to his ventriloquism. Slavery's violations, Jacobs laments, "are inflicted by fiends who bear the shape of men" (27). And indeed in this section the mistress must take on both the Master's shape and his voice. Once again, this scene is merely a re-creation of the Master's attempts to seduce Linda, a confirmation of even the *white* Southern female's incapacity to sculpt a sexual persona outside his. The commingling of male and female roles in the mistress's espionage should remind us of the "masculine" agency attributed to female abolitionists, but the mistress's agency is here predictably leased from the master and spirals back to him as the scene ends.

Mrs. Flint's obsessive perusal of Linda's body, and of the unconscious murmurs she imagines will designate it seductive or innocent, designates the point at which the reader and the vigilant, judgmental mistress most dangerously converge. The reader, *too*, surveys Jacobs's black body and seeks to establish its relationship to her narrative credibility, that is, to the text itself, its jeremiads, and its interpolated conversations. In the letter to Post, Jacobs indirectly rues this correspondence between her sullied flesh, not that of a "Heroine," and a sullied discourse. Since Brent's body has been compromised for her readers, they might reflexively disown her as the text's didactic tracker of slavery's monstrosities. The meetings between Brent and Mrs. Flint do more than remind the audience that its protection of its own virtuous "ears" is akin to Mrs. Flint's vaulted self-pity. The conversations between the mistress and Linda also present the readership with duelling voices, each tuned to a different interpretation of the sexual dynamics of captivity. Certainly, Jacobs's nuanced insights into events are designed to clarify the mistress's epic confusion, her wobbly slide down the hermeneutic slope. Both Mrs. Flint's misplaced sense of herself as the lone victim in the "confession" with Brent and her fractured comprehension of the relationship between her husband and Linda prompt her to use a beleaguered slave girl to extract facts her husband denies her. Even Mrs. Flint's subsequent ravings to Aunt Martha wrongly target the doctor as the father of Linda's infant. Misinterpretation and malice in Mrs. Flint are damning mirror-images of the same reprobate essence; as the text's sign-readers, the audience must rescue the hermeneutic enterprise from the mistress's misinterpretations.

In encountering two competing versions of authority, the audience must decide whether the white female racist – duplicating the envy, rape, murderousness, and baroque miscalculations exhibited by her husband – or the harried slave narrator should be sanctioned as the American sibyl, the official mouthpiece, of captivity. The choice is by no means abstract, for how one reads generates human consequences outside the narrative's parameters. The reader countenancing the mistress's epistemological and moral maze, and not the instructive map of Jacobs's narration, becomes a participant in the continued seduction, rape, and child-selling that are the sordid constituents of Mrs. Flint's "peculiar institution." Much like the doctor's muffling of his slaves' disclosures, the audience's refusal to listen to the slave woman's teachings resubmits the captive body to the humiliations the narrative vilifies. At stake is whether the demure reader will exploit Brent as the suspicious Mrs. Flint exploits her, using Linda to recoup the concept of the black body as inherently sexual and the black voice as its carnal echo, or whether that reader will find in *Incidents* the narrative habitat for her *own* partial refurbishment. Two focal constituents of "True Womanhood" – sexual purity and candor – must be seen as distinct, not symbiotic, constructs for the slave woman whose chastity is jeopardized and invariably frustrated by law.

Jacobs hardly confers upon black speaker and white listener the naive familial egalitarianism of Child's "sister[hood]"; the author gradually builds toward an implicit and tenuous pact with her reader in which the captive, not the white apologist of Southern patriarchy or the white reader, secures a pedagogical austerity. Hearing no longer conforms merely to Child's figuration of the ear as the conduit of sexual debasement. In the elided lines of the *Isaiah* epigraph the women's nakedness was perceived as punishment for a sinful deafness. The former reluctance of Jacobs's listener to hear sexual "Incidents" should convert to a penitent's consent to unveil her complicity in slavery even as she veils the author's body – that once teeming site of judgment which, on the narrative auction block, awaited the reader's scrutiny.

The bond between the ear and the speech invading it, however, continues to provide not only a source of redemption, but also a metonymic figure for the inevitable agon between master and slave. Violation, whether it threatens Linda or her black sisters, is so potent that it sends its reverberations, as we have witnessed, through the triangle of mistress, master, and chattel; yet it also affects traditional abolitionist chapters, like "Fear of Insurrection," which seem irrelevant to the feverish chases and epithets at the doctor's house. Just as the mob's ripping open of a versified letter is the base realization of the upper-class's laws against reading and writing, so the crew's oaths and "malediction[s]" become bumpkin litanies of Flint's lascivious curses – those breaches of the ear, and the body it signifies. Even the lash, as it breaks the slaves' flesh into a bloody pool, is the physical correlative of Flint's verbal lacerations, which "tear and rip" Brent as if they were rape articulated. The exploitation perpetrated by the literate demi-aristocrat and that of the lurid rural class defending him by eliciting screams in the night are tactically muddled. This canny transference – this extrapolation of one context onto another – compels each encounter, private and public, high and low class, to assume the "monstrous" countenance of the other. The mob captain, in his scathing, illiterate curses before the pseudo-army, or his commands to break into doors, linens, and gardens, merely subs for the literate and fornicating doctor he claims to serve.

Just as she inverts the master–slave hierarchy in her "secret history" with the Flints, so Linda restages a reversal within the more public spectacle of the aftermath of Turner's rebellion. In these scenes Linda's admissions that she can read, write, and choose whether to respond to her white correspondents make her again the momentary master-speaker in a predicament that should merely advertise her slave status.[56] That Linda's keenest triumph derives from the mob's violent purloining of a letter is no surprise in a narrative that so consistently pairs word and assault. When the mock-regiment discovers a particular missive, Brent advertises it as a sign of status with the same choreography as that with which she draws attention to her Grandmother's cleansed linens – using a literate speech about her literacy to elaborate her own ego while plucking that of the illiterate whites:

There was a general rush for the supposed letter, which, upon examination, proved to be some verses written to me by a friend. . . . When [the mob's] captain informed them of [the verses'] contents, they seemed much disappointed. He inquired of me who wrote them. I told him it was one of my friends. "Can you read them?" he asked. When I told him I could, he swore, and raved, and tore the paper into bits. "Bring me all your letters!" said he, in a commanding tone. . . . Nobody

shall do you any harm." Seeing I did not move to obey him, his pleasant tone changed to oaths and threats. "Who writes to you? half-free
niggers?" inquired he. I replied, "O, no; most of my letters are from
white people. Some request me to burn them after they are read, and
some I destroy without reading." (65–6)

With their "oaths and threats" the posse reprises Flint's and the mistress's
verbal sorties.[57] But Brent's retorts about her literacy, like her strategic revelations to doctor and mistress, force her auditors into a series of capitulations.
Primed for tearful confessions, the mob is first "disappointed" by the letter's
verses. It then discovers that Linda is not the perpetrator of the crime of writing, but the recipient of someone else's letter; that she can read while the mob
cannot; that the letter is not from a "'half-free nigger'" but from one of the
white elite; that she has decided to read only certain letters from white correspondents and "'destroy[s]'" other letters, "'without reading.'" The implication lingers, to be sure, that certain versified letters contain sexual or romantic invitations from white suitors and thus encode the threat of miscegenation
the poor rowdies hotly reject. During Linda's speech about literacy, just as
significant as literacy itself in this segment, the mock-captain's vile "malediction" redounds as a curse against himself, as he "swore, and raved." The imperative propriety of her speech – "'You were not sent here to search for
sweetmeats'" – overturns his expletives and the mob's hobbled colloquialisms: "'We's got 'em! Dis yaller gal's got letters!'" (65).

Linda's suave admission of literacy, of course, fails to wed slave and free
pauper in a bond of deprivation, a mutual epiphany of the American
damned. The rabble is frozen into the role of lackey in a minstrel show, where
it plays blackfaced boaster at one moment, harassed buffoon the next. Linda,
in turn, takes on the persona of a minstrel "endman," lampooning the ignorance of those her literacy and Grandmother's bounty have reduced to naive
"straightmen." The din of the mock-regiment's drum and fife recalls the coerced music and "darkie" cheer engineered at slave coffles, where the pain
accompanying the legalized selling of loved ones was traditionally disguised
as jubilant performance. Yet here the sense of black disenfranchisement is
partially shared by the white rowdies whom Jacobs whittles into bathetic subordinates denied access to the ruling corps they ostensibly represent.

Such rhetorical turnabouts entitle Linda to a brief hegemony over the
class that would subdue her. Unfortunately, like the confrontation between
Brent and her mistress, which collapses into a dazed enmity, Linda's manipulation of the envious white crew merely augments her auditors' rage. They
decipher not only in the Grandmother's "'sheet an' table clarf'" (65), but also
in Linda's uncolloquial speech, their tottering supremacy. Wresting a private
laurel from class aggression, Linda can still do little to salvage the less privileged black community, whose screams resonate through the dark. Moreover, to utter her sovereignty she must pay homage to her white masters,

their literacy, and a possible liaison with them. In staging her reversals, then, she also enacts her own systemic entanglement in the paternalistic binary of master and slave.

Regardless of this cycle of exploitation, however, Jacobs ultimately endorses a revised dynamic between speech and hearing that invokes another understanding of the entrenched codes between master and slave or speaker and listener. In "The Confession" of Chapter Thirty-nine, Brent's attempt to reveal to her daughter her "great sin" with Sands functions as a revised template for the exchange between speech and ear that Jacobs wishes her white audience to imitate and for which her narrative, with its array of faulty listeners, has steadily prepared that audience:

> "Listen to me, Ellen; I have something to tell you!" I recounted my early sufferings in slavery, and told her how nearly they had crushed me. I began to tell her how they had driven me into a great sin, when she . . . exclaimed, "O, don't mother! Please don't tell me any more. . . . I know all about it, mother." (188–9)

Jacobs's mention in her letter to Post of the hypothetical ear of "a very dear friend" is literalized in Ellen's receptive listening. Like Jacobs in that letter, Brent dreads the "diminish[ment]" of her auditor's "affection," an elitist separatism which might reside in the "delicacy [Ellen] had manifested toward the unfortunate mother" (189). Yet "delicacy," here dissociated from the self-fixation of Child's reader and aligned with filial affection, provides an alternative mode of reader response. Ellen's delicacy is not the residuum of white privilege but a sympathy born of the deprivations of a racist milieu. Jacobs, earlier hoping for reunion with her son Benjamin, distinguishes between chattel and white maternity: "O reader, can you imagine my joy? No, you cannot, unless you have been a slave mother" (173). Now, again both embracing and alienating the reader, she privileges Ellen's filial respect as that, not just of a daughter, but of a slave's daughter caught in an eternal return to the captivity from which her mother tried to liberate her. The shadow of her mother's former slave-self, Ellen has been privy to Sands's carelessness, as well as to the sexual pressures incurred by her role as a black subordinate in a white family. If "delicate," Ellen has been severely tested as a maid-servant up North, her ear scarred by the "vile" whispers that once polluted the young Linda at Flint's. It is the very inequity between a white audience hymning its own maternity and the black mother–daughter kinship that should prompt those readers to adjust their orthodox code of "delicacy" to the accepting girl's more knowing alternative.

Despite the consciousness of the disequilibrium between reader and characters,[58] this chapter between *black* females restores to "Confession" its sentimental cachet – as the sign of communion and regeneration.[59] In doing so, it revises at least two of the thwarted examples of attempted womanly rapport seen previously in the text: that between Mrs. Flint and Brent in Linda's "confession" about the doctor in Chapter Six, "The Jealous Mistress," and between Brent and the grandmother, who in Chapter Ten banishes Linda for her pregnancy and consigns her to muteness. As Jacobs turns from "slavery" to the saga of her daughter's parentage, Ellen, unlike Mrs. Flint, requires no details, dismissing as extraneous speech not only her mother's sexual incidents, but also the granting of forgiveness to one who should not ask for it. Mrs. Flint has contorted Linda into a wench-collaborator in her husband's "perfidy"; Ellen unabashedly maintains that her mother is immune to disgrace. Indeed, Ellen reserves her scorn for Sands, whose refusal to recognize her as his daughter erodes familial identity. Ellen's response serves as a corrective to Mrs. Flint's corrupted role as auditor in Brent's early bedroom confession, wherein the mistress jealously solicits facts about her husband that allow her ego a victimized self-fashioning. In addition, the fact that this reformed model of teller and listener is conveyed in familial terms marks a quiet revolution within the ubiquitous cultural fantasy of the slave as a perennial child guided by a surrogate white parent. The reader is meant to emulate the black daughter Ellen's reaction, the child's "delicate" reticence to scan the sexual history of a mother whose brave attentions to parenthood are enhanced by Sands's oversights as father.

The grandmother hardly shares the mistress's blinding vanity. Yet her bristling repudiation of the pregnant Linda should also be read in terms of the intimate meeting between Linda and Ellen. Linda refrains from telling her grandmother about Flint's trespasses because Aunt Martha's ears, much like the white audience's, are too sensitive to the speech of violation, or about her pregnancy by Sands, because Linda "fear[s]" Martha's righteous anger as much as she craves her love. Though the grandmother's concern for her own aural integrity is, of course, less venial than Mrs. Flint's view of herself as the exclusive casualty of the doctor's lust, Aunt Martha's refined hearing, her implicit ukase of silence regarding sexual matters, is an impediment to Brent's desire for maternal advice. "I went to my Grandmother," Jacobs sighs. "My lips moved to make a confession, but the words stuck in my throat" (56). Ellen, on the contrary, curtails Brent's disclosures not out of this porcelain politesse, but out of an insight into her mother's excruciating history. Silence, as Ellen evokes it, actually encompasses a *caritas* contrary to the Grandmother's imperious refusal to listen to sexual accounts. While "confession" throughout has often been implicated in Linda's nimble will to power, even in her cool brag of literacy to the rabble, the dialectic between speaking and hearing is here purged of that will. Ellen becomes the sanctified icon for the audience that releases confession from the "degradation" Jacobs bemoans in her letter to Post.

The brief rapprochement of Mrs. Flint and Aunt Martha, of immoral auditor and the sentimental slave matriarch who unwittingly becomes her accomplice, is most vividly displayed in Chapter Ten, in which the two women appear together – a diptych of melodramatic indignation. Mrs. Flint tells the grandmother, already suspicious, that Linda is carrying the doctor's child. The grandmother is as quick to believe the mistress's story as the mistress was to portray Linda as scheming concubine. The mistress's and Aunt Martha's "suspicions" are here disturbingly in sync, and just as Linda sat on a stool to tell Mrs. Flint of her husband's infidelity, so she now longs to "throw myself at my [Grandmother's] feet, and tell her all the truth!" (57). Although one would expect the grandmother to be Mrs. Flint's haloed antithesis, the fixed point around which sentiment and its interpretative reason gravitate, Aunt Martha bars Linda from her property, the domestic Paradiso whose "gate" the slave girl must now "close." Pariah from both the Flint house and Martha's home, Linda wanders across a stark topography with the same "sickness," "chilliness," and "horrid thoughts" (57) that shadow her nightmare in the wilderness after her botched escape, as well as her anguish in the garret, with its onus of capture, paralysis, and death. As such ostracism affirms, sentiment's Gothic underside is a melodramatic exclusion of the fallen.

This long passage circles frantically around Brent's, and by implication Jacobs's, ache to be heard: The Grandmother's ire "left me no chance to answer"; Linda longs to "tell her all the truth"; "I told her [Linda's mother's kind friend] why I was there"; "I thought if she [Aunt Martha] could know the real state of my case . . . she would perhaps judge me less harshly"; "[I] told her [Aunt Martha] the things that had poisoned my life" (57). Mrs. Flint and the grandmother, united in the misapprehension that Flint is the father of Linda's child, deny Brent speech and withhold listening and counsel. Linda's role in this section oscillates between that of banished Eve and that of deserted Christ bleeding on the cross of domestic indictment – "Had she [Aunt Martha] utterly forsaken me?" (57). Brent finally begs her grandmother for the "forgive[ness]" she wished from Mrs. Flint in the earlier confession, though then the girl had a "clear conscience." But whereas the grandmother eventually bestows "pity" with her restorative exclamation of "Poor child!" and ushers Linda into the genealogy of dignified females in which Brent's "dead mother" is enshrined (57), Martha, like the mistress, withholds Christian "forgiveness."

Jacobs not only associates the heinous Mrs. Flint and the good grandmother in the same gestures of rejection and misapprehension; she also extends her appeal, through Linda's repetitive cry for a genial listener in this section, to the white reader who might exile the author Jacobs as well. That reader is faced with her own subterranean affinities with the castigating grandmother when Martha indicts Linda through the either / or orthodoxy of the sentimental ethos: the lean alternatives of purity or death. The choice Jacobs earlier argued was inapplicable to slave women is now fiercely enunciated by Aunt Martha, who has imbibed the code of white sentiment: "'I had rather see you dead than to see you as you are now'" (56). For Aunt Martha, Linda is presently "just like" other black female chattel. The girl's supposed descent in caste suggests that Martha, while constantly aching for the slaves' misfortune, has deemed herself and her clan a dignified mulatto/a elite for which the mass of blacker slaves, especially those in the field, would be ineligible. The reader whose righteousness might be affronted by Jacobs's narrative is here flush with the implications of her own exclusionary credo. Jacobs then offers her audience, in the figure of her mother's "soothing" friend, an alternative auditor prefiguring Ellen's exemplary listening. And through them *Incidents* grants priority to the collective understanding of "true womanhood" over its consecration of inviolability. As "delicacy" is redefined, so too is "degradation," negotiating the gulf between a "fallen" black writer *and* her shamed white reader. In the spirit of self-scrutiny, the latter should comprehend that Linda's "degradation" was imposed by the pernicious complications of slavery, but that her own deafness to the slave woman's plight was willingly adopted. At this point, the imperatives in *Isaiah* – "Rise up" and "Give ear unto my speech" – are suggestively reversed, for one is to "Give ear" and then, herself, "Rise up" to speak of slavery's violations. The reader is asked to exchange the insulating prerogatives of womanly indifference for the polemical force of abolitionism. Jacobs's speech, which shielded and exposed the "delicate" ear, exhorts the listener herself to tell. The woman orator whom the wary reader once suspected is the figure the reader herself can now become.

Jacobs was largely denied the oral format other abolitionists exploited, the performative élan and momentum of the lectures in which others tested their material and forged reputations promoting their written oeuvre. A plausible result of this denial is that the interaction between ear and speech prohibited to her on the abolitionist circuit is insinuated into the script of her autobiography: its verbal confrontations, confessions, warnings to a prim reader, and translations of the rift between Jacobs and the white working-class into a linguistic volley between poised articulation and promiscuous illiteracy. It is true that these conversations are in part derived from those animating the sentimental novel, yet they often move briskly beyond that mode's most quotidian examples.[60] The immediacy of *parole* infiltrates her text and permits Jacobs a magisterial esprit over the numerous auditors in the narrative, the readers outside it, and the live audience she may never have addressed.[61] Through the symbolic exchange between utterance and the hesitant ear, Jacobs tinkers with the sexuality of abolitionist narration in order to oversee the terms of her own sexual identity, rather than permit them entirely to fix her. We are but "delicate" listeners if we hesitate to lend our ears to the calculated whispers of this slave woman's *talking book*.

Notes

Part of this essay originally appeared in *Arizona Quarterly* (Summer 1994).

1. January 21, 1838, in *The Letters of Theodore Dwight Weld, Angelina Grimké Weld, and Sarah Grimké*, ed. Gilbert Barnes and Dwight Dumond (Gloucester, MA: Peter

Smith, 1965), Vol. 2, 523–24, hereafter cited as *Weld-Grimké Letters*. Grimké here refers first to the need for a particular fugitive slave to speak in England about his experience, "burning from his own lips," so that his account might be published in narrative form in America. She then champions the speech of other "slaves" by mentioning two "interesting" tales from Uxbridge, one about "a Mother pining after" her lashed son, another about a young man's yearning for his enslaved sister (523–4). For more information on this letter, see Larry Gara, "The Professional Fugitive in the Abolitionist Movement," *The Wisconsin Magazine of History* 9 (Spring 1965): 196–204, and Gerda Lerner, *The Grimké Sisters from South Carolina* (New York: Schocken Books, 1967).

2. Angelina Grimké, quoted in *The History of Pennsylvania Hall, which Was Destroyed by a Mob on the 17th of May, 1838* (Philadelphia: 1838; rpt., New York: Negro Universities Press, 1969), 123–5.

3. John A. Collins, letter to William Lloyd Garrison, January 21, 1842, quoted in *The Liberator*. For vital works on, among other issues, slave orators and their relation to white abolitionists, see William A. Andrews, "The First Fifty Years of the Slave Narrative, 1760–1810," in *The Art of Slave Narrative*, ed. John Sekora and Darwin Turner (Macomb, IL: *Essays in Literature* Books, 1982), 19–22; Henry Louis Gates, Jr., "Introduction," *The Classic Slave Narratives* (New York: New American Library, 1987); and John Sekora, "Black Message / White Envelope: Genre, Authenticity, and Authority in the Antebellum Slave Narrative," *Callaloo* 10 (1987): 482–515. Sekora's thesis – that the oral and, to a large degree, the written slave narrative were fitted into the form dictated by the white abolitionists' questionnaires and interviews – is thoroughly documented and beautifully proved. Although I agree with his assertion that the pre–Civil War narratives were invariably scripted according to "white" strategies, his argument that Harriet Jacobs, too, wrote her text for "persons other" than herself is complicated by her double strategy of appeasing the white reader and critiquing the standards by which that reader interprets.

4. This particular advertisement is quoted in full in Sekora, "Black Message," 498.

5. *The Life of Josiah Henson, Formerly a Slave, Now an Inhabitant of Canada, as Narrated by Himself*, ed. Samuel A. Eliot (Boston: A. D. Phelps, 1849).

6. Phillip Foner, ed. *The Life and Writings of Frederick Douglass* (New York: International Publishers, 1975), Vol. 1, 55. My emphasis on the agents' voice is not meant to detract from the theatrical impact of their physical presence on stage. For an imaginative scrutiny of Douglass's finesse at orchestrating his body for public display – its abuses, female vulnerability, and auspicious virility – see Jenny Franchot, "The Punishment of Esther: Frederick Douglass and the Construction of the Feminine," in *Frederick Douglass: New Literary and Historical Essays*, ed. Eric J. Sundquist (Cambridge University Press, 1990), 141–65. Franchot offers, as well, a solid bibliography on the visual uses to which Douglass's appearance was put – by himself and others.

7. The understanding of the competition between utterance and narrative is thoroughly articulated by Derrida, who questions the medieval dialectic between writing (écriture) and speech (phone) and sums up the debate concerning the two by asserting that the former was seen by theologians in the Middle Ages as the *made*, the latter as *revealed*. According to this point of reference writing was consid-

ered self-obsessively creative, "artful" and akin to Satan, speech a more instan-
taneous, if humble, outpouring of faith, the "good" and unpremeditated product
of conversion. The medieval mind conceived of the "good and natural [as] the
divine inscription in the heart and soul; the perverse and artful is technique. . . . "
See Jacques Derrida, *Of Grammatology*, trans. Gayatri Spivak (Baltimore: Johns
Hopkins University Press, 1976), 17–18. Relevant, of course, to the sexual reading
of the body are Satan's malignant whisperings into Eve's ear and consequently an
Augustinian displacement of hearing by reading (*tolle lege* – take up and read – in
his *Confessions*) and by the Protestant consecration of what is *read* by what is *spoken*,
that is, the written by the heard.

    The black agents' speech, drawn from the excoriating experience of slavery
but orchestrated by white abolitionists, marks an intriguing confusion between
the two discursive modes defined by Derrida. The agents' speech derived its power
from the theological tradition that conceived of utterance as a natural articulation of the "heart." Yet such performances, amended by white abolitionists, rendered speech a crafted, if necessary, construct for the refurbishing of the white
masses. Such testimonies from ex-slaves therefore appealed to the audience's need
for revelation and truth while being partially "made" by external supervisors.

8. William L. Andrews skillfully examines the way in which the written slave narrative, because of the earlier lecture format, began to resemble oratory. See
William L. Andrews, *To Tell a Free Story: The First Century of Afro-American Autobiography, 1760–1865* (Urbana: University of Illinois Press, 1986).

9. Despite the focus on the female speaker in my essay, I do not mean to dismiss the
infamous reactions to male abolitionist orators – from the violent hazing of William Lloyd Garrison to the murder of Elijah Lovejoy. I would contend, however,
that the connection between the male body and his speech was often less problematic than what became a ubiquitous correspondence for audiences between
the woman's flesh, chaste or not, and her oratory.

10. The reprimand, issued in a well-known first "Pastoral Letter" (Boston: 1837), was
not merely a personal affront to the Grimkés alone, since the indictment did not
specify them by name. The "Letter," read in churches and published in journals,
alienated the conservative clerical abolitionists from Garrison and thus sent rip-
ples throughout the movement itself. The second Clerical Appeal, emanating
from Andover Theological Seminary, more explicitly targeted the Grimkés.

11. Quoted in Elizabeth Cady Stanton, Susan B. Anthony, and Matilda Gage, *History
of Woman's Suffrage* (New York: Fowler and Wells, 1881–1922), Vol. 1, 85–86, hereafter cited as Stanton et al. Whittier's poem on "The Pastoral Letter," along with
other abolitionist verse, is given an interesting context in Jean Fagan Yellin,
Women and Sisters: The Anti-Slavery Feminists in American Culture (New Haven and London: Yale University Press, 1989), 66–70, hereafter cited as Yellin.

12. Samuel J. May, *Some Recollections of the Anti-Slavery Conflict* (Boston: Fields, Osgood
and Co., 1869), 234. Usually attuned to his own biases, May quickly retracted his
views and attributed them to "nothing but miserable prejudice." He carried
through with the sense of apology by inviting the Grimké sisters to his home and
Angelina in particular to lecture from his pulpit and to other congregations. May
claimed that he "had never heard from other lips, male or female, such eloquence
as that of her closing appeal" (235–6).

13. *Letters of James Gillespie Birney: 1831–1857*, ed. Dwight Dumond (New York: Appleton-Century, 1938), 478–9. Birney reports that he and Bacon, pastor of the New Haven Congregational Church, had this exchange on a boat traveling to New Haven. Put off by Bacon's remarks, Birney terminated the conversation angrily. Bacon, like other ministers and journalists of the time, was disturbed by the unseemly conjunction between women's and slave's rights. For an account of this relationship, see Blanche Glassman-Hersh, *The Slavery of Sex: Feminist-Abolitionists in America* (Urbana: University of Illinois Press, 1978); Yellin's *Women and Sisters*; and Karen Sánchez-Eppler, "Bodily Bonds: The Intersecting Rhetorics of Feminism and Abolition," *Representations* 24 (Fall 1988): 28–59, hereafter cited as Sánchez-Eppler.

14. The Boston *Morning Post*, 25 August, 1837.

15. Elijah Lovejoy, quoted in *The Emancipator*, 14 September, 1833.

16. Ronald Walters analyzes slavery's infectious threat to the chaste white female. Northerners perceived the various sins of chattelhood as a foreshadowing of an increasing promiscuity in those women and men residing outside the slave states. See his "The Erotic South: Civilization and Sexuality in American Abolitionism," *The American Quarterly* 25 (May 1973): 177–201. A writer in *The Genius* encapsulates this fear of national contamination, even in 1831, and cites the danger of the Northern woman's attraction to the plantation system's "luxury and wealth": "The debasing effects of slavery on those who are its victims, are too painfully obvious. . . . [We] may turn at once to their fairer, and more fortunate sisters." Slavery, though "foul" for the black captive, is seen as more insidious because of its immoral translation up North into a desire for "fashion," a womanly fetish for the Southerner's ornamented body, versus one for the "proper sphere of woman," i.e., "a knowledge of 'household good.'" See Elizabeth Margaret Chandler, "The Influence of Slavery on the Female Character," *The Genius of Universal Emancipation*, 1 (February 1831): 170, hereafter cited as *Genius*.

17. Caroline Healey Dall, "The Inalienable Love," *The Liberty Bell* 15 (n.d.): 83–114.

18. *Liberator*, 17 May, 1834.

19. July 22, 1837, *Weld-Grimké Letters*, Vol. 1: 411–12. Married to Angelina the same year, Weld also surmised that part of the controversy with the committee derived from the Grimkés' Quakerism, with its mix of enthusiasm and sexless, "impenetrable drab" clothing (411). The assessments of the sisters were frequently in almost comical conflict: too sexual, asexual, masculinely sexual and thus "unnatural." Martha Banta persuasively accounts for the contradictory readings of the political female in *Imaging American Women: Idea and Ideals in Cultural History* (New York: Columbia University Press, 1987), 92–139.

20. Stanton et al., Vol. 1, 81.

21. The relative approval of black women on the circuit, however, did not preclude sporadic surges of violence against them. As Shirley Yee remarks, "Black women speakers, like other abolitionist men and women, were often at the mercy of hostile audiences who harassed them physically as well as verbally." Even Frances Harper, so often deflating the ire against women orators through her own genteel countenance and voice, wrote of "rowdyism" in the small towns of Ohio. Yee soundly attributes such outbursts to the triple resentments of "anti-black feelings, anti-abolitionist sentiment, and hatred of 'public' women." See Shirley J. Yee,

Black Women Abolitionists: A Study in Activism, 1828–1860 (Knoxville: University of Tennessee Press, 1992), 113–14, hereafter cited as Yee.

22. Yee, 114. Shirley Yee is especially convincing in targeting the criteria that determined the status of black female speakers. African American male leaders prohibited free black women on the speaking circuit from "directly" (114) excoriating the black man as lazy, inebriated, or licentious – a characterization that Stewart and others had deployed in their speeches. Stewart aimed at what she saw as the renovation of the black male as a fit provider in a family simulating that of a stable white unit and also urged the female to secure her own economic autonomy. Her male cohorts and audience, however, winced at a version of African American masculinity that relegated it to the familiar quintessence of erotic body, the woman to pioneering entrepreneur.

23. Dorothy Sterling, ed., *We Are Your Sisters: Black Women in the Nineteenth Century* (New York: Norton, 1984), 170–1; *Provincial Freeman*, March 7, 1857, BAP, reel 10, fr. 0097, quoted in Yee, 179.

24. *Provincial Freeman*, March 29, 1856, BAP, reel 10, fr. 0097, quoted in Yee, 119.

25. Anna Dickinson, *What Answer?* (Boston: Field, Osgood, 1869).

26. Nathaniel Hawthorne, *Selected Tales and Sketches*, ed. Michael Colacurcio (New York: Penguin, 1987).

27. The girlish and prophetic power of Francesca's pure oratory resembles that of Dickinson's Joan of Arc, who in #33 of the holograph "Jeanne d'Arc," elevates her audience through a "voice, that brought comfort to the fainting hearts of men, [and] was a woman's voice: – that of a girl, young and beautiful" (Michael C. Leff and Fred J. Kauffeld, eds., *Texts and Contexts: Critical Dialogues on Significant Episodes in American Political Rhetoric* [Davis, CA: Hermagoras Press, 1989], 282). Her death, true to Dickinson's wish-fulfillment of a female's prophetic speech, is portrayed as a sublime meeting between the enraptured ears of the bystanders and the "broken murmurings of her voice" (309), scattered to the hearing of God.

28. Jean Fagan Yellin's "note" in *Women and Sisters* confronts our later discoveries in the novel about Francesca's "mixed" blood. Yellin perceptively wonders if, since the heroine is later identified as a quadroon, Dickinson's belief in the pure power of oratory might be undermined by her speaker's black status: "does a woman who mounts the platform become conventionally black . . . ?" (196). Though this remark certainly has its merits, Dickinson might well have deferred the secret of Francesca's race to surprise the now sympathetic reader into a retrospective realization that there is no disparity between a heroine's race and sentimental inviolability.

29. *Genius*, 171.

30. In her own empathic rites Angelina Grimké at least offers "knees [that] smote together" and bound hands (Diary, April 1829, Weld-Grimké Collection, Clements Library, University of Michigan; quoted in Yellin, 186), Chandler the punishing code words of lashes and "spouting blood" (*Genius*, 171). Such depictions served both as mimetic records of slavery and as veiled substitutions for the sexual act. The descriptions also, however, steeped the female orator in what the public viewed as unfeminine gore, not in the more cloistered patriotism of institutional domesticity.

31. Though Surrey's reaction is a heady blend of political and amorous sentiment, the

captives' cries are absorbed by the helpless allure of the feminine voice, even though other male listeners berate it as "bad taste" (93).

32. Harriet Beecher Stowe, "Preface," *Uncle Tom's Cabin, or Life Among the Lowly* (New York: Harper and Row, 1965), 10.

33. Kelley to "Brother Rogers," July 8, 1841, New-York Historical Society. Quoted in Yellin, 50, who is indebted to Dorothy Sterling, in her ongoing biographical study of Kelley. Kelley married the fiery Stephen Symonds Foster in 1845, and most books about her address both her feminism within this marriage and the humiliations she endured as a woman whose public speeches caused members of the clergy and press to brand her a "harlot."

34. Harriet Jacobs, *Incidents in the Life of a Slave Girl*, ed. and introduction by Jean Fagan Yellin (Cambridge: Harvard University Press, 1987), hereafter cited as *Incidents*.

35. Hazel Carby lucidly establishes the criteria for the cult of true womanhood in her indispensable chapter on Jacobs in *Reconstructing Womanhood: The Emergence of the Afro-American Woman Novelist* (Oxford: Oxford University Press, 1987), 45–61; and she implies the racist implications underscoring the code and thus the black woman's inability to feel at ease within its strictures. Carby, like Yellin in her Harvard "Introduction" to *Incidents*, argues that Jacobs reattaches true womanhood to freedom and shows the relative nature of "purity."

36. Lydia Maria Child, *The Child's Anti-Slavery Book* (New York: Carlton and Porter, 1859), 67, hereafter cited as *Anti-Slavery Book*.

37. P. Gabrielle Foreman, "The Spoken and the Silenced in *Incidents in the Life of a Slave Girl* and *Our Nig*," *Callaloo* 13 (Spring 1990): 317, hereafter cited as Foreman.

38. I am indebted to Mitchell Breitweiser, who addresses the costly ambivalence of national representation for male icons in *Cotton Mather and Benjamin Franklin: The Price of Representative Personality* (Cambridge University Press, 1984). Jacobs's self-portrait in "Linda Brent" factors race, gender, and the slave's obscurity into the losses involved in representative identity.

39. Foreman, 242.

40. The narrative's title is the first of such deflections, since it turns, among other actions, Jacobs's sexual liaisons into *Incidents* and her selfhood into that of a typical *Slave Girl*. The generic title hints at a certain impersonality, discrete segments of experience functioning more as examples than autobiographical revelations.

41. Child's "Tragic Mulatto" tales include, among others, "The Quadroons," "Elizabeth Wilson," and "Rosenglory," all of which appeared eventually in *Fact and Fiction* in 1847. Through abolitionist giftbooks like the famous *Liberty Bell*, Child published "Slavery's Pleasant Homes" (1843), which dramatizes the conflict between race and family bonds. A far more radical Child wrote *A Romance of the Republic* (1843), her final novel, on miscegenation as a cure for the racial problem.

42. Valerie Smith, *Self-Discovery and Authority in Afro-American Narrative* (Cambridge: Harvard University Press, 1987), 40.

43. Jane Tompkins, *Sensational Designs: The Cultural Work of American Fiction, 1790–1860* (Oxford: Oxford University Press, 1985).

44. Jacobs thus becomes the female avatar for what Robert B. Stepto sees as the "distrustful" slave-author. Jacobs's "distrust" is grounded both on a skepticism about race and on one about the differences between a female slave's sexual knowledge, her victimization within the slave system, and the reader's relative isolation from

such desecrations. See Stepto's "Distrust of the Reader in Afro-American Narratives, *Reconstructing American Literary History*, ed. Sacvan Bercovitch (Cambridge: Harvard University Press, 1986), 309–15. Elizabeth Fox-Genovese, in focusing exclusively on the issue of African American female autobiography, spotlights "the chasm between the autobiographer's intuitive sense of herself and her attitude toward her probable readers." See Fox-Genovese's "To Write My Self: The Autobiographies of Afro-American Women," *Feminist Issues in Literary Scholarship*, ed. Shari Benstock (Bloomington: Indiana University Press, 1987), 169.

45. See Sánchez-Eppler, 2–4; Sánchez-Eppler, "Harriet Jacobs: Righting Slavery and Writing Sex" (paper delivered at the Georgetown Race and Ethnicity Conference, 1989), 1–11; and Foreman, 318–19. Foreman also evaluates the word's status as a "sphere" of "redemption" (319). Amy Post includes this recognition in her assertion that Jacobs "passed through a baptism . . . in recounting her trials to me." (209). Thus, the speech that sexually penetrates the ear can also foster the soul's rebirth. We discern this linguistic redemption in Brent's confession to her forgiving daughter.

46. Despite this linguistic sublimation, Flint is said to inflict open violence upon Linda by, among other acts, beating her or tossing her son Benjamin across a room. Yet these acts are infrequent in the text when contrasted with the multiple instances of verbal abuse.

47. In fact, Sands's "Eloquence" also serves as the mode of physical seduction and thus conflates word and flesh. Words, however, are also the sign of his betrayal, as Linda, later fearing that he has failed to liberate their children, recalls how "persuasively he once talked to the poor helpless slave girl" (145).

48. Responding to the dictates of a black female's autobiography and its audience, Jacobs manipulates the relationship between literacy and liberation discussed so provocatively by Robert B. Stepto, *From Behind the Veil: A Study of Afro-American Narrative* (Urbana: University of Illinois Press, 1979), and by Henry Louis Gates, Jr., *The Signifying Monkey: A Theory of African-American Literary Criticism* (New York: Oxford University Press, 1988).

49. Bruce Franklin reads *Incidents* as a direct critique of the differing fates of the taunted slave and the curious, but protected, reader of the romantic "novel of victimization" (24–30). See his *The Victim as Criminal and Artist: Literature from the American Prison* (New York: Oxford University Press, 1978), 24–9.

50. The command of recitation, however, is one Linda usually manages to resist.

51. Jacobs thus seems to know that the "true" bourgeois white reader was adept at decoding and interpreting. Karen Halttunen shrewdly argues that the American public after 1850 was, in its parlor games, theater and funerals, increasingly schooled in elaborate signification. Halttunen errs, I think, in not differentiating between regions of the country (New England, New York, the South), with their distinct codes of conduct. But even her book's study of the pre-1850 era – the sentimental initiate's training in dress and demeanor – suggests that "true womanhood" was, at a relatively early time, an intricately cultivated "fashion," not simply a transparent endeavor of the heart. See Karen Halttunen, *Confidence Men and Painted Women: A Study of Middle-Class Culture in America, 1830–1870* (New Haven: Yale University Press, 1982).

52. Among those who recognize the machinations of a "trickster" or conjure narrator

in *Incidents* are Houston A. Baker, Jr., with his emphasis on Brent's economic maneuvers, in *Blues, Ideology, and Afro-American Literature: A Vernacular Theory* (Chicago:
University of Chicago Press, 1984), 53–5; William Andrews, with his plotting of
the female slave's "secrets," in *To Tell a Free Story*, 257–9; and Valerie Smith, in
Self-Discovery and Authority, 29–39, in her scrutiny of the veil metaphor and of the
transformation of the garret to a site of narrative empowerment. Carla Kaplan
critiques such modes of recuperating Jacobs from the crippling practices of slavery and from its "ambivalent and wary" inscriptions. See her recent "Narrative
Contracts and Emancipatory Readers: *Incidents in the Life of a Slave Girl*," *The Yale
Journal of Criticism* 6: 1 (1993): 93–119, esp. 116.

53. As I was working on the strategies of female discourse in this narrative, so was
Karen Sánchez-Eppler. In a paper delivered at Georgetown University, 1989,
"Righting Slavery and Writing Sex," she tellingly scrutinized the sexual nuances
enlivening the scenes between Linda and Mrs. Flint, especially Linda's confession
of the doctor's seduction and Mrs. Flint's nocturnal eavesdropping. Sánchez-
Eppler's lecture has now appeared in more extended form in *Touching Liberty: Abolition, Feminism, and the Politics of the Body* (Berkeley: University of California Press,
1993).

54. The relationship between slave and mistress is analyzed in, among other works,
Minrose C. Gwin, "Green-eyed Monsters of the Slavocracy: Jealous Mistresses in
Two Slave Narratives," in *Conjuring: Black Women Writers and Literary Tradition*, ed.
Marjorie Pryse and Hortense Spillers (Bloomington: Indiana University Press,
1985), and Elizabeth Fox-Genovese, "To Write My Self," 166–70.

55. Hortense Spillers, in a comprehensive survey of the ways in which patriarchal
sexual models determine the densely symbolic relations in African and African
American literature, includes Jacobs in her analysis. Mrs. Flint's show of white
female power in her eavesdropping on Linda is infiltrated by the compulsion to
emulate her husband's phallic domination in the slavocracy. See Spillers,
"Mama's Baby, Papa's Maybe: An American Grammar Book," *Diacritics* 17
(Summer 1987): 65–81.

56. William L. Andrews examines how interior dialogues within slave texts signify the
machinery of "power which goes on in discourse," the negotiations waged between master and slave, reader and writer. See Andrews's "Dialogue in Antebellum Afro-American Autobiography," in *Studies in Autobiography*, ed. James
Olney (New York: Oxford University Press, 1988), 91. Not just Jacobs's counter-
attacks with the rabble, but the retorts to the master and mistress, derive from an
aggression that is barely concealed in the sometimes splenetic warnings to the
myopic or ill-informed audience.

57. Listening in the text is not always a sign of victimization, as witnessed in the white
girl's metamorphosis, through hearing her parents quarrel, into an active sexual
being. Especially relevant in this regard is Linda's auditory power in the garret
when she overhears Flint's lies about her. This species of listening, by implication,
suggests that the reader, too, is not merely vulnerable to listening, but also stimulated by the mastery of eavesdropping.

58. I note the imperfection of such contracts between slave-narrator and white reader
in response to Carla Kaplan's probing essay, "Narrative Contracts." Kaplan repeatedly views contracts between slaves and their audience as "impossible," and

the scholarship on Jacobs's redemptive narration as an almost quixotic tic in African American letters: "Jacobs parodies – even as she seems to invite – the collapse of ideal and implied readers. . . . [Scholars have] risked obscuring [slavery's] tragic conditions" (116). Yet Jacobs endorses not an ideal contract between reader and slave writer, but a pragmatic *possibility* for her audience's political revision. Her construction of motherhood, and of slavery as a whole, leaves a host of experiences outside the circumference of white maternal sentiment, while still allowing the audience a recognition based on its prizing of motherhood. Inside and outside, the reader is permitted maternal sympathy while being refused a perfected identity with the more tormented slave-mother. In a sense, then, the inequity Kaplan rightly claims lies behind contracts is deployed by Jacobs to her own advantage in her narrative, if not in her life. The reader, mother or not, is the inferior who must simply imagine the ruptured bonds of chattel maternity. Superior in suffering, however, the *slave woman* underscores the white reader's inadequacy in comprehending the slave-mother's special ordeals. For a persuasive analysis of Jacobs's sense of the white reader's shortcomings, see Dana D. Nelson, *The Word in Black and White: Reading "Race" in American Literature, 1683–1867* (New York: Oxford University Press, 1992), 131–45.

59. Jane Tompkins and Gillian Brown convincingly portray regeneration as the empowering force behind sentimentalism. See, respectively, *Sensational Designs: The Cultural Work of American Fiction, 1790–1860* (Oxford and New York: Oxford University Press, 1985), 122–46, and *Domestic Individualism: Imagining Self in Nineteenth-Century America* (Berkeley and Los Angeles: University of California Press, 1990). Tompkins suggests that confession sets into motion a cycle of spiritual and political salvation.

60. For a telling assessment of the novelistic bent of early African American narrative, see William Andrews's "The Novelization of Voice in Early African American Narrative," *PMLA* 105 (January 1990): 23–34.

61. Indeed, many of Jacobs's verbal encounters build toward the excitement of the seemingly endless questions Lewis Clarke fielded from auditors, questions he attached to the second edition of his autobiography (1846). John Sekora gives an adept playback of such queries in "Black Message," 502.

READING AND REDEMPTION
IN INCIDENTS IN THE LIFE
OF A SLAVE GIRL

SANDRA GUNNING

The post–Civil War version of Olive Gilbert's *Narrative of Sojourner Truth* in-cluded a curious letter by Indiana abolitionist William Hayward describing an 1858 confrontation between Truth and proslavery forces: During a rural antislavery meeting, a Dr. T. W. Strain declared "that a doubt existed in the minds of many persons present respecting the sex of the speaker"; according to Strain, Truth should "submit her breast to the inspection of some of the ladies present, that the doubt may be removed by their testimony."[1] When Truth inquired about the basis for his opinion, Strain continued: "'Your voice is not the voice of a woman, it is the voice of a man, and we believe you to be a man'" (*Narrative*, 138).

Facing an unruly crowd, the indefatigable Truth replied

> that her breasts had suckled many a white babe, to the exclusion of her own offspring; that some of those white babies had grown to man's es-tate; that although they had sucked her colored breasts, they were . . . far more manly than they (her persecutors) appeared to be; and she quietly asked them, as she disrobed her bosom, if they too, wished to suck!

Truth thus uncovers herself before the crowd, "not to her shame . . . but to their shame" (*Narrative*, 139). With Truth's sex verified, Hayward gloats that Strain loses a forty-dollar bet on her masculinity.

Though undoubtedly included by the *Narrative*'s white editors as a testi-monial to Truth's courage, Hayward's anecdote speaks ironically to the ways in which the ostensibly opposing elements of abolition and slavery could rely on the same mechanism for self-enhancement: On the one hand Strain set out to discredit anti-slavery activists by the obliteration of Truth's voice through a deliberate misreading of her body, a misreading firmly set within a context of de-sexualization provided by slavery, where male bodies became interchangeable with female, where gender was acknowledged only for the convenience of sexual and reproductive exploitation.[2] But on the other hand Hayward ignores the assault on Truth's modesty and makes the issue instead Truth's willingness to combat slavery by any means available – even with her body. At the same time, however, Hayward is quick to recognize that a physical examination of an unclothed black body by female audience members is an attack on white female modesty: "a large number of ladies present . . . appeared to be ashamed and indignant at such a proposition" (*Narrative*, 138). When he proudly reports on the proslavery advocate's loss of face through the public revelation of Truth's breasts, he inadvertently confirms that Truth's own credibility as an abolitionist speaker must rest finally not with her testimony as an ex-slave, but on the white reading of her body. Whether the incident ends in favor of the proslavery supporters or the abolitionists, successful political agitation seems destined to occur through the medium of Truth's body, the body of the slave interlocutor.

Although abolitionist objectification appears to win out over proslavery fetishization, there is a crucial dimension to this incident produced by Truth's decision to disrobe publicly. Challenging the objectifying gaze of the hostile Indiana audience (and with the publication of Hayward's letter, future generations of white readers also), Truth reunites the ex-slave's body with its voice through an articulation of bodily secrets that confirm white links with black physicality. Truth appropriates the linguistic moment by reinterpreting her breasts not as markers of biological identity, but as signifiers of the long American history of exploitative sexual and maternal contact between black and white bodies. As the crowd insists on their moral obligation to know the truth of her body, Truth's invitation to suckle the crowd recontextualizes that white desire for knowledge as pruriently sexual, as exploitative of her maternity. Thus under Truth's bodily language of critique the distinction between the North and South as ideological opposites in their attention to the slave begins to blur as the black abolitionist resembles the denuded slave woman on a Northern auction block, and the false ideal of slavery as the patriarchal institution merges with and consequently begins to falsify white middle-class idealization of domesticity and maternity.[3]

If we move from this narrated incident in the life of Sojourner Truth to the self-authored narrative of Harriet Jacobs in *Incidents in the Life of a Slave Girl* (1861), we find Jacobs confronting, through the voice of her alter ego Linda Brent, the very similar challenge of a white audience intent on replacing her interpreting voice with her already overinterpreted black body. However, as

I argue in this essay, if for Truth the ability to assert herself as a social critic rests on the capacity to interpret the black female body's history as a narrative about masked relations, a similar strategy is employed by Jacobs to highlight and to challenge her audience's unwillingness to accept the authority of a slave speaker. Like Truth, Harriet Jacobs uses the story of her body's exploitation in slavery as a critical moment to call into question the supposed distances between black and white bodies, and especially the Northerners' (especially Northern white women's) conception of themselves as ideologically distinguished from their Southern neighbors on the subject of slavery. Working to make visible the seemingly invisible, disembodied white reader through the medium of the physically exploited Linda Brent, Jacobs achieves a critique of Northern models of white female domestic activism that in the end establishes hers as the true voice of reform, to which all whites must attend if they are concerned about moral salvation.[4]

Ironically, Jacobs's credibility as a social commentator is compromised not by doubts about her sex, but by the fact of her identity and experience as a female ex-slave. According to the narrative, as a young woman in Edenton, North Carolina, Jacobs (represented through Linda Brent in the story) chooses to escape a lascivious master by encouraging the affections of a sympathetic white admirer.[5] Eventually, in an effort to secure the freedom of their resulting two children, as well as in a final bid to put a stop to her master's continued sexual advances, Jacobs confines herself to an attic hiding place. Only after spending almost seven years in hiding does Jacobs finally escape to the North.

But as Jacobs and some of her supporters well knew, Northern white readers of the narrative would ignore her analysis of slavery's criminality and instead fix upon her "immoral" black body and her apparently willful complicity in sexual relations with a white man. Indeed, the problem was that instead of defining Jacobs as she defined herself, that is, as a mother who has led her children out of slavery and who now seeks to create a subjective role as an abolitionist writer and social critic, her white audience would construct her as the contaminated product of slavery's moral decadence – an object of white scrutiny, of white contempt for her violation of moral codes of female conduct, but certainly not an authoritative commentator on slavery, much less Northern morality.

Like Truth, Harriet Jacobs aims, as she enters the political arena, to become the interpreter of her own body's experience of slavery. But in Jacobs's case, the female ex-slave is determined to provide readings of her sexual conduct that compete with the already established white middle-class patterns of judging correct female behavior. As virtually all modern readers of *Incidents* have noted, Jacobs's commentaries are strategically embedded within Linda Brent's language of domesticity, a language imported into the text to high-

light the black female slave as mother, all in an effort to make her acceptable
to a Northern audience. Indeed "it is not surprising," Jean Fagan Yellin suggests, "that Jacobs presents Linda Brent in terms of motherhood, the most
valued 'feminine' role" of the antebellum period, given the need to enlist
white sympathy for a story which many might find outrageous.[6] As an escaped slave Jacobs confronts an American cultural setting that defines black
femininity as everything white womanhood was not: publicly exposed, sexualized, unable or unwilling to create a domestic space of its own.

Jacobs's presentation of the black woman as mother is not simply an attempt to embrace a white cultural icon of respectability. Within the narrative
Jacobs appears to fall into line behind such women as Harriet Beecher Stowe
and Lydia Maria Child in using the language of domesticity to build a platform from which to agitate for social justice. Yet the text's political aims are
continually at odds with the format of the domestic novel, which precludes
discussions of sexual exploitation and miscegenation as subjects unmention-
able in a white familial setting, despite their importance to any discussion of
slavery. Instead of submission to silence, however, *Incidents in the Life of a Slave
Girl* uses the continual conflict between form and content to problematize the
position of white readers with respect to their role as private spectators to the
public story of Linda Brent and her exploitation as a slave, and, as a result,
their political identity as Northern, supposedly antislavery advocates.[7] In the
end, *Incidents in the Life of a Slave Girl* gives special meaning to a black woman's
physical flight from slavery to freedom and a home by contextualizing such
experiences within a continuum of moral corruption where racism, wrongful
persecution, and sexual exploitation flourish. This pattern of suffering begins
in North Carolina but, as the narrative works to emphasize, it extends even to
Northern cities, despite the strong presence of abolitionists. In the narrative,
the same terrible hardships that Jacobs and her children must endure regardless of whether they live in the North or the South suggest that the regions
might be similar in their moral and indeed their political treatment of black
slaves.

And yet *Incidents* does not merely set out to condemn Northern white
readers; rather, it is a critique of the traditional practices of reading blackness
as a severed relationship between voice and body, as the epitome of powerless
victimization. And if Jacobs's text calls into question the patterns of representation for blackness, then it does so for representations of whiteness as well:
On what foundation is white privacy based within the context of race? What
is the basis of white political self-constructions with regard to liberty and slavery? Why is agency racialized as white with regard to abolitionists? These are
some of the questions Jacobs addresses in her narrative, and they are designed to lead readers beyond inane stereotyping of black victimization or
black culpability, beyond deluding self-constructions, toward a sense of
Northern white moral and political self-scrutiny.

I

Jacobs's project of re-reading posed a challenge to mid-nineteenth-century literary and social ideologies that fetishized the black female body. White women agitating for suffrage employed the image of the chained, denuded, helpless black female slave as a metaphor to describe their own perceived position as patriarchal wards without the social and political power to control their economic and physical lives.[8] Although these representations also epitomized Southern slavery, visions of chained black women did not necessarily encourage white women to empathize with the material condition of female slaves. For example, even though Harriet Beecher Stowe set out in *Uncle Tom's Cabin* (1851) and the 1853 *Key* to the novel to demonstrate black exploitation during slavery, her own dealings with real black women (and Jacobs in particular) suggests that Stowe was not always inclined toward sensitivity, or antiracist feelings.[9]

For most Northerners, black enslavement (as opposed to the figurative "slavery" of marriage) was made vivid through the numerous descriptions of public slave auctions, the violation of black families, beatings, and allusions to rape and incest within the pages of popular male-authored slave narratives and antislavery fiction by white abolitionists.[10] Such scenes of moral chaos no doubt provided a comforting contrast for Northern whites between their life and the life of the degraded South, a contrast abolitionists capitalized on by presenting slavery as a national threat to traditional concepts of family and personal liberty; indeed slavery marked "the outer limits of disorder and debauchery," and if left unchecked it might spread moral pollution even to the North.[11] Certainly although whites in the North were not necessarily hostile to slaves, blackness and black women in particular signified victimization (hence, as Jean Fagan Yellin and Karen Sánchez-Eppler have shown, the need to act on behalf of the slave, especially the slave-mother), but also the threat of racial pollution (hence the need to keep the de facto miscegenation practices of the South out of the North).[12]

When Lydia Maria Child (who served as the narrative's editor) and Jacobs's white friend Amy Post composed the literary addresses that frame *Incidents,* their presentations of the ex-slave as Linda Brent were clearly shaped by dual Northern attitudes to black women as pariahs and victims.[13] Lydia Maria Child recognized the problem of audience reception, no doubt from her own experience as an abolitionist writer shunned for the publication of her controversial *An Appeal in Favor of That Class of Americans Called Africans* (1833).[14] In the "Editor's Introduction" to *Incidents* Child instructs white readers to look beyond the ex-slave's narration of offending horrors and interpret *Incidents* so as to focus on the injustice of slavery. Indeed, in her role as editor Child reorganized certain aspects of the narrative as part of a strategy against audience alienation, putting "savage cruelties into one chapter . . . in order that those who shrink from 'supping upon horrors' might omit them, without interrupting the thread of the story."[15]

Nevertheless, as her own introduction suggests, Child recognizes that even with the "savage cruelties" pruned, the story of Linda Brent might itself be offensive:

> I am well aware that many will accuse me of indecorum for presenting these pages to the public; for the experiences of this intelligent and much-injured woman belong to a class which some call delicate subjects, and others indelicate. . . . [B]ut the public ought to be made acquainted with . . . [slavery's] monstrous features, and I willingly take the responsibility of presenting them with the veil withdrawn. (I, 3–4)

In her effort to protect Jacobs and justify the publication of *Incidents*, Child bypasses Jacobs's authorship – and therefore the notion of Jacobs as a self-conscious critic of an American political and social system – altogether, thereby constructing Linda Brent as an anonymous woman defined not by her role as speaker, but by her (presumed) bodily "experiences" in slavery.[16] These are the real issues of the narrative, according to Child. By focusing on the problem of audience reception (the problem of indecorousness), Child draws attention not to the slave narrator's authority to determine the meaning of her slavery, but to the privatized privilege of the white reader to interpret and pass judgment on Brent's life and – if we follow the gist of Child's metaphor of the unveiling – on Brent's body as well.[17] The white reader's authority (especially that of the white female reader) is constructed through the metaphoric presentation of the unveiled slave woman: Her location within the public realm signifies female contamination, racialized in this context as black, while their location within the realm of shielding domesticity signifies spirituality and moral purity.[18]

At the same time, if Child unveils the "monstrous features" of slavery made visible upon the body of a slave woman, this woman is both an object of charity and a pariah, as her life story vacillates between the "delicate" and the "indelicate" – categories that move the white audience either to protect the victimized Brent or to protect their own sensibilities from her offending presence. The problem here is Child's appeal to the conscience of the white reader and her or his interpretation of the narrative; the success of the narrative rests not on Brent's telling, but on how the white reader chooses to read the meaning of the narrative, in effect the meaning of Brent's body as it is exposed in the text.

Child's strategy of mediation becomes clear when she phrases her final appeal to the audience as a celebration of the power of Northern whites to effect correct moral judgments:

> I do this for the sake of my sisters in bondage, who are suffering wrongs so foul, that our ears are too delicate to listen to them. I do it with the

hope of arousing conscientious and reflecting women at the North to a
sense of their duty in the exertion of moral influence on the question of
Slavery, on all possible occasions. (*I*, 4)

Child's final proposal for the proper response to her "unveiling" of Brent
identifies the "indelicate" (the offensiveness of Jacobs's story) with the slave
testimony ("our ears are too delicate to listen to them"), since the pronoun
"them" refers both to the black speakers and to the atrocities committed under slavery. At the same time, since Child has described the readers' proposed encounter with stories of slavery through the visual metaphor of gazing
at unveiled images, the suggestion then is that within *Incidents* the mere sight
of Brent's enslaved body, unadorned with commentary, will be less offensive
than hearing about it from Brent herself. What is indelicate, then, is the black
eye-witness interpretation of slavery, the notion of the authoritative voice of
the slave narrator.[19]

Only when Brent is silenced can she become the object of charity. Her
situation can be perceived as "delicate" (and therefore worthy of sensitivity)
only when thoughtful white women readers are allowed to contemplate
safely the transparent text of Brent's life for themselves, and in so doing assign
what whites would consider to be proper meaning to the ex-slave's experience. In other words, the public body of the slave woman, the site of the
grossly physical, becomes the site of intervention and mystification for the
disembodied white female reader to "exert" protective moral influence.

If in her "Introduction" Child attempts to win audience support by validating the white right to assign correct meaning to the "monstrous features"
of slavery through the construction of a silenced Brent as literally a physical
specimen for sympathetic white consideration, Amy Post tries a seemingly
different tactic in her appendix. In a statement of support for the slave narrator that attempts to remain faithful to Jacobs's directives from an 1857 letter,
Post seems at first to destabilize the terms of Child's introduction by completely submerging the notion of Brent's physicality.[20] Referring directly to
Jacobs through the pseudonym of Linda Brent, Post stresses the slave narrator's perfect assimilation into the private world of Northern middle-class
white true womanhood.

As "a beloved inmate" of Post's house, Brent's physical characteristics are
referred to in passing as "prepossessing," but in large part the testimonial
constructs Brent as a spiritual creature with "remarkable delicacy of feeling
and purity of thought" whose body responds to the more acceptable somatic
sensations of grief and modesty, rather than to sexual exploitation (*I*, 203).
But whereas the evidence of slavery is concealed in the suppression of bodily
knowledge, such suppression seems to have rendered Brent inarticulate and
even mute – this after the "incidents" themselves have just been delivered in
the ex-slave's own words: "she passed through a baptism of suffering . . . in

private confidential conversations"; "even in talking with me, she wept so much, and seemed to suffer such mental agony, that I felt her story was too sacred to be drawn from her by inquisitive questions" (*I*, 203–4).[21] Even though she is ethereal, Brent is being read for what is unsaid about her body. Indeed, her tears and shrinking modesty, even as they signify her rightful place in a white domestic setting, might also betray incriminating secrets. After all, though she is accepted into Post's female community, Brent's claim to true womanhood is always mediated by her race.

Brent's body seems to have been recouped by Post's narrative strategy, yet the slave narrator's interpreting voice is still depicted as nonexistent, since the political foresight to write and publish the narrative is unmistakably stressed as Post's rather than Brent's. In the end, though Brent performs the manual labor of tracing "secretly and wearily . . . a truthful record of her eventful life" (204), Post takes the credit by constantly harping on "the [moral] duty of publishing" *Incidents*. As such, though Brent occupies the favored place of adopted white daughter, though she displays the necessary spiritual grace of white women, she still lacks the moral strength that defines the ideal of white domestic feminism. Thus Post's appendix suggests that Brent may be the daughter, but it is the white mother who leads her toward political action.[22]

Despite the disturbing implications of their testimonials, Child and Post offer their respective construction of the slave narrator from a genuine commitment to assisting Jacobs with the publication of her text. Jacobs was no doubt grateful to both women for their encouragement and assistance in helping her with *Incidents*, and she describes them affectionately as "whole souled."[23] However, her own discussion of the writing of the narrative and her implied instructions to the audience about what, who, or how to "read" with regard to her autobiography contradict the interpretive practices employed by Child and Post, and also clearly foreground her awareness of the problems of writing for a Northern audience not likely to grant her respect as a competent social commentator.

Through the persona of Linda Brent in the "Author's Preface," Jacobs's terse description of her past and present condition suggests a woman who has survived physically and intellectually the hardships of drudgery and denial imposed by life in both the North and the South:

> I was born and reared in Slavery. . . . Since I have been at the North, it has been necessary for me to work diligently for my own support, and the education of my children. This has not left me much leisure to make up for the loss of early opportunities to improve myself; and it has compelled me to write these pages at irregular intervals, whenever I could snatch an hour from household duties. (*I*, 1)

In describing her confinement to domestic service Jacobs does not focus on physical tortures, but instead makes clear her dedication to political action ("I want to add my testimony to that of abler pens to convince the people of the Free States what Slavery really is"), and her desire to claim for herself the role of the moral and intellectual authority who will lead the audience to a proper understanding of the complex issue contained within the narrative: "I do earnestly desire to arouse the women of the North to a realizing sense of the condition of two millions of women at the South, still in bondage" (*I*, 1–2).

In an 1857 letter to Amy Post, Jacobs describes the persona she has created for herself in *Incidents* as "a poor Slave Mother [who comes] not to tell you what I have heard but what I have seen – and what I have suffered" (*I*, 243). The oxymoronic appellation Slave/Mother ironically gestures toward the two entities split in Child's introduction and racialized as opposites: the sexually degraded, commercialized body that Child would unveil, and the intuitive, disembodied nurturing image of female moral force.[24] In the public body of the narrator Linda Brent, both mother and slave will be united as witness and participant. And it is precisely Jacobs's experience as a participant (the same experience which might repulse the audience) that her preface argues is the premiere qualification for assigning her the role of judge: "Only by experience can any one realize how deep, and dark, and foul is that pit of abominations" (*I*, 2). Clearly, what Child sees as the point of danger for white women becomes a source of authority for Jacobs.

II

In her effort to problematize the authority of a white audience that deems itself empowered by the privatized moral force of domestic feminism, the narrator Linda Brent situates both the Southern and Northern portions of *Incidents* within the interior spaces of the home. Her tactic here is to highlight that setting as the special context of black female exploitation. Representational patterns begin shifting from the very opening of the text, when Brent's first owner turns out to be a godly woman having more in common with the mothers among the audience than with slaveholders like Simon Legree. In her introduction Lydia Maria Child identifies her as Brent's first benefactor who, along with many white Northerners, provides the slave with "opportunities for self-improvement" by teaching her to read and educating her in "the precepts of God's Word" after the death of Brent's parents (*I*, 3, 8).

But Brent herself is quick to discuss the full extent of her "opportunities" when as a surrogate daughter within the white family unit she is bequeathed to the white woman's niece, the infant daughter of the infamous Dr. Flint. Unlike Brent's former mistress, who is ultimately disappointing in her actions because she appears to be falsely the ideal white mother, Flint and his wife take on demonic proportions from the start: the doctor tries to sell Brent's grandmother after her mistress's death, even though both blacks and whites know that the mistress had intended to free Aunt Martha. A fitting consort to Dr. Flint, Mrs. Flint has no "strength to superintend her household affairs," but she is strong enough to "sit in her easy chair and see a woman whipped, till the blood trickled from every stroke of the lash" (*I*, 12).

Brent's description of life in the Flint household lifts Child's metaphoric veil of decency to reveal not just brutalized slave bodies, but the nature of the victimization process developed and sustained as part of the means of constructing white privacy. Her first discussion of Dr. Flint's sexual misconduct in the slave quarters makes clear this connection. After only a short time in the Flint household, she witnesses the torture of a male slave:

> There were many conjectures as to the cause of this terrible punishment. Some said master accused him of stealing corn; others said the slave had quarreled with his wife, in presence of the overseer, and had accused his master of being the father of her child. They were both black, and the child was very fair. (*I*, 13)

Eventually Flint sells both husband and wife:

> The guilty man put their value into his pocket, and had the satisfaction of knowing that they were out of sight and hearing. When the mother was delivered into the trader's hands, she said, "you *promised* to treat me well." To which he replied, "You have let your tongue run too far; damn you!" (*I*, 13)

Flint conceals his indiscretion by prohibiting the woman from speaking of the crime, so that even the slave community must whisper and conjecture about what has really occurred. Under this system of reversals the pregnant slave bears the guilt of sexual misconduct. Indeed the protection of Flint's private life as father and husband is predicated on the exposure and punishment of black female bodies; they become criminalized, while white paternity is replaced by irresponsible, immoral black maternity. However, Brent's narration works to undermine the careful protection Flint has constructed for himself by moving the narrative beyond the public exhibition of the slaves (the man who is beaten, the woman who is sold), an exhibition that, in its reliance on stereotypical images of victimization, suppresses rather than facilitates truth. Her vocalization finally allows the lost story of the slave couple to surface, despite Flint's prohibition. Brent's motive for speaking out in the case of the slave couple becomes the context for the telling of her own experiences: clearly, as in the case of the slave woman who is sold away, for Brent *not* to reveal the details of her relationship with Flint would be to allow her (potential) bodily corruption to stand as a means of shielding his moral degradation.

Though regional and political differences seem to separate the degenerate Flints from the apparently purer communities of Northern white readers, Brent's emphasis throughout her narrative on Flint's obsession with the silencing of black (especially black female) speech about sexual exploitation suggests frightening parallels in the Northern white readers' own resistance to *hearing* about the horrifying details of slavery as they read the narrative within a familial setting. Indeed, if they resist Brent's authority as narrator, the morally righteous audience addressed by Child's introduction, who are appealed to as saviors but whose ears will be contaminated by slave accounts of oppression under slavery, ironically risk appearing in collusion with Flint, the evil slavemaster so often vilified in abolitionist literature.

This implication has important consequences with respect to how white readers supportive of familial harmony can claim to be innocent spectators to the perversion of their ideals in the Southern patriarchal "family" of slavery. Brent's narrative continually seeks to implicate them in a racial conspiracy against black female modesty that undermines the notion of white sectional difference. She begins by appropriating the concept of delicacy and assigning it to black femininity. Then she depicts this delicacy under assault by the white master "father" who seeks to suppress the detailed discussion of sexual – and therefore incestuous – exploitation of a surrogate daughter: "My master began to *whisper* foul words in *my ear*. . . . He tried his utmost to corrupt the pure principles my grandmother had instilled" (emphasis added; *I*, 27):

> I saw a man forty years my senior daily violating the most sacred commandments of nature. He told me I was his property; that I must be subject to his will in all things. . . . But where could I turn for protection? No matter whether the slave girl be as black as ebony or as fair as her mistress. In either case, there is no shadow of law to protect her from insult, from violence, or even from death. . . . The degradation, the wrongs, the vices, that grow of slavery, are more than I can describe. They are greater than you would willingly believe. (*I*, 27–8)

The penultimate sentence of this passage re-echoes Flint's own silencing of his victim: "Dr. Flint swore he would kill me, if I was not as silent as the grave" (I 28).[25] And since decency, or more precisely "delicacy," is the same watchword mediating between the audience / slave master and the slave narrator (neither wants their home contaminated by Brent's story), then in the North as well as the South discretion rather than justice remains the better part of valor. Thus, white readers, who shy away from full disclosures from the mouth of the slave narrator, could well be accused of an identical acceptance of a hypocritical standard of public morality.

With regard to Brent's reticence concerning the details of Flint's attempted seduction, her silence cannot be attributed solely to her desire to avoid reliving a distressing situation.[26] Precisely because Flint's prohibition occurs within the context of white middle-class privacy, which is dependent on the annihilation of the slave family and the poisoning of black female morality, Brent seems compelled to speak. Her silence is therefore dramatized as an imposed one – in the past by Flint, in the present moment of *Incidents in the Life of a Slave Girl* by the antislavery audience itself: "The degradation, the wrongs, the vices that grow out of slavery, are more than I can describe. They are greater than you would willingly believe."

In many ways Brent's compelled silence forces her to be the guardian of the white reader's morality, since she keeps to herself all the unpleasant, unseemly details that insult a pure sensibility. Consequently, the exploited slave girl is transformed into the physical receptacle of slavery's contamination, standing as the victim abolitionists want to rescue, the pariah they feel compelled to keep at arm's length.[27] But it is precisely in dramatizing how the protection of both Northern and Southern white morality is constructed through the particular usage of the slave body in tandem with the silencing of the slave's voice that Brent resurrects herself as social critic. This point is made clearer when we read the rest of her comments to a disbelieving audience:

> Surely, if you credited one half the truths that are told you concerning the helpless millions suffering in this cruel bondage, you at the north would not help to tighten the yoke. You surely would refuse to do for the master, on your own soil, the mean and cruel work which trained bloodhounds and the lowest class of whites do for him at the south.
> (*I*, 28)

Thus Brent, artless, reticent, bowed down by shame, uses the apparently limiting construction of herself as mute victim to reveal her binary opposite, the depraved tyrant whose "monstrous features" depict not just Flint, but also the moral citizens of the North who tolerate the Fugitive Slave Law. So when Brent describes Flint as a fiend, Northerners, because of their own hypocrisy and their refusal to listen to "truths," are likewise constructed as the monstrous bloodhounds and uncivilized slave-catchers in antislavery territory.

This refiguration of the well-meaning readers is particularly devastating with respect to its implication for white women. Their participation, as readers, in the silencing of Brent sanctions her sexual exploitation by Flint; the identification of their need for silence with his recontextualizes these women's popular representation as saviors. They have, in fact, joined the ranks of Brent's male tormentors, a shift that threatens to defeminize them. So, clearly, Brent's appeal is not solely for the protection of the slave victim: What is at risk also is the very notion of femininity and true womanhood white Americans have hitherto idealized.

Since Brent wants to arrest the attention of her audience without alienating it, she provides a vivid but distanced dramatization of white female collusion in a half-sarcastic, half-regretful description of Mrs. Flint as the failed maternal figure who might protect her from the doctor's torments. When her husband's sexual designs on Brent become too obvious, Mrs. Flint's anger is aroused. Up to this point Brent has represented Flint's sexual harassment as incestuous, a violation of the codes of familial decency. He demands to have his four-year-old daughter sleep in his chamber, as an excuse for Brent to remain in the room; here one wonders if Flint expects the child to be present while he tries to rape her nurse. The narrative thus creates the need for a response from Mrs. Flint, the family's moral guardian, not just to save Linda, but indeed to save the white family as well.

Brent has already painted Mrs. Flint as the stereotypically lethargic but cruel slave mistress; here she urges the need to understand the secrets of slavery and to act against the institution as a necessary self-protective measure. Mrs. Flint's (and the white female reader's) salvation as the moral center of the family will depend on her ability to uncover the master's secrets, despite his subterfuge. If she depends on her own abilities of discernment, she will fail: Mrs. Flint "watched her husband with unceasing vigilance; but he was well practiced in means to evade it" (*I*, 31). Her only hope of comprehending the problem and shifting her position from accommodating ignorance to effecting change is to allow herself to heed the words of the slave narrator.

Significantly, in the same chapter in which Brent teaches herself to write (and thus begins her journey to the present white audience as author/commentator), Mrs. Flint finally allows a painful interview with Brent that lays bare the details of her husband's debauchery. Brent's words also suggest their commonality as virtuous females who have been violated by exposure to a slaveholder's conduct:

> As I went on with my account her color changed frequently, she wept, and sometimes groaned. She spoke in tones so sad, that I was touched by her grief. The tears came to my eyes. . . . She felt that her marriage vows were desecrated, her dignity insulted. (*I*, 33)

But because Mrs. Flint is a model of white female ineptitude, she is unable to grasp the connection between herself and Brent: "She pitied herself as a martyr; but she was incapable of feeling for the condition of shame and misery in which her unfortunate, helpless slave was placed" (*I*, 33).

Rather than trust the testimony of a slave who has raised the first blow against the master's evasions by disobeying the order of silence, an angry Mrs. Flint becomes obsessed with observing Brent's body, a move that links her unmistakably with the readers addressed in Child's introduction. Mimicking her husband's construction of the slave woman as the object of (sexual) desire, Mrs. Flint situates Brent "in a room adjoining her own," keeping a constant watch on the slave victim, rather than on her husband. Enacting an "especial care" of Brent, Mrs. Flint scrutinizes Brent's body in hopes of a more comforting version of events that will somehow contradict what she has already heard. And when her attention parallels Flint's own lascivious obsession with Brent ("Sometimes I woke up, and found her bending over me"),

Mrs. Flint is transformed into the corrupting seducer intent on tricking Brent into becoming the site of sexual contamination (*I*, 34).[28]

But in a clever repositioning of herself as the reader of Mrs. Flint's body, Brent carefully describes the slave mistress's self-seduction by the details of her own falsely constructed narrative of sexual misconduct. Working under the delusion that Brent is the corrupter of Dr. Flint, the slave mistress attempts to elicit unconscious responses from her (at night "she whispered in my ear, as though it was her husband who was speaking to me, and listened to hear what I would answer"), responses that will confirm her "truth" that Brent is the real threat to the sanctity of her marriage and home (*I*, 34). But when Brent is represented as the seducer, Dr. Flint is shielded once more by an "audience's" refusal to listen to slave testimony. With the unwitting Mrs. Flint working hard to support her husband's deceptive practices, Brent becomes the only resister holding out for a true account of the events.

Brent's narrative suggests that, as an ideal method of misreading, Mrs. Flint's self-consoling validation of white interpretive powers through an invalidation of the black voice reinforces white visions of racial superiority, but it has little to do with the freeing of slaves or with national moral reform. The story of Mrs. Flint's failure stands as a textual lesson for Brent's readers about how Northern domestic morality can quickly become ineffective (indeed self-annihilating) when whites fail to recognize the folly of designating the victim's, rather than the slaveholder's, testimony as the source of offense. At moments such as these the text forces a confrontation between the dual myths of a manifestly present white authority and a manifestly absent black authority to interpret the meaning of slave speech. The interview between Mrs. Flint and Brent provides the Northern audience with two choices: either they participate in the exploitation of the slave body and remain deaf to the only credible interpreter available (Brent herself), in which case they are identified with the duped and demonic slave mistress, or they admit to the necessity of allowing Brent not just to speak to but to guide them, as part of the initial step toward abolition.

If we are indeed meant to read this failed interview between Mrs. Flint and Brent as a representation of the reader's rejection of the black female slave narrator, what is at stake finally is not Mrs. Flint's (and the Northern audience's) misplaced obsession with the artificial dichotomy of white spiritual morality versus black bodily immorality, but rather the hope that there might exist a national moral landscape where respect and protection for white ideals will translate into respect and protection for the black victim. I am not suggesting here that *Incidents in the Life of a Slave Girl* is voicing a simplistic call to interracial unity. Rather, I am suggesting that the text questions the character of a white nation that establishes its moral ideals on a victimizing construction of blackness.

Earlier, in describing her plight as an unprotected slave girl, Brent has evoked the traditional contrasts between the sexually exploited female slave and her supposedly more fortunate white counterpart: The black slave accepts "the cup of sin, and shame, and misery," whereas the white child becomes "a still fairer woman" whose life is "blooming with flowers, and overarched by a sunny sky" up until the moment of her marriage (*I*, 29). But although the ideal of the white true womanhood depends on the perceived existence of its opposite, the sexualized black female, how ideal an image is sanctified, privatized white ladyhood, and thus domesticity, if it has to be safeguarded through the silencing of slave discourse on rape and sexual terror, and a tolerance of slavery?

The notion that white ladyhood will have no real value in any community supporting slavery is made clear by Brent when she analyzes the implication of Flint's attempt to bribe her with promises of fair treatment: "'Have I ever treated you like a negro? . . . I would cherish you. I would make a lady of you.'" (*I*, 35). Brent suggests that Flint's offer of a falsified female respectability is not that of the pampered quadroon mistress but that of white femininity itself. At this point Brent drops the personification of corrupted white womanhood as exclusively Southern by referring directly to Northerners supportive of slavery through acceptance of the Fugitive Slave Law. They willingly jeopardize the sensibilities of their own women when they "proud[ly] . . . give their daughters in marriage to slaveholders" (*I*, 36). Lulled into ignorance by "romantic notions" about Southern life, these woman (again note the connection with Mrs. Flint) enter brothellike settings: "The young wife soon learns that the husband in whose hands she has placed her happiness pays no regard to his marriage vows. Children of every shade and complexion play with her own fair babies. . . . Jealousy and hatred enter the flowery home, and it is *ravaged* of its loveliness" (*I*, 36; emphasis added). Brent's choice of words unmistakably implies that through white moral neglect, the rape of the slave woman will translate into the rape of the Northern/Southern home.

III

In recounting her life with the Flints, Brent demonstrates the futility of white analyses that address neither the sexual politics of slavery nor the right of slaves to speak. Such avoidance cannot lead whites to effective agency in the abolition of slavery and, in the face of the audience's failure to act its part (as exemplified by Mrs. Flint), *Incidents in the Life of a Slave Girl* suggests that without white sympathy Brent is not only compelled to enact her own strategy for emancipation; she must succeed on the very terms of what whites perceive to be black female moral failure. In contrast to those who interpret black bodies as merely metaphors for slavery, Linda Brent works to achieve her own liberation by dictating a radical resignification of black physicality against the fundamentally linked expectations of both Dr. Flint and Northern white readers. Though the moral vacuum created by Mrs. Flint's retreat forces Brent to take a white lover to save herself from Flint, this moment of the female slave's apparent physical self-abasement is transformed by the narrative into an articulation of staunch resistance: "I knew nothing would enrage Dr. Flint so much as to know that I favored another; and it was something to triumph over my tyrant even in that small way" (*I*, 55).

To authorize her appropriation of the white power to liberate, Brent enacts a second moment of confrontation when she addresses offended readers who, like Mrs. Flint, come across distasteful information (her decision to submit to Sands's overtures). Will the readers blame Linda for sexual promiscuity, or will they accept her pronouncement that "the slave woman ought not to be judged by the same standards as others" (*I*, 56) in the struggle for her freedom? At this point the narrative exhibits an oft-noted schizophrenic quality, retreating back and forth between a very matter-of-fact, dispassionate detailing of a material strategy of manipulation and admissions of guilt and emotional appeals for the audience's forgiveness:

> I thought he [Dr. Flint] would revenge himself by selling me, and I was sure my friend, Mr. Sands, would buy me. . . . Pity me, and pardon me, O virtuous reader! . . . I know I did wrong. No one can feel it more sensibly than I do. (*I*, 55)[29]

But does such a duality signify regret for mistaken action and a desire to be seen as a truthful, virtuous witness, or does it dramatize the conflict between, on the one hand, Brent's desire to record in her own words the transformation from victim to actor on the very terms of the slave woman's oppression (that is, her sexuality), and, on the other, her white audience's determination to reject that transformation and its implied transference of agency from the abolitionist to the slave? *Incidents* is patterned after novels of domesticity but, as Carolyn Karcher has shown, Brent's literary tradition is the domestic novel specifically politicized as antislavery fiction.[30] Thus, although Brent's problematic apologies would seem to refer to the indelicacy of her sexual choices, they stress that such acts of self-liberation are unacceptable only within the context of antislavery fiction that would value the passivity rather than the resistance of the exploited female slave.

Up to this moment, Brent's role as victim is crucial to effect the construction of the white savior. Up to this moment, the fairly traditional presentation of Brent as the silent, shamefaced slave girl whose ordeal remains inoffensive as long as it is discreetly unvoiced has exemplified, at least superficially, Child's promised history of bodily horrors presented in the slave's silence. But Brent's body becomes offensive in the text precisely when the narrative begins to articulate a different system of bodily representation, one that jeopardizes the political role of the reader. Thus what is now offensive in Brent's account is her claim to agency: the move toward self-ownership that transforms her body from an emblem for white self-construction to the enabling tool for black action. Again, the implied sense of the Northern reader's affront to, condemnation of, and even anger at Brent is also shared by Dr. Flint, revealing that even as Brent appears to pay homage to pure Northern sensibilities, she questions those sensibilities by aligning them with a designated foe of domestic morality. Such an alignment also implies that anger at her action must come from the same basic source: a resentment for her defiance of white power over the slave.

After the narrative's indictment of the reader's authority to comprehend Brent's situation or to act on her behalf, the slave suggests an alternative audience and agent of salvation: female slaves themselves. If Mrs. Flint is a failed reader, Aunt Martha is cautiously styled as her opposite – cautiously, because even though she receives Brent's story of sexual manipulation with "an understanding and compassion readers are meant to share," she does not grant Brent her forgiveness.[31] Nevertheless Aunt Martha's acceptance of Brent's narrative (which has a cathartic effect for Brent) signals the potential for a transformed relationship between speaker and reader and provides the next step in Brent's achievement of physical freedom from the Flint household.

Once she acknowledges the conditions from which Brent has emerged, Aunt Martha – along with other women in her community – offers her shelter as Brent enacts a scheme to free her two children by Sands. In her effort to disappear from sight and thereby convince Flint he has nothing to gain by refusing to sell her children, Brent retreats to an attic crawl space of Aunt Martha's house. What is important here is the fact that Brent removes her body from the relations between herself and Flint, so that the master's power is now diminished precisely because the material basis for his role has vanished. In a narrative dramatizing the struggle to tell a supposedly sympathetic audience about the need to abolish slavery, Brent demonstrates the power of her voice as Flint is forced to follow the directives of her discourse via letters sent from various Northern locations by the "escaped" slave Linda. When her manipulations eventually lead a frustrated Flint to sell the children to Mr. Sands, Brent emerges as the true liberator in the narrative.

It is important that as a mother herself, Brent achieves her children's freedom by both enacting and critiquing the central metaphor of maternity which describes the abolitionist platform for social reform. From her hiding place Brent watches over her children, appears mysteriously to urge their father to take them north, and visits them at night as if she were an apparition. As the "disembodied" matron who must literally watch her children from above, Brent ridicules Northern white metaphoric self-construction (abolitionists supposedly watch over the slaves) as "maternal" saviors. In describing herself as the ethereal mother within the relative privacy of her grandmother's home, Brent continually indicates the white impediments to safe-guarding that privacy, as Aunt Martha's domestic peace is regularly violated by Dr. Flint and other enforcers of white law. Brent's self-construction here registers a warning against an idealization of the spirit of maternity that severs it from the material conditions of the body. Lest we romanticize her role as maternal figure in the "Loophole of Retreat," Brent continually re-minds us that she is actually cut off from her children and that she also suffers a confinement of the body that is tortuous: enduring sickness, painful insect bites, extremes of heat and cold, and frostbite, she has to accept that her limbs might never recover from their imprisonment (*I*, 114).

Her articulation of bodily torture in the performance of maternal duty becomes a plea for a new construction of maternal power that includes black women; idealized maternity, like idealized womanhood, cannot function for black women if it celebrates moral action but denigrates attempts at physical survival. Brent acts like a mother while she is hiding, but she achieves liberat-ing motherhood for her children only when she is reunited with them. Other-wise Brent is destined to imitate in part the life of her deceased Aunt Nancy, whose physical connection to motherhood has been stolen by slavery until she is "stricken with paralysis" (*I*, 144), and finally dies without the ability to speak.

The text stresses the need to attend to the slave woman's body, as well as her soul, when Brent's position is juxtaposed with that of the dead Nancy: she calls herself "a poor, blighted young creature, shut up in a living grave for years" (*I*, 147). Although some readers have recently argued that Brent's con-finement can be read partially as a metaphor of birth in that Aunt Martha has provided "a protective womb for Linda's birth to freedom," or that Brent "manages to convert that tomb into a womb" by reaffirming ties with her family, by remaining in the attic she risks a still-birth into inertia, rather than physical freedom or active motherhood.[32] Eventually, when Brent goes north, her escape from slavery is framed within the specific context of the need to address the alienated black body. Indeed, the freedom signified by the North can be tangible only if it signals a reclamation, a reversal of that alienation.

Brent goes north in 1842, after her daughter has been sent to New York to live with relatives of Mr. Sands, where she is later joined by her son. Yet what will become of her ultimate search in the North for "a home and freedom," a material situation first promised by Dr. Flint when he tried to bribe Brent into sexual submission (*I*, 83)? Her search for the genuine article beyond the South is constantly frustrated by Northern conditions that duplicate almost exactly those survived by Brent and her family in North Carolina. Even be-fore the passing of the Fugitive Slave Law in 1850, these conditions of "free" life included fear of physical capture, constant confinement, subterfuge, racism, and – for Brent's daughter Ellen – direct enslavement and even the threat of sexual harassment from white relatives. When Brent obtains a post as nursemaid in the Bruce household (the same post she occupied with the Flints), she must accept the position of surrogate mother. Such characterizations of Brent's experiences as essentially repetitions of slave life, despite the shift in region, demonstrate the narrative's active critique of the "freedom" offered to blacks by the North.

An important variation within the text's repetitive moments is Ellen's shift into Brent's former role, and Brent's into that of her grandmother. While Brent's own position improves (she has a kind employer), Ellen's condition worsens. Evoking a tangle of blood, capital, and control that characterized Brent's position in the Flint household, Mr. Sands's relative Mrs. Hobbs echoes Flint in her insistence on a tie of ownership between her family and their cousin Ellen: "I suppose you know that . . . Mr. Sands, has *given* her to my eldest daughter. She will make a nice waiting maid for her when she grows up" (*I*, 166). In addition, to hide their own alcoholism, Mr. Hobbs and his Southern brother-in-law Mr. Thorne employ Ellen to fetch their liquor, so much so that "she felt ashamed to ask for it so often" (*I*, 179). Though she suppresses this information so as not to burden her mother, Ellen is distressed by such concealment. This situation recalls Brent's own discomfort about, and concealment of, similar experiences during her girlhood: "I did not discover till years afterwards that Mr. Thorne's intemperance was not the only annoyance she suffered from him. . . . He had poured vile language into the ears" of the young girl (*I*, 179).

Brent's metaphoric description of the exchange between Thorne and Ellen exactly mirrors those she used earlier in describing Dr. Flint's attempts to seduce her. Such reoccurrences challenge the notion of regional and political differences (Brent will soon call New York under the Fugitive Slave Law "the City of Iniquity"), since the use of the silenced black "slave" Ellen as a shield for white sins provides a parallel between the domestic life of slavery in the South and the domestic life of "freedom" in the North.

This pattern of duplicated suffering occurs in the vacuum created by white inaction, a vacuum that again demands that Brent emerge as the liberator. When it is discovered that Mr. Thorne has betrayed her location to Dr. Flint, Brent goes into hiding, but this time she takes Ellen with her. This rescue of another "slave girl" is achieved through "a mother's observing eye" (*I*, 178), since Brent has read distress on Ellen's face: Replaying both the failed role of Mrs. Flint and the problematic role of Aunt Martha, Brent again defines the ideal of liberating maternity as one that must be informed by a willingness to come to terms with the physical nature of black female exploitation. Because of her own experience in slavery, she alone can claim the power of bodily interpretation. Also, Brent's recognition of Ellen's pain is mirrored by the daughter's own attempt to quiet her mother's silent fears about revealing the circumstance of her birth: "I know all about it mother. . . . All my love is for you" (*I*, 189). Thus the acknowledged suffering of mother and daughter enables isolating silences to be replaced with mutual understanding and comfort. In a sense Ellen and her mother do not need to speak of their experiences: the nature of their slavery – and Brent's ability to understand the terms of black female exploitation and to use them as the basis for a successful rescue of herself and her family – has already been voiced by the narrative's account of their reunion.

Long before Brent obtains her legal freedom, then, she articulates a particular kind of salvation that reunites the voice with the body of the slave, celebrates black actions against slavery, and finally appropriates the domestic discourse of maternity in order to reform it for the use of black women. But if Brent is now the successful mother, the successful speaker, and the successful abolitionist (at least in the sense of obtaining a relative freedom for herself and her children), what role then does the Northerner play? Although *Incidents* suggests that Northern whites might actually represent a negative social force against the abolition of the slave's condition, the text does not finally accept rigid binaries as the only ground for black–white interaction. Throughout Brent has been helped in small ways by Southern slave mistresses, slave traders, and others who empathize with the slave's plight. But for Brent effective white empathy must be accompanied with an activism that acknowledges a connection rather than a dislocation between black and white bodies.

After the death of his English wife, Mr. Bruce remarries, and Brent's new American mistress serves as the narrative's closing model for the ideal white abolitionist. When Brent is forced into hiding to escape the Flint family, the new Mrs. Bruce, like her Southern counterpart, is called upon to offer protection. However, unlike Mrs. Flint, who recoiled from any connection to Brent, Mrs. Bruce embraces a strategy of redemption that causes her to risk her own domestic peace for the sake of resisting the North's moral ineptitude.

Mrs. Bruce allows her own child to accompany Brent into hiding as a scheme to force the slave-catchers to alert the white mother should the slave be caught. For Brent this is not a paternalistic act, but one of self-sacrifice: "How few mothers would have consented to have one of their own babes become a fugitive, for the sake of a poor, hunted nurse, on whom the legislators of the country had let loose the bloodhounds" (*I*, 194). Mrs. Bruce's temporary abandonment of her child for the sake of a slave's freedom redefines the possibility of domestic feminism's role in abolition, because it forces Mrs. Bruce, even in a limited way, to experience the same sense of maternal loss that Brent experienced when she left her children in pursuit of their freedom. By breaking the Fugitive Slave Law, Mrs. Bruce invites imprisonment and financial penalties, and in doing so she demonstrates a willingness to endure a kind of physical suffering that does not duplicate slavery, but comes close to it: "I will go to the state's prison, rather than have any poor victim torn from *my* house, to be carried back to slavery" (*I*, 194).[33] Yet, although Brent's representation of Mrs. Bruce's active sympathy suggests that whites can help through a more sincere and deliberate sharing of risks, the fact that the slave's freedom can be secured only by a bill of sale between her benefactress and the Flint family still indicts the North: "the bill of sale is on record, and future generations will learn from it that women were articles of traffic in New York, late in the nineteenth century of the Christian religion" (*I*, 200).[34]

In concluding her critique, Brent refuses to validate the freedom offered to her in the North, but instead problematizes this freedom almost to the last sentence: "We are as free from the power of slaveholders as are the white people of the north; and though that . . . is not saying a great deal, it is a vast improvement in *my* condition" (*I*, 201). Brent's ambivalence arises from the fact that "the dream of my life is not yet realized. I do not sit with my children in a home of my own" (*I*, 201). These bitter reflections (Is the North really free of slavery? Do homelessness and the struggle to overcome poverty in the North represent a major improvement?) challenge naive notions of freedom and as such affirm the black critiques Jacobs has been working to uncover through the narrative of Linda Brent. Revering the memory of Aunt Martha, and fully aware of the new struggles that await her on the "dark and troubled sea" signified by Northern black life, Brent ends the narrative by validating herself as a survivor and an active critic of both the North's and the South's peculiar forms of social injustice.

Notes

My thanks to Keith L. T. Alexander, Barbara Christian, M. Giulia Fabi, and Stephanie Smith for their sensitive commentary on early drafts of this essay.

1. [Olive Gilbert, ed.], "Book of Life" in *Narrative of Sojourner Truth; A bondswoman of Olden times, With a History of Her Labors and Correspondence Drawn from Her "Book of Life"* (1878; rpt., New York: Oxford University Press, 1991), 138. Cited in text henceforth as *Narrative*, followed by page number.
2. See Hortense J. Spillers's "Mama's Baby, Papa's Maybe: An American Grammar Book," *Diacritics* 17 (Summer 1987): 65–81, for an excellent discussion of the popular construction of black women.
3. Truth had been a slave in New York state before the abolition of slavery in that region. She escaped in 1827.
4. In her book *The Word in Black and White: Reading "Race" in American Literature, 1638–1867* (New York: Oxford University Press, 1992), Dana D. Nelson also addresses Jacobs's critique of traditional notions of racial difference, and the complacency of readers. Although she and I arrive at what I feel are complementary conclusions, Nelson focuses more on the notion of how "sympathy" mediates Jacobs's critique of the reader: "The text repeatedly appeals to the sympathy of its readers, but at the same time it warns them to be careful about the motives and critical of the results of that sympathetic identification" (142).

5. Recalling her "deliberate calculation" to choose a sexual partner in order to maintain control over her life, Jacobs remarks through Linda Brent's narration that "it seemed less degrading to give one's self, than to submit to compulsion"; in Harriet Jacobs, *Incidents in the Life of a Slave Girl Written by Herself* (1861; rpt., Cambridge: Harvard University Press, 1987), 54, 55. Cited in this essay henceforth as *I* followed by page number.

6. Jean Fagan Yellin, "Introduction," *Incidents in the Life of a Slave Girl, Written by Herself* (Cambridge: Harvard University Press, 1987), xxvi. See also Bruce Mills, "Lydia Maria Child and the Endings of Harriet Jacobs's *Incidents in the Life of a Slave Girl*," *American Literature* 64:2 (June 1992): 255–72. Standard discussions of the cultural binary constructions of black and white womanhood include Barbara Christian, *Black Women Novelists: The Development of a Tradition, 1892–1976* (Westport, CT: Greenwood, 1980), specifically 7–14; Paula Giddings, *When and Where I Enter: The Impact of Black Women on Race and Sex in America* (Bantam, 1985), 47–55; Hazel Carby, *Reconstructing Womanhood: The Emergence of the Afro-American Woman Novelist* (New York: Oxford University Press, 1987), chapter 2.

7. According to Karen Sánchez-Eppler, "the acceptability [of stories from slavery] . . . depends upon their adherence to a feminine and domestic demeanor that softens the cruelty they describe and makes their political goals more palatable to a less politicized readership." See "Bodily Bonds: The Intersecting Rhetorics of Feminism and Abolition," *Representations* 24 (Fall 1988): 35. For other discussions of Harriet Jacobs, Linda Brent, and their relationship to the narrative's audience, see Carby, *Reconstructing Womanhood*, 45–61; Valerie Smith, "'Loopholes of Retreat': Architecture and Ideology in Harriet Jacobs's *Incidents in the Life of a Slave Girl*," in *Reading Black, Reading Feminist: A Critical Anthology*, ed. Henry Louis Gates, Jr. (New York: Meridian, 1990): 212–26; P. Gabrielle Foreman, "The Spoken and the Silenced in *Incidents in the Life of a Slave Girl* and *Our Nig*," *Callaloo* 13 (Spring 1990): 313–24; Beth Maclay Doriani, "Black Womanhood in Nineteenth-Century America: Subversion and Self-Construction in Two Women's Autobiographies," *American Quarterly* 43 (June 1991): 199–222; Fanny Nudelman, "Harriet Jacobs and the Sentimental Politics of Female Suffering," *ELH* (59) 1992: 939–64; Harryette Mullen, "Runaway Tongue: Resistant Orality in *Uncle Tom's Cabin, Our Nig, Incidents in the Life of a Slave Girl*, and *Beloved*" in *The Culture of Sentiment: Race, Gender, and Sentimentality in Nineteenth-Century America*, ed. Shirley Samuels (New York: Oxford University Press, 1992): 244–64, 332–5.

8. See Yellin's *Woman and Sisters: The Antislavery Feminists in American Culture* (New Haven: Yale University Press, 1989). Also, Ronald G. Walters, "The Erotic South: Civilization and Sexuality in American Abolitionism," *American Quarterly* 25 (May 1973): 177–201. For a useful look at the rhetoric of white feminist abolitionists and its relationship to the bodies of male and female slaves see Sánchez-Eppler, "Bodily Bonds," and William Andrews, *To Tell a Free Story: The First Century of Afro-American Autobiography, 1760–1865* (Urbana: University of Illinois Press, 1988), 241–7.

9. See Stowe's rebuff of Jacobs over the publication of the latter's story in the *Key to Uncle Tom's Cabin* in Yellin, "Introduction," xviii–xix. Jacobs's letters to Amy Post also reveal her anger and distrust for Stowe. They are reprinted in *Incidents*, 233–37.

10. See Frances Foster's "'In Respect to Females . . . ': Differences in the Portrayals of Women by Male and Female Narrators," *Black American Literature Forum*, 15: 2 (Summer 1981): 66–70.

11. Walters, "Erotic South," 189. According to Carolyn L. Karcher, one of the many challenges faced by white abolitionist writers was the problem of even discussing the occurrences of rape, torture, incest, or murder under slavery, since any representation of these issues would have been insulting to the sensibilities of American white women of the North. See her "Rape, Murder and Revenge in 'Slavery's Pleasant Homes': Lydia Maria Child's Antislavery Fiction and the Limits of Genre," *Women's Studies International Forum* 9: 4 (1986): 323.

12. See Yellin, *Women and Sisters*, and Sánchez-Eppler, "Bodily Bonds."

13. Whereas Child and Post see Harriet Jacobs and Linda Brent as the same person, I would argue that to some extent Jacobs is fictionalizing her life experiences through the character of Brent, or, according to P. Gabrielle Foreman, at least shielding herself through the narrator. See Foreman's "The Spoken and the Silenced."

14. See Carolyn L. Karcher's discussion in "Censorship, American Style: the Case of Lydia Maria Child," *Studies in the American Renaissance, 1986*; ed. Joel Myerson (Charlottesville: University Press of Virginia, 1986), 283–303.

15. Quoted in Yellin, "Introduction," xxii. Karcher also discusses this practice in the context of antislavery fiction in "Rape, Murder and Revenge," 330. Bruce Mill's "Lydia Maria Child and the Endings to Harriet Jacobs's *Incidents*" is the most recent discussion of Child's role as editor.

16. For other readings of Child's introduction, see Valerie Smith, "Loopholes of Retreat," 218–23, and Foreman, "The Spoken and the Silenced," 316–17.

17. Child is acting the part of the conscientious editor, given the traditional expectations of white readers. According to William Andrews, "nineteenth century whites read slave narratives more to get a firsthand look at the institution of slavery than to become acquainted with an individual slave." Indeed, a "reliable slave narrative would be one that seemed purely mimetic, in which the self is on the periphery instead of at the center of attention, . . . transcribing rather than interpreting a set of objective facts" (*To Tell a Free Story*, 5–6).

18. Though he fails to underscore the importance of race in the determination of privacy, Richard H. Brodhead nevertheless offers an important discussion on the subject of (un)veiled presentations in "Veiled Ladies: Towards a History of Antebellum Entertainment," *American Literary History* 1 (Summer 1989): 273–94.

19. In a letter to the *National Anti-Slavery Standard*, one reader of *Incidents* objected to the existence of slave commentary: "A few sentences in which the moral is rather oppressively displayed, might have been omitted with advantage. These, it is to be wished, Mrs. Child had felt herself authorized to expunge. They are the strongest witnesses who leave the summing up to the judge, and the verdict to the jury" (quoted in Yellin, "Introduction," xxiv–xxv).

20. In her letter to Post, Jacobs writes: "I think it would be best for you to begin with our acquaintance and the length of time I was in your family   your advice about giving the history of my life in Slavery   mention that I lived at service all the while that I was striving to get the Book out . . . . – my kind friend I do not restrict you in anything for you know far better than I do what to say" (reprinted in *I*, 242).

21. In an earlier letter to Post in 1852, which mentions Post's "proposal" that Jacobs make her story public, the latter says: "dear Amy if it was the life of a Heroine with no degradation associated with it   far better to have been one of the starving poor of Ireland whose bones had to bleach on the highways than to have been a slave with the curse of slavery stamped upon yourself and Children" (reprinted in *I*, 232). Is Jacobs just ashamed of her experience under slavery, as Post's appendix seems to imply, or is she instead trustful of the Northern reading public?

22. Although Post did urge Jacobs to write the narrative, Jacobs had never doubted the need for her own political activism: "My conscience approved it but my stubborn pride would not yield   I have tried for the past two years to conquer it and I feel that God has helped me or I never would consent to give my past life to any one for I would not do it without giving the whole truth   if it could help save another from my fate it would be selfish and unchristian in me to keep it back" (reprinted in *I*, 232). One of the chief causes she lists for not writing is her situation on the household staff of proslavery Nathaniel P. Willis.

23. Harriet Jacobs's 1860 letter to Amy Post, reprinted in *I*, 247.

24. While acknowledging for a moment the critical explanation that Brent/Jacobs embraces maternity within her narrative as a strategy to engage Northern sympathies, we need to recognize that maternity itself is a highly problematic category in *Incidents*. Although she has been acting in the capacity of a mother since the birth of her children during slavery, Brent is not officially allowed to accept the status of mother until the final pages of the narrative when, as a free woman, she can own herself and so own her children. The category of the slave-mother embodied by the character Linda Brent functions not just as a category for her presentation to American readers, but also as a metaphor for instability to describe Brent's lifelong struggle against social processes that govern her identity.

25. For an illuminating recent discussion of Southern etiquette around miscegenation and the rape of slave women by white men, see Catherine Clinton, " 'Southern Dishonor': Flesh, Blood, Race, and Bondage," in *In Joy and in Sorrow: Women, Family, and Marriage in the Victorian South, 1830–1900*, ed. Carol Bleser (New York: Oxford University Press, 1991): 52–68, 281–84.

26. Certainly the descriptions of Flint's initial attempts to corrupt Brent are marked with what other readers have called "omissions and circumlocution" designed to give some modicum of protection to the narrator – who seems unwilling to relive the details of the event – or to encourage the potential voyeurism of the white reader regarding Brent's experience of a distressing situation. See Yellin, "Introduction," xxi, and especially Foreman, "The Spoken and the Silenced," 317.

27. I am grateful to M. Giulia Fabi for helping me develop this idea.

28. Though Hortense Spillers gives a different but related reading of Mrs. Flint's role as seducer, I am indebted to her discussion for the formulation of my own.

29. Contemporary scholars have long been fascinated by Brent's discussion of her affair with Mr. Sands, because it seems to be a curious mixture of shame, regret, defiance, and "deliberate calculation" (*I*, 24). For illuminating discussions of Brent's description of her affair with Sands in the context of a domestic narrative that shuns any discussion of sexuality, see Yellin, "Introduction," xxix–xxxi; Foreman, "The Spoken and the Silenced," 322–3; Valerie Smith, "Loopholes of Retreat," 222; Andrews, *To Tell a Free Story*, 254–6. See also Laura E. Tanner,

"Self-Conscious Representation in The Slave Narrative," *Black American Literature Forum* 21: 4 (Winter 1987): 415–24.

30. See her "Rape, Murder and Revenge," esp. 330.

31. Mills, "Lydia Marie Child . . .," 259.

32. Ibid.; see also Stephanie A. Smith, "Conceived in Liberty: Maternal Iconography and American Literature, 1830–1900" (Ph.D. dissertation, University of California, Berkeley, 1990), 179.

33. Interestingly, Jacobs originally ended her narrative with a chapter on John Brown, the white militant abolitionist executed for his attack on Harper's Ferry. In a letter to Jacobs, Child said she thought it "had better be omitted," adding that "Nothing could be so appropriate to end with, as the death of your grandmother" (reprinted in *I*, 244). Arguing for the appeasement of the audience through an appeal to their sympathies, Child wanted to steer Jacobs away from discussions about direct political action by encouraging her to end with "tender memories of my good old grandmother, like light fleecy clouds floating over a dark and troubled sea" (*I*, 201). For a discussion of Child's reaction to John Brown see Mills, "Lydia Marie Child . . .," 255–72.

34. Echoing William Andrews, Dana D. Nelson argues that Mrs. Bruce is still a slave-holder and that for Brent, "serving, whether under compulsion or privilege, remains servitude: the structure of this sympathetic identification is one of hierarchy, not equality." However, although Brent articulates an unmistakable resentment by the narrative's end, her anger is directed not at Mrs. Bruce herself, as some critics have suggested, but at the contradictory legal and social "circumstances" allowed to develop in the North, so that Mrs. Bruce's genuine act against the slaveholders is itself compromised by its resemblance to slavery. For Nelson's comments, see *The Word in Black and White*, 141. See also Andrews, *To Tell a Free Story*, 260–2.

HARRIET JACOBS, FREDERICK DOUGLASS, AND THE SLAVERY DEBATE

BONDAGE, FAMILY, AND THE DISCOURSE OF DOMESTICITY

DONALD B. GIBSON

My master had law and power on his side; I had a determined will. There is might in each.

Harriet Jacobs[1]

The kindness of the slave-master only gilds the chain of slavery, and detracts nothing from its weight or power.

Frederick Douglass[2]

The power of the master must be absolute to render the submission of the slave perfect.

Judge Thomas Ruffin[3]

Ulrich Bonnell Phillips was the earliest, most widely read, and most influential twentieth-century historian of Afro-American slavery. An extraordinarily well-read, well-educated, shrewd, and intelligent white native of South Carolina, he was also an apologist for slavery, a man who believed that slavery was just and right because Africans were an inherently inferior people and slavery offered the best possibility for civilizing them. He was thus a participant – a key one, while ostensibly merely writing history – in the slavery debate. Although he wrote many decades after the publication of the narratives here considered – those of Harriet Jacobs and Frederick Douglass – he is still engaged in struggle with them. They join with many others before and after them in a debate of long standing about what slavery is, about its nature or its character.

Phillips's book, *American Negro Slavery* (1918), his first major salvo in the debate, emerged from a tradition of thinking about Southern slavery that began long before he first drew breath.[4] The tradition's inception extends back to the eighteenth century, when slaveholders responded to attacks on slavery by attempting to justify slaveholding to themselves and to the world. Many slaveholders began to feel the need to answer questions that others began asking, especially Quakers – Benjamin Lay, Jonathan Woolman, and others – about the justice and rightness of enslaving people who by common sense and Biblical injunction could not be other than human beings, God's creatures.

As one reads the history of slavery, and sees its developments reflected in, for example, colonial statutes from the early seventeenth century onward, it becomes increasingly clear that nobody in colonial America knew what American slavery was. Hence the beginning of a debate, a contention of opposing forces intent on capturing the meaning of slavery and convincing the world of its truth. There were literal definitions derived from Biblical examples and existing within the boundaries of ordinary experience and knowledge, but the complexion of New World slavery had yet to be worked out through economic, political, social, and moral contingencies.

Confusion and moral indecision about what slavery was in the United States are reflected, during the whole period of slavery's legal existence, in the unsettled usage of the terms "slave" and "servant." Throughout slavery's duration (whenever it might be imagined actually to have begun) the terms were frequently used interchangeably, "servant" often functioning as a euphemism for the harsher and more opprobrious term "slave,"[5] though among individuals less concerned about politeness, there would likely be no compunction about referring to blacks using terms far less polite than "slave."[6] The simultaneous usage of the two terms lays open the slavery debate: If the Africans brought to the United States were "slaves," the institution was one thing; if they were "servants," it was quite another.

The slavery debate, in which Jacobs and Douglass became in its nineteenth-century phase essential participants, grew especially intense in the later eighteenth century. During that period colonists were carving out their own freedom through reference to the natural rights doctrine, reflected in the word and deed: in *word* through the Declaration of Independence and the Constitution, in *deed* through the Revolution. The connection between slavery and the Revolution is revealed in the fact that thinking about the rightness of slavery changed at this time in some colonies. Rhode Island ended slavery in 1774, shortly before the war began, and Massachusetts in 1777, during it. Revolutionary ideology, though it resulted in many slaves being freed, did not serve to end slavery. Its existence served instead to require a counter-response to the issue. If the political philosophy of natural rights allowed for the freedom of men throughout the country, then how could black men justifiably remain anywhere enslaved?

In opposition to natural rights doctrine, slaveholding ideology portrayed slavery as deriving its character not from philosophical principle but from institutional mandate, its relation to family. Slavery was defined as an extension of the traditional patriarchal family. The slave occupied a station within the family hierarchy of the "domestic" institution, not entirely unlike that customarily belonging to servants or apprentices.[7] Not only did such an analogy allow one to subject the relationships between slaves and others to order and understanding (as imagining God as father leads to an order and understanding – of sorts – of the universe), it also justified imagining slaves as subservient, as children who, as such, needed parental control, direction, and support.

Despite the peculiarity of the slave's status as property and family member, during the nineteenth century the analogy-to-family argument became one of the chief and most frequently employed to justify slavery. In their descriptions of slavery, Harriet Jacobs and Frederick Douglass, to a much greater extent than most other narrators, insist that, whatever slavery might be, there is little of the character of benevolent domesticity associated with family life about it.[8] Both narrators make it abundantly clear that slavery and family life, as conceived in the antebellum South, are much at odds, the property relationship between slave and slaveowner precluding any such analogy. Jacobs and Douglass draw descriptions of life within their own families that stand in sharp contrast to the apologists' claims. In so doing, both challenge and deny those claims. As the historian Willie Lee Rose puts it,

> Proslavery philosophers intended to suggest a benign institution that encouraged between masters and slaves the qualities so much admired in the Victorian family: cheerful obedience and gratitude on the part of the children (read slaves), and paternalistic wisdom, protection, and discipline on the part of the father (read master). . . . So, in the nineteenth century, the phrase "domestic institution" came to mean slavery idealized, slavery translated into a fundamental and idealized Victorian institution, the family.[9]

The admission of "peculiarity" to the institution is a confession of variation from historical norms. Jacobs and Douglass both insist that slavery impedes the family relation, not promoting but obstructing and subverting it at every turn. This is the main thrust of the characterizations of slavery in both Jacobs's *Incidents in the Life of a Slave Girl* and Douglass's *My Bondage and My Freedom*.

William Andrews maintains that the 1855 edition of Douglass's autobiography differs from the 1845 version in the portrait of Douglass that emerges as one "who had been all too ready to attach himself to paternal figures whom he identified unconsciously with all that home signified."[10] I would modify this proposal to emphasize that Douglass's exposure to the women's movement, its influence on his thinking, and his immersion in Victorian values surrounding domesticity, led him to emphasize the effect of slavery on the family to such an extent that it becomes a far more major theme in the second edition of his autobiography than in the first, though even there it is prominent.[11] I would also argue that if we consider *My Bondage and My Freedom* in light of the political perspective from which both of its versions were written, it then becomes clear that, whatever the psychological motivations driving the narrative, the ideological ones, because conscious and intentional, must of necessity be regarded in interpreting the text.

The kind of discourse that Jacobs and Douglass write against is aptly represented in the sentiments expressed by one of the most widely known and most extreme of the Southern apologists for slavery, George Fitzhugh, who contends that

> The slaves are all well-fed, well clad, have plenty of fuel, and are happy. They have no dread of the future – no fear of want. A state of dependence is the only condition in which reciprocal affection can exist among human beings – the only situation in which the war of competition ceases, and peace, amity and good will arise. A state of independence always begets more or less of jealous rivalry and hostility. A man loves his children because they are weak, helpless and dependent. He loves his wife for similar reasons. . . . He ceases to love his wife when she becomes masculine or rebellious; but slaves are always dependent, never the rivals of their masters. . . . He [the slave master] would scorn to put on airs of command among blacks, whether slave or free; he always speaks to them in a kind of subdued tone. . . . His whole life is spent in providing for the minutest wants of others in taking care of them in sickness and in health. . . . Nature compels master and slave to be friends.[12]

Every word of Douglass's and Jacobs's narratives is testament against Fitzhugh's and countless others' claims regarding not only the benevolence of the Southern slave-holding patriarch but the nature and character of slavery itself. Fitzhugh's representation of slavery, the prototype of its popular image in the American mind in innumerable nineteenth- and twentieth-century characterizations, belies the facts. Most slaveholders were not the grand patriarchs Fitzhugh conjures up; few in fact belonged to the planter class. Eighty-eight percent of slaveholders owned fewer than twenty slaves.[13] For example, Booker T. Washington's owner in 1860, John Burroughs, possessed four adult slaves, two men and two women. He and his sons worked in the fields alongside them.[14] Such a situation was by no means unique. Many slave owners, for that matter, owned only one slave. The large majority of Southerners, nearly 75 percent, contrary to popular opinion, owned none.[15]

Comparison of the openings of the 1845 and the 1855 editions of Douglass's narrative reveals between them a somewhat altered focus, the revision accountable finally to an emphasis on family and sharply at odds with Fitzhugh's picture. Whereas the 1845 *Narrative*, when it focuses on the narrator, dwells on the system of slavery as by definition withholding the knowledge belonging to any person who is not a slave, the 1855 *My Bondage and Freedom*'s personal focus is on the lack of knowledge specifically accruing from circumstances far more specific than the existence of slavery itself, the absence of the father: "genealogical trees do not flourish among slaves. A person of some consequence here in the north, sometimes designated *father*, is literally abolished in slave law and practice" (28). In other words, the fact that "I never met with a slave who could tell me how old he was" does not stem from the desire on the part of the slaveowner to withhold knowledge but from the deleterious effect of slavery on the family.

In *Bondage and Freedom* Douglass thus reinterprets his experience of slavery by describing its role in impeding the existence of normal domestic relations. The place given to his mother in *Narrative* is filled and enlarged by his grandmother in the later work; since he hardly knew his mother (slavery took her away), it was his grandmother who filled the mother's role, who was the center of the domestic space he occupied as a child. She is a mother who provides a home that offers not only support and nourishment but also the knowledge useful for survival – she is a skilled weaver of fishing nets and highly knowledgeable about planting, a subject explored at length by the historian Sterling Stuckey.[16]

> In this little hut [his grandmother's carved out domestic space] there was a large family of children. . . . My grandmother – whether because too old for field service, or because she had so faithfully discharged the duties of her station in early life, I know not – enjoyed the high privilege of living in a cabin, separate from the quarter, with no other burden than her own support, and the necessary care of the little children, imposed. She evidently esteemed it a great fortune to live so. The children were not her own, but her grandchildren – the children of her daughters. She took delight in having them around her, and in attending to their few wants. (*Bondage and Freedom*, 29)

The line that follows tells of the common practice of separating children from their mothers, so this motherly refuge is at least for a while a defense against the evils of slavery. The fact that the grandmother later delivers Douglass to "old master" and abandons him reveals little about his grandmother's disposition. He hears talk that informs him that "old master" allows children to live with the grandmother for only so long, until they were "big enough." Douglass's primary intent is not to call attention to a childhood betrayal, as some commentators suggest,[17] but rather to point to the insidious effect of slavery on the closest family ties. Separation from his grandmother is the first of many sunderings of family ties yet to come. Douglass looks back at the separation:

> My grandmother! my grandmother! and the little hut, and the joyous circle under her care, but especially *she*, who made us sorry when she left us but for an hour, and glad on her return, – how could I leave her and the good old home? (31)

We might ignore the obvious sentimentality here ("how could I leave her and the good old home?") in order to point to our specific interest, our concern being not so much with Douglass's sentimentality as with his use of it. Sentimentality is called upon when Douglass's grandmother points out to him his siblings at Colonel Lloyd's plantation, when he indicates that he has no sense of kinship with them because he does not know them, that no family relationship has been allowed to evolve:

> I really did not know what they were to me or I to them. We were brothers and sisters, but what of that? Why should they be attached to me, or I to them? Brothers and sisters we were by blood; but *slavery* had made us strangers. I heard the words brother and sisters, and knew they must mean something; but slavery had robbed these terms of their true meaning. (36)

The emphasis on home, present in the 1845 *Narrative*, is maximized in *Bondage and Freedom*. Comparison of the passages in the earlier and later works describing the moment of Douglass's leaving Colonel Lloyd's plantation for Baltimore reveals an expansion of the idea of home and a deepened significance of the concept. The family is described by absence, by negativity. What the family is is what Douglass does not have, and this is reflected in the negative inflection of the language. Consider the language of the first sentence ("dead," "far off," "seldom") and note how the diction carries through the following passages.

> My mother was dead, my grandmother lived far off, so that I seldom saw her. I had two sisters and one brother, that lived in the same house with me; but the early separation of us from our mother had well nigh blotted the fact of our relationship from our memories. I looked for home elsewhere, and was confident of finding none which I should relish less than the one which I was leaving. (73)

Bondage and Freedom expands the idea of the incompatibility of slavery and reasonably amiable familial relations. Again the family is defined in negative terms, by absence.

My mother was now long dead; my grandmother was far away, so that I seldom saw her; Aunt Katy was my unrelenting tormentor [not the mother he might have had]; and my two sisters and brothers, owing to our early separation in life, and the family destroying power of slavery, were, comparatively, strangers to me. The fact of our relationship was almost blotted out. I looked for *home* elsewhere, and was confident of finding none which I should relish less than the one I was leaving. (86)

The emphasis in both *Narrative* and *Bondage and Freedom* is *not* on Douglass's obsession with the identity of his father, and on the recovery of a lost patrimony, as so many recent commentators have insisted,[18] but on his wish to establish a family. What might appear to western critics inclined to Freudian interpretations to be a search for the father for the individual's bearings and orientation, is in fact a wish to establish community, a mode of response far more compatible with an Africanist bent, more in keeping with the subject's historical connection to his African past, a relation drawn out in *Bondage and Freedom*.[19]

The whole line of thinking, as reflected in the work of Peter Walker and Annette Niemtzow,[20] that identifies Douglass's aspirations simply with nineteenth-century mainstream individualism and white patriarchalism, does not take into account Douglass's relationship to his African heritage.[21] Binary thinking is at its least productive moment here because the naive assumption is that Douglass is choosing between black and white. In reality, he is mediating among far more complex alternatives. He is not choosing between black and white; he is not choosing between upper and lower class (black or white); he is not choosing between a vernacular and a mainstream cultural orientation; he is not choosing between men – in pursuing Emerson's clearly male scheme of self-reliance[22] – and women through his life-long identification with and support of the rights of women.

I contend that every reference in the narratives to needs ordinarily met by the family, according to Victorian standards, is a reference to family. Thus every reference to hunger relates to family: Hunger comes about because slavery does not allow the family to feed its young; lack of warmth comes about when parents are not allowed to provide it for children: "The great difficulty," Douglass tells, "was to keep warm during the night. I had no bed. The pigs in the pen had leaves, and the horses in the stable had straw, but the children had no beds" (84–5). Who supplies the meaning of the beds, not their "fact" but their "meaning"? The family, the missing ones: the mother, the father.

Harriet Jacobs's *Incidents in the Life of a Slave Girl* is no less focused on family; indeed it is even more intensely so.[23] Let us begin by emphasizing the two texts' similarities rather than their differences by insisting that differences stemming from the prerogatives of gender existing outside of and apart from the texts themselves do not of necessity set the texts at odds. Because Douglass is able to take the first step toward establishing a family immediately upon his escape to the North whereas Jacobs is not, should not set the two authors in antagonistic relation.[24] Douglass's first significant gesture after his escape from slavery is to marry Anna Murray.[25] Jacobs, in large part because she is both woman and black, has no such choice. We may hate the circumstance, but only lack of clear distinction between race and gender issues, and the assumption that considerations of gender must supersede considerations of race, will lead us to conclude that we must privilege one narrator or text over the other because one narrator finds it possible to be more free than the other. The salient point is that both Jacobs and Douglass choose to cast their narratives within the discourse of domesticity, both insisting on the connection between humanitarian and family values and decrying the deleterious effect of slavery on values associated with the home. The extent and degree of Jacobs's focus on domestic discourse is utterly pervasive for many reasons, but it is primarily because of considerations of gender that the scope of her narrative is far narrower than the scope of Douglass's second narrative.[26]

She begins her narrative, "I was born a slave; but I never knew it till six years of happy childhood had passed away" (5). This opening line allies Jacobs's narrative with many, many others, yet sets it immediately apart.[27] Most other slave narratives opening with the phrase "I was born" mean to make a comment about family: "I was born . . . " binds the child to a mother but sets it off from a surname and, in a patriarchal society where the surname bears such significance, a culture. The "I was born" is almost immediately followed by a declaration of ignorance about the identity of the father. The implication points to cultural, familial, discontinuity. Most narrators mean to suggest that their births lie unrecorded, their parents unknown, and their siblings unrecognized in a society where the condition of the child follows the status of its mother. Harriet Jacobs revises these opening words to mean something else. She immediately joins the antislavery debate; her salvo juxtaposes the opposition between slavery and domestic bliss: "I was born a slave; but I never knew it till six years of happy childhood had passed away." Slavery breaks in upon and destroys "happy childhood," a happy childhood that would have continued except for the rude intrusion of the realities of slavery. "I was born a slave" likewise means that slavery obtrudes into her life; for the first six years of her life she was not a slave because she did not *know* she was a slave.

The language of the opening chapters highlights the incongruity between slavery and family by contrasting, in the very language Jacobs chooses, the contradictory nature of the two institutions: a slave is by definition a commodity; a relative is entirely not a slave.[28] Much of the content of the opening paragraphs is intended to contrast domestic and marketplace values, to demonstrate through the act of speech itself the utter nonhuman character of slavery. Jacobs's argument is as much in her diction as in her logic.

His [her father's] strongest wish was to *purchase his children*; but, though he several times *offered his hard earnings* for that purpose, he never succeeded. . . . They lived together in a *comfortable home*; and, though we were all *slaves*, I was so *fondly shielded* that I never dreamed I was a *piece of merchandise*, *trusted* to them for *safe keeping*, and *liable* to be *demanded* of them [as goods may be, or silver or gold for a note] at any moment. (5, my emphasis)

The following words, relating to family and domestic affairs, occur (some of them several times) in the first three paragraphs of *Incidents* (5–7): "childhood," "father" (or its pronoun), "children," "parents," "together," "home," "fondly," "shielded," "brother," "child," "maternal," "grandmother" (or its pronoun), "daughter," "mother," "cook," "wet nurse," "seamstress," "cooking," "crackers," "bake," "uncle," "cakes," "preserves," "sister," "nourished," "breast," "babe," "food," "sewing."

The following words relating to market economy and commodity occur within the same space: "slave," "trade," "work," "paying," "dollars," "manage," "affairs," "purchase," "earnings," "merchandise," "demanded," "planter," "money," "captured," "sold," "master," "mistress," "interest," "valuable," "property," "profits," "terms," "business," "profitable," "laid by," "saved," "fund," "divided," "heirs," "dower," "service," "portion," "dollars and cents," "paid," "sale," "laid up," "loan," "pay," "property," "lent," "trusted," "slaveholder," "indebted," "sell," "servant," "labor," "chattel." This homely language of domesticity and the contrasting language of marketplace exchange are intended to raise the questions of human value around which the narrative revolves.

The question of the terms of the value and worth of a human being is raised persistently throughout the narrative. Under what circumstances may a person be bought or sold in the manner of a commodity? One is tempted to say "never." But the circumstances presented by the narrative disallow such a simple response. As it turns out, there is no single, clear, and obvious answer to the question, for slavery has so poisoned and perverted human values, in both North and South, that subversion of the institution or the thwarting of its claims may require one's participation in its machinations. In order, for example, for Harriet's children to be saved from slavery and for her family to have had the least possibility of being held together, they needed to be transferred from one slave owner to another. Their biological father is also their owner and master, a man who proves finally to be more slavemaster than father. The very first word of the narrative is "I"; the very last word of the third paragraph is "chattel." The character of the intervening discourse is meant to insist upon the moral and ethical distance between the terms and slavery's confounding of them. Had clear delineation of the terms been possible, then Harriet Jacobs's fate and the fate of her family might have been a different one. She is never able to escape the ramifications of her original status as chattel.

The word offsetting "chattel" and most frequently occurring within the first paragraphs of *Incidents* is the word "grandmother," appearing forty times. The references intend not only to point to the relation between the narrator and her forebear but to establish the major theme of the narrative as well, for the space given to the grandmother is in effect space given to the mother, since the relationship between Harriet and her grandmother is more like that between mother and child than otherwise. ("My grandmother had, as much as possible, been a mother to her orphan grandchildren," 17.) The grandmother's place in Jacobs's narrative is much greater and more central on the whole than in Douglass's, largely because of their relations of both blood and gender. We might imagine that the role of Douglass's grandmother in his life would have been greater had he been able to maintain contact with her during the whole time of his enslavement. It must also be allowed that Jacobs's focus on family is more involved because she was engaged with her family to an extent that Douglass could not have been.

Throughout Harriet's life, her grandmother is by precept and example the champion of domestic values.[29] She owns her own home, a circumstance practically unheard of among slaves; and that home is the center around which the lives of her grandchildren and great-grandchildren revolve, if not literally, narratively, for the first chapter focuses on values surrounding the home even though the grandmother does not initially own one.[30] She firmly believes that even slavery should be endured if its alternative means the rending of family bonds: it is better to submit to the yoke of slavery than to sever family ties.[31]

When Harriet's brother William escapes slavery by leaving Mr. Sands, the father of Harriet's children, while on a Northern trip, Harriet's grandmother reacts in such a way as to suggest she values family over freedom: "If you had seen the tears, and heard the sobs, you would have thought the messenger had brought tidings of death instead of freedom. Poor old grandmother felt that she should never see her darling boy again" (134). "It seems," the grandmother says to a slave neighbor regarding William's escape, "as if I shouldn't have any of my children or grandchildren left to hand me a drink when I'm dying, and lay my old body in the ground. My boy didn't come back with Mr. Sands. He staid [*sic*] at the north" (135).

Harriet's grandmother has, through strength, endurance, intelligence, perseverance, frugality, and faith been able to reconcile herself to her condition and even to carve out a space allowing her to survive comparatively well within the confines of the peculiar institution. She expects Harriet, no less than William and other family members, to adjust to the requirements of the situation. When Harriet's initial plan to escape is put into action, her grandmother reacts in a highly emotional although not entirely irrational manner.

The grandmother's response comes totally out of domestic values centering around the primacy of family relations: "Linda, do you want to kill your old grandmother? Do you mean to leave your little, helpless children? I am old now, and cannot do for your babies as I once did for you" (91). She analyzes, in a highly correct and reasonable way, as subsequent events reveal, Harriet's understanding of her own situation. She tells her grandmother that if she were to disappear, the children's father, Mr. Sands, would be able to "secure their freedom" (91). Her grandmother, evincing the wisdom of her age, replies:

> "Ah, my child . . . don't trust too much to him [a Southern white man whose name – Sands – evokes images of the least substantial of foundation materials]. Stand by your own children, and suffer with them till death. Nobody respects a mother who forsakes her children; and if you leave them, you will never have a happy moment. If you go, you will make me miserable the short time I have to live. . . . Do give it up, Linda. . . . Things may turn out better than we expect." (91)

A rupture appears here between Jacobs's emotions and her ideology. The narrative reveals that whereas Jacobs does not agree ideologically with her grandmother, she fully understands and sympathizes with the grandmother's response to her grandson's flight. It is clear enough that Jacobs partly agrees and partly disagrees with her grandmother. Before her Uncle Benjamin's first attempt to escape, Harriet, failing to dissuade him with other arguments, finally appeals to his sense of loyalty to family and to his mother: "Go," said I, "and break your mother's heart" (21). The chapter's title, "The Slave Who Dared to Feel Like a Man," makes it clear enough that his unwillingness to accept the terms of slavery and his desire to escape are worthwhile values. Yet the grandmother's perspective is also "right." It is only normal and natural, the narrative makes clear, that her grandmother should desire overwhelmingly that her family should remain intact. It would be perverse if the grandmother were content never to see her grandson again. But slavery renders impossible the pursuance of right and ordinary family goals. Slavery turns reasonable desires regarding family upside down, making moral judgments so complex as to be finally incapable of clarity. It is a perversity stemming from slavery, the narrative argues, that the grandmother should be forced into the position of rejoicing that she will probably never see her son again! The disparity between abstraction and felt experience does not at all constitute paradox or logical inconsistency, it merely signals slavery's utter disdain for and utter incompatibility with ordinary, family values.

The implicit belief on the part of the author of *Incidents*, that domestic values prevail by nature and *should* prevail politically over marketplace values, is continually insisted upon throughout the narrative. The point is brought to bear in the implicit comparison Hazel Carby makes between Harriet's grandmother and Mrs. Flint insofar as their maternal roles as nourishers are concerned.[32] The narrator tells us that "Little attention was paid to the slaves' meals in Dr. Flint's house. If they could catch a bit of food while it was going, well and good. I gave myself no trouble on that score, for on my various errands I passed my grandmother's house, where there was always something to spare for me" (10). Mrs. Flint, in stark contrast, exhibits not the good but the evil mother's attitude toward the nourishing of dependents: "If dinner was not served at the exact time on that particular Sunday, she would station herself in the kitchen, and wait till it was dished, and then spit in all the kettles and pans that had been used for cooking. She did this to prevent the cook and her children from eking out their meagre fare with the remains of the gravy and other scrapings" (12).

As might be expected in a narrative so intensely focused on slavery as filtered through the lens of domesticity, food, because that was always one of the basic issues of slavery, is of central significance. (In all the slave narratives, of course, food is a cardinal concern.) Mrs. Flint's perverse denying of adequate food to her slaves stands in sharp contrast to Harriet's grandmother's supplying of food to Harriet's mother's foster sister. Harriet's mother is weaned at three months in order that her white foster sister might be adequately fed: the slave feeds the enslaver; the enslaver denies adequate nourishment to the enslaved. Dr. Flint's use of food as a means of control is no less aberrant than his wife's. Mrs. Flint spits in the pots as punishment for meals not being served on time. Dr. Flint, an epicure, forces the cook to eat every mouthful of any dish felt by him to be inadequately prepared. Not only is the cook forced to eat the mush that the family's slavering dog refuses to eat, but she is sometimes punished by being locked away from her nursing baby "for a whole day and night" (13). Elements of the narrative involving food create the distinction between friend and enemy. When she is conveyed into hiding in the home of her friend Betty's mistress – the unnamed benefactress – Harriet's welcome and safety are assured by shibboleths involving food. The person who offers food rather than withholding it can be trusted to protect and sustain in all other ways.

> Her [Betty's] first words were: "Honey, now you is safe. Dem devils ain't coming to search *dis* house. When I get you into missis' safe place, I will bring some nice hot supper. I specs you need it after all dis skeering. (100)

Shortly thereafter the benefactress appears, saying:

> "I will keep the girls busy in the morning, that Betty may have a chance to bring your breakfast." . . . Betty came with the "nice hot supper," and the mistress hastened down stairs to keep things straight till she returned. (100)

It is only when she is most deeply in the clutches of slavery that food becomes a major issue. Once Harriet is in the hands of friends, in either the North or the South, food is not a problem; the closer Harriet is to slavery, the more confined she and her compatriots are, the less control they have over their status, the more likely is food to pose a problem of great significance.

Two early episodes intended to represent the moral necessity and desirability of domestic values prevailing over market values or values antithetical to familial ones exist in (1) the scene where Harriet's brother William is called at the same time by his father and his mistress; (2) the scene in which Aunt Martha goes by choice upon the auction block. In Chapter Two, when the first incident occurs, the narrator makes clear what the issues are:

> One day, when his father and his mistress had happened to call him at the same time, he hesitated between the two; being perplexed to know which had the strongest claim upon his obedience. He finally concluded to go to his mistress. When my father reproved him for it, he said, "You both called me, and I didn't know which I ought to go to first."
>
> "You are *my* child" replied our father, "and when I call you, you should come immediately, if you have to pass through fire and water." (9)

It is clear where the narrator's values lie. Is the child's allegiance to the slavemaster? The values of domesticity, according to the narrator's unequivocal implication, prevail over those of the marketplace. The child should answer to the real, social, and biological parent, not to the pseudo, ideologically spawned parent – the slavemaster. If the child must answer to the master, then the extent of the compulsion to do so reflects the degree of perversity of slavery.

The narrative focus on drawing the contrast between slavery and domestic values is nowhere better illustrated than in the scene where Aunt Martha, Harriet's grandmother, takes control of the very symbol of slavery, the auction block, for that site in its context brings into sharp relief the conflicts immediately emerging when people are treated as commodities. She confronts slavery head on with an antithetical cluster of values.

> When the day of sale came, she took her place among the chattels, and at the first call she sprang upon the auction-block. Many voices called out, "Shame! Shame! Who is going to sell *you*, aunt Marthy? Don't stand there! That is no place for *you*." (11)

She can't be sold because she is shown to possess human attributes. The auction block is not objected to, in this scene, because it is a site for the exchange of money for black human flesh in general, just hers. "Every body who knew her respected her intelligence and good character" (11). Thus the auction block, a gateway into slavery or a point of exchange between one slave circumstance and another, becomes for Aunt Martha the turnstile out. She is bought for a token amount and set free by virtue of her capacity to pit the power of true domestic values against that of slavery, cleverly knowing how, in one dramatic gesture, to counterpoise her status as person against her status as slave. The seemingly mixed metaphors of the narrator's description of this scene actually reflect Martha's choreographing her movement among the different modes of perception of her situation.

Whereas Linda's grandmother comes close to having what she most desires – freedom and a home for her family – she does not achieve all; slavery will not allow that, will not allow her to live unfettered with her children, grandchildren, and great-grandchildren in one domestic space. She acquires the space, even within the confines of the institution of slavery, yet she is never allowed to fill the space with all its proper occupants. She cannot become one of these "careless daughters" of the North, for slavery will not allow her freedom from care. Her daughter, Linda's mother, dies, it is implied, as a result of her enslavement. Her son-in-law, Linda's father, also dies a victim of slavery, another instance of slavery's impingement upon the protections ordinarily accruing from institutional domestic arrangements.

The limits standing between Linda and the literal obtaining of a physical space that she can call home are reflected in the legal, physical, and psychological boundaries confining her. The legal boundaries confining her are the laws giving sanction to her confinement as a slave and supporting the slaveowner in his ownership of slaves. These are not merely the state statutes forbidding assembly and denying the sanctity of slave marriage, but all laws and legal proceedings supporting slave-holding interests, such as the Dred Scott decision, and, above all insofar as Linda is concerned, the Fugitive Slave Act. These are not abstract obstructions to black people; they have specific and definable effects on Linda. The impingement of law upon Linda is specifically manifested in her daily interaction with Dr. Flint, to the extent that their legal relationship sets out the parameters within which they act out their roles. Not slavery alone but the laws upholding it and empowering slaveowners impede Linda's efforts to establish a home and thus live in proper relation to her family and a society.

Linda's physical and psychological confinement are not separable from her legal confinement, since the former proceed from the latter. Her psychological confinement consists in being compelled to live within the Flint household, where her free space is constricted by Dr. Flint's real or imagined presence – literally within the house, but also anywhere in the area, in the town and its environs, and ultimately, with the passage of the Fugitive Slave Act, in the nation. Where he is, is suspected to be, or plans to be, whether his is an actual or presumed presence, wherever his agents are or are suspected to be, constitute the boundaries of Linda's space, the literal areas where she may in fact not feel safe, at first in his house and its environs, then in the South, and aeventually anywhere within the country.

The psychological boundaries, again inseparable from the physical and

the legal, force her to feel constrained. Her physical confinement is metaphorically rendered in her enclosure in the small spaces characterizing her
mode of existence during literal enslavement.[33] Chief among these is her en-
capsulation for seven years within the garret of her grandmother's house.
Prior to this "grand enslavement" is her "escape" into restricted territories,
spaces of confinement but not homes. The places she squeezes herself into –
spaces beneath floors, attics, closets – are far less than abodes, hardly houses,
and absolutely not homes. In contrast to her grandmother's home, they are
called in turn: "cell" (100), "small room" (100), "shallow bed" (103), "retreat"
(103), "place of confinement" (110), "den" (114), "prison" (121), "dark hole"
(131), "dungeon" (133), "dismal hole" (140), "grave" (147), and "nook" (155).

They are "loopholes of retreat" – an exact designation, a term fully in
keeping with the multifarious meanings of key aspects of the text, some of
them touched upon above. Valerie Smith points to various complexities of
meaning surrounding Jacobs's term for her place of sojourn. A "loophole" is
indeed, as Smith observes, "in common parlance an avenue of escape" (29),
and, as Jacobs redefines it, "a place of withdrawal," a "retreat." But a loophole is also a small opening in a *fortress* wall through which arms may be fired,
a place allowing defensive action, and also, because it conceals observer from
observed, unobserved offensive action. In other words the term "loophole of
retreat" has about it denotations and connotations that are opposite in meaning. "Retreat" means withdrawal, yet, in connection with "loophole" it suggests offensive intent. "Loophole" may suggest at once evasive and direct action.

The multifarious (not "ambiguous," since the word is too easily interpreted in binary terms) meanings inherent in the term "loophole of retreat"
reflect not the unwillingness or inability of the author to fit her story into the
existing forms, but rather they reflect her desire to stretch the boundaries of
the genres of slave narrative and novel of sentiment to whatever extent necessary to accommodate her particular experience. The slave narrative, as encouraged by the abolitionists, depicts the movement of the slave from bondage to freedom; the sentimental novel depicts the movement of a young
woman through problematic romance to marriage and the eventual establishment of a home. Jacobs's narrative chronicles neither in any clear-cut
fashion. By the narrative's end, she is only nominally free, and her prospects
for establishing the hearth and home she desires for her family are indeed
dim. Early in the narrative she expresses her desire:

> By perseverance and unwearied industry, she [grandmother] was now
> mistress of a snug little home, surrounded with the necessaries of
> life. . . . We longed for a home like hers. (17)

Because she is *bought* by her friend and benefactor, the second Mrs. Bruce,
and because the discrimination and segregation she finds in the North, espe-

cially following the implementation of the Fugitive Slave Law, are demeaning and constricting, Jacobs does not consider herself wholly and entirely free. The pride expressed by her Uncle Benjamin in his entire unwillingness to be paid for and in that way freed from slavery is shared by Linda, bequeathed to her, as noted by Elizabeth Becker,[34] by her father. When uncle Phillip implores the escaped Benjamin to return South with him to buy their relatives out of slavery, he replies, "No, never!" Unlike his mother (Harriet's grandmother), he chooses freedom over family: "Phil," he says finally, movingly, "I part with all my kindred" (26). Before Mrs. Bruce pays Mr. Dodge for her, Harriet has expressed her feelings about the issue:

> In a few days one [a letter] came to me from Mrs. Bruce, informing me that my new master was still searching for me, and that she intended to put an end to this persecution by buying my freedom. I felt grateful for the kindness that prompted this offer, but the idea was not so pleasant to me as might have been expected. The more my mind had become enlightened, the more difficult it was for me to consider myself an article of property; and to pay money to those who had so grievously oppressed me seemed like taking from my sufferings the glory of triumph. (199)

When Harriet learns that Mrs. Bruce has paid for her and that she is no longer subject to capture and return to the South, her response is not the jubilation we might expect, but mortification. Her response gives an ironic twist to the final chapter's title "Free at Last":

> "The bill of sale!" Those words struck me like a blow. So I was *sold* at last! A human being *sold* in the free city of New York! The bill of sale is on record, and future generations will learn from it that women were articles of traffic in New York, late in the nineteenth century of the Christian religion. (200)

She cannot but be thankful for her deliverance: "I had objected to having my freedom bought, yet I must confess that when it was done I felt as if a heavy load had been lifted from my weary shoulders" (200). Her sense of freedom is a qualified one:

> I and my children are now free! We are as free from the power of slaveholders as are white people of the north; and though that, according to my ideas, is not saying a great deal, it is a vast improvement in *my* condition. (201)

Perhaps Linda recalls here the observation she made earlier when she discovered the realities of Northern discrimination: "It made me sad to find how the north aped the customs of slavery" (163). The sentence immediately following her comment saying that merely to be free from the power of slaveholders does not alone constitute freedom refers to the "dream of [her] life," establishing a connection between a legal freedom and freedom as she conceives it:

> The dream of my life is not yet realized. I do not sit with my children in a home of my own. I still long for a hearthstone of my own, however humble. I wish it for my children's sake far more than for my own. (201)

She never finds true freedom. But, of course, she does not seek such an abstraction as "freedom"; she seeks, as Elizabeth Becker suggests, "home," a state of being that she sensed from earlier existence,[35] had even tasted in the savor of her grandmother's crackers. The ideal domestic state was somewhat achieved in the living situation of her grandmother but not quite. Her grandmother possessed the house, but her children were never able to share "the snug little home." Presumably slavery stands in the way of the achievement of the domestic ideal. Jacobs discovers, however, that even in the North her longings go unfulfilled. The intermingling of positive and negative currents captured in the grammar, syntax, and diction of her final image intimates the depth and variegation of the narrative's emotional hues:

> Yet the retrospection [occasioned by the narrative] is not altogether without solace; for with those gloomy recollections come tender memories of my good old grandmother, like light, fleecy clouds floating over a dark and troubled sea. (201)

Let me draw my comparison of these two narratives to a close by reference to my main point, that both are engaged in furthering the progress of historically antislavery forces in the slavery debate. More than most other literary opponents of slavery, they have chosen to focus on the pernicious effects of slavery on the family as a means of centering and buttressing their argument. Nearly all slave narratives comment to some degree or another on slavery's destructive effect on the families of both the slave and the slaveowner, but none focuses so intensely on the subject as do Jacobs's and Douglass's.

The two narratives, notwithstanding their similarities, are not entirely consonant in their representation of the effects of slavery on the family. Their differences have primarily to do with each author's sense of mission and purpose. Jacobs wishes to follow the usual method of the slave narrative as it had developed by the late 1850s, describing the horrors of slavery and showing the slave's eventual escape from the dungeon of slavery (whether, contrary to some current thinking on the matter, literacy was achieved or not).[36] Her focus on family lends her a vision that does away completely with the distinction between freedom and the establishment of a home. The two motives become wholly one. This she learned through observation of her grandmother, whose establishing of a household occurs inside the space she carves out within the confines imposed by slavery. The activities her grandmother pursues (earning and saving money, buying and selling, and owning property – including herself) are universally denied to slaves in the United States. Such activities are generally reserved not only for the free, but for men. How astounding that Jacobs's grandmother is able to operate to such a large extent beyond the boundaries of race and gender. Her class affiliations allow such leeway.

Douglass, on the other hand, writes in the second version of his autobiography from quite different motives. Autobiography always has a motive, but in this case the motive may not always be so clear as it becomes when we think of Douglass's second narrative in relation to his first. The first narrative is much more like Jacobs's in that it aims primarily to present the horrors of slavery and to show how one slave escapes those confines. The second is more complicated in that it intends to move beyond the goals of the slave narrative and to begin recounting Douglass's later experience as abolitionist leader in the antislavery movement.

Finally, it must be said that the heavier emphasis on domestic issues in the Jacobs narrative results from a gender difference. The prerogatives of males in nineteenth-century America (even black males) allowed them more individual freedom than was allowed to women. Once Harriet had begun to establish her family, with the births of Ellen and Benny, she was fixed within the boundaries of her sphere as woman and mother so that she could not have emulated Douglass even if by temperament, will, inclination, and ability she was able to do so. The common denominator of their circumstance is slavery and, whatever we might think, it was opposition to that antagonist that brought them together. Their specific gender distinctions, until shown to be otherwise, are part of our ideology, not theirs, and are social, not personal. They both knew that slavery was destructive to family, and they joined on that score to battle it. The gender differences, so tenderly sensitive and alive for us, were in their personal relations less alive and active for them. They would have no problem in agreeing that their enemy was a common one. "My master had power and law on his side; I had a determined will," Jacobs says. "There is might in each" (85). Douglass might well have voiced the same words.

Notes

1. *Incidents in the Life of a Slave Girl, Written by Herself*, ed. Jean Fagan Yellin (Cambridge, MA: Harvard University Press, 1987), 85. Yellin explores in detail the theme of domesticity in the narrative, and I am indebted to her for initiating my thinking along these lines. Yellin's edition makes it abundantly clear that a reader of the text literally cannot understand it without knowing the historical context supplied by her introduction, appendix, and notes.

2. *My Bondage and My Freedom* (Urbana: Illinois University Press, 1987), 166. I use Douglass's second edition of his autobiography rather than the first because in

expanding his life story, he not only brings it up to date, but he elaborates on various features of his early life, especially matters relating to domestic issues.

3. Quoted in Eugene Genovese, *Roll, Jordan, Roll: The World the Slaves Made* (New York: Random House, 1974), 35.

4. In a widely noted article published in the early forties the historian Richard Hofstadter revealed that without doubt U. B. Phillips, though in many ways a highly skilled and gifted historian, wrote history from a transparently biased perspective. The article opens with an epigraph, a quotation from Phillips expressing his predisposition: "We are concerned with Southern civilization and its cherishing." After pointing out that Phillips's *American Negro Slavery* (New York: Appleton, 1918) and *Life and Labor in the Old South* (Boston: Little, Brown, 1929) "are the most widely read scholarly studies of the slave system, and have become classic sources of information and propaganda about antebellum Southern life," Hofstadter goes on to say, "Professor Phillips's interest was clearly centered in the planter class, so much so that his popular study *Life and Labor in the Old South* gives only casual attention to those classes, slaveholding and non-slaveholding small planters and farmers, which comprised the vast majority of the white population of the antebellum South." In other words, insofar as his predisposition toward the support of Southern values is concerned, he might just as well have based his history on the view of slavery expressed in Margaret Mitchell's *Gone with the Wind*. "U. B. Phillips and the Plantation Legend," *Journal of Negro History* 29 (April, 1944): 109–24.

5. Nehemiah Adams, D. D. , though his book raises questions about his judgment, reason, and sensitivity, writes in 1854, "I had always noticed that Southerners seldom used the word 'slaves' in private conversation." *A South-Side View of Slavery* (New York: Negro Universities Press, 1969), 30–1. With all due respect, I would differ with the historian Winthrop D. Jordan, whose distinction between "servitude" and "slavery" is more linguistic than historical. He says that "Slavery was a power relationship; servitude was a relationship of service." Such a distinction holds up linguistically but not in actuality, for it makes no sense to imagine that the relation between master and servant is not a "power relationship." *White Over Black: American Attitudes Toward the Negro, 1550–1812* (1968; rpt. Baltimore: Penguin, 1969), 55.

6. Good examples of the use of the terms "slave" and "servant," as well as some other names she uses to designate the status of the black people she notes, are contained in *The Private Mary Chesnut: The Unpublished Civil War Diaries*, ed. C. Vann Woodward and Elisabeth Muhlenfeld (New York: Oxford University Press, 1984). She most frequently refers to blacks as "negroes" – often "our negroes." She never uses the term "nigger" in her own voice but reports others doing so, usually as a marker indicating the user's social class. When she uses the word "slave," which she rarely does, it is always used for some special purpose, as when she writes, "The Bible authorizes marriage & slavery – poor women! poor slaves!" (21). But she never calls her own slaves "slaves."

7. Willie Lee Rose comments on slavery and domesticity: "Certainly in time defenders of slavery had so distinct a preference for the term 'domestic slavery' that when they referred to their 'domestic institution' the phrase absorbed the color of

a euphemism, and was more often enunciated with pride than apology"; *Slavery and Freedom* (New York: Oxford University Press, 1982), 21.

8. See Frances Smith Foster's discussion of this theme in the slave narrative in *Witnessing Slavery: The Development of Antebellum Slave Narratives* (Westport, CT: Greenwood Press, 1979), 131–7.

9. *Slavery and Freedom*, 21.

10. "Introduction to the 1987 Edition," *My Bondage and My Freedom*, xix.

11. See Eric Sundquist's discussion of father and family in "Frederick Douglass: Literacy and Paternalism," in *Critical Essays on Frederick Douglass*, ed. William L. Andrews (Boston: G. K. Hall, 1991), 126–7. Waldo E. Martin, in *The Mind of Frederick Douglass* (Chapel Hill: University of North Carolina Press, 1984), 3–17, interprets Douglass's concern with fathers and families as largely psychological. Those interests are political too, and one is likely to diminish the political by too great an emphasis on the personal and psychological.

12. *Sociology for the South* (1854; rpt. ed. Donald M. Scott and Bernard Wishy, New York: Negro Universities Press, 1982), 332. There is some question about Fitzhugh's representativeness as a defender of the institution of slavery. Some thought of him as a "crackpot"; others have felt that he articulated the fundamentals of slaveholding ideology. See Drew Gilpin Faust, *Southern Stories: Slaveholders in Peace and War* (Columbia: University of Missouri Press, 1992), 84–6.

13. See Kenneth M. Stampp, *The Peculiar Institution: Slavery in the Ante-Bellum South* (New York: Random House, 1956), 30.

14. Louis R. Harlan, *Booker T. Washington: The Making of a Black Leader* (New York: Oxford University Press, 1972), 8.

15. "Nearly three-fourths of all free Southerners had no connection with slavery through either family ties or direct ownership. The 'typical' Southerner was not only a small farmer but also a nonslaveholder." Kenneth Stampp, *The Peculiar Institution*, 30.

16. "'Ironic Tenacity': Frederick Douglass's Seizure of the Dialectic," in *Frederick Douglass: New Literary and Historical Essays*, ed. Eric J. Sundquist (Cambridge University Press, 1990), 25–7.

17. See, for example, Waldo Martin, *The Mind of Frederick Douglass*, 6, and William S. McFeely, *Frederick Douglass* (New York: Norton, 1991), 10.

18. These critics have followed Dickson J. Preston, *Young Frederick Douglass: The Maryland Years* (Baltimore: Johns Hopkins University Press, 1980). The most recent is McFeely, 8, who seems to follow Peter Walker, *Moral Choices: Memory, Desire, and Imagination in Nineteenth-Century American Abolition* (Baton Rouge: Louisiana State University Press, 1978), 254–7. Eric Sundquist finds Douglass not searching for a lost patrimony but in a struggle to the end with all fathers: his biological father, the founding fathers, and Abraham Lincoln as the emancipating "father." Introduction to Sundquist, *Frederick Douglass*, 16–17.

19. The connections between Douglass's early life and his African past are brilliantly drawn out in Sterling Stuckey's essay, "'Ironic Tenacity': Frederick Douglass's Seizure of the Dialectic," in Sundquist, *Frederick Douglass*, 23–46.

20. Walker, *Moral Choices*, 244–7. Niemtzow even goes so far as to suggest that Douglass has no true self, that he must assume the role of a white, bourgeois male by

virtue of the fact of literacy. Does this mean that if one dwelling in the United States wears leather shoes or a cravat, writes, or reads, then he or she wants to be white? "The Problematic Self in Autobiography: The Example of the Slave Narrative," in Modern Critical Interpretations, *Frederick Douglass's Narrative of the Life of Frederick Douglass*, ed. Harold Bloom (New York: Chelsea House, 1988), 116–24.

21. Consider Houston Baker's perspective at this moment, "Autobiographical Acts and the Voice of the Southern Slave," in his *The Journey Back: Issues in Black Literature and Criticism* (Chicago: Chicago University Press, 1980), 27–52. Slaves are not existential creatures; they each bring a culture and a past with them.

22. Beginning in about 1859 and throughout his life (according to John Blassingame's brief note to an 1860 transcription in the *Frederick Douglass Papers*, New Haven: Yale University Press, Vol. 3, 289), Douglass delivered a speech called "Self-Made Men." This speech was intended to be inspirational, to encourage others to make themselves as he had made himself. Waldo Martin analyzes the speech in great detail in *The Mind of Frederick Douglass*, chap. 10.

23. The notion that Harriet Jacobs's editor Lydia Maria Child asserted specific influence on Harriet Jacobs's focus on "domesticity," "feminine virtue," or "family" fails to take into account that Jacobs did not need to be influenced by any individual to engage in the discourse of domesticity. The discourse was available to anyone who breathed the bourgeois air of the time. It is extraordinarily unfortunate that after Jean Fagan Yellin's brilliant and exhaustive research on the subject (see the introduction to her edition of *Incidents*) a less knowing critic, Bruce Mills ("Lydia Maria Child and the Endings of Harriet Jacobs's *Incidents in the Life of a Slave Girl*," *American Literature* 64 [1992]: 255–72), would attempt to undercut it, claiming that Child had a greater role in Jacobs's narrative than she could by any stretch of the imagination possibly have had. Mills does, to his credit, explore in detail the theme of domesticity, though he seems not to know that knowledge of such values would be no less well known to Harriet Jacobs than to Lydia Maria Child.

24. Valerie Smith establishes convincingly and in detail some of the chief differences between Jacobs's narrative and narratives written by males. See *Self-Discovery and Authority in Afro-American Literature* (Cambridge: Harvard University Press, 1987), 33–43.

25. I am not sure Douglass need be taken to task, as he frequently is, because Anna Murray does not have a larger role in his autobiographies. I do know that he was not at liberty to reveal her role in his escape because he feared that disclosing the details might block that path for others and because he did not want to risk putting her friends and family in jeopardy. Some critics seem to find fault with Douglass for what I infer to be misogyny, without taking into account that he was a stronger advocate of women's rights than practically any other nineteenth-century male. See, for example, Nellie Y. McKay, "The Souls of Black Women Folk," *Writing Black, Writing Feminist*, ed. Henry Louis Gates, Jr. (New York: Meridian, 1990), 228–9, and Rafia Zafar, "The Afro-American as Representative Man," in Sundquist, *Frederick Douglass*, 109.

26. Annette Niemtzow's discussion ignores – as do others of its kind – the political dimensions of Jacobs's text largely because it focuses on gender alone. See "The

Problematic of Self in Autobiography: The Example of the Slave Narrative," in *The Art of the Slave Narrative,* ed. John Sekora and Darwin T. Turner (Macomb: Western Illinois University Press, 1982), 98–104. The essay does, however, make significant distinctions between men's and women's narratives resulting from gender differences.

27. "The opening chapter of her account focuses not on the solitary 'I' of so many narratives but on Jacobs's relatives. And she associates her desire for freedom with her desire to provide opportunities for her children." Smith, *Self-Discovery,* 34.

28. The paradox lies largely in the ownership of slaves by blacks. Most of the slaves owned by blacks were family members who were owned because state laws that forbade the emancipation of slaves unless they left the state forced "freed" (bought or willed) slave relatives (wives, husbands [rarely], children, siblings) to be owned by their free relatives.

29. Joanne M. Braxton discusses in detail the relationship between Harriet and her grandmother in *Black Women Writing Autobiography: A Tradition within a Tradition* (Philadelphia: Temple University Press, 1989), 30–1.

30. Harriet's grandmother actually came to own the house on June 21, 1830, when Harriet was about 17. The evidence presented by Jean Fagan Yellin suggests that Harriet's grandmother had lived in the house with other people (presumably her relatives, some children, and perhaps grandchildren) for some time before, perhaps beginning in 1827, the year in which the person named "Molly" in fact, "Aunt Martha" in the narrative, was bought and freed (see *Incidents,* 260, n. 5; 262, n. 6; 264 n. 13). In any case, it is clear that Jacobs intends to engird the image of the mother/grandmother with domestic, familial values.

31. On the eve of the Civil War there were 250,000 free African Americans in the South. Most were in Virginia and Maryland, with decreasing numbers in the more southern and southwestern states. But there were free black people in every state (see Eugene Genovese, *Roll Jordan, Roll: The World the Slaves Made* [New York: Random House, 1974], 400). Why did these freed persons not move north or west, especially given the difficulties that free African Americans underwent while living in slave territory? I would venture that family, hence communal, relations were responsible for keeping them in the South.

32. Hazel Carby, *Reconstructing Womanhood: The Emergence of the Afro-American Woman Novelist* (New York: Oxford University Press, 1987), 56–7. Minrose C. Gwin discusses Mrs. Flint in detail in "Green-eyed Monsters of the Slavocracy: Jealous Mistresses in Two Slave Narratives," in *Conjuring: Black Women, Fiction, and Literary Tradition,* ed. Marjorie Pryse and Hortense J. Spillers (Bloomington: Indiana University Press, 1985), pp. 45–8.

33. Note Valerie Smith's interpretation of Jacobs's confinement as also empowering, *Self-Discovery,* 32.

34. Elizabeth Becker, "Harriet Jacobs's Search for Home," *CLA Journal,* 35:4 (1989): 414.

35. When "Linda Brent discovers that she is a slave, she says that she will seek freedom, which she defines as a 'snug little home' like her free grandmother's. . . . " Becker, "Harriet Jacobs's Search for Home," 411.

36. Robert B. Stepto formulated this widely accepted view that the meaning of the

quest of the escaped slave lies in his search for freedom and literacy. I would argue that there is no necessary connection between freedom and literacy. Most slaves who escaped were not literate, and literacy is just as likely to follow as to precede the achievement of freedom; *From Behind the Veil: A Study of Afro-American Narrative* (2nd ed.; Urbana: University of Illinois Press, 1991).

MOTHERHOOD BEYOND THE GATE

JACOBS'S EPISTEMIC CHALLENGE IN
INCIDENTS IN THE LIFE OF A SLAVE GIRL

JOHN ERNEST

In 1837, at the Anti-Slavery Convention of American Women,[1] Mrs. A. L. Cox put forth a resolution proclaiming that "there is no class of women to whom the anti-slavery cause makes so direct and powerful an appeal as to *mothers*." Responding to this appeal, the resolution calls for women to "lift up their hearts to God on behalf of the captive, as often as they pour them out over their own children in a joy with which 'no stranger may intermeddle.'" The same resolution warns women to "guard with jealous care the minds of their children from the ruining influences of the spirit of pro-slavery and prejudice, let those influences come in what name, or through what connexions they may."[2] The dual mandate here – for hearts to be lifted upward to God's purifying realm, and for jealous care to be directed outward against Man's *corrupting* realm – points us in turn to what Jean Fagan Yellin calls the "double tale" in Harriet Jacobs's 1861 narrative *Incidents in the Life of a Slave Girl*. As Yellin notes, Jacobs dramatizes "the triumph of her efforts to prevent her master from raping her," but she also presents the story of "her failure to adhere to sexual standards in which she believed."[3] In other words, although Jacobs might hope that the story of her "triumph" would lift up her readers' hearts, she knew also that her "failure" would cause her readers to guard those same hearts with jealous care, and to turn God's realm against Jacobs in judgment.

It is this other double story, her white readers' inevitably dual response of approbation and judgment, that complicates Jacobs's attempt to "be honest and tell the whole truth,"[4] and that qualifies any common bond she might claim as a mother. Certainly, resistance to the institution of slavery required

179

mothers to protest the habitual violation of an ideologically sanctified relationship – in effect, a matter of insisting upon the enslaved woman's right to
the privileges and duties of motherhood. But Jacobs knew well that many
antislavery white women, in their search for injustice, did not even think of
looking beyond the visible violation of the sacred relationship of mother and
child. In other words, they saw only those horrors that threatened the ideological security of the domestic sphere, and from that sphere they judged such
horrors. To maintain the sphere, the horrors (including both the act of violating and the act of being violated) must remain outside. Thus distanced,
Jacobs could not hope to "tell the whole truth" unless she could teach her
readers to *hear* and understand the whole truth.[5]

If Jacobs were to present something more than an object lesson in the horrors of slavery, she would have to inspire her readers to trace to their own
homes the "ruining influences of the spirit of pro-slavery and prejudice," and
to question not only their willingness but even their ability to fulfill the duties
of motherhood in a culture that sanctions slavery. In other words, motherhood, as viewed from Jacobs's perspective, does not provide an unproblematic bond between narrator and reader, for Linda Brent, the pseudonymous
author and subject of this story, cannot help but represent the most threatening and pervasive vice.[6] No reader, no matter how sympathetic, can change
Brent's cultural identity; the progression available to her is that from slave girl
to concubine to slave mother to fugitive slave to "free Black." Each new phase
is a resounding echo of her previous condition: a restricted identity, the terms
of which Brent can try to adapt to her needs but can never hope to control.
Nor can Brent offer the dubious protection or comfort of a closing moral, for
such closure was not available either to her or to the larger community whose
story she represents. Instead, the lesson of *Incidents* is that white mothers and
daughters cannot identify with Brent, but that they must learn to do so if they
are to achieve their own moral ideals, if they are to fulfill the terms of their
own self-definition.[7]

Incidents directs itself toward this paradox and operates in the space it at
once opens and closes, thereby creating a need for the perspective that only
Jacobs, and others like her, can offer. The choice for white women and
mothers concerned about the immorality of slavery – the choice between taking the high moral ground of, say, an Esther, and being the victim of a prophecy – cannot be accomplished by way of a sympathetic engagement in
Brent's story, a self-assuring response to what Joanne M. Braxton terms "outraged motherhood."[8] Rather, this choice requires white women to learn
from Brent not only a new language but also a new mode of understanding,
one characterized not by separation of subject and object but rather by a
reciprocal relationship between two differently knowing subjects. Ultimately,
Jacobs issues to her readers an epistemic challenge to change the nature of

their knowledge by changing the way they look at and learn from African Americans.

I

Fundamentally, Brent's experiences remind us that the nineteenth-century American institution of motherhood was a racialized, class-based concept. As such, the concept of motherhood presented both possibilities and problems as a vehicle for social change. As Lori D. Ginzberg notes, "To those who worried that benevolent activities would weaken women's effectiveness in the home, reformers replied that benevolent work merely extended the job of motherhood."[9] However, the problem women faced in applying the concept of motherhood to new cultural contexts was that the ideology of motherhood carried with it its own contextualizing apparatus, and this could be turned back against reforming mothers. Not only men but many "benevolent women" themselves "were quite prepared," as Ginzberg demonstrates, "to use the ideology of femininity as a weapon against female organizing that served interests they thought too radical."[10] The question of a mother's duty in relation to social order was one of both praxis and principle. How one defined one's principles, in turn, defined one's representative identity as the individual embodiment of intermeshed political and religious ideologies.

The career of Jacob's editor, Lydia Maria Child, might itself be viewed as an extension of the job of motherhood; but Child's own public entrance into the antislavery movement, the publication of *An Appeal in Favor of That Class of Americans Called Africans*, came at the expense of her position as a trusted guardian of the practice of motherhood, causing many mothers and fathers to cancel their subscriptions to the *Juvenile Miscellany*, which Child edited.[11] But the relationship between Child's early career and her antislavery work was even more intimately problematic. With no culturally sanctioned way to negotiate the differences between class and caste and between reified womanhood and sexual exploitation, Child could hardly hope to apply to enslaved women the defense of middle-class motherhood that led her to argue in her 1827 guidebook for "middle class" women, *The American Frugal Housewife*, that

> most of us could obtain worldly distinctions, if our habits and inclination allowed us to pay the immense price at which they must be purchased. True wisdom lies in finding out all the advantages of a situation in which we *are* placed, instead of imagining the enjoyments of one in which we are *not* placed.[12]

Of course, Child wrote this early in her career, and demonstrates a culturally delimited understanding of the possibilities of "wisdom" and the contingencies of social position. When Child writes of "a situation in which we *are* placed," she refers to fate, to the mysterious influence of Divine providence as enacted by human agency. Enslaved Blacks, on the other hand, were placed in their situation by human hands that claimed the authority of Divine agency and the power of fate, while directing themselves toward the most vulgar of human motives. For black women, who indeed were admonished by their lascivious so-called *protectors* and holders to realize the "advantages" of the "situation" in which they were placed, the brand of homespun wisdom of which Child speaks would (and often did) constitute self-victimization at its most specific and, in general, a reminder of the multifarious degradation of enslavement. [13]

Motherhood, I am suggesting, was the essential condition of what I have called "reified womanhood," by which I mean the culturally determined attributes by which women could know themselves as Woman. These attributes are what Barbara Welter terms the "four cardinal virtues" of "True Womanhood": "piety, purity, submissiveness and domesticity." [14] But it is important to remember that these virtues did not exist in an ideological vacuum, a separate sphere reserved for social constructions of gender. Rather, they existed in relation to the state – that is, they served both practical and ideological functions in the maintenance of social order and of national identity. Ideals of what is often called "true womanhood," and the related reification of the woman's sphere of virtue in the home, at once worked to forestall social change and to place at the heart of American society an ahistorical realm, a world untouched by the increasing complexities of material and political culture. [15]

Outside the realms of the public institutions and events that defined human history, and inside the home, women's virtue served as the ideological womb of civic virtue. [16] In an 1853 essay in *Putnam's Monthly* on "Woman and the 'Woman's Movement,'" the anonymous writer argues that the woman's life "is always a present one"; and "Hence the first woman was named *Eve*, that is, LIVING." [17] Woman therefore stands as "the expressive type or symbol of that lustrous life which shall one day redeem him [her husband] from earth, and ally him with divinity." [18] Through the republican woman, the republican man maintains an intimate relationship with the eternal. As it is idealized in the essay "The Homes of America the Hope of the Republic," which appeared in *The United States Democratic Review* in 1856, home "is a place, apart from and beyond the world"; "the spirit of home is the pervading spirit, which lends high aim and purpose to our lives, and makes an aggregate of virtue sufficient to sustain a pure form of republicanism." [19] It was the republican duty not only of domestic education but of motherhood itself both to ennoble and to protect, but not to participate in, the political sphere.

To redefine womanhood as historical agency released the ideologically ahistorical anchor that secured what many women took to be their historical roles. Deliberately private, representing a simplicity of faith and virtue that belies the complexity of life, the culturally constructed domestic sphere served the most public of purposes. To many women as well as men in the antebellum United States, for women to leave the home and enter the political arena was a matter not of leaving the private sphere to enter the public, but rather of redefining one's role in the public sphere, for women were thought to serve distinctively public roles by holding to private spheres. Essentially, motherhood was both a condition and a duty, both noun and verb; it was the ongoing, delicate negotiation of the relationship between the historical and the ahistorical by way of domestic education. True womanhood involved the embodiment of timeless virtues; true motherhood was the expression of womanhood in history, the preparation of children for lives in the world.

In 1859 one of the many attacks on the increasing public prominence of women was an article published in the *Southern Literary Messenger* on the "Intellectual Culture of Woman." This article was designed ultimately to argue that it is the mother's role, within the context of domestic education, to defend the institution of slavery. Asserting that "it is no slight duty . . . to which woman is called, in the discharge of her offices to society," the author strategically amplifies the implicit responsibilities inherent in the ideology of femininity, arguing that "the social problems which are the subject and the origin of laws, the manners and customs of the people which originate and produce these laws, are the product, directly or indirectly, of the women."[20] As this appropriation demonstrates, the ideology of motherhood – like religion itself, like law, like republican philosophy – proved infinitely flexible. Whether or not a woman accepted the role of a true woman, the task of applying this generalized role to the concerns of the day was unavoidably political. To be a mother in opposition to law and custom was to announce an ideological reconstitution of motherhood.

On these terms, Brent (and Jacobs) cannot claim the cultural authority of motherhood; she can only struggle to undermine the readers' own claims to authority. As Hazel V. Carby reminds us, at the end of her narrative Brent remains "excluded from the domain of the home, and the sphere within which womanhood and motherhood were defined. Without a 'woman's sphere,' both were rendered meaningless."[21] However, the unspoken assertion behind Jacobs's self-presentation is that her white motherly readers themselves cannot claim the power of reified womanhood because the ideological vessel of that power is falsely constructed. Accordingly, as Brent promises not "to try to screen [herself] behind the plea of compulsion from a master" (54), so Brent's female readers must learn to step out from behind their own ideological screens. To do so means to confront the actual conditions and events of their world, in all their disturbing and disruptive ideological contradictions, and, more to the point, to acknowledge responsibility for these contradictions. The screens themselves, woven of coarse ideological threads, provide a unified public diorama to cover the many private stories that would reveal the nation's failure to live up to its professed ideals. And as Jacobs knew well, yet another screen – in some ways, the most deceptive of all, and most capable of undermining the individual sense of moral responsibility – was the abolitionist belief in the possibility of understanding the "monstrous features" of slavery once the "veil" of propriety is "withdrawn," as Child puts it in her introduction to the narrative (4). For the "monstrous" is always the other; and, as the other, Jacobs would have no real voice, no way to penetrate the screen between narrator and reader. White readers would need to learn to see the monstrous at home before Jacobs could extend her own cultural identity beyond that of a representative and victimized site of monstrous exchanges.

By all cultural standards, ideological motherhood in *this* narrative of national life has been violated and corrupted, and Jacobs argues that it is only by acknowledging and studying the terms of that violation and corruption that motherhood can be restored to integrity. After all, *Incidents'* central character, Linda Brent, has no living mother, and can look for her maternal guidance only from her grandmother. Indeed, Brent notes early in the narrative that "if I knelt by my mother's grave, [Flint's] dark shadow fell on me even there" (28). Instead of providing the moral entrance into history, motherhood in this narrative marks the violent intrusion of history into a woman's life. For Brent, the state does not await the performance of motherhood; rather, the state has become sexually implicated in the condition of womanhood and the conception of motherhood. When telling of her attempt to avoid Flint's demands by submitting herself to relations with a future statesman,[22] Brent notes significantly that without slavery she would have nothing to confess. Asserting that her own deliberate moral transgression was the only avenue for self-determination, Brent reminds the reader again that "the condition of a slave confuses all principles of morality, and, in fact, renders the practice of them impossible" (55). Her grandmother's own rejection of Brent after this transgression emphasizes the strictness with which American Christianity defines that which it creates, forcing Brent outside the moral sanctuary of the domestic sphere.

Banished from that culturally determined domestic sphere, Brent leaves her grandmother's house and, as the gate closes behind her – "with a sound I never heard before" (57) – she enters into a new stage in her relationship with her grandmother, history, and selfhood. Jacobs's readers are seemingly left within the gate, with little more to offer than sympathetic echoes of the grandmother's lamentation after the two are reconciled: "Poor child! Poor child!" (57). Brent herself is left with the experience that will produce the children who will motivate her eventual escape from the South. But the internal logic of *Incidents* comes to a point here, as Brent completes her identity as a highly determined product of the American Christian slave culture, literally embodying its moral and social contradictions in the children she soon carries. Jacobs's task is to draw her readers themselves beyond the gate, to show that they reside there already, and thereby to make Brent their representative and her quest theirs as well.

II

To perform this task, Jacobs must re-educate her readers, teaching them to see the invisible by giving voice to the unspeakable, forcing them beyond the gate of moral security and into a realm where all is uncertain, and where nothing can be addressed directly. What is needed is not merely the familiar argument that slaves and whites alike are taught in the "school of slavery" to accept and participate in the moral corruption of the system. Although Jacobs indeed works to reveal the baseness of these lessons learned in school, she argues further that the mode of thought one acquires in this school is inadequate to change the course of these lessons. Whereas Harriet Beecher Stowe argued that her readers should *"feel right,"*[23] Jacobs (perhaps fortified by her own disillusioning experience with Stowe, and certainly by her attenuated enslavement as a "free Black" in domestic service)[24] begins with the assumption that it will matter little if readers "feel right" if they do not also challenge fundamentally the nature and terms of their self-definition. Drawing her readers into an awareness of their own identities as U.S. citizens, Jacobs challenges the reader's ability even to know whether he or she does "feel right." If one is produced by this culture, then "feeling right" is a matter of aligning one's behavior (both physical and intellectual) with one's conception of moral law. As Stowe argues through her characterization of Marie St. Clare in *Uncle Tom's Cabin*, when one's conception of moral law is distorted, then so too is one's "conscience," and feeling right will mean simply that this dual distortion is perfectly aligned.

Jacobs could not simply appeal to a true application of Christian precepts, for the "all-pervading corruption produced by slavery" (51) made such appeals, in and of themselves, worthless. The dominant culture's ability even to understand those precepts was itself in question. Moreover, the many "Christian" slaveholders and proslavery ministers throughout both the Northern and Southern states demonstrated daily that such appeals could easily be redirected back to the enslaved. Well versed in the multifarious ways in which slavery is capable of "[perverting] all the natural feelings of the human heart" (142), Jacobs has little hope of appealing to that heart for justice. She knows that the justice of the heart can only echo, even at its best, the conceptions of justice defined by culture and habit. The ideological system that both requires and sustains the figurative heart would be the interpretative filter through which any appeal must pass. As Carby argues, not only white Southern women but also the Northern women "who formed Jacobs's audience were implicated in the preservation of this [ideological] oppression."[25] Unable to trust in relationships engendered by the fundamental commonalities of women's condition and experiences, Jacobs needed to reshape the ways in which women relate their individual experience to the concept of gendered commonality.

The problem was that many, blinded by custom, could not see what they were doing to blacks; in fact, they were incapable of imagining that the dominant culture's ethical standards could even apply to blacks. Early in *Incidents*, Brent notes that her otherwise solicitous and kind original mistress had taught her "the precepts of God's Word: 'Thou shalt love thy neighbor as thyself,'" and "'Whatsoever ye would that men should do unto you, do ye even so unto them'" (8). The mistress commits her "one great wrong" (bequeathing Brent to her sister's daughter) not because she fails to believe in the "precepts of God's Word," but rather because she does not recognize Brent as her neighbor in the moral sphere (8). Brent's later mistress, worried about Dr. Flint's interest in the girl, forces her to act as a moral agent by swearing on the Bible and "before God" to tell the truth; but this episode is fundamentally similar to the earlier one, for Brent's account simply leads Mrs. Flint to "[pity] herself as a martyr." Brent adds pointedly that Mrs. Flint "was incapable of feeling for the condition of shame and misery in which her unfortunate, helpless slave was placed" (33).

Certainly, Jacobs writes in the hope that the exposure of immorality will inspire in her readers a renewal of moral character, leading to reformative actions. But she signals her awareness also that this is a rather tenuous hope. Christian "precepts" can be applied to African Americans for the purposes of intellectual and spiritual colonization, but the flexible logic by which those precepts are applied belongs to the dominant culture, the members of which determine – at times consciously, at times not – which aspects of black bodies and black lives shall be visible. Dehumanized enough to be viewed as a slave, Brent was still human and woman enough to be the object of Flint's lust; still invisible, however, remained the human heart and divine soul that would make it impossible for Flint to fulfill his desires without sacrificing his community standing. Jacobs had long been in the North when she wrote *Incidents*, and Northerners, she notes through Linda Brent, are all too ready to "satisfy their consciences with the doctrine that God created the Africans to be slaves" (44). And those who could see more than a slave often had trouble seeing more than a servant. Jacobs knew that exposure simply uncovered one layer of black invisibility, one more dimension of the fullness of human experience that whites had not learned (or did not care) to recognize in blacks.

At issue is not only *what* knowledge the reader gains from this text, but also *how* the reader conceptualizes the acquisition of that knowledge. In *What Can She Know?*, Lorraine Code joins many looking to construct a feminist epistemology in arguing that "the subject–object relation that the autonomy-of-reason credo underwrites is at once its most salient and its most politically significant epistemological consequence."[26] In traditional approaches to knowledge acquisition, Code argues, "the subject is removed from, detached from, positions himself at a distance from the object; and knows the object as other than himself."[27] This subject–object relation characterized the nineteenth-century relationship between white reader and black author. In this highly politicized relationship, the black author served as the ostensibly self-voicing object of knowledge. However, the tenor and quality of that voice was itself an object of knowledge, obliged to obey the demand that Thoreau complains of in *Walden*: "that you shall speak so that they can understand you."[28] The conventions of cultural communication carry with them the cultural assumptions and prejudices that can undermine true communication between white and black. As Karen Sánchez-Eppler argues compellingly, the "moments of identification" that characterized the feminist/abolitionist alliance led easily and invisibly to "acts of appropriation."[29] Jacobs's task was to redefine the terms of this identification by reappropriating the authority to define the experience of oppression.

She approaches this task by redefining knowledge – replacing, in effect, the gaze as the central perspectival figure for acquiring knowledge, drawing instead on the visual mode sometimes referred to as "locking eyes." As Lorraine Code notes, "direct eye contact between people" is

> a symmetrical act of mutual recognition in which neither need be passive and neither in control. Such contact is integral to the way people position themselves in relation to one another and signify the meaning of their encounters. Through it, they engage with one another, convey feelings, and establish and maintain, or renegotiate, their relationships.[30]

Throughout *Incidents*, working behind the screens of their official relationship, Jacobs looks to establish such contact with her women readers, which requires that she first break through their subject–object mode of knowing. To initiate such a breakthrough, Jacobs must rely upon the power of the stories *suggested* by the stories one tells. By saying indirectly that which she cannot communicate directly, Jacobs deflects the reader's attempt to acquire knowledge from her text; she disrupts the subject–object dynamic of the gaze, and locks eyes, if only momentarily, in a quiet glance of mutual understanding. Through this indirect mode, Jacobs accomplishes what might be called *deferred* discourse, a suspended communication which first addresses unspeakable bonds, formed of common experiences, between (black) narrator and (white) reader, so that later the task of truly reciprocal discourse might be possible. These unspeakable bonds, formed of the gendered experiences for which women have no recognized public language, provided Jacobs with a possible mode of communication beyond the words contained and defined by the dominant, patriarchal culture, as if to exchange knowing looks with those female readers gazing at her pages.

Consider, for example, Brent's brief sentimental plot about a "young lady" who inherits both a fortune and seven slaves, a mother and her six children. Brent presents her as one of the conspicuous exceptions to the rule of cruelty, one for whom "religion was not a garb put on for Sunday," as "there was some reality in her religion" (50). Caught in the contradictions of the system, the lady tries to act according to her beliefs, and tries to inculcate those beliefs by example as well as by word. However, she falls victim to love, marrying a man who is interested in her wealth. Before her marriage, she offers to manumit her slaves, "telling them that her marriage might make unexpected changes in their destiny" (50), but the enslaved family does not know enough of the world of slavery to seize the opportunity. When the lady's new husband assumes control over the slaves – who had "never felt slavery," but were now "convinced of its reality" – she can only admit to the "free" patriarch of the enslaved family, "I no longer have the power I had a week ago" (50). Power lost to marriage, including the power to act upon one's moral beliefs, was, of course, a prominent concern of feminist abolitionists who drew from the rhetoric of enslavement. The sequel of this story, in which the young lady cannot but recognize that "her own husband had violated the purity she had so carefully inculcated" (51), provides an embodied reminder that one cannot negotiate a privileged moral relationship within the system of slavery. The face of the child reveals the unspoken bonds that characterize the system's invisible community. In this story, the wife finds herself "locking eyes" with the product of the system and the evidence of her own implication in that system.

In the silent reciprocity of locked eyes, Jacobs could speak through the stories she tells and, yet more powerfully, through those untold and untellable stories she implicitly draws from her readers. In the most intimate chapter of *Incidents*, under the decidedly objectified title "A Perilous Passage in the Slave Girl's Life," Brent argues that the reader cannot understand the "deliberate calculation" by which she chose to take Mr. Sands as her lover (54). Certainly, her readers will want to stand at a distance from such calculated transgressions of the ideology of moral relations between the sexes. And yet, as Brent explains *why* they cannot understand her motives, her language echoes not only feminist abolitionist rhetoric but also the rhetoric and plot of many a sentimental romance:

> Pity me, and pardon me, O virtuous reader! You never knew what it
> is to be a slave; to be entirely unprotected by law or custom; to have
> the laws reduce you to the condition of a chattel, entirely subject to
> the will of another. You never exhausted your ingenuity in avoiding
> the snares, and eluding the power of a hated tyrant; you never shud-

dered at the sound of his footsteps, and trembled within hearing of his voice. (55)

This appeal for understanding sends a covert message to the many women who have either read about or experienced the stratagems of a "hated tyrant," and who have felt the consequences of being "unprotected by law or custom," "subject to the will of another." Her readers' unspoken, responding narratives are likely to begin in sympathy when Brent confesses "I know I did wrong," and to extend to empathy when she claims, "No one can feel it more sensibly than I do" (55). Critics looking at this passage have noted the assertion that ends the paragraph – "I feel that the slave woman ought not to be judged by the same standards as others" (56) – and have rightly argued that Jacobs suggests that such standards are inadequate to account for the reality of the black subject's life.[31] I would add that Jacobs suggests as well that such standards are inadequate to account for the reality of *any* woman's life. Seeing their own experiences behind the veil of this confession, they see also the failure of their own culture to provide them with a sense of moral closure, let alone justice.

Moral closure, in the form of mutual understanding and a truly reciprocal relationship, comes when Brent confesses a second time, not to the presumably Christian reader but rather to her daughter Ellen. This time, in the brief chapter entitled "The Confession," Brent addresses herself to someone who neither needs nor wants to hear the confession, someone who understands the world that necessitated and shaped Brent's decision. The reader gazes on as an informed spectator, waiting, perhaps, to see Ellen's reaction.[32] But Brent and the reader alike discover that the confession is unnecessary – at least, as an *informative* act. Ellen knows of her mother's past, and she knows who her father is. But Brent's confession still has value as a *moral* act, the act of confessing one's sins for the sake of those who listen. Ellen's experience has provided her with a different knowledge of the world than that known by Brent's white readers, and therefore with a different standard for judgment. "I thanked God," Brent tells us, "that the knowledge I had so much dreaded to impart had not diminished the affection of my child" (189). Ellen, after all, knows the world well enough to say of her former belief that a father should love his child, " 'I was a little girl then, and didn't know any better' " (189). In this case, Brent's confession makes possible the reciprocity of trust:

> I had not the slightest idea she knew that portion of my history. If I had,
> I should have spoken to her long before; for my pent-up feelings had
> often longed to pour themselves out to some one I could trust. But I
> loved the dear girl better for the delicacy she had manifested towards
> her unfortunate mother. (189)

Reading this chapter, we see Ellen's reading of her world, an understanding born of experience that strengthens her relationship with her mother. Far from endangering the relationship, Brent's confession signals an unspoken understanding between mother and daughter that both had suspected but not fully realized. Through this exchange, the two give voice, and a shared consciousness, to the history of a relationship that might otherwise have seemed always imminent, always unfulfilled.

Jacobs's point is that different standards of judgment, capable of accounting for the actual lives concealed behind the moral and behavioral screens of reified womanhood, will not come from the dominant culture; they can come only from "the knowledge that comes from experience" in slavery (17). Certainly, Jacobs's readers still do not know any better than to hold to a belief in the natural love of a parent for a child, a love to be expressed according to established cultural codes of behavior.

Transgression of the codes constitutes transgression of parental duty and love. Even Brent's own grandmother warns her that her plans to escape constitute a double blow to motherhood, damaging Brent's role and reputation as a mother, and hurting her grandmother in the bargain. "'Nobody,'" her grandmother informs her, "'respects a mother who forsakes her children'" (91). Aware of this, and in spite of the rewards of her confession to her daughter, Brent still hesitates when the time comes to tell the reader. She knows that the white reader's judgment, even when directed at the system of slavery, necessarily encompasses herself as well. But as Brent, writing "only that whereof I know," describes the "all-pervading corruption produced by slavery," her readers may find themselves encompassed by their own standards of judgment, wondering who has forsaken whose children. For the sins enabled by slavery are both individual and systemic, extending beyond individual families to pervert the roles and relationships that give meaning to the *concept* of family: "It makes the white fathers cruel and sensual; the sons violent and licentious; it contaminates the daughters, and makes the wives wretched" (52). Clearly, history has invaded not only Brent's life but that of each of her readers as well. Brent's point is that she is valuable to those contained by the ideological American home precisely because she stands outside that home, and therefore knows it differently than those inside.

III

It is here, in this moral realm born of her struggles, that Jacobs works to transform herself from the object of knowledge to a subject of mutual understanding. In this narrative that is celebrated for its frank depiction of the experiences of enslaved women, Brent works to train her readers to read their world and themselves indirectly. For as experience shapes knowledge, so knowledge, in turn, shapes experiences; that is, her white readers' "knowledge" of themselves and their world tells them what to see in Brent's story, and how to understand it. White readers must learn to read their way out of the self-fulfilling prophecies of racialized knowledge and into the world of Brent's experience. This, of course, requires a heightened state of self-consciousness, which Brent encourages by emphasizing the necessity of considering one's response to Brent's confessions. For example, when she meets with Mr. Durham in Philadelphia, Brent "frankly" tells him of her life, noting that "it was painful for me to do it; but I would not deceive him" (160). Mr. Durham's response is significant, and his last word burns Brent "like coals of fire": "'Your straight-forward answers do you credit; but don't answer every body so openly. It might give some heartless people a pretext for treating you with contempt'" (160). As Jacobs makes painfully clear, this advice still stood as she wrote this narrative.

Equally clear is the extent to which apparently straightforward discourse can prove threatening. When Brent seeks to recover her daughter, who is staying with Mrs. Hobbs, she makes a point of noting that she had to contrive a story to present in her note. It was important, she emphasizes, that no one know that she had recently arrived from the South, "for that would involve the suspicion," she explains to the reader, "of my having been harbored there, and might bring trouble, if not ruin, on several people" (165). And having thus presented this reading of the cultural text, Brent explains the necessity of deception in her response to this text:

> I like a straightforward course, and am always reluctant to resort to subterfuges. So far as my ways have been crooked, I charge them all upon slavery. It was that system of violence and wrong which now left me no alternative but to enact a falsehood. (165)

Straightforwardness may be best, but experience has taught her when to practice and when to avoid it. In a system based on deception, straightforwardness can be dangerous, opening one not only to contempt but also to violence. All that is stated directly in such a system is held to the logic of the dominant ideology, in which anything Brent might say is held to be either inconsequential or threatening to the standing order. Brent's security, and the security of her extended community, depends upon careful reading, and equally careful narration.

Appealing to the deferred narratives of women's actual lives, the encoded stories that they can whisper to one another but not reveal to the world,[33] Jacobs draws her female readers into an unspoken realm contained and silenced by the ideological boundaries of cultural womanhood, a realm with its own mode of discourse (for communication both behind and across gender lines) and of knowledge. Wounded and sexually violated by Dr. Flint's words, Brent is "made . . . prematurely knowing, concerning the evil ways of the world" (54); in writing *Incidents* she uses the conventions of sentimental discourse to suggest the evil beneath the smooth patriarchal veneer. But she learns also that the subterranean realm of the actual "ways of the world" has its own silent codes, its own system of relations: the sensual vortex not only of the "secrets of slavery" but also of the secrets of women's experience. The second Mrs. Flint, Brent notes, "possessed the key to her husband's character before I was born," and "she might have used this knowledge to counsel and to screen the young and the innocent among her slaves" (31). Instead, she carries her struggle to the visible cultural apparatus for assigning guilt and maintaining order: she punishes the female slaves and watches her husband "with unceasing vigilance" (31). Dr. Flint, himself, when under his wife's eye, simply takes his violations to the subterranean realm of communication: "What he could not find opportunity to say in words he manifested in signs. He invented more than were ever thought of in a deaf and dumb asylum" (31). Jacobs knew the power of this mode of discourse not only as a slave but also as a "free" black in the North where she lived daily with unspoken signs of prejudice. If *Incidents* were to be transformative, this is the realm it would need to transform, and this the discourse it would need to appropriate.

Incidents offers its readers ample opportunity to practice Brent's mode of interpretation – that is, to reread apparently straightforward discourse, to question and interpret the cultural text guided by the hermeneutical map of Brent's narrative. Consider, for example, this one of many examples, toward the end of the narrative, when Brent receives a letter from her former enslavers. Brent copies the letter, and then comments on it, though telling her readers nothing they could not have determined from the letter itself:

> This letter was signed by Emily's brother, who was as yet a mere lad. I knew, by the style, that it was not written by a person of his age, and though the writing was disguised, I had been made too unhappy by it, in former years, not to recognize at once the hand of Dr. Flint. O, the hypocrisy of slaveholders! Did the old fox suppose I was goose enough to go into such a trap? Verily, he relied too much on "the stupidity of the African race." I did not return the family of Flints any thanks for their cordial invitation – a remissness for which I was, no doubt, charged with base ingratitude. (172)

Note that Brent withholds the information – the signatory, the appearance of the handwriting – that *might* have led the reader to misread the veiled text of this letter. The reader guesses the identity of the writer, and sees through the feigned affection and cordiality of the letter, simply noting these characteristics associated with the mythology of the paternalistic Southern system. Brent simply affirms this reading after she presents the letter, and adds at the end her own ironic rendition of formal courtesy, concerning their "cordial invitation," as an inside joke for the reader to enjoy.

But however threatening Flint's duplicitous letter may be, yet more threatening are those whose straightforwardness serves as simply the most direct example of a well-trained, restrictive perspective, as when Mrs. Hobbs, a Northern woman and mother, looks Brent "coolly in the face" to inform her that Ellen has been "*given*" to Hobbs's eldest daughter (166). In so doing, Mrs. Hobbs exemplifies the limited hopes one could place in the justice that might come to "enraged motherhood." If Jacobs had hoped to appeal to mothers through this narrative, this experience certainly reminded her how tenuous the power of that appeal might be. As Brent puts it, questioning the very bond of motherhood that she seems to count on for understanding elsewhere in the narrative,

> How *could* she, who knew by experience the strength of a mother's love, and who was perfectly aware of the relation Mr. Sands bore to my children, – how *could* she look me in the face, while she thrust such a dagger into my heart? (166)

A partial answer, of course, is that Mrs. Hobbs's experience is insufficient for understanding the very injustice of which she is aware. One could say that she is fundamentally *incapable* of looking Brent in the face, for she can look into only the face her experience has prepared her to see. She lacks the knowledge that comes from the experience of slavery, and she cannot attain this knowledge. As Brent puts it when she is reunited with her son Benjamin, "O reader, can you imagine my joy? No, you cannot, unless you have been a slave mother" (173).

Brent's experience has trained her differently; she is able to recognize Mrs. Hobbs's gaze for what it is, even though she is astounded to encounter it. More significantly, Brent's experience enables her to read the broader cultural text from an informed rather than a merely theoretical perspective. Consider Brent's discussion of the relative condition of American slaves and the European laboring classes, a comparison that dominated debates about slavery, and which was therefore a standard feature of many slave narratives. Brent ends by emphasizing that she will address only the relative condition of the two groups, and not the actual experience of European laborers. She does so to contrast her account of the laborers with uninformed accounts of slavery in America:

> I do not deny that the poor are oppressed in Europe. I am not disposed to point their condition so rose-colored as the Hon. Miss Murray paints the condition of the slaves in the United States. A small portion of *my* experience would enable her to read her own pages with anointed eyes. (184–5)

Without such experience, one lacks the eyes to read not only Brent's experience but also one's own pages, one's *own* experience. And can we imagine? No, we cannot. At best, we can recognize that we are incapable of reading our world without the "small portion" of Brent's experience that we gain by reading this narrative. We need Brent's help if we are to read "with anointed eyes" not only the system of slavery but also the broader system that has informed our identities.[34]

Brent underscores this need for a "small portion" of her experience not only by reminding her reader that the act of interpretation is a moral act but also by emphasizing the fragmentation of the cultural text. One might take as the symbol of this text the letter that Mr. Thorne writes to Dr. Flint, informing him of Brent's whereabouts. Thorne tears up the letter, and Ellen retrieves the fragments, telling Mrs. Hobbs's children that Thorne is out to expose her mother. The children do not believe that she can be right until they "put the fragments of writing together, in order to read them to her" (179). Similarly, Brent argues throughout *Incidents* that we are faced with a fragmented cultural text, and that we cannot read it until we reassemble the fragments. Moreover, we cannot put the fragments together without Brent's help. Earlier in the narrative, when William accompanies Mr. Sands to Washington and then runs away, Brent presents us with varying accounts of William's escape. She presents the reader first with William's letter to his family; next with Mr. Sands's account to Brent's Uncle Phillip; and, finally, with William's unwritten account to Brent herself when later they meet. The first is a conditioned account, for one could not afford to assume that the letter would be read only by one's intended audience. The second is a version of the dominant culture's interpretation of the event. The third is a frank account – to one who knew how to read the situation, one who had experienced enslavement – that deconstructs the authorized explanation. The true account of this event is not the last but the combined implications of all three. Brent presents the reader with a series of conditioned readings, each of which works to encompass, undermine, or otherwise account for the others. The fragmented text, in other words, is not simply a puzzle waiting to be pieced together; rather, it is a series of overlapping pieces that collectively form no single picture but indicate pictures that must be envisioned.

If Linda Brent cannot claim the knowledge of cultural privilege and education, she can claim the knowledge that forms the contours of her readers' lives, the knowledge gained from moral and ideological transgression, the transgression by which the dominant culture defines the enclosing boundaries of social order. Ostensibly, *Incidents,* like other works produced and endorsed by the abolitionist movement, argued that stories of experience will arm empowered white readers with the knowledge they need to struggle for the right. Brent herself acknowledges this possibility of empowering knowledge, noting that "never before had my puny arm felt half so strong" as when she understood Flint's implicit demand that she was "made for his use, made to obey his command in *every* thing" (18). But Brent shows also the limited value of this forearming knowledge when she becomes the victim of knowledge. Resolving "never to be conquered," able to "read the characters, and question the motives, of those around me" (19), she resists Dr. Flint by taking up with Mr. Sands (whose motives she also reads and understands). Thus she accepts the same situation she had tried to resist, with only the comfort of knowing that she had deliberately chosen, from a strictly limited field, her sexual partner. As the object of knowledge, Brent embodies the significations of both official cultural discourse and the more intimate subterranean codes, both order and its underlying chaos. Public discourse defines her; private whispers surround her. She is the Other that embodies the unspeakable experiences of the Self. In short, she is the fully determined product of the will to know – so determined, in fact, that she stands at the other side of the gate of knowledge, where the imminence of sexual and social violation is brought not only to consummation but also to public display. And it is from this public platform that she gazes back at the reader, locking eyes to begin the mutual task of re-forming knowledge, discourse, and community.

Notes

1. Dorothy Sterling has called the convention not only "the first public political meeting of U.S. women" but also "the first interracial gathering of any consequence" (*Turning the World Upside Down: The Anti-Slavery Convention of American Women* [New York: Feminist Press, 1987], 3). *Incidents'* editor, Lydia Maria Child, attended the convention, as did many other prominent women. The convention passed resolutions denouncing prejudices against color, promoting the renewal and practice of Christian principles, and arguing against the practice of many churches. The convention delegates also "organized a campaign to collect a million signatures on petitions to Congress asking for the abolition of slavery in the District of Columbia and the Florida Territory," and "prepared six pamphlets and 'open letters' for publication" (Sterling, *Turning the World Upside Down*, 4). Significantly, agreements about the public efficacy of Christian virtue and sympathetic motherhood were more easily reached than agreements about attendant redefinitions of women's social role. On the 1837 convention in the context of women's reform activism generally, see Lori D. Ginzberg, *Women and the Work of Benevolence: Morality, Politics, and Class in the 19th-Century United States* (New Haven: Yale University Press, 1990), chap. 1; on the 1837 convention and the justification and political influence of petitions, see Ginzberg, chap. 3, and Gerda Lerner, *The Majority Finds Its Past: Placing Women in History* (Oxford: Oxford University Press, 1979), chap. 8.
2. Sterling, *Turning the World Upside Down*, 17.
3. "Introduction," in Harriet Jacobs, *Incidents in the Life of a Slave Girl*, ed. Jean Fagan Yellin (Cambridge: Harvard University Press, 1987), xiv. All quotations from *Incidents* are taken from this edition, and are cited parenthetically in the text.
4. The phrase is from a letter from Jacobs to Amy Post; in *Incidents in the Life of a Slave Girl*, 232.
5. As Robert B. Stepto argues, "The risks that written storytelling undertakes are . . . at least twofold: one is that the reader will become a hearer but not manage an authenticating response; the other is that the reader will *remain a reader* and not

only belittle or reject storytelling's particular 'keen disturbance,' but also issue confrontational responses which sustain altogether different definitions of literature, of literacy, and of appropriate reader response" ("Distrust of the Reader in Afro-American Narratives," in Sacvan Bercovitch, ed., *Reconstructing American Literary History* [Cambridge: Harvard University Press, 1986], 308).

6. Much has been written about the role of motherhood in Jacobs's attempt to reach her white female readers, for as Jean Fagan Yellin rightly observes, "motherhood is central to *Incidents*" (*Women & Sisters: The Antislavery Feminists in American Culture* [New Haven: Yale University Press, 1989], 89). As Bruce Mills argues, Lydia Maria Child's editorial advice to Jacobs – particularly, that a closing chapter on John Brown be omitted – "underscores her conviction that a female slave narrative would be most forceful if it invoked the sanctity of motherhood" ("Lydia Maria Child and the Endings to Harriet Jacobs's *Incidents in the Life of a Slave Girl*," *American Literature* 64:2 [1992]: 256). See also Sarah Way Sherman, "Moral Experience in Harriet Jacobs's *Incidents in the Life of a Slave Girl*," *NWSA Journal* 2:2 (1990): 178–82.

7. I agree with Yellin that "*Incidents* was written and published to foster a community of women who would act to oppose slavery." As Yellin argues, "Both the author and editor of *Incidents* urge their female readers to move beyond the private sphere and to emulate their example by engaging in the public debate on slavery and racism. Informed not by 'the cult of domesticity' or 'domestic feminism' but by political feminism, *Incidents* is an attempt to move women to political action" (*Women & Sisters*, 92). The question, of course, is how to negotiate the significant transition into the "public sphere." At base, this is a question about Jacobs's conception of the "community of women," and the implicit terms of that community. As Hazel V. Carby argues, "'Sisterhood' between white and black women was realized rarely in the text of *Incidents*. Jacobs's appeal was to a potential rather than an actual bonding between white and black women" (*Reconstructing Womanhood: The Emergence of the Afro-American Woman Novelist* [New York: Oxford University Press, 1987], 51). See also William L. Andrews on Jacobs's and Frederick Douglass's desire "to qualify themselves for admission into [an] idealized marginal community," an appeal that includes the recognition that the conditions of that community must be carefully defined (*To Tell A Free Story: The First Century of Afro-American Autobiography, 1760–1865* [Urbana: University of Illinois Press, 1986], 253–4). In what follows, I argue that Jacobs makes a point of deferring that community to define the terms by which the *potential* bonding between women of different races and varying classes could be realized.

8. Braxton presents "the archetype of the outraged mother" as "a counterpart to the articulate hero," noting of this archetype that "She is a mother because motherhood was virtually unavoidable under slavery; she is outraged because of the intimacy of her oppression" (*Black Women Writing Autobiography: A Tradition Within a Tradition* [Philadelphia: Temple University Press, 1989], 19).

9. Ginzberg, *Women and the Work of Benevolence*, 16.

10. Ibid., 25.

11. Karen Sánchez-Eppler, "Bodily Bonds: The Intersecting Rhetorics of Feminism and Abolition," *Representations* 24 (1988): 43.

12. Lydia Maria Child, *The American Frugal Housewife. Dedicated to Those Who Are Not Ashamed of Economy* (Boston: Carter, Hendee, and Co., 1832), 106.

13. See Sherman on Brent's position "between the brutal, exploitative bonds of slavery and the idealized, altruistic bonds of true womanhood" (167).

14. Barbara Welter, "The Cult of True Womanhood: 1820–1860," *American Quarterly* 18:2 (1966): 151–74; 152. On black women and the cult of true womanhood, see Shirley J. Yee, *Black Women Abolitionists: A Study in Activism, 1828–1860* (Knoxville, TN: University Press of Knoxville, 1992).

15. The domestic sphere – and the woman in it – is, of course, involved in history, and this is accounted for by the reciprocity of republican domestic ideology in the context of ideals of human progress: the vision of history that informed much of American political and historiographical thought, presenting the United States as the culmination of human history and looking forward to the increased perfection of the race. Basically, men could hope to be refined *by* women only insofar as they worked to create a world that would refine women themselves, and that would refine also men's appreciation of women. As one anonymous commentator put it, the "original and coarse appreciation" of women "has been refining all along the stream of history"; by 1853, this process had refined itself to the point where the author could exclaim, "She is Eve, or living still, but with how much diviner a life than she ever knew before!" ("Women and the 'Women's Movement,'" *Putnam's Monthly. A Magazine of Literature, Science, and Art* 1 [March 1853]: 287). This reciprocal relationship provided the conduit by which history was allowed and encouraged to enter the home. As Nina Baym has argued, "history made the American republican home coextensive with the body politic. Because republican women in republican homes could not do their work without history, they praised, valued, and disseminated it in their writings" ("At Home with History: History Books and Women's Sphere Before the Civil War," *Proceedings of the American Antiquarian Society* 101:2 [1991]: 278).

   On nineteenth-century American assumptions about the progress and perfection of history, see David Levin, *History as Romantic Art: Bancroft, Prescott, Motley, and Parkman* (1959; rpt. New York: AMS, 1967); on women, theology, American historiography, and the "escape from history," see chap. 5 of Ann Douglas, *The Feminization of American Culture* (Anchor Books, 1977; rpt. New York: Doubleday, 1988). On American republican ideologies of womanhood, see Douglas; Maxine L. Margolis, *Mothers and Such: Views of American Women and Why They Changed* (Berkeley: University of California Press, 1984), 33–9, 115–24; and especially Linda K. Kerber, *Women of the Republic: Intellect and Ideology in Revolutionary America* (Chapel Hill: University of North Carolina Press, 1980).

16. See Ruth H. Bloch, "The Gendered Meanings of Virtue in Revolutionary America," *Signs: Journal of Women in Culture and Society* 13:1 (1987): 37–58, on "the conflation of the virtuous with the feminine" in Revolutionary America – the process by which conceptions of republican civic virtue gave way to feminine virtue "in an increasingly competitive male political system" wherein "the distinction faded between virtuous men committed to public service and unvirtuous men pursuing narrow self-interest" (57). As Bloch argues, "the representation of public virtue as a feminine trait hinged on the exclusion of women from institutional public life. If virtue was regarded as outside politics, what better way to conceive of it than as feminine?" (57).

17. "Women and the 'Women's Movement,'" 287.

18. Ibid.

19. "The homes of America the Hope of the Republic," *The United States Democratic Review* 7:4 (1856): 296–7.

20. "Intellectual Culture of Women," *Southern Literary Messenger: A Magazine Devoted to Literature, Science and Art* 28:21 (1859): 329.

21. Carby, *Reconstructing Womanhood*, 49. Similarly, Sherman refers to Brent's double bind of slavery and true womanhood, noting that "Both systems denied her a self-hood; neither had words to authorize her choices" (168). As I argue, to create choices, Jacobs (through Brent) had to reconfigure authorized modes of discourse and knowledge.

22. Mr. Sands (identified by Yellin as Samuel Tredwell Sawyer) runs for and is elected to Congress as the Whig candidate (*Incidents*, 189).

23. *Uncle Tom's Cabin; or, Life among the Lowly* (Library of America, New York: Vintage, 1991), 515.

24. On Jacobs's experiences with and comments about Stowe, and on her situation after reaching the North, see the letters collected in the appendix of Yellin's edition of *Incidents*; see also Yellin's introduction; *Women & Sisters*, chap. 4; and "Texts and Contexts of Harriet Jacobs' *Incidents in the Life of a Slave Girl: Written by Herself*," in *The Slave's Narrative*, ed. Charles T. Davis and Henry Louis Gates, Jr. (Oxford: Oxford University Press, 1985), 262–82. See also Carby, 47–61.

25. Carby, *Reconstructing Womanhood*, 55.

26. Lorraine Code, *What Can She Know? Feminist Theory and the Construction of Knowledge* (Ithaca: Cornell University Press, 1991), 139.

27. Ibid.

28. Henry D. Thoreau, *Walden and "Resistance to Civil Government,"* A Norton Critical Edition, 2nd ed. (New York: Norton, 1992), 216. See William L. Andrews on the differences between Thoreau's concept of autobiography and that of black auto-biographers, in Andrews, *To Tell a Free Story*, 2.

29. Sánchez-Eppler, "Bodily Bonds," 31.

30. Code, *What Can She Know?*, 144. See also Code's source, Evelyn Fox Keller and Christine Grontkowski, "The Mind's Eye," in Sandra Harding and Merrill Hintikka, eds., *Discovering Reality: Feminist Perspectives on Epistemology, Methodology, and the Philosophy of Science* (Fordrecht: Reidel, 1983).

31. See, for example, Yellin, "Text and Contexts," 274, and *Women & Sisters*, 93; see also Carby, *Reconstructing Womanhood*, 58.

32. Consider, in this context, the nineteenth-century eroticization of the vice of slavery, making the slave narrative, in Robin Wink's phrase, "the pious pornography of their day" (quoted in Andrews, *To Tell a Free Story*, 243); see also Andrews, 242–3.

33. I am referring, of course, to Jacobs's letter to Amy Post, in which she says that "Woman can whisper – her cruel wrongs into the ear of a very dear friend – much easier than she can record them for the world to read" (*Incidents*, 242).

34. On Jacobs's attempt to "structure an alternative vantage of understanding, an alternative epistemology, that mirrors Linda's reconstituted Subjectivity," particularly as it relates to the relationship between (black) author and (white) reader, see Dana D. Nelson, *The Word in Black and White: Reading "Race" in American Literature, 1638–1867* (New York: Oxford University Press, 1992), chap. 7. As Nelson argues, "The text repeatedly appeals to the sympathy of its readers, but at the same time it warns them to be careful about the motives and critical of the results of that sympathetic identification" (144, 142).

"THIS POISONOUS SYSTEM"

SOCIAL ILLS, BODILY ILLS, AND INCIDENTS IN THE LIFE OF A SLAVE GIRL

MARY TITUS

———

> Unless we can get rid of this poisonous system, there will be no health left in us.
>
> Lydia Maria Child

Relations between the poisonous social system of slavery and the individual afflicted body lie at the heart of Harriet Jacobs's narrative *Incidents in the Life of a Slave Girl*. Throughout, Jacobs depicts incidents of illness, physical and moral, personal and social. In its story of individual suffering, Jacobs's text can be fruitfully identified as an illness narrative. As defined by physician Arthur Kleinman, an illness narrative is "a story the patient tells, and significant others retell, to give coherence to the distinctive events and long-term course of suffering. The plot lines, core metaphors, and rhetorical devices that structure the illness narrative are drawn from cultural and personal models for arranging experiences in meaningful ways."[1] *Incidents in the Life of a Slave Girl*, however, tells not only of a "long-term course of suffering" personal and familial, but of an entire culture disordered and polluted. These several levels of illness are both interactive and made synonymous, each caused by a destructive order that affects both the individual and social constitution. As illness forms a core of meaning in *Incidents*, bodily relations of authority and powerlessness are played out in the relation of physician with patient, which is also, in Jacobs's text, the relation of master with slave.

Jacobs's illness narrative draws on the rich variety of nineteenth-century discourse, from the stern language of Garrisonian resistance to the appeals of

199

sentimental sisterhood. Her recurring depiction of illness simultaneously speaks the actuality of her suffering and reflects another important discourse of her cultural moment, particularly through its employment of medical language to name social disorder. Illness was a favorite abolitionist trope; typically, abolitionist writing describes slavery as a poison or disease that affects both the body and politic of the nation and the body natural of each citizen. As Martha Banta has established, such analogies form a tradition in American political argument, epidemic in the periodic arguments over the health or disease of the nation's "constitution."[2] In the mid-nineteenth century, abolitionist writers joined a rich tradition of political diagnosis as they delineated the disease of slavery and argued for various remedial actions.

That Jacobs was extremely familiar with abolitionist rhetoric is apparent from the eighteen months she spent directing a reading room in Rochester, New York. As Jean Fagan Yellin confirms, during this time Jacobs "read her way through the abolitionists' library of books and papers 'The latest and best work on slavery and other moral questions.'"[3] Throughout *Incidents in the Life of a Slave Girl*, Harriet Jacobs employs and revises the rhetorical relations between disease and slavery common to abolitionist argument. Because hers is a narrative of personal experience, illness simultaneously expresses her literal suffering, represents the affliction of the body as the disease of slavery, and speaks figuratively of a wider social malady. Through her narrative, Harriet Jacobs painfully questions whether health – personal or national – can ever be regained after the long illness of slavery, "that blight which too surely waits on every human being born to be chattel" (7).[4]

Turning briefly to nineteenth-century medical theory, we can readily comprehend why illness imagery appealed to abolitionist writers, such as Harriet Jacobs. Contemporary medicine tended to unite individual illness with both moral character and environmental influence. Charles Rosenberg argues that in eighteenth- and early-to-mid-nineteenth-century medical theory, "Just as man's body interacted continuously with his environment, so did his mind with his body, his morals with his health. The realm of causation in medicine was not distinguishable from the realm of meaning in society generally."[5] Not only were personal and social illness mutually contagious, but one, according to Bryan Turner, could be an expression of the other: "Sickness in the individual was intimately linked with disorder and mismanagement of the social body."[6] As a result, abolitionist writers could freely mingle environmental, moral, and physical illnesses in their discourse; the relations were intimate, the boundaries permeable, the terms ultimately interchangeable. In the same discourse, for example, contamination might be depicted as arising, simultaneously, from unclean food practices and the less visible, but no less pernicious, pollution of immorality.

Because the body was viewed as a "system of intake and outgo" taking in food and flagitiousness alike, medical practices frequently involved bitter potions, the ingestion of emetics, cathartics, and diuretics to produce cleansing excretions.[7] Not surprisingly, attention to diet was crucial to health; in general, there was a strong focus on what went into the body, predominantly orally, as well as what came out. Of all the so-called heroic measures to combat disease by arousing comparable but opposing physical distress, the most notorious was bleeding, using cutting or the application of leeches and often prolonging treatment until the sign of victory – unconsciousness. In the words of medical historian John Haller, "Armed with cups, lancet, and leech and provided with calomel, tartar emetic, arsenic, and an assortment of other drugs, doctors proceeded to bleed, blister, puke, purge, and salivate patients until they either died from the combined disease and treatment or persevered long enough to recover from both."[8]

Abolitionists frequently invoked heroic medical practices in their discourse, arguing for various vigorous remedial actions to combat the spreading blight of slavery. To cite a few from the wealth of examples, in "Revolution the Only Remedy for Slavery," the fiery Stephen Foster proposes bleeding over quarantine as a political model, arguing that action analogous to the latter would ultimately fail to halt the spread of "this terrible disease," slavery: "Our first great work is to cut this Gordian knot, – the Union. . . . Talk of confining slavery? As well might you talk of regulating the cholera, or of confining the plague within certain limits, or say to intemperance, 'In such and such localities seek your victims, and we will defend you there; but pass not those boundaries.'"[9] Medical discourse also helped the New England Anti-Slavery Society shape its call for immediate emancipation. The Society labeled emancipation the ideal curative. One dose "will banish the poverty of the South, reclaim her barren soil, and pour new blood into all her veins and arteries . . . will renovate the whole frame of society. There is not a slave State but will exhibit the flush of returning health, and feel a stronger pulse and draw a freer breath."[10] Agricultural, economic, and political vigor will all attend the curative of emancipation.

Like their contemporaries, abolitionists not only viewed social and individual health as interdependent, but also believed both depended on the health of that crucial nineteenth-century institution, the home.[11] Thus national moral vigor could also be attained through abolition, for healthy order in the social body would follow healthy order – physical and moral – in domestic arrangements. In abolitionists' minds, according to Ronald Walters, "slavery was a guidepost, marking the outer limits of disorder and debauchery."[12] Slavery promoted licentiousness and thus threatened the health of the family. Perhaps no one evoked the spreading infection of debauchery more fervently than James Thome, who cried "pollution, pollution! . . . let it be felt in the North, and rolled back upon the South, that the slave States are Sodoms, and almost every village family is a brothel." Thome's horror ultimately lies in his view of the contaminating proximity of uncivilized blacks to the white family. As he makes clear: "I refer to the inmates of the kitchens, and not to the whites." All night long in Thome's heated imagination, slaves carouse in "the kitchens of church members and elders!"[13] To diagnose the health of a society, investigate its kitchens. There, the medical view of the well-regulated body as a balanced system of intake and output finds expression in well-regulated domesticity: a family in clean, nutritional order. Such a family suffuses health over their surroundings, personal and political. Thus Thome's focus on kitchens is fully explicable. A debauched slave presence there, where food is prepared, suggests to him the potential for infection of first the familial and then the social body.[14]

Like her fellow abolitionists, Harriet Jacobs employs the language of illness to condemn slavery, writing her individual illness narrative into a contexture of disorders. Her text is rich throughout with the language of disease and contamination. Dr. Flint is a "plague"; "cruelty is contagious"; slavery is an "all-pervading corruption" or, most commonly, a "blight." Moral pollution is repeatedly invoked, for slavery is "deep, and dark and foul" (2), or in Lydia Maria Child's prefatory words, a "loathsome den of corruption and cruelty" (4). Diseased, this slave society consumes poisons rather than medicinal concoctions: The slave girl drinks the "cup of sin"; visitors to the South "imbibe" a tolerance for slavery. Because of the ill-health of the Southern social body, individual bodies experience suffering that is simultaneously literal and an expression of an overall disorder.

Perhaps the most striking representation of bodily suffering occurs in Chapter Nine of Jacobs's narrative, "Sketches of Neighboring Planters." Composed of multiple, graphically described incidents of the abuse of bodies – whipped, scalded, starved, clubbed, torn apart, and devoured by vermin – the chapter's language echoes the precision of medical discourse, noting a "form . . . attenuated by hunger," and a man "faint with loss of blood . . . too sick to walk" (46–7). In fact, medical knowledge is regularly employed by slaveholders; in one instance, a man "cut with the whip from his head to his feet" is "then washed with strong brine, to prevent the flesh from mortifying, and make it heal sooner than it otherwise would" (48–9). Through these descriptions of irrational violence delineated with the language of rational medical discourse, Jacobs depicts the perversion of slave society, where a diseased system presents itself as social health. This is a world with no true order governing relations between persons or the treatment of bodies. In the nexus of medical–political language mapped by Martha Banta, it is a world with "no therapies in operation; no political or medical system in effect; no social codes, contracts, or covenants."[15] It is important to note that Chapter Nine of *Incidents* is more marked by Lydia Maria Child's editorial hand than are other sections of Jacobs's text, for Child urged Jacobs to "put the savage cruelties into one chapter, entitled 'Neighboring Planters.'"[16] The result is certainly powerful, a concentration of horrors. Yet at the same time Child's editing may have effectively diminished some of the overall power and unity of Jacobs's original design. If the bodily abuses collected in Chapter Nine were instead dispersed, they would further enhance the atmosphere of social illness and perverse governance that pervades the entire text, and connect more overtly with the abuse and illness of Jacobs's body in particular. Lydia Maria Child ostensibly compiled Chapter Nine "in order that those who shrink from 'supping upon horrors' might omit them, without interrupting the thread of the story."[17] Her phrase "supping upon horrors" gives pause when one considers that many of the abuses in the chapter are related to the preparation and consumption of food. Through her imaging of perverse feeding, Jacobs employs the cultural association of nutritional disorder with social disorder, foregrounding the breakdown of salubrious domestic practices under slavery.

Chapter Nine, shaped no doubt by Child's editorial hand, becomes a litany of food abuse. From the first specific incident in which "a piece of fat pork" is cooked, so that its "scalding drops of fat" burn a bound slave, food serves as an instrument of torture or as contributor to incidents of violence. Repeatedly, Jacobs figures slave bodies consumed by animals, thereby pointing to slavery's inhuman consumption of human beings. Her climactic image comes with the death of a slave pinned within a cotton gin and "partly eaten by rats and vermin" (49). The image encapsulates Jacobs's argument, uniting in a single horrific image the slave, the verminous slaveholder who consumes him, and the central machine of the cotton economy.

Jacobs more directly describes the subversion of eating within the slaveholding family when she turns to individual experience, following her pattern of depicting specific, personally related incidents of illness within a general cultural contamination. In the Flint household, food is repeatedly polluted and used for punishment, part of the perversion attending to white domination. For example, the Flints punish their cook by compelling her to consume the meals they reject; even more terribly, they force her to eat food their dog has slavered on and rejected. As punishment for a late Sunday dinner, Mrs. Flint "would station herself in the kitchen, and wait till it was dished, and then spit in all the kettles and pans that had been used for cooking . . . to prevent the cook and her children from eking out their meagre fare with the remains of the gravy and other scrapings" (12). The slaveholding Flints' negative sense of nourishment is most apparent when they lock their cook "away from her nursing baby" (13), essentially violating the very heart of domestic harmony and physical nurturance.

Throughout her narrative, Jacobs also exposes the contagious nature of immorality. Her text responds to and indeed reverses the assumptions shaping abolitionist moral diatribes such as James Thome's. Where Thome, as noted, locates immorality in the black community, fearing the infection of the white home through the debauched inhabitants of the kitchen, Jacobs forcefully and repeatedly identifies white men as the source of contagion. According to Thome, in the "unrestrained communication" between "female slaves and the misses . . . the courtezan feats of the over-night are whispered into the ear of the unsuspecting girl, to poison her youthful mind."[18] With the marked contrast of her own daughter, Jacobs shows us a white man, named Thorne, "pour[ing] vile language into the ears" of an innocent black child (179). Likewise Flint, "peopled [Jacobs's] young mind with unclean images" (27), and his wife crouches by Jacobs's bedside whispering in her ear. It is the "slave girl [who] is reared in an atmosphere of licentiousness and fear" (51), according to Jacobs, for she must listen to the talk of white men. Although white girls are likewise infected, it is not from the general proximity of slaves, but from the specific practices of fathers. "White daughters early hear their parents quarreling about some female slave," and "They are attended by the young slave girls whom their father has corrupted" (52). As a result, Jacobs asserts – in a startling reversal of white ideology – white daughters follow their fathers' examples and corrupt male slaves. Moral disease originates with white men, spreading outward through white and black communities alike. All are infected: "Yet few slave-holders seem to be aware of the widespread moral ruin. . . . Their talk is of blighted cotton crops – not of the blight on their children's souls" (52). Like the "whited sepulcher" of Matthew 23:27 to which Jacobs alludes, Southern white society may "appear beautiful outward," but disease and death hide within this charnel house, full of "dead men's bones, and all uncleanness" (36).

Against the moral disorder and abuse of food characteristic of white domination Jacobs sets her grandmother's harmonious, loving household, with its jars of delicious preserves and "grand big oven . . . that baked bread and nice things for the town" (17). Yet abiding health cannot be found in this household either, for slavery infects its members as well. Most of Jacobs's family members are enslaved, and again the diseased social order is manifested in individual, physical suffering. In the first chapter, Jacobs's mother dies; in the second, her father, "so suddenly [she] had not even heard that he was sick" (10). Soon her uncle Benjamin is "taken sick" (24), and his namesake, little Benny, is "very ill" in infancy (62). Likewise Ellen is twice sick, her bout of measles badly affecting her eyes. Aunt Nancy is "stricken with paralysis," her health ruined "by years of incessant, unrequited toil" (144, 146), and the grandmother becomes critically ill during Jacobs's long confinement, breaking "down under the weight of anxiety and toil" (123).[19] The illness that strikes at all members of Jacobs's family expresses the diseased social system that surrounds them and that denies them healthy and harmonious domestic practices. As nineteenth-century domestic ideology espoused and medical theory concurred, the family represents the locus of health – physical, emotional, and spiritual; its decay expresses the breakdown of society as a whole.

Slavery is a spreading blight, and thus, in the words of one abolitionist, "when the family 'falls into decay' . . . no other true institution can be preserved in a healthful state."[20] Lacking the protected space of "a home shielded by the laws" (54), neither Jacobs nor the members of her family can depend on the salutary benefits of secure domesticity.

The general illness of Jacobs's family expresses the social upheaval brought by slavery at the same time that the pain of individual members carries more specific meanings. Her uncle Benjamin, for example, should be a robust young man, but his "condition" makes him ill. Locked in jail because he so powerfully desires freedom – the physical imprisonment making concrete his legal condition – Benjamin's health declines. "Long confinement had made his face too pale, his form too thin" (23). When he heads northward, he is "taken sick" in Baltimore and confines himself, fearful of capture. Yet he cannot recuperate without physical freedom: "How could he get strength without air and exercise?" (24). The ironies implicit in Benjamin's illness and quest for health are easily apparent. Slavery makes him ill, confining his body, denying him "one breath of free air" – a phrase Jacobs employs repeatedly, no doubt for its mixing of medical prescription with physical liberation. Yet in seeking light, air, and mobility – all necessary for literal health and signs of the healthy state of freedom – Benjamin risks greater imprisonment. The counterpoint of healthy freedom is paralysis, suffered by Aunt Nancy later in the text, as well as by Jacobs herself.

At the center of *Incidents in the Life of a Slave Girl* lies Harriet Jacobs's own illness narrative shaped by her relationship with Dr. Flint. That the master–slave relationship she endured was also that of doctor–patient no doubt intensified her focus on the illness occurring under slavery. At the same time, it provided a rich, often ironic means to comment on questions of authority and the body. In very general terms, both doctors and slavemasters are assigned the "right" to decide the physical treatment of persons who have been defined as not normal, persons who have been denied autonomy "for their own good" and who are perceived as being in need of external control from those of greater knowledge and authority. Both slave and patient are asked to be passive and obedient, accepting their treatment; in short, both are defined as unequal. It is crucial to acknowledge that the hierarchical relations of physician and patient cannot be completely equated with the extreme inequality of master and slave; yet the former can function as analogous to the latter. Medical practice no less than slavery arises from theories about acceptable and unacceptable bodily conditions and likewise represents a system inscribed with cultural assumptions about power and authority, expressed in language of order, disorder, and remedial action. As Martha Banta argues in her reading of "Medical Therapies and the Body Politic," looking at the relations "binding citizens to society, [or] patients to physicians . . . concerns 'authority' because it asks in different ways, who is in command and by whose consent? It asks, What is being done, and in what manner, to the 'body'? – whether the physical body of the individual or the body of the community."[21]

In her *Incidents in the Life of a Slave Girl* Harriet Jacobs is well aware of and indeed exploits as a central and powerful irony the fact that her slavemaster is a physician. Jacobs consistently refers to Flint as "the doctor," for his professional identity further adds to the sinister reversals symptomatic of slavery. Where food becomes punishment, where fathers corrupt daughters, where illness is a cultural norm, doctors are the source of disease, not the servants of health. Both the repeated claims made by the "wily doctor" – "You are mine and you shall be mine for life" – and his repeated interest in treating her illnesses suggest Doctor Flint's (the slavemaster's) desire to dominate Harriet Jacobs's (the slave's) body, to define her "condition," and to choose her treatment.

Flint, or Dr. James Norcom, received his training at the Medical School of the University of Pennsylvania, and under his tutelage, Harriet Jacobs's brother Benjamin learns to "leech, cup, and bleed" (61). As is clear from Benjamin's achievement, Norcom performed the very common practice of bleeding patients; he was a typical practitioner of his time, employing "heroic" measures to wrestle illness into submission. It is interesting that during her escape Jacobs receives medical treatment from two other sources besides Dr. Flint, both sources offering therapies in opposition to those of the slavemaster/physician. After she is bitten by a reptile, she turns to "an old woman, who doctored among the slaves," and receives a folk remedy: "steep a dozen coppers in vinegar, over night, and apply the cankered vinegar to the inflamed part" (98). Slave practitioners, who often provided remedies inherited from African forebears, were often more trusted by slaves, for they were members of their community. Receiving treatment from a slave practitioner could represent both a form of resistance to white domination and an affirmation of black cultural heritage. As Todd L. Savitt suggests, "To offset the failures and harshness of white remedies or the negligence of masters, or perhaps to exert some control over their lives, some slaves treated their own diseases and disorders or turned to other trusted blacks for medical assistance. . . . Black home remedies circulated secretly through the slave quarters and were passed down privately from generation to generation."[22] After Jacobs escapes to her attic hideaway, she receives medical assistance from a homeopathic or Thompsonian doctor. The nineteenth century saw the rise of homeopathic medical theory – part of the powerful lay movement that opposed the solidifying professionalization of medicine. In both politics and practice, homeopathy sought to democratize medical treatment, returning knowledge and authority to the hands of laypersons, and approaching illness with gentler, more egalitarian therapies. It is intriguing that Thompsonians were also concerned with women's rights and that several Thompsonians aided in an 1835 slave revolt in Mississippi.[23] In his flight toward freedom, William Wells Brown is also assisted by "Thompsonian friends" in the Quaker household of Wells Brown, whose name he adopts.[24]

As a slavemaster and thus the source of the systematic illness of slavery, Doctor Flint dispenses disease, not health. Those around him must breathe "his contaminating atmosphere" and suffer from the contagion. Repeatedly, Jacobs enacts the irony of a doctor's coming to treat the symptoms of a disease that originates in his own actions, that is essentially caused by his treatment. In fact, "treatment" occurs frequently in Jacobs's text, the term taking on a rich double meaning, denoting simultaneously violent medical action and violent physical domination, the authoritarian rule of doctor/master forced upon the patient/slave. Doctor Flint "treats" Jacobs with violence. He prescribes punishment – "such treatment that you would forget the meaning of the word *peace*" (40) – rather than healthy freedom. Most ironic are the incidents in which he treats the consequences of his own vicious treatments – for example, after Jacobs gives birth to her second child. Stopping by her childbed, Doctor Flint first verbally and physically abuses her, forcing her to rise and stand before him; then, when she collapses he "dashed cold water in my face, took me up, and shook me violently." As Jacobs concludes, "I suffered in consequence of this treatment; but I begged my friends to let me die, rather than send for the doctor. There was nothing I dreaded so much as his presence" (77–8). In the world of domination and unfree bodies, the doctor is also the slavemaster; his visits bring sickness, not recovery; slavery, not emancipation. They perpetuate the endless cycle Jacobs delineates, in which there can be no cure under slavery, only treatment that requires treatment. Other paradoxes are played out elsewhere in the text. For example Ellen, suffering from eye disease brought on by measles, is taken from jail by Doctor Flint to receive treatment in his home. The cure threatens more than the disease, and "Poor little Ellen cried all day to be carried back to prison" (102). For this child, incarceration promises more physical vitality and freedom than does the doctor's "care."

Under the specific "treatment" of Dr. Flint and more generally the "treatment" of slavery, Jacobs suffers particularly from two forms of illness: impaired mobility and physical contamination. Both are complexly related to her social "condition." Jacobs's impaired mobility both results from and speaks to the issues of her physical enslavement.[25] At the same time, it participates in a metaphorical tradition of mobility and freedom that runs through the rhetoric of political well-being; as one historian notes, "Lawful systems are like muscles of the body that function to produce a mutually beneficial ease of motion. 'Motion' is 'desire,' and desire is made possible when each man's liberty is shielded by the state from the encroachment of others' 'liberties' on his own 'motion.'"[26] In Doctor Flint's restless desire to take "liberties" with Harriet Jacobs's body her own "desire" is denied; she becomes immobilized.

It is one of the book's striking paradoxes that Harriet Jacobs's means to freedom is through greater physical limitation: The loophole of retreat both confines and liberates her. As confinement, it suggests her increasingly limited physical freedom under Doctor Flint's power. Out of his house, she escapes the full paralysis that ultimately afflicts her Aunt Nancy, but she does not achieve full and healthy freedom; her bodily movement is incredibly restricted and, briefly, she also loses her ability to speak. The "free air," that recurring symbol of health and unlimited mobility in the text, is denied to Jacobs in her den. As she bitterly comments, watching Flint through her loophole, "I longed to draw in a plentiful drought of fresh air, to stretch my cramped limbs . . . the laws allowed *him* to be out in the free air" (121). It is notable that as Doctor Flint's power over Jacobs diminishes, her physical abilities increase. After her letters convince him that she is safe in the North, she slips "down into the storeroom more frequently, where I could stand upright, and move my limbs more freely" (141). During her passage northward, she slowly regains the use of her limbs, nourished by the free "air and sunlight" as well as the "constant exercise" that bespeaks her less restrained political condition (158).

More complex is Jacobs's second form of illness, bodily contamination. It is imbibed with the "cup of sin and shame and misery" she must swallow as a slave woman, a dose imparting not just the general "condition" of slavery, but a more specific moral contamination from contact with the white men who perpetuate the disease of slavery and sexually exploit her. Throughout her narrative, Jacobs must repeatedly sip from "the bitter cup of my life" (104, 170, 249). Not curatives, these doses, like all the slavemaster's "treatments," spread infection. The central trope of bodily contamination in *Incidents in the Life of a Slave Girl* builds around a conventional image of abolitionist rhetoric, the slaveholder as a snake. As Jean Yellin notes, "Abolitionists, who characterized slavery as 'the national sin,' routinely symbolized the institution as a serpent."[27] Jacobs is unstinting in employing this image, not only in generalized proclamations – "Hot weather brings out snakes and slaveholders, and I like the one class of venomous creatures as little as I do the other" (174) – but also in specific references, for example, one describing Dr. Flint as "the venomous old reprobate" (76). Most notably, however, Jacobs employs the figure to make personal – as she does all the general imagery of cultural illness – her own bodily connection to the slavemaster's venom. Several times in her narrative, Jacobs's flesh is literally bitten and contaminated. In the Snaky Swamp, hundreds of mosquitoes "poisoned [her] flesh" as, horrifyingly, "snake after snake" crawled around her (112). These particular invasions speak metaphorically of her sense of being physically infected by slavery, an infection communicated to her through her sexual relations with white men – not just the venomous Flint, but also the only somewhat less reprehensible Mr. Sands. In her confession to her grandmother shortly after her announced first pregnancy, Jacobs attempts to describe all "the things that had poisoned my life" (57); after the child's birth she weeps for her lost virtue, a loss that began with sexual harassment and culminated in a retaliatory, but no less contagious, sexual contact: "I shed bitter tears that I was no longer worthy of being respected by the good and pure. Alas! slavery still held me in its poisonous grasp" (76).

Jacobs's references to her own bodily contamination often occur in connection with her motherhood. The venomous reptiles that seize her in the snakey world of slavery pass on their poisons from her pain-racked flesh to that of her children. Describing her first child, she follows her confession that "I could never forget that he was a slave" with a description of the child's illness, an illness suggesting the inherited condition of slavery. Jacobs concludes the incident with the words, "O, the serpent of Slavery has many and poisonous fangs!" (62). Again, lamenting that "slavery still held me in its poisonous grasp," she thinks bitterly, "'the child shall follow the condition of the *mother*'" (76). One of her most painful early recognitions occurs when she imagines having children with her "first love," the free-born carpenter. "For *his* sake" – her words – she ends their relationship, thinking, "if we had children, I knew they must 'follow the condition of the mother.' What a terrible blight that would be on the heart of a free, intelligent father!" (42). As the slave mother, Jacobs sees her body as the source of her children's "condition." Slavery denies her the right to pass on to her children a healthy physical and social order: free air, mobility of limb, social, environmental, and political well-being. Instead she communicates her own "slave condition." As bringer of blight, a body poisoned by venomous slavemasters, Jacobs is immersed in the tainted world identified by abolitionists as the slave South, infected with the general malaise of slavery.

When John Jacobs first saw his sister Harriet in the North, "living with a family as a nurse at the Astor House," he found her appearance markedly changed: "At first she did not look natural to me, but how should she look natural, after having been shut out from the light of heaven for six years and eleven months!"[28] His testimony confirms what Jacobs suggests everywhere in the final chapters of her narrative, that her recuperation from slavery is slow, perhaps never complete. Although she gains in mobility as she moves out of the grasp of Flint in particular and Southern slavery in general, Jacobs continues to suffer "whenever I walked much" (168). Her physical limitation speaks specifically of the confinement she endured; however, it also suggests the continued denial of full freedom. In the North she remains dependent to a degree on white authority, albeit expressed as benevolence. At the same time her physical freedom is compromised by the racism she encounters in travel and hotels. Her children, too, are denied complete mobility. Particularly after the implementation of the Fugitive Slave Law, neither she nor her children can "go out to breathe God's free air without trepidation" (195); they dread "the approach of summer when snakes and slaveholders make their appearance" (193).

An important part of Harriet Jacobs's narrative is her experience of stigma in the North. According to Erving Goffman's classic study, *Stigma: Notes on the Management of Spoiled Identity*, stigma may be defined as "the situation of the individual who is disqualified from full social acceptance."[29] Most obviously, the physical limitations Jacobs encounters in the North express the ways in which she is stigmatized because of her race. As Orlando Patterson notes of cultural responses to freedmen, "Nominally granted almost complete equality, politically and legally, with 'free' persons, freedmen nonetheless remained stigmatized. . . . In well over 80 percent of all significant slaveholding societies freedmen suffered some civil disability."[30] Harriet Jacobs's response to the stigmatizing racial practices in Northern society is a clear and rightful indignation.

What is less clear is Jacobs's anxiety that she will be stigmatized because the illness that is slavery leaves some permanent infection; she remains contaminated from her contact with white men. In Goffman's terms, she not only suffers from "the plight of the discredited," those whose appearance automatically invokes stigmatizing responses, but also from the anxiety of the "discreditable," those whose "differentness is not immediately apparent, and is not known beforehand." For the discreditable individual, according to Goffman, anxiety surrounds the "unwitting acceptance of himself by individuals who are prejudiced against persons of the kind he can be revealed to be."[31] In the South, Jacobs experienced both Flint's harassment and her sexual relationship with Sands as incidents in which she was forced into most immediate contact with the disease of slavery, a disease contracted from white men and communicated to her children. Although in the North she might be free of the primary infirmity, she does not feel cured. As slavery becomes background, her extramarital sexual relations and her children's illegitimacy move to the foreground. In her new environment, both represent unacceptable moral disorders. For Harriet Jacobs, full well-being does not simply follow physical recovery; it requires emotional struggle with feelings of shame and unacceptability as well.

Few issues in *Incidents in the Life of a Slave Girl* have received as much critical attention as Harriet Jacobs's response to her relationship with Mr. Sands. As Jean Yellin rightly states, "It is difficult to determine the extent to which Linda Brent's characterization of her action as 'a headlong plunge' and a 'great sin' are merely conventional, and the extent to which these articulate a serious endorsement of a sexual standard that condemns her."[32] Readers have focused on Jacobs's blunt statement, shortly following the anguished passages describing her relationship with Sands, that "in looking back, calmly, on the events of my life, I feel that the slave woman ought not to be judged by the same standards as others" (56). In these few words, they have found Jacobs's challenge to "ideologies of female sexuality" and her "development of an alternative discourse of womanhood."[33] It is true here, and elsewhere in the first half of her narrative, that Jacobs adapts to her own moral condition the "environmentalist" theories espoused by many abolitionist writers. According to Ronald Walters, theories that environment markedly influences behavior helped "abolitionists to hold fast to their belief in human unity while explaining why groups of people looked and acted so different from one another."[34] As Lydia Maria Child affirmed, "human nature is essentially the same in all nations and ages; being modified only by the laws that control and regulate it, and the social conditions under which it is developed."[35] One can hear this environmentalist position clearly not just in Jacobs's comments on her own sexual choices, but in her defense of other slaves. At one point she addresses the reader: "Do you think this proves the black man to belong to an inferior order of beings? What would *you* be, if you had been born and brought up a slave, with generations of slaves for ancestors?" (44). However, despite general attestations that moral choices must be read within environmental context and only subsequently excused or condemned, Harriet Jacobs cannot fully exonerate herself for her relationship with Sands. In genteel Northern society, she suffers the feelings of the "discreditable," perceiving herself as an individual whose "condition," if fully known, would damage the possibilities of full social acceptance.

Again and again in the North, Jacobs considers telling and then most often withholds her story. As Goffman notes, for the potentially discreditable individual, "the issue is . . . that of managing information about his failing. To display or not to display; to tell or not to tell; to let on or not to let on; to lie or not to lie; and in each case, to whom, how, when, and where."[36] After her first frank confession in Philadelphia, Jacobs thinks often about concealing her story. Jeremiah Durham's advice, "don't answer every body so openly," is well heeded, although what she hears most is the word "contempt": " 'It might give some heartless people a pretext for treating you with contempt.' That word *contempt* burned me like coals of fire" (160–1). Thereafter she repeatedly fears that those whose esteem she desires will learn her story and will shrink from her as one morally contaminated, potentially contagious. When she parts from Mrs. Durham, foremost in her mind is a longing "to know whether her husband had repeated to her what I had told him" (162). Likewise with Mrs. Bruce, "I valued her good opinion, and I was afraid of losing it, if I told her all the particulars of my sad story" (180). As her twinned confessions to her daughter Ellen suggest, in the South the "condition" of illness Jacobs must confess is that of her slave status; in the North her "condition" is one of a former moral failing, her sexual relationship with Sands. In the first moment, she took her daughter in her "arms and told her I was a slave"; in the second, with a "shrinking dread of diminishing my child's love," she begins to give Ellen "the knowledge" that she "dreaded to impart" (140, 188–9). It is a knowledge that Jacobs, like most who suffer the anxiety of being discreditable, feels is so potentially stigmatizing that her daughter will join society in setting distance to avoid being contaminated by her.

Harriet Jacobs's sense of her discreditable condition finds expression in her correspondence as well as in her text. As Hazel Carby notes, when Jacobs wrote to Amy Post, she hesitated to ask "one so good and pure" to have editorial contact with her text, expressing in Carby's words, a fear that "her own history would contaminate the reputation of her white friend."[37] In another letter to Post, Jacobs confesses her anxiety, her phrasing revealing her emotional agony:

> dear Amy if it was the life of a Heroine with no degradation associated with it far better to have been one of the starving poor of Ireland whose bones had to bleach on the highways than to have been a slave with the curse of slavery stamped upon yourself and Children your purity of heart and kindly sympathies won me at one time to speak of my children. . . . I had determined to let others think as they pleased but my lips should be sealed and no one had a right to question me for this reason when I first came North I avoided the Antislavery people as much as possible because I felt that I could not be honest and tell the whole truth.[38]

Jacobs cannot free herself of her felt sense that contact with the "curse of slavery" has left her permanently contaminated or impure. It is a painful fact that her beloved children potentially testify by their presence to her "degradation." It is anguish for Harriet Jacobs to tell her story. Telling moves her from the potentially safe status of the discreditable to that of the discredited. As Amy Post describes her experience of listening to Jacobs, "Even in talking with me, she wept so much, and seemed to suffer so much mental agony."[39]

Erving Goffman suggests, however, that in ceasing to hide his or her stigma, the discreditable person moves toward health, for "the stigmatized individual can come to feel that he should be above passing, that if he accepts himself and respects himself he will feel no need to conceal his failing. . . . It is here that voluntary disclosure fits into the moral career."[40] Some such awareness finally motivated Harriet Jacobs to write. She told Amy Post about her battle with self-protective pride: "I have tried for the past two years to conquer it and I feel that God has helped me or I never would consent to give my past life to any one."[41] Telling her illness narrative, her moral and physical infection from the disease of slavery, Harriet Jacobs further moves herself toward full freedom, toward full health.

Employing abolitionist rhetoric of cultural disease and contamination to shape the language and incidents of her narrative, Harriet Jacobs found a means to express her personal bodily experience under slavery as part of a general social malaise. She diagnoses slavery as a contagious, insidious illness that moves throughout the slave community. From the white men, those masters / doctors authorized to prescribe "treatment," the disease of slavery infects all members of the community: white and black, male and female, parent and child. In her depiction of cultural disorder, Jacobs expresses a communal vision akin to that of Lydia Maria Child, who likewise argued that "Unless we can get rid of this poisonous system, there will be no health left in us."[42] Yet general social health will come slowly and painfully, Jacobs makes clear, as slowly and painfully as her own progress toward healthy freedom. To tell her illness narrative is to perform a curative act, both in her individual struggle with stigma and in the way that all slave narratives work toward general social health – encouraging the sympathy that might lead to remedial action. Yet Harriet Jacobs's illness narrative, exposing the course of her suffering, from infection to recuperation, suggests most of all the difficulty of healing, both for herself and for her society. In the very act of therapeutic composition, Jacobs feels pain. As she tells her reader: "It is a fact; and to me a sad one, even now; for my body still suffers from the effects of that long imprisonment. . . . I had lived too long in bodily pain and anguish of spirit" (148, 150). For Harriet Jacobs, and perhaps for her country as well, there can be no complete cure. The disease that she suffered was too terrible, its course too prolonged, its symptoms still lingering.

Notes

1. Arthur Kleinman, *The Illness Narratives: Suffering, Healing, and the Human Condition* (New York: Basic, 1988), 49. Elaine Scarry's exploration of the relationship between pain and imagination provides another perspective on illness and narrative in Jacobs's text. According to Scarry, "One can say that pain only becomes an intentional state once it is brought into relation with the objectifying power of the imagination: through that relation, pain will be transformed from a wholly passive and helpless occurrence into a self-modifying and, when most successful, self-eliminating one" (*The Body in Pain: The Making and Unmaking of the World*, New York: Oxford University Press, 1991, 164). Eluding language, pain becomes known primarily through descriptive analogues, or through a "language of agency" (Scarry, 15), naming a perpetrator of the pain. From this perspective, Jacobs's text may be seen as an effort at self-healing, externalizing, objectifying, and thus beginning to control her experience of pain. Drawing on Scarry, Athena Vrettos's brilliant essay, "Curative Domains: Women, Healing, and History in Black Women's Narratives" (*Women's Studies* 16:4 [1989]: 455–73), situates physical and spiritual suffering in Harriet Jacobs's text within a tradition of African American women's writing on the subject. Vrettos argues that illness and healing are recurring metaphors in texts by African American women, part of their labor to heal and give authoritative voice to a history silenced by pain.
2. Martha Banta, "Medical Therapies and the Body Politic," *Prospects: The Annual of American Cultural Studies*, Vol. 8 (Cambridge University Press, 1983), 59.
3. Jean Fagan Yellin, "Introduction," *Incidents in the Life of a Slave Girl* (Cambridge: Harvard University Press, 1987), xvi.

4. References to *Incidents in the Life of a Slave Girl*, cited parenthetically, will be to the following edition: *Incidents in the Life of a Slave Girl: Written by Herself*, ed. Jean Fagan Yellin (Cambridge: Harvard University Press, 1987).

5. Charles Rosenberg, "The Therapeutic Revolution: Medicine, Meaning, and Social Change in Nineteenth-Century America," in *The Therapeutic Revolution: Essays in the Social History of American Medicine*, ed. Morris Vogel and Charles E. Rosenberg (Philadelphia: University of Pennsylvania Press, 1979), 10.

6. Bryan Turner, *The Body and Society: Explorations in Social Theory* (Oxford: Basil Blackwell, 1984), 219.

7. Rosenberg, "The Therapeutic Revolution," p. 6.

8. John S. Haller, *American Medicine in Transition, 1840–1910* (Urbana: University of Illinois Press, 1981), 98–9.

9. Stephen S. Foster, "From *Revolution the Only Remedy*," in *The Antislavery Argument*, ed. William H. Pease and Jane H. Pease (New York: Bobbs-Merrill, 1965), 476–8.

10. "From 'Declaration [of Sentiments] to the National Anti-Slavery Convention'" in Pease and Pease, *The Antislavery Argument*, 63.

11. Medical theory supported the connections between social health, familial health, and individual health. According to Joan Burbick, for example, "Domesticity in the antebellum world often stands for protected space, offering health and peace of mind from an otherwise turbulent culture." Joan Burbick, "'Intervals of Tranquility': The Language of Health in Antebellum America." *Prospects: The Annual of American Cultural Studies*, Vol. 6 (Cambridge University Press, 1981), 178. On slavery's threat to the family see Ronald Walters, *The Antislavery Appeal: American Abolitionism After 1830* (Baltimore: Johns Hopkins University Press, 1976), 91–110.

12. Walters, *The Antislavery Appeal*, 78.

13. James A. Thome, "From 'Speech . . . Delivered at the Annual Meeting of the American Anti-Slavery Society'" in Pease and Pease, *The Antislavery Argument*, 92–3.

14. Food preparation and consumption can be perceived as the locus of the second most intimate possible bodily relation under slavery. This perception helps to explain the frequently expressed anxiety of white abolitionist writers about slave presence in kitchens, more particularly in food preparation, as an expression of their anxiety about the overall physical proximity of blacks and whites under slavery. For more extended discussions of food and race in Harriet Jacobs and other nineteenth-century texts see Mary Titus, "Groaning Tables and 'Spit in the Kettles': Food and Race in the Nineteenth Century South," *Southern Quarterly* 30 (Winter–Spring, 1992), 13–21, and Anne Bradford Warner, "Harriet Jacobs's Modest Proposals: Revising Southern Hospitality," *Southern Quarterly* 30 (Winter–Spring, 1992), 22–28. For a reading of disorderly Southern kitchens as signs of the intersection of political economy with domestic economy under slavery, see Gillian Brown's *Domestic Individualism: Imagining Self in Nineteenth-Century America* (Berkeley: University of California Press, 1990), esp. 13–38.

15. Banta, "Medical Therapies and the Body Politic," 62.

16. Lydia Maria Child to Lucy [Searle], Feb. 4, 1861. Quoted in Yellin, "Introduction," *Incidents in the Life of a Slave Girl*, xxii.

17. Ibid.

18. Thome, "From 'Speech . . . Delivered at the Annual Meeting of the American Anti-Slavery Society," 92–3.

19. For the convenience of the reader, here and elsewhere in this essay I use Jacobs's pseudonyms for members of her family and other individuals. For actual names see the explanatory apparatus in Jean Fagan Yellin's edition of *Incidents in the Life of a Slave Girl*, in particular the helpful chronology on pages 223–35.

20. William Goodell, *National Principia*, quoted in Walters, *The Antislavery Appeal*, 92.

21. Banta, "Medical Therapies and the Body Politic," 59–60.

22. "Black Health on the Plantation: Masters, Slaves and Physicians," in *Science and Medicine in the Old South*, ed. Ronald L. Numbers and Todd L. Savitt (Baton Rouge: Louisiana State University Press, 1989), 352. For further discussions of folk medicine and resistance, see also Anne Bradford Warner, "Carnival Laughter: Resistance in *Incidents*," this volume; Lawrence Levine, *Black Culture and Black Consciousness: Afro-American Folk Thought from Slavery to Freedom* (New York: Oxford University Press, 1977), 63–7; and Athena Vrettos, "Curative Domains: Women, Healing and History in Black Women's Narratives," 456–60.

23. Barbara Ehrenreich and Deirdre English, *For Her Own Good: 150 Years of the Experts' Advice to Women* (New York: Doubleday, 1978), 48–68.

24. "Narrative of William W. Brown" (1847), rpt. in *Five Slave Narratives*, ed. William Loren Katz (New York: Arno Press, 1969), 104.

25. To physical confinement, Athena Vrettos adds spiritual oppression as represented by Jacobs's suffering under slavery: "Physical pain is insistently present in Brent's narrative, becoming inseparable from the conditions of slavery. . . . Injuries also function as symbols of slavery's spiritual maiming" (459). Vrettos also points to the connections Jacobs builds between healing and freedom.

26. Banta, "Medical Therapies and the Body Politic," 77.

27. Yellin, "Notes," *Incidents in the Life of a Slave Girl*, 269.

28. Ibid., 285.

29. Erving Goffman, *Stigma: Notes on the Management of Spoiled Identity* (Englewood Cliffs, NJ: Prentice-Hall, 1963), i.

30. Orlando Patterson, *Slavery and Social Death: A Comparative Study* (Cambridge: Harvard University Press, 1982), 247.

31. Goffman, *Stigma*, 42.

32. Yellin, "Introduction," *Incidents in the Life of a Slave Girl*, xxxi.

33. Hazel Carby, *Reconstructing Womanhood: The Emergence of the Afro-American Woman Novelist* (New York: Oxford University Press, 1987), 58–9.

34. Walters, *The Antislavery Appeal*, 64.

35. Lydia Maria Child, *The Patriarchal Institution*, quoted in Walters, *The Antislavery Appeal*, 67.

36. Goffman, *Stigma*, 42.

37. Carby, *Reconstructing Womanhood*, 48.

38. Harriet Jacobs to Amy Post [1852?], in Yellin, *Incidents in the Life of a Slave Girl*, 232.

39. Yellin, *Incidents in the Life of a Slave Girl*, 204.

40. Goffman, *Stigma*, 101–2.

41. Harriet Jacobs to Amy Post [1852?], in Yellin, *Incidents in the Life of a Slave Girl*, 232.

42. *Lydia Maria Child: Selected Letters, 1817–1880*, ed. Milton Meltzer and Patricia G. Holland (Amherst: University of Massachusetts Press, 1982), 413.

CARNIVAL LAUGHTER

RESISTANCE IN INCIDENTS

ANNE BRADFORD WARNER

Every child rises early on Christmas morning to see the Johnkannaus. Without them, Christmas would be shorn of its greatest attraction.

Harriet A. Jacobs[1]

[The carnivals] were the second life of the people, who for a time entered the utopian realm of community, freedom, equality, and abundance.

Mikhail Bakhtin[2]

The Negroes have no manner of religion by what I could observe of them. It is true that they have several ceremonies, as dances, playing etc., but these for the most part are so far from being acts of adoration of a God that they are for the most part mixed with a great deal of bawdy and lewdness.

Sir Hans Sloane[3]

The Johnkannau festival of the New World seems as diverse in its origins as in its interpretations. In itself a heteroglossia of African languages and rituals re-created in the hostile environment of New World slavery, the Johnkannau has been perceived as children's amusement, godless bawdy, sacred ritual, and folk resistance.[4] Occurring in a critical middle chapter in *Incidents in the Life of a Slave Girl*, Harriet Jacobs's description of the johnkannau becomes a central trope for the multiple concerns of her slave narrative. She deliberately blends her narrating voice with this all-male raillery,[5] suggesting Linda

Brent's female appropriation of an African American trickster figure. And in this role Linda Brent enacts the ritual, undertaking – through dialogue and disguise in the narrative – diverse voices. The dance, music, and song of the festival, both in action and language, become a multidimensional medium of expression for the African American in slavery. The fact that the ritual is polyphonic and diversely understood demonstrates Jacobs's own awareness of an indeterminacy in language and the war that must be fought for reversal of authoritarian uses of it. The festival functions as trope for the oral and literary resistance not only within the slave community but within *Incidents* itself. This representation of the festival reveals further dimensions of the literary process called "novelization," traced by Bakhtin in Western narrative and skillfully applied by William L. Andrews to mid-nineteenth-century slave narrative.[6] Jacobs's parody of the official society in the middle chapters of her narrative, her evocation of diverse authorities and texts, and her undermining of the sanctity of authoritarian texts are conducted not only through "dialogization" of the narrative but through intertextual "narrative parody" and an "internal polemic" famously described by Henry Louis Gates as "signifyin(g)."[7]

"Christmas Festivities," the central chapter of *Incidents*, signals Jacobs's shift in the text to an African-retained authority and intensifies the process of parody of earlier events and other texts. The assertion of folk authority suggested by Brent's description of the Johnkannau not only exposes Flint's perverse excesses as a slaveholder, but also constitutes a bit of burlesque against Douglass's dour comments on the slave holidays in both *Narrative* and *My Bondage and My Freedom*. For Douglass observes to his Northern reader, in a voice attuned to abolitionist puritanism, that at jubilee time "only those wild and low sports, peculiar to semi-civilized people, are encouraged."[8] For Jacobs the Johnkannau – with other signifying in this chapter – becomes a trope for all the purposes that will be implied in current views of carnival and for the vibrancy and regeneration of the community she, much more than Douglass, esteems.

Mikhail Bakhtin defines the European Catholic carnival in Rabelais as "a vast and manifold literature of parody."[9] The "ritual spectacles," "comic verbal compositions," and "various genres of billingsgate" are closely linked forms of folk humor that mock the civil and social ceremonies of the authoritarian culture.[10] Through laughter and mock ritual, carnival unmasks authority.[11] As Jacobs describes the Johnkannau, the carnival provides the one day that slaves may be lawless, may capture "many a pig or turkey" and "regale [the] ears" of "any white man or child who refuses to give them a trifle" (119). Innocent of violence, it does mimic the appropriations by the opposing culture of man, woman, and animal. The spectacle is described in some detail:

> Two athletic men, in calico wrappers, have a net thrown over them, covered with all manner of bright colored stripes. Cows' tails are fastened to their backs, and their heads are decorated with horns. A box,

covered with sheepskin, is called the gumbo box. A dozen beat on this, while others strike triangles and jawbones, to which bands of dancers keep time. For a month previous they are composing songs, which are sung on this occasion. (118)

The ritual, which, for Douglass, is the sort that converts men to animals, is here a vital, creative commentary on the infernal reduction of the human to the animalistic devouring of the slaveholder. But for Jacobs, the ritual also represents a fluidity and a playful version of metamorphosis, which is not a sign of the community's reduction, but of its ability to change form, to avoid stasis – a stasis seen in the paralysis of Brent's limbs in the garret.

Sterling Stuckey observes that often the masked dancers of this ritual affirmed its relation to a West African means "of relating to ancestral spirits and to God."[12] In fact, the very actions that lead the slave Linda Brent to the moment of observing the Johnkannau from her loophole are guided by her dead "father's voice . . . bidding me not to tarry till I reached freedom or the grave" (91). Ancestral guidance and spiritual vision direct Brent at critical moments and point to the blend Jacobs found in her own life between African-retained values and the Quaker Spiritualism practiced by Amy and Isaac Post.[13] In her description of the Johnkannau, Brent confirms the dual origins of her visionary moments and demonstrates her capacity for what Mae Henderson describes as "glossolalia," or a "private, closed, and privileged communication between the congregant and the divinity" – a kind of communication produced by the need for black women to "speak in a plurality of voices."[14] *Incidents* not only offers this language of vision but also suggests its sources, among them, the powerful authority of folk religion practiced in the Johnkannau. With the trope of the Johnkannau, Jacobs commits herself to finding a public voice and visible ritual for the expression of personal experience and the recovery of energies of subversion and resistance present but silenced at other seasons.

There is a certain comedy in the fact that Dr. James Norcom (Jacobs's Flint) views the Johnkannau in terms of an absence rather than a presence:

> It is to be regretted . . . that drunkenness is too common on these occasions: but this also is habitually overlooked and never punished, unless it [becomes] outrageous or grossly offensive.[15]

"Flint's" opinion of the Johnkannau reflects an awareness of the absence of official constraint; of the laughter, raillery, and communal ritual he says little. Thus, he has "overlooked" more than the drunkenness of the Johnkannau celebration, for he fails to see in it the exercise of an authority prior to the authoritarianism of his own official society. The briefly empowered folk of Jacobs's description, in their huge plantation bands, express their resistance to American slavery with their African survivals and parody the oppressive institutions of the South.

It is necessary to see in Jacobs's treatment of the Johnkannau her drama of transformation, an overturning of power structures and an assault on their integrity. Like the dual world of comic and official ritual Bakhtin describes in Rabelais, the Johnkannau in the world of patriarchal slavery enjoys a temporary privilege. Its role in Jacobs's narrative demonstrates "the 'unmasking' and disclosing of the unvarnished truth under the veil of false claims and arbitrary rules."[16] The authority of these folk forces preexists the authority of those who license the carnival.[17] Jacobs places this folk laughter in a chapter that unmasks figures of authority by showing them as gulls. Chapter Twenty-two opens with a child's pointed assertion that "Santa Claus ain't a real man. It's the children's mothers" (118). The constable and the betraying "free colored man" in the town are feasted by Aunt Martha in the house where Linda hides. They are given a tour upstairs "to look at a fine mocking bird" (119), with the hare and the spider, an African American trickster figure.[18] At the end of the chapter, as the narrator observes that "So passed the first Christmas in my den" (120), she hints at the reversed roles of hunter and hunted and at her appropriation of the animal identity of the trickster figure. Like the clown or fool of the carnival, Linda Brent disrupts and reverses the transactions of power by the official society. In the noisy revels of the Johnkannau and in Brent's silent revelry, the folk triumph.

There is another disguised resistance in this description as Jacobs orchestrates her values for the slave holidays against the text of Frederick Douglass, who abhors the drinking and carousal (not in the specific celebration of the Johnkannau, but in a general "jubilee") of the slaves he observes in Maryland – though he acknowledges the occasional satiric jibe "among a mass of nonsense and wild frolic."[19] Unlike Jacobs, Douglass concludes, "These holidays are conductors or safety valves to carry off the explosive elements inseparable from the human mind, when reduced to the condition of slavery."[20] About sixty years later Bakhtin leveled his argument about carnival as a revolution against the "safety valve" theory of Anatoly Lunacharsky in *The Social Role of Laughter*.[21] Bakhtin argues what Jacobs implies: It is clear in Chapter Twenty-two of *Incidents* that the Johnkannau is a sign of continued, cooperative effort of the folk to resist the goals of official society. With this central trope Jacobs affirms the ongoing resistance in the folk culture against Douglass's idea that such temporary liberty affords a more effective enslavement. This position allows Jacobs to privilege the integrity of a folk culture that Douglass perceives as degraded.

This Johnkannau episode appears in a section of the narrative that transforms the terms of what the narrator calls "the war of my life" (19). The "Loophole of Retreat" is both a chapter and a place of transformation and rebirth – a grave for the victim and a womb for the child of freedom. Writing to Amy Post in 1854 about the state of her narrative, Jacobs says, "The poor book is in its Chrysalis-state and though I can never make it a butterfly I am satisfied to have it creep meekly   among some of the humbler bugs" (238).

The narrative, like the narrator, moves from enslavement to freedom, changing forms in the company of the "humble," the less literate but sharp-eyed folk upon whom Brent's deliverance depends. Sally, "an old woman who doctored among the slaves" (98), and Betty are among the folk elements of support; they work (and speak) with the style of the slave community. The language of the resisting slave takes many forms, from standard English in Chapter Twelve, satirizing the poor whites who conduct reprisals against Nat Turner's revolt (64–6), to the folk vernacular of the slave Luke, who "stole" his wages and himself (192–3). Trusting the cleverness of the folk, the concealed Brent "sleeps" through the revolution like Rip Van Winkle, also mentioned in this "chrysalis" letter to Amy Post. In *Incidents* it has been precisely Linda's loophole of apparent passivity and real dependence on community that have allowed the disguised faces and voices of the folk to be "seen" and "known."

Thus, in *Incidents*, Harriet Jacobs uses the feast day of Christmas and the advent of the Johnkannau to mark the beginning of Linda Brent's long and subversive confinement in her grandmother's attic space. These two celebrations also mark the "double-vision" of the narrator and suggest a shift from the Bible to African folk tradition for rhetorical authority.[22] The representation of the Johnkannau in *Incidents* signifies the full extent of Jacobs's resistance and the strategies she employs to communicate it. Jacobs's text is decidedly radical and literary, self-consciously intertextual and signifying. In deadly serious play, it opens the range of warring ideologies to reveal the distortions of the slaveholding society and to embrace the African American folk as a community of resistance rather than dependency.

The folk laughter of the Johnkannau, like the laughter in the European carnival analyzed in Bakhtin, reveals

> the world anew in its gayest and most sober aspects. Its external privileges are intimately linked with interior forces; they are a recognition of the rights of those forces. This is why laughter could never become an instrument to oppress and blind the people. It always remained a free weapon in their hands.[23]

Like the folk in the festival she describes, Brent acts within the text as agent for this disruptive laughter. The trickster's ventriloquism becomes a comic literary weapon against the killing instruments of official society.

Recent scholarship has made readers aware of the deeply revisionist impulse within *Incidents* as Jacobs reworks the genres she inherited, writing under the weight of discourses not her own.[24] Focusing on the genre most closely related to *Incidents*, Andrews argues that early African American autobiography itself constitutes a kind of scripture, "the sanctified record and directing text" of the diaspora experience, that "misreads" the "essential texts of oppressive American culture" – the Bible and the Declaration of Independence.[25] If this view of slave narrative is accepted, then Jacobs creates her own narrative under an even greater weight of "scriptures" that inscribe her as victim even while engaged in her defense. Efforts to define Jacobs's construction of a representative female hero articulated in the figure of Linda Brent include Braxton's formulation of the "outraged mother" and Smith's of the "self-in-relation."[26] Though each of these interpretations illuminates some phases of the narration, neither fully describes the narrator. Rather, it seems that Jacobs herself is undermining the static notion of a representative heroine in *Incidents;* she heightens the level of indeterminacy in her own text by creating a figure in transformation, in metamorphosis, a multiple and many-voiced figure of folk authority and festive laughter that moves among masks, breaking barriers, and working always toward regeneration and away from definition. Andrews's commentary on *Incidents* addresses the narrator's changeability when he describes Jacobs as on "a precarious margin" and moving between "antipodes of 'concealment' and 'confidence' in her narrative posture before her reader," whom the narrator apprises of her own distrust.[27] Brent, as trickster, is both marginal and empowered; her changeability is a product of her power and regenerative metamorphoses rather than her victimization; and her articulated distrust of the readers dramatically includes them in the drama of Brent's self-construction. Thus, Jacobs's rhetorical positioning invites the reader to participate in her drama of reversals, parody, shifting authorities.

In fact, the dynamic of the text's heightened indeterminacy is to offer repeated rereadings as the narrator subverts the textual inscriptions from the official culture, rereads the "misreadings" of her kindred slaves, and also draws into question her own bases of authority in the first and last sections of narration. The festive laughter of the middle chapters, in the midst of the paralyzing attic confinement, forms a radiant map of rereadings. It shows Jacobs's world in its "gayest and most sober aspects," articulating the spirit of community. She ends the absence of a literary tradition for the silenced black woman with an open text and a voice that, because it questions the nature of official authority, will not silence others.

Jacobs's narration varies according to the location and condition of her persona Linda Brent in the three phases of *Incidents:* from the diabolically un-Christian world of enslavement, to the concealed and confined freedom of her seven years in hiding, to the final journeys northward. Such formalist archetectonics are important not just for a comprehension of the narrative's general order, but also for a specific recognition of the placement of the John-kannau episode – and of its subtle strategies as a map of rereading the surrounding parts. The first section (Chapters One through Fifteen) tells the story of an inverse Eden; the second (Chapters Sixteen through Thirty) shows transformed perspectives on slave and slaveowner from The Loophole of Retreat; the third (Chapters Thirty-one through Forty-one) works as a Northern travelogue. Jacobs invokes the authority of the Bible first, the authority of the

African trickster tradition second, and the authority of objective observation last. Still, the transformations of the middle section undermine the reader's ability to rely on the bases of authority in the others.

Jacobs maintains her subversions of the reigning documents and reigning notions of the age throughout her narrative and enters an intertextual dialogue with two major figures, ending her long avoidance of public debate in the North. Both Stowe and Douglass, immensely popular and eminent figures with "representative" texts, furnish the contexts for Jacobs's revision of racial politics.[28] As Robert Stepto has pointed out in an essay about the "antislavery textual conversation" between Stowe and Douglass, their texts constitute a dialogue of differences beyond the shared task of abolition. Jacobs's narrative becomes a part of this exchange. It clearly aligns itself with Douglass on the sinister role of the Southern church and the impossibility of colonization – two major issues in the antislavery movement outlined by Robert Stepto in his essay on Douglass and Stowe.[29] More strongly than Douglass, Jacobs assaults the possibility of an idealized domesticity in the Southern white community. But a more significant intertextual dialogue emerges on biases that undermine the integrity of the folk culture. Jacobs uses her own dialogism to oppose both Stowe's and Douglass's tendency to equate command of standard English with heightened sensibility and intellectual capacity. Similarly, Jacobs undermines the enlightenment or romantic individualism that distinguishes the heroes and heroines of Douglass and Stowe.

In her transition from South to North Jacobs parodies the now famous hyperbolic passage in *Narrative* where Douglass's narrator, in the highly stylized diction of the Romantics, articulates his longing to escape. In a countertext Brent, as she becomes assured of her own safety in her voyage to freedom, speaks with an ecstatic lyricism:

> The balmy air of spring was so refreshing! And how shall I describe my sensations when we were fairly sailing on Chesapeake Bay? O, the beautiful sunshine! the exhilarating breeze! and I could enjoy them without fear or restraint. I had never realized what grand things air and sunlight are till I had been deprived of them. (158)

Jacobs signifies upon Douglass's apostrophe to the sailboats on the Chesapeake and, in a sense, sails right past him. Jacobs shows the rhetoric of triumph, rather than of longing; and she does not conceal her means of escape through a community of assistance as Douglass does. Long before Zora Neale Hurston, Jacobs, too, took exception to the lone male "Watcher," who "traced, with saddened heart and tearful eye, the countless number of sails moving off to the mighty ocean."[30] The loneliness in *Incidents* relates to loss of community, not to longing for freedom: "We were alone in the world, and we had left dear ties behind us: ties cruelly sundered by the demon Slavery" (158). Brent reverses the conventional closure of a sentimental plot when her fugitive life in the North does not recover the home and hearth lost to her. Here, Jacobs's intertextual play creates a far more complex notion of freedom than Douglass defines with his *Narrative*.

Another context for intertextual parody involves Stowe's romance of race, her suggestion that the African has gifts that enable a mystical kinship with nature and ability to endure hardship. For instance, when her ship to freedom navigates the Albemarle Sound, Brent enters into this brief exchange with the captain:

> As we passed Snaky Swamp, he pointed to it, and said, "There is a slave territory that defies all the laws." I thought of the terrible days I had spent there, and though it was not called Dismal Swamp, it made me feel very dismal as I looked at it. (158)

Through his statement about Snaky Swamp, the captain shares with Stowe the vision of safety and control conveyed in *Dred,* an 1857 novel based on the figure of Nat Turner. Dred, a visionary with "preternatural keenness and intensity,"[31] presides over a fugitive camp in the Great Dismal Swamp where "the whole air is flooded with a golden haze, in which the tree-tops move dreamily to and fro, as if in a whispering reverie. The wild climbing grapevines, which hang in thousand-fold festoons round the inclosure, are purpling with grapes."[32] This tiny cultivated plot of civil and agricultural order is a far cry from Brent's "wretched" night in the swamp, her "seat made among the bamboos," the poisonous mosquitoes, the snakes that she is "continually obliged to thrash . . . with sticks" (113). The text of *Incidents* challenges this Northern construction of race, with its apparently benign romance of life in a swamp and of a people with the special gifts for surviving there.

To check the sentimentalized portraits of slaves but affirm the viability of the African American folk culture in the South and the constructive role of the black woman within it, Jacobs revises these texts with her own. Her intertextual dialogue sets politics flying and complicates complacencies while the reader's probable assumptions undergo increasing authorial challenge.

Yet it is the Loophole chapters of *Incidents* that demonstrate most actively Jacobs's resistance to Southern institutions and her revision of texts about slavery. The Loophole chapters are the most deeply disruptive, encoded, and intertextual. They form the spiritual center of the work. In this darkly comic middle section of the narrative Jacobs most clearly revises language and reverses conventional relations between appearance and act, act and language. It is in this section that the narrator–trickster reveals the power of community to sustain the revolutionary impulse through a plenitude of disguises.

Both William Andrews and Joanne Braxton have shown how language is reclaimed and self-esteem preserved in the "verbal warfare" or "sass" of the dialogues throughout the narrative.[33] But in the middle section of *Incidents,* as the trickster–narrator, Linda Brent, gains a measure of control over the events through her spying from "the loophole of retreat," a larger warfare between signifier and signified, act and appearance, is orchestrated. Here, particularly, Jacobs affirms the authority of the folk community, dismantles any notion that virtue has a systematic relation to class identity, and reveals a resistance invisible to the official society. Brent, the orchestrating female trickster, reverses temporarily the victimizing dynamic of chattel slavery, suggests the irrepressibility of a natural impulse toward freedom, and reworks in her own plot passages from Stowe and Douglass that undervalue the spirit and force within the slave community.

The revolution in plot is set up in Chapter Sixteen when Brent resolves upon escape. The comedic quality of this long middle section of narration emerges as Brent reverses the outcomes for her grim meditation upon Ellen's future and the prospect of death as the sole release from oppression. The impetus for Brent's flight, as Braxton points out, is "the projection of her daughter's life under slavery."[34] The event that inspires her decision becomes a trope for Brent's changed relationship to Dr. Flint. In Chapter Sixteen, after the disconsolate Ellen has been found asleep and withdrawn from the crawl space beneath the great house, Flint's son "kill[s] a large snake, which crept from under the house" (87). The death of this phallic threat signals Brent's decision to send Ellen home and plan her own escape. Only a little later, when Miss Fanny's solicitude for Linda's family leads to the wish that they "were at rest in [their] graves," the narrator reveals her contrary intention to put the old woman's mind at peace "not by death, but by securing our freedom" (89). Slavery moves, symbolically and literally, behind Brent when she leaves the plantation, resists a reptile's bite with a folk cure from an old slave woman, and survives the Snaky Swamp. Despite the pursuit by "snakes and slaveholders" (193), she appears to disappear and attains a haven from both.

The "loophole" represents both a tiny portion of attic in her grandmother's house and an opening Brent drills to spy upon events outside, affording her both concealment and a point of observation. She now undergoes a series of bodily trials because of her close quarters. Brent's crippling discomfort and periodic loss of physical function cannot help but comment on the gothic romance and trickery of Cassy's escape episode of *Uncle Tom's Cabin*. Surely Stowe wanted Jacobs's story for the *Key* to fill the absence of a slave's narrative to give credence to the novel.[35] Just as surely, Brent's "little dismal hole, almost deprived of light and air, and with no space to move [her] limbs, for nearly seven years" (148) revises the fictive comforts of the "immense box," shared by Cassy and Emmeline and "plentifully stored with candles, provisions and all the clothing necessary to their journey."[36] The box that served as a means of escape in other slave narratives and a place of safety and comfort for Cassy is rendered here in terms of unmitigated physical suffering and near paralysis.

More significantly, the loophole that allows Brent to spy and plot her deception of Flint reverses the function of Cassy's "knot-hole," through which she helplessly witnesses Legree's attempt to extract information from Uncle Tom. As Valerie Smith implies in her discussion of confinement in sentimental fiction and in Jacobs, one attic is not so very like another.[37] Jacobs's attic is no fiction, but personal history turned to a trope. Cassy escapes, as Gilbert and Gubar point out, first by "manipulating [the] familiar fiction" of the madwoman and later by feeding Legree's guilt for denying his mother.[38] By contrast, Brent never feigns madness. She does not haunt Flint, who lacks a moral sense, but exploits his greed and obsession: his vices, not his latent virtue or fear. Confinement in Jacobs is the confinement of a "Chrysalis-state" before transformation, a metaphor she applies to her book in a letter to Post (238). The attic space is an ironic trope for freedom in a perverse world. To the slaveholding community Brent is invisible; and the property that has disappeared is now the unseen mover.

In this middle portion of the narrative, events in Edenton, unchanged on the surface, take on new significance. Brent's loophole narrative reveals beneath the dire appearance of the family's imprisonment and the sale of her children a second, subversive plot. In a comic reversal of expectations, the imprisonment of Brent's relatives arranged by Dr. Flint is ineffectual: the jailed family becomes an image of community, not of suffering, and Ellen, who had been carried off to the doctor's house to be "cured" of the measles, "cried all day to be carried back to prison" (102). Similarly, the portrait of the family sold off into slavery, with "William handcuffed among the gang, and the children in the trader's cart" (106), frightens Aunt Martha but actually signals the children's first journey toward safety, toward the freedom implied in their purchase by Mr. Sands. These events confound the sinister goals of Flint, revealing a steady and effective resistance enacted within the community and a reversal of official power.

In these chapters of disguise and reversal, acts of rebellion transpire unnoticed within the voice and touch of those representing official society. Brent hears Flint as she hides, and fears imminent capture, but the doctor is negotiating a loan for his journey to New York, where he "will merely lighten his pocket hunting after the bird he has left behind" (104). The woman and slaveholder who lends Flint the money for pursuit harbors the slave he pursues. In such moments Jacobs fuses drama with comedy, fear with exhilaration. The trickery intensifies as the trickster herself walks the streets of Edenton twice, disguised as a man, a sailor:

We were rowed ashore, and went boldly through the streets, to my grandmother's. I wore my sailor's clothes, and had blackened my face with charcoal. I passed several people whom I knew. The father of my children came so near that I brushed against his arm; but he had no idea who it was. (113)

Jacobs's female raillery here targets her most intimate connection with a culture that has failed to "see" her. Brent's presence and condition are as obscure to Sands in the street as they are elsewhere in the narrative. This self-portrait suggests, too, the androgyny of her trickster. Jacobs claims this em-powering role for a woman but also shows her ability to "mask" gender. Moreover, this womanish sailor who moves twice through the town without leaving it or her children comments upon an event outside the text. For, as Mary Helen Washington has pointed out, Frederick Douglass escaped as a sailor at the close of his narrative. He left through his fiancee's financial sup-port and wore a suit of her making, but Douglass's construction of the solitary male hero de-emphasized his ties to the community and mandated silence about the support for his escape.[39]

The false appearances of people and events in the loophole section allow the narrator to revise the history of her escape and the history of subversion in the community. The disguises abound. Brent's battery of false letters en-hances her safety and puts Flint to much expense and trouble. Unlike the earlier lies about life in the North (43), Flint's lie is known and becomes a source of amusement when he brings Aunt Martha a false letter from Linda. Those who would be betrayers are exposed; false suspicions about betrayal are disproved. In Linda's final escape, the captain of the departing vessel in-terprets Peter and the hired boatmen as "officers . . . pursuing his vessel in search of the runaway slave he had on board" (153). When the chase is re-vealed as an effort to put *another* slave on board, the captain comments, "That's the name of the woman already here. . . . I believe you mean to be-tray me" (153). There are two Lindas, doubled escapes. None of the antici-pated betrayals – of the captain by Peter, of Fanny, of Linda by the captain – takes place. Much betrayal is unmasked as loyalty that crosses boundaries of race, class, and gender. Thus, these middle chapters of apparent confinement represent a revolution in language and image – and an assault on every offi-cial social construct.

Because Jacobs's loophole chapters undermine both the established au-thorities of the culture and conventional wisdom about slavery, they map re-readings of the surrounding narrative. Her parody of exclusive or authori-tarian systems disrupts the function of scripture in the first section and of objective observation in the last. Her politics of inclusion radiate from this central narration to overthrow the linear certainty such constructs require. Thus, what begins as conventional narrative (I was born a slave, but I never knew it [5]), with a conventional appeal to Biblical authority, undermines its own conventions with recursive gestures embedded in the middle section.

In the first section of the narrative Jacobs directly quotes from the Bible more than twenty times, in addition to making allusions that are less direct. The incidence of such passages is far higher throughout this portrait of slav-ery than anywhere else in the text, except in the last chapter, where freedom is obtained. The multiple quotations from Matthew in this section suggest a Christian community persecuted by the authorities: Brent speaks in the moral rhetoric of the besieged Christian, a familiar posture in black and white, male and female abolitionist circles.

At the same time, the "sass" or heteroglossia of the novelized voice undermines the language of Flint and others, challenging a Biblical context that commands a servant's obedience yet makes that virtue dishonor, converts a slave's chaste beauty to ruin, and makes fatherhood enslavement. Jacobs undermines the traditional promise of literacy and access to the Bible by showing Flint's letters and Brent's ability to read them as a part of the design of seduction. For Brent literacy is not, at first, a pathway to Old Testament freedom but one to loss of sexual innocence. Moreover, Jacobs's picture of the church, its failed communion, and Mrs. Flint's spitting in the Sunday pots and pans alter not only the benign proslavery description of the patriarchal family but Stowe's Edenic and Christianized portraits of the Shelbys and St. Clares of *Uncle Tom's Cabin* and the Gordons and Claytons of *Dred*. The kitchens and churches of slaveholders in Edenton offer little sustenance, less communion.[40] Though *Incidents* begins with the trust of a kind and religious mistress, it moves quickly to betrayal.

Unlike that of conventional slave narrative, the chief feature of this first section is not only the fall into an understanding of enslavement, but the highly dramatized fall from sexual innocence. Jacobs describes the slave Linda's twenty-one years in this "cage of obscene birds" (52), encoding the inverted Eden of Edenton. Though the town is never named, it is represented as a perverse Eden,[41] with the devil as Flint, "whose restless, craving, vicious nature roved about day and night, seeking whom to devour" (18). The fall into knowledge is the plight of the enslaved woman who becomes "prematurely knowing of evil things. Soon she will learn to tremble when she hears her master's footfall" (28).

Jacobs parodies *Paradise Lost* and revises Genesis in the descriptions of the devil and his wife: Brent explains that Flint "began to whisper foul words in my ear. . . . He peopled my young mind with unclean images, such as only a vile monster could think of" (27). Like Milton's Eve, Brent is approached awake and in sleep.

> Sometimes I woke up, and found [Mrs. Flint] bending over me. At other times she whispered in my ear, as though it was her husband who was speaking to me, and listened to hear what I would answer. If she startled me, on such occasions, she would glide stealthily away; and the next morning she would tell me I had been talking in my sleep, and ask who I was talking to. (34)

In Edenton, as in Milton's garden, the devil is a sophist, confounding language and logic, putting poison in the ear of the innocent. But here there is no providential hand. As a writer who quotes both Byron and Cowper, Jacobs reveals her awareness of the inscribing power of literary texts and undermines their authority with reversals of plot and context.

When Jacobs does describe Brent's fall from sexual innocence in the first section, she has already deconstructed the Biblical context for the slave's choice. In *Incidents* the reader is free to see that the Bible is one of multiple texts used by official society to mandate female obedience, submission, martyrdom. When Brent states, "I feel that the slave woman ought not to be judged by the same standard as others" (56), she has already questioned the basis for that standard. Jacobs has reread and exposed the conflict and contradiction in the official order. Her text resists reductive solution. Stowe's Little Eva and Uncle Tom, for instance, do not "tell the half" of the moral complexities in such a fallen world. Whatever consolation Stowe offers her reader for their martyrdom is denied the witness to the many martyrs in this first section of *Incidents*. Instead, the nearly psychotic malice of Flint inspires resistance, escape, and concealment for Brent in a world of folk authority, a prior authority which lies beneath and repeatedly undermines the sinister foundations of Edenton.

Less apparent but essential to an understanding of Jacobs's narrative technique is the persistence of the parodic voice of the Johnkannau and the dynamics of reversal in the last section of the narrative. Here, Jacobs performs a very basic function of laughter and carnival, to break down "any distinction between actors and spectators."[42] Geographically Brent breaks through the northern boundaries, playing with the pieties, perhaps, and social constructions of the readers she has previously addressed from a comfortable distance and warned of her distrust.

In "Incidents in Philadelphia," a chapter which suggestively echoes the title and perhaps theme of the work, Jacobs dramatizes the occasion for her long silence in the North. Brent first reveals her past troubles to the minister who assists her. The act suggests that, in this new setting, such a story of her life can be told; the minister's response conveys caution: "Your straightforward answers do you credit; but don't answer every body so openly. It might give some heartless people a pretext for treating you with contempt" (160). This lesson opens Brent's Northern education, and it was years before she whispered her story a second time.

Telling the story of freedom requires the politics of inclusion, and most particularly, the inclusion of the silenced black woman warned against the contempt of her listener. With her own sleight of hand, Jacobs has challenged her reader's role as observer and closed the distance; here the reader is cast in the role of participant. If the Johnkannau is an adequate trope for the narrative itself, then it "is not a spectacle seen by the people; they live in it, and everyone participates because its very idea embraces all the people."[43] In many voices, the text itself invites revisionist responses and challenges all natural authority that has become arbitrary or authoritarian. The existence of *Incidents*, its comedy and violation of official boundaries, assumes the moment of festivities; it assumes a long and painful silence broken with play rather than piety and the eruption of parody for the sake of regeneration. The terrible politics that made *Incidents* necessary are bound up in its hope for transformation. Such a vision requires an inspired trickster.

Notes

1. Harriet A. Jacobs, *Incidents in the Life of a Slave Girl*, ed. Jean Fagan Yellin (Cambridge: Harvard University Press, 1987), 118. Subsequent uses of this work will be cited by page number in the text of the article.

2. Mikhail Bakhtin, *Rabelais and His World*, trans. Helene Iswolsky (Cambridge: MIT Press, 1965), 9.

3. Quoted in Sylvia Wynter, "Jonkonnu in Jamaica," *Jamaica Journal* 4 (1970): 36.

4. For discussions of the Johnkannau festivals in the New World, see Wynter, "Jonkonnu in Jamaica," 34–48; Dougald Mac Millan, "John Kunners," *Journal of American Folklore* 39 (1926): 53–7; Ira De A. Reid, "The John Canoe Festival," *Phylon* 3 (1942): 349–70; Sterling Stuckey, *Slave Culture* (New York: Oxford University Press, 1987), 68–73. For a discussion of the "anti-social" qualities of festivals of many kinds, see Jean Duvignaud, "Festivals: A Sociological Approach," in *Festivals and Carnivals: The Major Traditions*, ed. Alfred Metraux (Paris: UNESCO, 1976), 13–25. I am indebted to Professor Maureen Warner-Lewis at the University of the West Indies–Mona Campus for insights into carnival celebrations in the Caribbean.

5. Sterling Stuckey, *Slave Culture: Nationalistic Theory and the Foundations of Black America* (New York: Oxford University Press, 1987), 68.

6. See William L. Andrews, *To Tell a Free Story* (Urbana: University of Illinois Press, 1986), 271–3, and "Novelization of Voice in Early African American Narrative," *PMLA* (June 1990): 23–34.

7. Henry Louis Gates Jr., *The Signifying Monkey: A Theory of African American Literary Criticism* (New York: Oxford University Press, 1988), 110.

8. Frederick Douglass, *My Bondage and My Freedom* (New York: Miller, Orton, and Mulligan, 1855; rpt. New York: Dover Publications, 1969), 255.

9. Bakhtin, "Introduction," *Rabelais and His World*, 4.

10. Bakhtin, "Introduction," *Rabelais and His World*, 4.

11. Bakhtin, "Foreword," *Rabelais and His World*, x.

12. Stuckey, *Slave Culture*, 104.

13. See Jacobs's reference to "Leah of the Spirits" in her June 18, 186[1], letter to Amy Post, Isaac and Amy Post Family Papers, Department of Rare Books, Manuscripts, and Archives, University of Rochester Library, Rochester, N.Y.; rpt. in *Black Abolitionist Papers*, 16:30271.

14. Mae Gwendolyn Henderson, "Speaking in Tongues: Dialogics, Dialectics, and the Black Woman Writer's Literary Tradition," in *Changing Our Own Words: Essays on Criticism, Theory, and Writing by Black Women*, ed. Cheryl A. Wall (New Brunswick, NJ: Rutgers University Press, 1989), 22.

15. Norcom, quoted in Stuckey, 106; taken from a quotation in Guion Johnson, *Ante-Bellum North Carolina: A Social History* (Chapel Hill: University of North Carolina Press, 1937), 558.

16. Bakhtin, "Foreword," *Rabelais and His World*, x.

17. Bakhtin, "Prologue," *Rabelais and His World*, xviii.

18. Stuckey, 18–19.

19. Douglass, *My Bondage and My Freedom*, 252.

20. Douglass, *Bondage*, 254.

21. Bakhtin, "Prologue," *Rabelais and His World*, xviii.

22. Like W. E. Burghardt Du Bois in *The Souls of Black Folk*, but forty years before him, Jacobs seeks a voice for the "double self" of "Negro and American" (New York: NAL Penguin, 1969), 45, but in the notably different representation of the silenced black woman.

23. Bakhtin, *Rabelais and His World*, 94.

24. For a discussion of Jacobs's reworking of sentimental fiction and slave narrative, see Jean Yellin's "Introduction" to her edition of *Incidents*, xviii–xxxiv; Mary Helen Washington's treatment of *Incidents* in *Invented Lives: Narratives of Black Women, 1860–1960* (Garden City, NY: Anchor, 1987), 3–15; and Hazel Carby's chapter in *Reconstructing Womanhood* (New York: Oxford University Press, 1987), 45–61.

25. Andrews engages Bloom's terms concerning the "misreadings" of "strong readers" in his argument about the scriptural relation and power of these texts in *To Tell a Free Story*, 13–14.

26. Joanne Braxton, *Black Women Writing Autobiography* (Philadelphia: Temple University Press, 1989), 18–38, and Valerie Smith, *Self-Discovery and Authority in Afro-American Narrative* (Cambridge: Harvard University Press, 1987), 26–43.

27. Andrews, *To Tell a Free Story*, 240.

28. In her Introduction to *Incidents* Jean Yellin discusses Jacobs's acquaintance with Frederick Douglass through her brother, John S. Jacobs, and her operation of the Anti-Slavery Reading Room above the office of the *North Star*. Jacobs's exchanges with Stowe are far more indirect and painful, as Yellin shows in the published letters. *Incidents* represents Jacobs's entry into the public dialogue and her decision to terminate the long silence compelled by her desire for privacy.

29. Robert Stepto, "Sharing the Thunder: The Literary Exchanges of Harriet Beecher Stowe, Henry Bibb, and Frederick Douglass," in *New Essays on Uncle Tom's Cabin*, ed. Eric J. Sundquist (Cambridge University Press, 1986), 136.

30. Douglass, quoted in Gates, *The Signifying Monkey*, 170–2, in a discussion of Hurston's signification on Douglass in *Their Eyes Were Watching God*.

31. Harriet Beecher Stowe, *Dred, A Tale of the Great Dismal Swamp*, Volume 2 (New York: Fireside Edition, 1910), 285.

32. Stowe, *Dred*, 468.

33. See Braxton on sass and the female trickster, *Black Women*, 30–1, and Andrews's discussion of "dialogizing," *To Tell a Free Story*, 277–80, and the discussion of de-privileging or relativizing a discourse in M. M. Bakhtin, *The Dialogic Imagination*, trans. Caryl Emerson and Michael Holquist (Austin: University of Texas Press, 1981), 411–14.

34. Braxton, *Black Women*, 35.

35. Jacobs comments on Stowe's request for the story of the "seven-year incarceration" and inquiry about its validity in a letter to Amy Post. Yellin notes that Stowe's request came during preparation of *A Key to Uncle Tom's Cabin*. Cited in *Incidents*, 234–5.

36. Harriet Beecher Stowe, *Uncle Tom's Cabin; or Life Among the Lowly* (Boston: J. P. Jewett, 1852; rpt. New York: Harper and Row, 1965), 409.

37. Smith, 28–32.

38. Sandra M. Gilbert and Susan Gubar, *The Madwoman in the Attic* (New Haven: Yale University Press, 1979), 534–5.

39. Mary Helen Washington mentions this contrast in her introduction of Jacobs in *Inverted Lives*, 8. Houston Baker describes Douglass's mode of escape and Anna Murray's financial assistance in his introduction to *Narrative of the Life of Frederick Douglass, an American Slave* (New York: Penguin, 1986), 18.

40. For discussions of this perversity in domestic and religious space, see Mary Titus, "'Groaning tables' and 'Spit in the kettles': Food and Race in the Nineteenth-Century South," *Southern Quarterly* 30 (Winter–Spring 1992): 13–21, and my article "Harriet Jacobs's Modest Proposals: Revising Southern Hospitality," in the same issue, 22–28.

41. I am indebted to Vernon Miles, with whom I worked in an NEH seminar directed by Eric Sundquist, for this insight. The first section of *Incidents* is not merely allusive to the Bible; it is an ironic reworking of the Creation. Vernon Miles drew my attention to the passage Jacobs paraphrased from I Peter 5:8.

42. Bakhtin, *Rabelais and His World*, 7.

43. Bakhtin, *Rabelais and His World*, 7.

Bibliography

Andrews, William L. "Novelization of Voice in Early African American Narrative." *PMLA* (January 1990): 23–34.

———. *To Tell a Free Story: The First Century of Afro-American Autobiography, 1760–1865*. Urbana: University of Illinois Press, 1986.

Bakhtin, Mikhail. *The Dialogic Imagination*. Translated by Caryl Emerson and Michael Holquist. Austin: University of Texas Press, 1981.

———. *Rabelais and His World*. Translated by Helene Iswolsky. Cambridge: MIT Press, 1965.

Braxton, Joanne M. *Black Women Writing Autobiography: A Tradition Within a Tradition*. Philadelphia: Temple University Press, 1989.

Carby, Hazel V. *Reconstructing Womanhood: The Emergence of the Afro-American Novelist*. New York: Oxford University Press, 1987.

Douglass, Frederick. *My Bondage and My Freedom*. New York: Miller, Orton, and Mulligan, 1855; rpt., New York: Dover Publications, 1969.

———. *Narrative of the Life of Frederick Douglass, an American Slave*. Edited with an Introduction by Houston A. Baker. New York: Penguin, 1986.

Duvignaud, Jean. "Festivals: A Sociological Approach." In *Festivals and Carnivals: The Major Traditions*, ed. Alfred Metraux. Paris: UNESCO, 1976.

Gates, Henry Louis, Jr. *The Signifying Monkey: A Theory of African American Literary Criticism*. New York: Oxford University Press, 1988.

Gilbert, Sandra M., and Susan Gubar. *The Madwoman in the Attic: The Woman Writer and the Nineteenth-Century Literary Imagination*. New Haven: Yale University Press, 1979.

Henderson, Mae Gwendolyn. "Speaking in Tongues: Dialogics, Dialectics, and the Black Woman Writer's Literary Tradition." In *Changing Our Own Words: Essays on Criticism, Theory, and Writing by Black Women*, ed. Cheryl A. Wall. New Brunswick, NJ: Rutgers University Press, 1989.

Jacobs, Harriet A. *Incidents in the Life of a Slave Girl*, ed. Jean Fagan Yellin. Cambridge: Harvard University Press, 1987.

———. "Letter from a Fugitive Slave. Slaves Sold under Peculiar Circumstances." *New York Tribune*, June 21, 1853, 6.

Mac Millan, Dougald. "John Kunners." *Journal of American Folklore* 39 (1926): 53–7.

Reid, Ira De A. "The John Canoe Festival." *Phylon* 3 (1942): 349–70.

Smith, Valerie. *Self-Discovery and Authority in Afro-American Narrative*. Cambridge: Harvard University Press, 1987.

Stepto, Robert. "Sharing the Thunder: The Literary Exchanges of Harriet Beecher Stowe, Henry Bibb, and Frederick Douglass." In *New Essays on Uncle Tom's Cabin*, ed. Eric J. Sundquist. Cambridge University Press, 1986.

Stowe, Harriet Beecher. *Dred, A Tale of the Great Dismal Swamp*. Boston: J. P. Jewett, 1856; rpt. *Novels and Stories by Harriet Beecher Stowe*, Volume 2. New York: Fireside Edition, 1910.

———. *Uncle Tom's Cabin, or Life Among the Lowly*. Boston: J. P. Jewett, 1852; rpt. New York: Harper & Row, 1965.

Stuckey, Sterling. *Slave Culture: Nationalist Theory and the Foundations of Black America*. New York: Oxford University Press, 1987.

Titus, Mary. "'Groaning tables' and 'Spit in the kettles': Food and Race in the Nineteenth-Century South." *Southern Quarterly* 30 (Winter–Spring 1992): 13–21.

Warner, Anne Bradford. "Harriet Jacobs's Modest Proposals: Revising Southern Hospitality." *Southern Quarterly* 30 (Winter–Spring 1992): 22–8.

Washington, Mary Helen. *Invented Lives: Narratives of Black Women 1860–1960*. New York: Anchor, 1987.

Wynter, Sylvia. "Jonkonnu in Jamaica." *Jamaica Journal* 4 (1970): 34–48.

HARRIET JACOBS, HENRY THOREAU, AND THE CHARACTER OF DISOBEDIENCE

ANITA GOLDMAN

Civil disobedience, or the public expression of dissatisfaction with the state through violation of particular laws, has assumed a central, familiar role in American politics. In the struggle for black liberation, civil disobedience has been upheld both as an organizing principle of action and as a crucial remedy for the failure of legal systems to secure necessary changes in their own structures. As Martin Luther King, Jr., observed in his 1963 letter written from the Birmingham City jail, the purpose of the civil disobedient is to "create a situation so crisis-packed that it will inevitably open the door to negotiation."[1] In the aftermath of the 1960s, a general description of civil disobedience has emerged in theoretical debate on the subject, but political philosophers have for the most part neglected questions of cultural context. They have failed to recognize a diverse field of conceptual possibilities: the untold variety of ways in which acts of disobedience have been rendered and critiqued in works of American literature.

In what follows, I compare two widely different nineteenth-century models of disobedience, both of which were constructed in response to a constitutional crisis arising from the fact of slavery in America. One model is Thoreau's famous example at Concord, which he describes in his 1849 essay "On the Duty of Civil Disobedience," originally published under the title "Resistance to Civil Government." The other is drawn from Harriet Jacobs's fictionalized slave narrative entitled *Incidents in the Life of a Slave Girl*, published in 1861. Broadly speaking, this discussion represents a contribution to ongoing efforts on the part of African-Americanist, feminist, and New Historicist scholars to develop interpretative frameworks that account for the political

233

effectiveness of rhetorics of protest in nineteenth-century American culture. The revisionary strategy of bringing Jacobs's insights to bear on Thoreau's model of disobedience, and vice versa, should result in a better understanding of the political sophistication and diversity of period writing as a whole.

More specifically, the comparison is designed to show how each writer's engagement with the problem of disobedience reflects a larger attempt to grapple with the conceptual premises of liberalism. In contemporary academic debates, critics of liberalism have made a philosophical distinction between the terms "liberal" and "democratic,"[2] but the major tenets of liberalism in the sense I am using it here are popularly identified with democracy. By "liberalism" I mean the constellation of ideals set forth in the philosophy of John Locke that was central to the politics and economic development of nineteenth-century American culture: the emphasis on voluntarism and individual rights (including the right to freedom, ownership, and self-ownership); and the notion that legitimate government and community are created by acts of consent to social contract. Careful attention to these premises will reveal the reciprocity that exists between literary texts and dominant cultural norms. Both Jacobs and Thoreau contest the conceptual limitations that inhere in liberal language just as they explore its contours and expressive possibilities.

The juxtaposition of Jacobs's account of her confinement in what she calls the "Loophole of Retreat" and Thoreau's description of his night in prison should allow for clearer specification and mapping of historical modes of resistance. There are at least three crucial points of difference between the two models, pertaining to criminality, freedom, and consent. As we shall see, the conceptual possibilities for disobedience as an organizing principle of action, and the form of political community or "nation" each model of disobedience promotes, are distinctive in each case.

Acts of disobedience abound in slave narrative. Mary Prince's 1831 narrative depicts the terrible dilemma she faced when, in response to her master's unfair beating, she once decided to speak up in her own defense. She recalls, "He struck me so severely . . . that at last I defended myself, for I thought it was high time to do so. I then told him I would not live longer with him, for he was a very indecent man. . . . So I went away to a neighboring house and sat down and cried till the next morning, when I went home again, not knowing what else to do."[3] Frederick Douglass in his 1845 *Narrative* describes the act of physical resistance, his battle with Mr. Covey, as a turning point in his career as a slave that revives his liberal faith in the inviolable right to freedom. "This battle . . . rekindled the few expiring embers of freedom," writes Douglass, "and revived in me a sense of my own manhood. It recalled the departed self-confidence, and inspired me again with a determination to be free. . . . He only can understand the deep satisfaction which I experienced, who has him-self repelled by force the bloody arm of slavery."[4]

The famous slave narrative account of the 1831 Southampton slave rebel-lion presented in *The Confessions of Nat Turner,* first published in Baltimore in 1831, is significant as a model of disobedience because it points up the fact that, as oppressed persons, slaves have no political obligations insofar as those obligations are to the state. As the political philosopher Michael Walzer ar-gues in "The Obligations of Oppressed Minorities," "There is a sense in which oppression makes men free, and the more radical the oppression the more radical the freedom. Thus slaves have a right to kill their masters, sub-ject peoples their tyrants. They are set loose from the normal restraints of social life, because any violence they commit against masters and tyrants can plausibly be called defensive."[5] What is important to note here is the utter incompatibility of the slave's act of disobedience and the legal system in which such acts are redressed. At the end of his account of the Turner trial, attorney Thomas Gray observes that "The court . . . having met for the trial of Nat Turner, the prisoner was brought in and arraigned, and upon his ar-raignment pleaded *Not guilty:* saying to his counsel that he did not feel so."[6]

In *Incidents in the Life of a Slave Girl,* Jacobs explicitly acknowledges Turner's 1831 rebellion as an event that marked a crisis in the meaning of disobedience for slaves in nineteenth-century America. She recalls the day Nat Turner's insurrection broke out, when the town she lived in was thrown into great commotion: "Strange that they should be alarmed, when their slaves were so 'contented and happy'! But so it was."[7] The critique of political obligation and disobedience Jacobs presents in *Incidents* is shaped by her experience of the legal and political consequences of the event. Rather than depict, as does Turner, her own situation of oppression as one of total violence which sanc-tions acts of violence in *Incidents,* Jacobs tells her readers at the outset that she writes primarily on behalf of "two millions of women at the South, . . . suffer-ing what I suffered, and most of them far worse" (*I*, 1). And rather than de-scribe, as Walzer suggests, a total lack of political obligation, Jacobs details the intimate complexities arising from the question of obedience which in her social world are present in the conduct of daily life. For example, she records an incident in which her brother William is called at the same time by his father and his mistress: "One day, when [my brother's] father and his mis-tress had happened to call him at the same time, he hesitated between the two; being perplexed to know which had the strongest claim upon his obe-dience." As Jacobs writes,

> He finally concluded to go to his mistress. When my father reproved him for it, he said, "You both called me, and I didn't know which I ought to go to first."

"You are *my* child," replied our father, "and when I call you, you should come immediately, if you have to pass through fire and water." Poor Willie! He was now to learn his first lesson of obedience to a master. (*I*, 9)

The problem of a slave's obedience as Jacobs presents it is paradoxical. Here the father's claim to his son's obedience, which arguably constitutes a powerful form of political, sentimental obligation, even though this obligation is not to the state, has contradicted a claim to obedience constructed in law and resulting from a contractual arrangement in which the slave has been exchanged as property. The father's emphasis on the word "my" – a word that Jacobs italicizes in her text – reveals a tension within the language of possession itself between rights to property defined by parenting and lawful owning. This tension within the meaning of property reflects a tension between conflicting claims to obedience raised by the father and the mistress. The father's claim, which arises out of the sentimental bond of kinship, has here been invoked as a means of resisting the mistress's claim, which arises out of the American law of slavery. Jacobs's father, by his assertion of parental over legal property, and of the sentimental duty of obedience to the patriarchal bonds of kinship over obedience to the so-called democratic law of contract, has established powerful grounds for his son's act of disobedience.

Jacobs's attempt to confront the question of obedience in this scene also registers her response to the incompatibility of Turner's act of disobedience and his represented position in a court of law – the fact that although Turner could exhibit his self-evident *feeling* that he was not guilty, this feeling could not be defended or accounted for in legal, theoretical terms. Because Jacobs knew that a son's duty of obedience to his father would be valued by her sentimental audience, she deliberately evokes a sentimental response. But Jacobs also knew that the mere feeling that her brother William should obey his father and deny his mistress would never hold up in a court of law. Viewed in these terms, Jacobs's acknowledgment of Turner's rebellion generates a narrative account of disobedience that invites but does not rely on a sentimental response to the disobedient slave's predicament. Her conceptualization of disobedience in *Incidents* discloses a persistent effort to negotiate between the competing claims of liberalism and sentimentality as contradictory but equally necessary value systems or rhetorics of representation, both of which were central to nineteenth-century American culture, and both of which Jacobs meant to invoke in her attempt to communicate with her readers. The insufficiency of sentimentality to articulate the meaning of disobedience and a legal argument against slavery also motivates Jacobs to have recourse to the liberal discourse of rights, and both rhetorics gain justification and force by the fact of this juxtaposition. Narrating her own act of disobedience, in which she escapes from her master and hides in her grandmother's attic garret for seven years, Jacobs designs a model of disobedience that expresses her dual and contradictory commitment both to the claims of sentimentality and to liberal ideas forming the conceptual basis for law in the United States.

Although Jacobs deploys the rhetoric of liberalism in *Incidents*, she does so in order to point out the extent to which existing political institutions fail to give full expression to liberal values and ideals. What is immediately striking about Jacobs's discussion of disobedience is that it provides her with the opportunity to point out the salient fact that, by law, a slave is not a citizen. Describing her uncle Phillip's obituary notice at the end of her narrative, she indirectly refers to an 1844 North Carolina Supreme Court ruling in *State* vs. *Elijah Newsom*, which states that "free persons of color in this State are not to be considered as citizens" (*I*, 292). Uncle Phillip's obituary "was written by one of his friends, and contained these words: 'Now that death has laid him low, they call him a good man and a useful citizen; but what are eulogies to the black man, when the world has faded from his vision?' So they called a colored man a *citizen*! Strange words to be uttered in that region!" (*I*, 201). In response to this obvious failure of American democracy to ensure equal access to the benefits of citizenship, the model of disobedience Jacobs presents in *Incidents* is structured on a central contradiction. On the one hand, she calls attention to the clear compromise of the liberal ideal of citizenship as it is constructed by law in the United States, thereby suggesting that the concept of civil disobedience is insufficient for her purposes: It has no relevance or applicability to her experience of American culture. On the other hand, Jacobs claims for herself the rights and full privileges of citizenship. Her identity as a disobedient entails what W. E. B. Du Bois would later call a self-contradictory state of "double-consciousness," one in which Jacobs articulates her exclusion from representation in society in order to work for her construction of a recognized position of representation within society as a "citizen," a position from which to claim her right to disobey. In Jacobs's cultural critique of liberal theory, then, the concept of civil disobedience is shown to be both insufficient to account for her own experience, and a necessary barrier to slavery that cannot be discarded.

An important point of difference thus emerges in this juxtaposition of Jacobs and Thoreau: whereas Thoreau works in his essay "Civil Disobedience" to construct a position in which he has, in his own words, been "put out and locked out of the State by her own act,"[8] Jacobs's task in *Incidents* is to construct a model of disobedience in which she has, by *her* own act, been locked into a prison of her own making. In order to establish the expressive possibility of civil disobedience, and thereby to fashion his essay as a useful tool for the purposes of reform, Thoreau must first find a way to speak from a position outside the state. He observes that "Statesmen and legislators, standing so completely within the institution, never distinctly and nakedly behold it. They speak of moving society, but have no resting-place without it" (CD, 87). Thoreau refuses to pay his poll tax and goes to prison, an act he regards as directed at the only possible site at which to "effectually withdraw [his] support, both in person and in property, from the government of Massachusetts" (CD, 74). By contrast, Jacobs constructs what she calls a "Loophole of Retreat," an attic garret where she hides as a fugitive slave, remaining in the slave South unseen for seven years. This Loophole functions both as a rhetorical device and as an actual hiding place; it is both a means of evasion from the law and a site for Jacobs's representation within the law.

Both Thoreau's account of his night in prison and Jacobs's invention of the "Loophole of Retreat" reveal distinctive utopian possibilities for political community in America. Both renderings of disobedience present us with the recasting and critique of concepts associated with liberal theories of government: concepts such as criminality, freedom, and the exercise of voluntary consent. The importance of these primary conceptual differences will become more apparent once we have considered each in isolation.

In her well-known philosophical account of civil disobedience, Hannah Arendt argues that civil disobedience can never be equated with criminal disobedience: "There is all the difference in the world," she writes, "between the criminal's avoiding the public eye and the civil disobedient's taking the law into his own hands in open defiance."[9] Thoreau concurs, arguing that the distinction between criminal and civil disobedience is evident in the fact that, in contrast to criminal disobedience, there exists no suitable and definite penalty for acts of civil disobedience: "One would think, that a deliberate and practical denial of its authority, was the only offense never contemplated by government; else, why has [government] not assigned its definite, its suitable and proportionate penalty?" (CD, 73). For Jacobs and other fugitive slaves, however, the only means of establishing a position within the law and of thereby constructing a model of civil disobedience resides in what is defined by law as a criminal act. The only way Jacobs can call herself into existence in legal terms, and establish a represented relationship to the law, is through her criminal act of stealing herself as her master's property.

This difference in thinking about criminality causes Jacobs and Thoreau to view incarceration in very different terms. For Thoreau, the Massachusetts prison is the only place where, in his own words, "freer and less desponding spirits" locked out by the state's own act can and should express their dissatisfaction. "It is there," he writes, "that the fugitive slave, and the Mexican prisoner on parole, and the Indian come to plead the wrongs of his race, should find them . . . – the only house in a slave-state in which a free man can abide with honor" (CD, 76). In contrast to Thoreau, for whom a Massachusetts prison is the only place the state provides for effective civil disobedience, the only form of prison in which Jacobs exercises a relative degree of freedom is a prison created by her own act of invention. As a site for disobedience, the state prison into which members of Jacobs's family are thrown is deemed insufficient.[10]

Much of the force of Jacobs's account of her confinement in the Loophole derives from the fact that it allows her to express her deep dissatisfaction with the imperfect realization of freedom as a cherished, invented value in liberal society.[11] We see this at the end of her narrative when, having finally escaped to New York City, Jacobs is shocked to discover that Mrs. Bruce has bought and freed her.

> My brain reeled. . . . A gentleman near me said, "It's true; I have seen the bill of sale." . . . So I was *sold* at last! A human being *sold* in the free city of New York! The bill of sale is on record, and future generations will learn from it that women were articles of traffic in New York, late in the nineteenth century of the Christian religion. . . . I well know the value of that bit of paper; but much as I love freedom, I do not like to look upon it. (*I,* 200)

Jacobs's ironic description of the "free city of New York" is not only a reference to the Fugitive Slave Law; it also reflects her outrage at the fact that in the very act of becoming legally free, she must affirm her slave status as an article of property. "The more my mind had become enlightened, the more difficult it was for me to consider myself an article of property; and to pay money to those who had so grievously oppressed me seemed like taking from my sufferings the glory of triumph" (*I,* 199). Whereas Thoreau finds freedom in jail, arguing that the Massachusetts prison is "the only house in a slave-state in which a free man can abide with honor," Jacobs finally insists upon the limits of freedom afforded her by existing social conditions.

Jacobs's preoccupation with the meaning of her freedom in the concluding pages of her narrative also registers her persistent attempt to negotiate between liberal and sentimental values.[12] For the sentimental heroine, the reward for moral constancy is often marriage or death and eternal bliss. By contrast, Jacobs adamantly celebrates her freedom.[13] "Reader, my story ends with freedom; not in the usual way, with marriage. I and my children are now free! We are as free from the power of slaveholders as are the white people of the north; and though that, according to my ideas, is not saying a great deal, it is a vast improvement in *my* condition. The dream of my life is not yet realized" (*I,* 201). And instead of promoting sentimental death as a valued reward at the end of her narrative, Jacobs turns to the liberal maxim that the individual's rights to life and liberty are self-evident and unalienable. When, for example, Jacobs tells us that Miss Fanny expressed a peculiar, sentimental wish that Jacobs and all her grandmother's family were at peace in their graves, Jacobs remarks that "The good old soul did not dream that I was planning to bestow peace upon her, with regard to myself and my children; not by death, but by securing our freedom" (*I*, 89).

Although Jacobs's profound awareness of her right to life, and her repudiation of the sentimentalization of death, reflect her stalwart belief in freedom as a liberal value, her act of disobedience expresses a powerful critique of this negative conception of freedom as unhampered autonomy.[14] In *Incidents* Jacobs broadens the liberal, individual conception of freedom so that it also accommodates her sentimental, maternal duties to children and to kin: "I could have made my escape alone; but it was more for my helpless children than for myself that I longed for freedom" (*I*, 89). By thus affirming both liberal and sentimental ideals, both free autonomy and familial obligation, Jacobs's model of disobedience strategically enlists both the sentimental reader's powers of sympathy and the liberal discourse of rights.

Jacobs's recognition of obligations arising out of love, obligations that are neither voluntarily assumed nor precisely involuntary, brings me to a third point of difference in this comparative analysis: namely, the important and unique role of consent in each writer's rendering of disobedience. The assumption that "consent" is the source of a government's legitimacy represents a conceptual keystone in liberal theory.[15] According to Locke's justification of the liberal state, individuals enter into a social contract only by means of rational, voluntary acts of consent. In the first stage of this process a new political association is formed; in the second, a liberal government is established and granted the right to make political decisions.[16]

Thoreau's attempt to have himself locked out of the state by the state's own act is an attempt to withdraw his consent, which forms the basis for law in liberal society. He argues that his primary task is to make sure that he does not himself contribute to the wrong that he condemns. "How does it become a man to behave toward this American government to-day?" he asks. "I answer that he cannot without disgrace be associated with it. I cannot for an instant recognize that political organization as *my* government which is the *slave's* government also" (CD, 67). Thoreau's recognition of a constitutional crisis marked by the existence of slavery in America is in some respects an attempt to remedy the original crime of excluding slaves from representation by his own refusal to be the condoning agent of social injustice: "As for adopting the ways which the State has provided for remedying the evil, I know not of such ways. . . . In this case the State has provided no way: its very Constitution is the evil" (CD, 74).

In "Civil Disobedience" Thoreau has recourse to highly symbolic actions – the refusal to pay his poll tax on the one hand, and the act of writing itself on the other – as a means of withdrawing his consent and challenging his government's legitimacy. This recourse to symbolic action may itself be regarded by some of his critics as problematic.[17] However, the function of Thoreau's symbolic action in "Civil Disobedience" is that it allows him to argue that slavery justifies the withdrawal of consent and the exercise of a right to revolution. "All men recognize," Thoreau observes, "the right of revolution; that is, the right to refuse allegiance to and resist the government, when its tyranny or its inefficiency are great and unendurable. In other words, when a sixth of the population of a nation which has undertaken to be the refuge of liberty are slaves . . . I think that it is not too soon for honest men to rebel and revolutionize" (CD, 67). Although, as we have seen, the *slave* has no political obligations to the state, Thoreau here argues that the existence of slavery warrants the dissolution of *his own* ties to the state: For Thoreau, slavery warrants a call to revolution, the invocation of liberal principles clarified and reformulated in Thoreau's own terms and applied to unique historical circumstances. That Thoreau's essay in this respect represents both a conceptual break from and a continuity within liberalism is evident in the fact that although Thoreau calls upon Locke's doctrine of the right of revolution in "Civil Disobedience," Thoreau's own political practices lead him to a consideration of circumstances that Locke himself could not have foreseen.[18]

According to contractarian thinkers such as Locke, consent is expressed in the first instance through ownership of property, because the consent to social contract that establishes legitimate government arises out of a desire for the protection of private property. Property in one's own person is the primary condition for admission to civil society. Property renders consent to civil society meaningful, because consent to the bonds of civil society occurs in exchange for its secure enjoyment. In his *Second Treatise of Government,* Locke insists that there can be no major cause for consent without property: "The great and *chief end,* therefore, of Mens uniting into Commonwealths, and putting themselves under Government, *is the Preservation of their Property.*"[19] One important implication of Thoreau's account of the disobedient's withdrawal of consent is that, for Thoreau, it requires that the disobedient refrain from the accumulation of property: "They who assert the purest right, and consequently are most dangerous to a corrupt State, commonly have not spent much time in accumulating property" (CD, 77).

For Jacobs, the disobedient's problem is that property rights are denied her because she is herself property; the fact that, as she puts it, "A slave, *being* property, can *hold* no property" (I, 6). In contrast to Thoreau, who explores the possibility of repudiating ownership as a means of withdrawing consent, Jacobs emphasizes the slave's present incapacity to consent to civil society. For Thoreau, the night in the Concord prison represents his withdrawal from society. For Jacobs, the "Loophole of Retreat" is a site at which to exercise her right to consent. Indeed, the entire account of Jacobs's life in the garret, although obviously a real and historical event, also functions as an allegory in which Jacobs self-consciously constructs, as Defoe did in *Robinson Crusoe*, her original act of consenting to civil society. Casting her lived experience as allegory, Jacobs describes her early experiences in the garret as follows:

> It was impossible for me to move in an erect position, but I crawled about my den for exercise. One day I hit my head against something, and found it was a gimlet. . . . I was as rejoiced as Robinson Crusoe could have been at finding such a treasure. It put a lucky thought into my head. I said to myself, "Now I will have some light. Now I will see my children." I did not dare to begin my work during the daytime, for fear of attracting attention. (*I*, 115)

Even if we choose to disregard the possibility of an allusion in this passage to the Emersonian state of uprightness as the state of self-reliance and freedom Jacobs has been denied, the labor of using the gimlet to make a loophole is clearly a means of her entrance into society. The light she lets into the garret with her own hands is light that allows her to work and to make garments and playthings, representing her connection to a larger social world.

Of the many things that might be said about the model of political community represented by the Loophole, two are relevant here. First, the Loophole stands as a critique of the liberal, contractarian view that the political sphere is separate from the rest of social life, and that property relations form the sole basis for ties that bind individuals together in civil society. Throughout *Incidents* Jacobs regards commercial negotiations as liberating,[20] and her disobedient retreat clearly registers this engagement with the premises of contract. But her account of life in the Loophole also presents the sentimental bonds of kinship or race as a means of resisting the purely contractual claims and obligations constructed in the liberal theory of government. The intimate web of relations she establishes in the Loophole are created not through economic exchange, but rather by free, loving, and unreciprocated acts of giving: The clothes she labors to produce are gifts that fill her children's Christmas stockings and afford Jacobs as their mother "the pleasure of peeping at them as they went into the street with their new suits on" (*I*, 118).[21] The obligations that provide the ground of Jacobs's disobedience in the Loophole, and which constitute her social and political world, are thus dual and contradictory: They represent both the liberal wish for freedom and the racial tie that attaches her to the family.

Second, this irreducible tie of kinship or race is, paradoxically, most visible to us at the very moment Jacobs consents to a social position and condition of invisibility, a condition in which she is both empowered and mute. I will not explore this important subject of invisibility in depth,[22] but we should note its centrality to the whole question of disobedience, insofar as philosophers such as Arendt define the public realm of politics as the space of visibility: "Everything that appears in public can be seen and heard by everybody. . . . For us, appearance – something that is being seen and heard by others as well as by ourselves – constitutes reality."[23] Thoreau's status as a free, taxpaying, white male allows him to be visible and, in Arendt's terms, public in his expression of dissatisfaction with the state. By contrast, Jacobs's entry into the public realm is complicated by the fact that her racial visibility endangers her by calling attention to her identity as a slave.[24] Her act of disobedience, by necessity, goes unseen. The powerful invisibility of the Loophole allows Jacobs to see and identify her rights in writing, but not in speech. For Jacobs, then, writing represents a crucial means of rendering the act of disobedience visible, public, and political.

The significance of disobedience for Jacobs's and Thoreau's respective critiques of liberal contractarianism becomes more apparent when we consider the larger attempt on the part of both writers to imagine an ideal "nation" of disobedients, and to confront the question of whether political obligations – the ties that bind disobedients together as a political community – are voluntarily or involuntarily assumed. In her discussion of civil disobedience, Arendt argues that, viewed collectively, civil disobedients are a form of voluntary association; that "In contrast to the conscientious objector, the civil disobedient is a member of a group, and this group, whether we like it or not, is formed in accordance with the same spirit that has informed voluntary associations."[25] Arendt asserts that Thoreau is not a disobedient in these terms because he represents only a single conscientious objector, and thus does not provide us with a model association of disobedients who have voluntarily consented to their political association.

But despite the fact that Thoreau looks like a lone conscientious objector, his imagination of an ideal political community is central to his project in "Civil Disobedience." At the end of his essay Thoreau articulates his vision of a nation of disobedients that is at once inside and outside the state, and whose "revolutionary" act of withdrawal is in fact compatible with the existence of the state:

> I please myself with imagining a State at last which can afford to be just to all men, and to treat the individual with respect as a neighbor; which even would not think it inconsistent with its own repose, if a few were to live aloof from it, not meddling with it, nor embraced by it, who fulfilled all the duties of neighbors and fellow-men. . . . A State which bore this kind of fruit, and suffered it to drop off as fast as it ripened, would prepare the way for a still more perfect and glorious State, which also I have imagined, but not yet anywhere seen. (CD, 89–90)

What is perhaps most striking about the form of political community Thoreau imagines in "Civil Disobedience" is that the political obligations that bind him to this community are not, as Arendt suggests, voluntarily assumed. Thoreau's appeal to conscience, a central and necessary aspect of his argument, functions to construct a conscience that is both private and collective, and thus the political obligations or dictates of conscience Thoreau invokes represent both his personal opinion and a universal moral law. "Can there not be a government in which majorities do not virtually decide right and wrong, but conscience?" Thoreau asks, "in which majorities decide only those questions to which the rule of expediency is applicable? It is truly enough said, that a corporation has no conscience; but a corporation of conscientious men is a corporation *with* a conscience" (CD, 65). This tension or contradiction between a private and a collective act of conscience is expressed by a grammatical ambiguity in Thoreau's construction of a pun on the phrase "majority of one":

> I do not hesitate to say, that those who call themselves abolitionists should at once effectually withdraw their support, both in person and property, from the government of Massachusetts, and not wait till they constitute a majority of one, before they suffer the right to prevail through them. I think that it is enough if they have God on their side, without waiting for that other one. Moreover, any man more right than his neighbors, constitutes a majority of one already. (CD, 74)

The central purpose of Thoreau's writing about his night in prison, his careful characterization of the act of disobedience, is the discovery in his essay of the intimate connection between obligations that arise out of an individual act of conscience and a powerful theory of national identity. In "Civil Disobedience" he discloses the political obligations that bind him to a nation of disobedients. During his night in prison, Thoreau tells us he was presented with a "closer view of [his] native town" and was "fairly inside of it," but this town is not the more perfect political community he finds in prison and to which he himself belongs (CD, 82). He recalls, "It was like travelling into a far country, such as I had never expected to behold, to lie there for one night. It was to see my native village in light of the middle ages, and our Concord was turned into a Rhine stream, and visions of knights and castles passed before me. They were the voices of old burghers that I heard in the streets" (CD, 82). This odd reference to the conventions of romance expresses Thoreau's nationalism precisely because it confirms our sense of his alienation from society, and his claim to have founded a freer and disobedient nation of one. "If there was a wall of stone between me and my townsmen," Thoreau writes, "there was a still more difficult one to climb or break through, before they could get to be as free as I was" (CD, 80).

In crucial respects, Thoreau regards his withdrawal into prison as a voluntary act: The imagination of a more perfect nation of disobedients in "Civil Disobedience" is in part made possible by Thoreau's voluntary withdrawal of consent to social injustice. But his strategic, coercive appeal to conscience would suggest otherwise, because this appeal entails an assumption of political obligations – obligations that bind him to a nation of disobedients – which cannot be regarded as a purely voluntary act. For Thoreau, political obligations and the ties of nationhood are not only voluntarily assumed; they are also, like the bonds of race, born into or found. The language of conversion through which Thoreau describes his experience inside the prison is also used to discover a self-evidently natural and already existing bond between the white, male disobedient, on the one hand, and the slave or the Mexican or the Indian on the other. He claims that

> The proper place to-day, the only place which Massachusetts has provided for her freer and less desponding spirits, is in her prisons, to be put out and locked out of the State by her own act, as they have already put themselves out by their principles. It is there that the fugitive slave, and the Mexican prisoner on parole, and the Indian come to plead the wrongs of his race, should *find* them. (CD, 76, emphasis added)

Indeed, once again outside the prison, Thoreau goes so far as to insist that he views the white people among whom he lives as "a distinct race from me by their prejudices and superstitions, as the Chinamen and Malays are" (CD, 83). The claim to a status within a race which is "distinct" from the white people among whom he lives is an essential gesture in Thoreau's strategy which has never, to my knowledge, been commented on. Thoreau's recourse to the discourse of race in this brief passage not only allows him to speak on behalf of the oppressed, and justify his act of disobedience by the fact of their enslavement, but also allows him to represent and rhetorically ensure the coherence of an exceedingly diverse nation of disobedients in racialist and deceptively unproblematic terms.

Having rhetorically equated his experience with that of the slave, Thoreau by his own admission adds justification and force to his own symbolic act of disobedience:

> If any think that their influence would be lost [in prison], and their voices no longer afflict the ear of the State, that they would not be as an enemy within its walls, they do not know by how much truth is stronger than error, nor how much more eloquently and effectively he can combat injustice who has experienced a little in his own person. (CD, 76)

Thoreau cannot and does not claim that *in fact* he speaks as one of the oppressed, nor does he need to. His purpose is to speak on *behalf* of the slave, and to register the existence of the political community he addresses and whose existence he thereby affirms – disobedients who are, like him, ready to find a more perfect society such as he imagines but has not yet seen anywhere.

Jacobs's position with respect to her readers and her rhetorical strategy for constructing an ideal nation of disobedients are fundamentally different from Thoreau's. Her task in *Incidents* is twofold: On the one hand, Jacobs attempts to form an association of disobedients by appealing to a white, Northern, and largely female audience whom she explicitly identifies throughout her narrative; on the other hand, Jacobs also brings into existence for her readers a community of slaves. With respect to her white, female reader, Jacobs's problem is whether and how she can appeal to this reader's conscience. Thoreau uses the voice of a private and corporate conscience to make this appeal, but this rhetorical vehicle is denied to Jacobs, because she is not in a position to be identified as a conscientious agent regarding the injustices of slavery. Instead of positioning herself above the white, female reader by displaying her moral superiority, Jacobs resorts to a strategic appeal to her readers for pity, which calls attention to the condition of slavery, a state that has forced her into what she portrays as her moral transgressions. Discussing her sexual relations with Mr. Sands, which are known to have occurred out of wedlock, she writes, "Pity me, and pardon me, O virtuous reader! You never knew what it is to be a slave; to be entirely unprotected by law or custom; to have the laws reduce you to the condition of a chattel, entirely subject to the will of another" (*I*, 55). Once again, in order to exhort her white, abolitionist readers to acts of disobedience Jacobs characteristically invokes values that are both liberal and sentimental. But at the same time that she invites the pitying, pardoning response of conventional sentimental readers, Jacobs also emphasizes the voluntarism implicit in her choice of Mr. Sands as a lover – the fact, as she so eloquently puts it, that "It seems less degrading to give one's self, than to submit to compulsion" (*I*, 55) – and thereby appeals to readers who admire her unwavering aspiration to the liberal ideals of individuality and freedom.

I have suggested that because Jacobs is the object and not the agent of oppression, her argument does not exhibit the same structure as Thoreau's, which relies on the dictates of an individual conscience that is also the corporate conscience of a more perfect society. One result of this disparity is that although Jacobs refuses to rule out the possibility of being powerfully representative, she does not, as does Thoreau, rely on the fact that she is representative. For Jacobs, the expression of a better world is forcefully justified even when that expression is highly personal. Despite the fact that she tells her readers that she speaks on behalf of those who suffer what she suffered and far worse, Jacobs does not need to speak on behalf of these others. For Jacobs, a better and more liberal world might be called "our" humanly possible world, but in order to have validity and effect her utopian vision need only be presented in terms of her personal experience – the personal, as yet unfulfilled, wish to have a hearthstone and home of her own.

In *Incidents* Jacobs, like Thoreau, imagines a political community or "nation" of disobedients bound together both by obligations that arise out of voluntary acts of consent and by obligations that are involuntarily assumed.

However, although both writers challenge the current prevailing theoretical view of disobedience as a purely voluntary act, each represents a historical mode of resistance in which positionality plays a central role. For Jacobs, the attempt to grapple with the meaning of disobedience entails her persistent negotiation between sentimentality and liberalism as contradictory but equally necessary rhetorics of representation. Moreover, by virtue of her position, Jacobs adds a crucial dimension to the character of disobedience that Thoreau cannot explicitly discuss. Insofar as Jacobs represents an oppressed minority, the obligations that bind her to this community of slaves are by her own description stronger than either the obligations of liberal contract or the ties of sympathy that bind her to an association of white, female readers. "There are no bonds so strong as those which are formed by suffering together," she insists (*I*, 170). Just as the obligations Jacobs invokes in her appeal to white, Northern women represent a critique of the purely contractual claims and obligations constructed in the liberal theory of government so, in her attempt to bring into existence a community of slaves, Jacobs invokes irreducible ties of race that represent an alternative notion of obligation because they are not assumed, in liberal terms, by acts of consent that are wholly voluntary.[26] The black community to whom Jacobs belongs and on whose behalf she writes is, paradoxically, made visible to her readers at the very moment she consents to a powerful, disobedient, and invisible position within the state – the only position from which she can claim her rights.

Notes

1. Martin Luther King, Jr., *A Testament of Hope: The Essential Writings and Speeches of Martin Luther King, Jr.*, ed. James M. Washington (New York: HarperCollins, 1991), 291–2.
2. In a thoroughgoing analysis of the problem of political obligation, Carole Pateman has argued that the habitual identification of liberalism with democracy is mistaken. "Liberal democratic societies are in origin, and remain today in institutional form and ideology, essentially *liberal* societies. Their one democratic element was introduced when universal suffrage was granted" (*The Problem of Political Obligation: A Critique of Liberal Theory* [Berkeley: University of California Press, 1979], 5). All future textual references to *The Problem of Political Obligation* will be cited parenthetically.
3. Mary Prince, "The History of Mary Prince," *The Classic Slave Narratives*, ed. Henry Louis Gates, Jr. (New York: Penguin, 1987), 202–3.
4. Frederick Douglass, *Narrative of the Life of Frederick Douglass*, ed. Benjamin Quarles (Cambridge: Harvard University Press, 1960), 104–5.
5. Michael Walzer, *Obligations: Essays on Disobedience, War, and Citizenship* (Cambridge: Harvard University Press, 1970), 62.
6. Nat Turner, "The Confessions of Nat Turner," in *Black Writers of America: A Comprehensive Anthology*, ed. R. Barksdale and K. Kinnamon (New York: Macmillan, 1972), 171.

7. Harriet Jacobs, *Incidents in the Life of a Slave Girl*, ed. Jean Fagan Yellin (Cambridge: Harvard University Press, 1987), 63. All future references are to this edition and will be cited parenthetically.

8. Henry David Thoreau, "Civil Disobedience," *Reform Papers*, ed. Wendell Glick (Princeton: Princeton University Press, 1973), 76. All future references are to this edition and will be cited parenthetically.

9. Hannah Arendt, *Crises of the Republic* (New York: Harcourt Brace Jovanovich, 1969), 75.

10. It is true that, because members of Jacobs's family have been put in jail as a result of Jacobs's crime, Jacobs describes the state prison as being for a time the only place where her daughter Ellen is loved: "I have always considered it as one of God's special providences that Ellen screamed till she was carried back to jail," she writes (*I*, 102).

11. In a recent analysis of freedom as a Western value, Orlando Patterson has shown that any coherent definition of the term must take into account three conceptually, historically, and sociologically related ideas. First, "personal freedom," in its negative and positive aspects, is defined both as the absence of restraints in the fulfillment of desires, and as the capacity to do what one pleases, insofar as one can without constraining others in the fulfillment of their desires. Second, "sovereignal freedom" entails the absolute power to act as one pleases, regardless of the wishes of others. And finally, "civic freedom" is expressed as participation within the life and governance of a political community. *Freedom in the Making of Western Culture* (New York, Basic Books, 1991), 1–5.

12. In her discussion of Jacobs's critique of the sentimental tradition, Valerie Smith has argued that although Jacobs incorporated the rhetoric of sentimentality, she also "seized authority over her literary restraints in much the same way that she seized power in her own life" (*Self-Discovery and Authority in Afro-American Narrative* [Cambridge: Harvard University Press, 1987], 28).

13. Compare Carla Kaplan's contention that the opposition of freedom and marriage in *Incidents* facilitates Jacobs's critique of "the nineteenth-century ideology of marriage as woman's 'sacred absolute,' the means of her personal fulfillment and proper end of her life" ("Narrative Contracts and Emancipatory Readers: *Incidents in the Life of a Slave Girl*," *The Yale Journal of Criticism* 6 [1993], 93). All future references to "Narrative Contracts" will be cited parenthetically.

14. As Kaplan has argued, Jacobs "challenges us to think about freedom and agency as specific and contextual, not as abstract and universal" ("Narrative Contracts," 93).

15. See Elaine Scarry, "Consent and the Body," *New Literary History* 21 (Autumn 1990), 867–96.

16. In her critique of liberal theory, Pateman presents two basic strategies adopted by political philosophers in order to deal with the significance of consent. One raises doubts about the relevance of consent as the sole basis for a citizen's obedience to the state; the other empties the concept of any genuine content by claiming that all citizens may be said to consent. Pateman argues that theorists who take this latter approach frequently identify "consent" with the existence of political practices such as voting, and as such provide "a very good illustration of the extent to which discussions of political obligation rest on the ideological assumption that

liberal democratic theory and practice coincide" (*The Problem of Political Obligation*, 82).

17. Although Thoreau's profound influence upon Martin Luther King, Jr.'s philosophy of nonviolent resistance presents us with clear evidence of Thoreau's expansion on possibilities for disobedience as a tactical strategy, African American writers such as Alice Walker have questioned the universal applicability and political effectiveness of symbolic action. In *Meridian* (New York: Simon and Schuster, 1973), which takes place in the aftermath of the Civil Rights Movement, Walker's acute awareness of the inadequacy of the symbol-making process to enact real changes in society is evident in her description of these responses to Meridian's act of disobedience:

> "God!" said Truman without thinking. "How can you not love somebody like that!" "Because she thinks she's God," said the sweeper, "or else she just ain't all there. I think she ain't all there, myself." (21–2)

For Walker, the political efficacy of symbolic action may be compromised by the limits of its comprehensibility. As an imaginative exploration of the radical potentiality of Thoreau's and King's theories of disobedience, *Meridian* offers us a bleak and startling ambiguity: as a civil disobedient, Meridian is either someone whom we thoughtlessly worship, as does Truman; or she is someone whom we dismiss, as the old sweeper does, for harboring grandiose and insane delusions about herself and utopian prospects for political community in America.

18. Compare Leonard Neufeldt's contention that Thoreau "accept[s] unreservedly the dialectic at the heart of the Revolutionary republican legacy. . . . On the one hand, one honors the North Bridge, the Concord and Acton rebels, and the republican sentiments and beliefs they have come to symbolize. On the other hand, one stands in alienation from, and sometimes in militia-like opposition to, many others who honor North Bridge, who utter republican sentiments and beliefs as platitudes. Republicanism consolidates and divides its adherents; it both centers and decenters their language." "Henry David Thoreau's Political Economy," *The New England Quarterly* 57 (1984), 363.

19. John Locke, *Two Treatises of Government*, ed. Peter Laslett (Cambridge University Press, 1960), 350–1.

20. Houston Baker, Jr., argues this point in *Blues, Ideology, and Afro-American Literature: A Vernacular Theory* (Chicago: University of Chicago Press, 1984), 54.

21. In her discussion of Jacobs's critique of social contract theory, Kaplan suggests that "while [Jacobs] rejects contracts to which she cannot be a fully equal and voluntary party, she does not reject the ideals to which such contracts allude. . . . Brent rejects contracts because, I believe, she endorses and even longs for the ideals and ideologies of individuality embodied by the idea of social contract" ("Narrative Contracts," 97).

22. The fact and possibilities of invisibility are vividly detailed in Ellison's *Invisible Man:* "Well, I *was* and yet I was invisible, that was the fundamental contradiction. I was and yet I was unseen. It was frightening and as I sat there I sensed another frightening world of possibilities" (*Invisible Man* [New York: Random House, 1947], 507; emphasis in original).

23. Hannah Arendt, *The Human Condition* (Chicago: University of Chicago Press, 1958), 50.
24. For a compelling sociological account of violent events from the 1940s up through the present that point up the dangers of racial visibility for black Americans engaged in acts of civil disobedience, see Manning Marable, *Race, Reform, and Rebellion: The Second Reconstruction in Black America, 1945–1990* (Jackson: University of Mississippi Press, 1991).
25. Arendt, *Crises of the Republic*, 96, 98.
26. In the novel *Iola Leroy*, published in 1892, Frances Harper explores the significance of racial identity for the question of political obligation during the Reconstruction Era by presenting us with the experience of various refugee slaves who are faced with the prospect of joining the Union Army. In the case of Robert, a light-skinned black man who has the option of passing into a white regiment but who instead decides to join the black regiment in the larger interests of his race, both forms of political obligation – those of race and citizenship – have been voluntarily consented to.

THE TENDER OF MEMORY

RESTRUCTURING VALUE IN HARRIET JACOBS'S INCIDENTS IN THE LIFE OF A SLAVE GIRL

STEPHANIE A. SMITH

Surely there must be some justice in *the man* . . .

Incidents (emphasis added)

In declaring that the "war of [her] life had begun,"[1] Harriet Jacobs, speaking as Linda Brent, describes this war as, in part, a consequence of her ripening ability to "read the characters" and so "question the motives" (*ILSG*, 19) of those around her – particularly those who call themselves her owners. Brent's first mistress, her mother's "whiter foster sister," had taught Linda how to "read and spell" (*ILSG*, 7–8). As Brent notes, these were rare skills for a slave, skills upon which Frederick Douglass's 1845 *Narrative of the Life of Frederick Douglass, American Slave, As Written by Himself* places an extremely high value.[2] However, this boon of early literacy, and Linda Brent's later, self-taught ability to write, does not grant her access to freedom in North Carolina. Nor does her literacy motivate her as much as that which she designates as another form of lived understanding. "I had not lived fourteen years in slavery for nothing" (*ILSG*, 19), she says, by way of explaining how she came to her war. Indeed, it is only through combining the powers of her literacy, her lived knowledge, and her retention of what she describes as the unruly "sparks of [her] brother's God-given nature" that Brent formulates heroism: "I resolved never to be conquered" (ILSG, 19).

Still, this militant vocalization evokes an immediate, sentimental lament of unspecified woe: "Alas for me!" (*ILSG*, 19), she says. Brent's foreshadow-

251

ing, formulaic cry of "alas" indicates the manifold, inevitable losses she will face. Yet she does not dwell on sorrow. Rather, she sets up a scene of noble conflict, highlighted by a clash of willpower: Uncle Benjamin's (Jacobs's Uncle Joseph) fight against his master, a story that prefigures her own struggles with Dr. Flint (Dr. James Norcom).[3] As she will say, "My master had power and law on his side; I had a determined will. There is might in each" (*ILSG*, 85). Thus, through her language, and in the narration of key "incidents," Brent's story promises to be a tale of thrilling moral uplift, a structure similar to many mid-nineteenth-century American abolitionist narratives. In fact, whether any of these works was deemed fictional, as in the case of Harriet Beecher Stowe's *Uncle Tom's Cabin*, or deemed authentic, like Stowe's later *Key to Uncle Tom's Cabin* – a distinction between fact and fiction to which I return below – such antebellum texts functioned as Books of Revelation. As Jacobs says, the "adventures" of Linda Brent's life might sound too thrilling to be true, but they were true, and meant to arouse the moral indignation of the "women of the North to a realizing sense of the condition of two millions of women at the South" (*ILSG*, 1).

Liberty or Death?

Strangely, though, Linda Brent's early declaration of a "girl's" war is made in a chapter of Harriet Jacobs's *Incidents in the Life of a Slave Girl* called "The Slave Who Dared to Feel Like a *Man*" (*ILSG*, 17, emphasis added). Indeed, Brent's declaration is not followed by an opening salvo from her own battle. Rather, she offers the account of her Uncle Benjamin's escape to the Free States, a story that follows what has often been called the classic slave-narrative quest pattern of fight-and-flight, enacted perhaps most famously in Douglass's 1845 *Narrative*.[4] In speaking of her uncle, Linda Brent allies her own experiences with his as thoroughly as if uncle and niece were twins. Uncle Benjamin, she says, was more "like my brother than my uncle," "a bright handsome lad, nearly white" (*ILSG*, 6), so fine in trade-parlance, and yet such a spitfire, that a slavetrader "said he would give any price if the handsome lad was a girl," since Benjamin's reputation as rebellious had made him an unsuitable masculine investment. In keeping with a popular image of the manly heroic slave,[5] Brent reports that the family "thanked God that he was not" a girl (*ILSG*, 23). Of course, given that Uncle Benjamin's tale is told within the context of *Incidents*, such thanks sits awkwardly, silently begging the question of Linda's condition as a high-spirited slave who *does* have the unfortunate fate of being a girl.

In aligning her "war" so closely with her uncle's both in this instance and in others throughout her narrative, Harriet Jacobs structures Brent's impulse for liberty as parallel to, if not the double of, a masculinized, martial exercise. At the same time, though, given how clearly Jacobs genders the subject of

Brent's narrative, she also questions the applicability of such a masculinized exercise to a slave woman's experience. Brent cannot physically "tackle" Dr. Flint the way her uncle does; as she soon reveals, physical "contact" between a slave and a master has different (often reproductive) consequences when the slave is a "girl" and not a "man." Yet, liberty appears to require that both men and women foster those rebellious sparks Brent has described as God-given only to men, an emotional state of "dar[ing] to feel like a man."

And not just any man! When Brent starts "upon this hazardous undertaking" (*ILSG*, 99) of emotional daring, she chooses to quote Patrick Henry: "Give me liberty, or give me death, was my motto" (*ILSG*, 99). Here, then, in 1861, Jacobs has Brent revoice Henry's 1775 speech to the Virginia Convention. Thus, on the verge of a second American Revolution – or, as the nascent Confederacy would soon name it, the Southern War for Independence – Brent appropriates an ennobled cultural sentiment about liberty taken from the mouth of an already mythologized, white, male American rebel. This was a sentiment that the slavocracy was attempting to manipulate for its own purposes.

But further, in using Patrick Henry, she also invites her audience to a reading of the character of the revered rebel, in order subtextually to question the motives[6] of those who, like Dr. Flint and his wife, would argue that a Linda Brent's situation is incommensurate with a Patrick Henry's. While Jacobs conjoins Brent's desire for liberty with a masculinized pattern of fight-and-flight, she also mobilizes an increasingly urgent critique of how this "will" to liberty has been logically structured. After all, if Patrick Henry's rhetoric offered a potentially suicidal either/or choice, the historical fact of the matter is that Patrick Henry himself did not die in the Revolution. His either/or of liberty or death was – and still is, if more recent displays of American nationalism are any indication[7] – traditionally deemed heroic. But this choice of liberty or death, an Enlightenment scenario that fueled, as well, Transcendentalist romanticism, falls curiously in line with the slavocracy's oft-repeated claim that African Americans were made to be slaves merely because they endured slavery. The romance of white supremacism would insist that the will of a true man would not allow him to put up with enslavement. A real man would rather die. Jacobs has even Brent voice such romantic logic when she and her family say to one another approvingly, "He that is *willing* to be a slave, let him be a slave" (*ILSG*, 26).

Yet the way Brent's family uses the verb "willing" in this textual moment follows upon a story of survival *within* slavery. Jacobs, in the process of narrating Brent's *Incidents*, redefines such culturally revered terms as "will" and "liberty," upon which such antebellum notions of identity ride. Contrary to a logic that would try to insist that one's survival as a slave denotes a cowardly lack of will, the various histories Jacobs places into relation represent intermeshed, complex patterns of living, survival, and strength, all of which revise the two-dimensional, simplified, one-way, masculinized liberty-or-death logic that antebellum cultural mores associated with nobility, willpower, and selfhood. By repeatedly demonstrating how liberty, within the context of racial slavery, can also mean separations that both resemble and replay the definitive, deliberate ones that slavery tried to force upon African Americans, Jacobs uses Brent's story to show that a wholesale restructuring of the value of individual liberty is necessary. The validity of the American democratic experiment depends on such a restructuring. Otherwise, Northern "freedom" will be no better than Southern "slavery."

Such a claim is clearly a staple of abolitionist texts. Antislavery politicians often warned that the slavocracy's unbridled authorities produced aristocratic, undemocratic tyranny.[8] However, Jacobs's rendition of this abolitionist warning demonstrates that it does not simply apply to the community that imagined itself as white, but impinges on future generations of African Americans, too. Therefore, and not surprisingly, Jacobs will show that Brent's reading of "liberty" is more accurate than the readings of those who claim to be the inheritors of Patrick Henry's legacy. As Jean Fagan Yellin claims, Jacobs was in the process of creating "a new kind of female hero . . . yok[ing] her success story as a heroic slave mother to her confessions as a woman who mourns that she is not a storybook heroine" (*ILSG*, xiv). And since, as both Yellin and Beth Maclay Doriani have demonstrated, early African American authors such as Harriet Jacobs and Harriet Wilson could not adopt the

> conventions of personhood as they were reproduced in the male slave narrative. Neither could they wholeheartedly embrace the definitions of womanhood that the popular genres of women carried to the American reading public in the 1830s, 1840s, and 1850s.[9]

Their projects necessitated narrative strategies of adaptation.

Indeed, using antebellum concepts of masculinized self-reliance very much the way Douglass does, Jacobs represents antebellum slave women who display resourcefulness – who, as Doriani claims, "take responsibility for the welfare of their children" – as "like the white, male Emersonian hero – shapers of their own destinies and responsible for their own survival."[10]

But why did Yellin use the term "female hero"? What of Doriani's syntactic frame that places the "personhood" of male slave narratives and the "womanhood" of Jacobs's text into such pro-forma structural opposition? Why compare Jacobs's story to a narrative of Emersonian self-reliance? What do these oft-repeated terms "hero" and "heroine" denote? These words track a potential interpretative paucity similar to those that Jacobs herself points to when she descants on the anomaly of the concept of "virtue" for a slave girl. Just as a virtuous slave girl or the term slave-mother[11] linguistically display the hypocritical violence of mid-nineteenth-century heterosexual ideology, so does a term like "female hero" indicate another, twentieth-century paradox that continues to shape how Jacobs's narrative has been *read* or what *questions* a reader might ask of it.

This is not to say that the critical focus on Jacobs's attempt to formulate a new, racially specific definition of "true" womanhood has not been vital. But if Linda Brent is a "new form of female hero" and a "black heroine," do such designations not occlude considerations of how this text also revises the character of such gender and racial designations? That is, no matter how often *Incidents* has been compared to either "classic" African American male slave narrative, or "classic" Anglo-American female domestic or seduction fiction, these comparisons have generally taken note of the ways in which *Incidents* deviates from one or the other without significantly questioning the gendered and racial assumptions made about those narrative patterns. Nor do such comparisons tend to grapple with how critics use their own historically determined language, a literary terminology that constructs the character of the previously mentioned narrative patterns and that may block interpretations regarding the extent of Jacobs's revisions.

Just as early commentary about this text invalidated its authenticity by declaring it to be too melodramatic to be a real slave narrative,[12] so designating Brent a "female hero" allows a reader the leeway to envision her decked out in Patrick Henry's conventional breeches, rather than to come to terms with how Jacobs may have, in fact, redesigned the garment. And if my image of a cross-dressing Brent decked out in breeches is meant to confuse gendered readings of this text, I would also point out that even when Jacobs stresses that racial identity is of consequence to lived social relations, she questions "race" as a category. In her oft-cited picture of two sisters, one of whose lives will be blighted because she has been designated a slave, Jacobs quietly makes the only difference between these children rest squarely on the designation "slave" and not on appearance, character, or familial role, thereby reinforcing the idea that race is a "legal fiction,"[13] determined by economic conditions, a commodity relation.[14] And what happens to the supposed purity of the term "white" if Brent's first mistress is, as Brent describes her, merely a little bit "whiter" than her foster sister, Brent's mother? In moments like this, while Brent insists that both "African" and "Anglo" have meaning, her text severely complicates a clear definition of either term.

Indeed, Jacobs's restructuring of mid-nineteenth-century racialized, gendered logic rescripts that logic, so that the basis of how all narrative identity, or how any constructed "character," accrues cultural value must change. As William Andrews claims, her process of linguistic retribution strives to appropriate "language for purposes of signification outside that which was privileged by the dominant culture."[15] If identifying, relational, gendered terms like "mother" or "sister," "father" or "son," have been bankrupted by the violence of slavery, so too have words such as "hero," "liberty," and "patriot"; all these words – those bearing specific gender or racial definitions (and those that some would claim are neutral) – are going to have an impact upon Jacobs's construction of that self named Linda Brent. Brent's value will ride on how these words signify. Clearly, Jacobs was interested in making gender and racial identities the special subjects of her narrative. However, while much twentieth-century commentary focuses on "gender" and "race" as Jacobs's subjects, those commentaries tend to use these words primarily to signify as simple synonyms for "woman" and "black." As Andrews writes,

> To facilitate the enslavement of people, the ideology of slavery must first master the potential meanings of key words in the language of the oppressing culture. Slavery must construct the free play of meaning that normally informs words like mother, home, lady or freedom so as to reduce the multivalent to the univocal.[16]

I would add to Andrews's statement this question: Doesn't using "gender" as a signifier for "woman," or "race" as a signifier for "black" also perform a reduction of the (Bakhtinian) multivalent to the univocal?

In his excellent study of *Incidents*, Andrews makes Jacobs's own interest in "signifying" clear when he demonstrates how her use of Southern dialect, when put in a "dialogic relationship with standardized usage that has become morally bankrupt or emotionally bogus" attains a new linguistic vitality.[17] Still, in concentrating on those dialogic moments in Jacobs's text that allow Linda Brent to "talk her way out of the most abject forms of humiliation,"[18] Andrews does not fully explore how Jacobs also revalues standard English, translating bankrupted terms back into a means of exchange valuable for her and her family. Such translations retool how character per se was narratively structured in cultural productions. Andrews's analysis does focus on those incidents – such as the invasion of Grandmother's home by, as he puts it, "feral white trash"[19] or Brent's command of the word "love" – that turn on domestic exchanges. However, although it is clear that Jacobs's interest did lie heavily within the antebellum sphere of "woman," what this analysis loses is how these revisions of the so-called private (fantasized as feminine) connect sharply to a revision of how an antebellum public (masculine) could be legitimately construed.

In other words, if familial dependency, culturally scripted as "private," must be abjured so that a "self" can rise to an individual liberty, isn't the resulting liberated self simply another form of the disfiguring disempowerment that slavery's logic has already enforced? Doesn't such a logic of masculinized solipsism threaten to undermine the ground of all personhood? If what antebellum mores claimed as most "human" was represented by a kinship tie – the tie between mother and child – what would happen if such bonds were as little regarded in the North as they were in the slavocracy? What conceptual stay remained to keep "person" from being translated into "property" – or, to use Jacobs's terms, to keep citizens from becoming nothing more than "God-breathing machines" (*ILSG*, 8)?

Ultimately, what Jacobs throws open to revision is the whole framework of individuality that has supported the value of "liberty" in nineteenth-century American culture. Freedom, *any* American's freedom, she will show, hangs in the balance of her revision. If Linda Brent's character, formulated as a result of strong interdependencies, can be read, interpreted, remembered, and valued as if she were a Patrick Henry (that is, if Linda Brent's name can signify a trope for Liberty) all justifications of enslavement, racial discrimination, and gendered degradation become more than simply points of sophistic debate. They become ludicrously hypocritical and, above all for that time and moment, dangerously unpatriotic, threatening, as they must, to debase the valuable tender underwriting Patrick Henry's cultural memory.

Translations and Relations

When Uncle Benjamin finally attains his liberty, he says to his brother, Phillip (Mark Ramsey), whom he meets by chance in New York, " 'Phil, I part with all my kindred.' " Jacobs has Brent remark dolefully, "And so it proved. We never heard from him again" (*ILSG*, 26). Benjamin disappears from the family just as completely as if he'd been sold down-river to a Georgia trader. Above all, Benjamin is lost to his mother, Aunt Martha (Molly Horniblow). Given the extreme emphasis abolitionist rhetoric and antebellum narrative in general placed on the bond of mother-and-child, this last separation is the most telling.[20] Without directly comparing Benjamin's new-found liberty in the North to his former condition as a slave in the South, Jacobs has pointed to their structural similarity. Although she rejoices that her Uncle has escaped being deemed a white man's property, Brent shows that Benjamin still loses what the slavocracy insisted a slave had no real cognizance of, outside, of course, the bonds in the "peculiar institution" – a family. All those kin-ties or affective terms upon which "white" identity and moral worth supposedly rested – words, in Benjamin's case, such as "uncle," "husband," "brother," "father" and "son," that have been rendered theoretically invalid (or indeed rendered sarcastically comic) by the volatile situation of slavery – are then made materially insubstantial.[21] Should Linda go, she would part from her kin.

Therein, of course, lies one of the most striking features of *Incidents in the Life of a Slave Girl:* Jacobs's insistence that Brent retain the material reality of the familial ties that exist, despite slaveholding fictions to the contrary, while also seeking and at last attaining freedom from enslavement. To do so, as more than a few critics have demonstrated since *Incidents* was reissued, Jacobs's 1861 narrative negotiates several forms of nineteenth-century discourse.[22] Many (if not most) evaluations of this text focus on how Jacobs had patiently to cross-stitch elements from what has often been read as a primarily masculine slave narrative of fight-and-flight with the feminine rhetoric of domesticity, in order to pattern a voice out of the "spoken and the silenced" pieces of both a "slave's" narrative and a "girl's" story.[23] As Jean Fagan Yellin writes, "The resulting text is densely patterned. Although slave narrative has been likened to the 'rootless alienated' picaro, Jacobs's Linda Brent locates herself firmly within a social matrix" (*ILSG*, xxvii), and, as William Andrews declares in *To Tell a Free Story*, the narrative skirmishes most prominent in Jacobs's work show "graphically the discursive nature of male–female power relationships."[24]

Still and all, in Jacobs's narrative, as in Douglass's, the concept of American "liberty" is most often concretely realized – if also consistently challenged – in masculinized representations.[25] The equation of "liberty = masculinity" is made evident in such moments as Jacobs's graveyard scene, where Linda Brent consolidates a determination to take Patrick Henry's motto for her own, and to follow her Uncle Benjamin's course. Note how Jacobs ties her resolution to heroic images of traditional, Americanized male courage:

> The graveyard was in the woods, and twilight was coming. . . . A black stump, at the head of my mother's grave, was all that remained of a tree my father had planted. His grave was marked by a small wooden board, bearing his name, the letters of which were nearly obliterated. I knelt down and kissed them, and poured forth a prayer to God for guidance and support in the perilous step I was about to take. As I passed the wreck of the old meeting house, where before Nat Turner's time, the slaves had been allowed to meet for worship, I seemed to hear my father's voice come from it, bidding me not to tarry till I reached freedom or the grave. (*ILSG*, 90–1)

Although Brent's deceased mother's "voice" has spoken to her at this same spot earlier, now, in the hour of crisis regarding an overt bid to escape, only her father's "voice" is heard. The dead mother is mute. Moreover, the paternal voice does not emanate from her father's grave, as one might expect, but rather erupts from the house of God, a sacred meeting hall desecrated by slaveholders out of their fear of rebellion – or fear of a righteous and noble revolution? Neatly conflating political freedom and rebellion (Nat Turner/ Patrick Henry), morality (the wrecked but sacred meeting hall), and the written word (her father's grave-marker) with paternal sanction (her father's voice crying "give me liberty or give me death"), Jacobs authorizes a fight for freedom multiply in the "Name of the Father."[26] Thus Jacobs validates a heroic course of action using traditionally paternal emblems that have very specific references to a rebellious African American context.

Yet, even as this passage upholds the validity of an ennobled, masculinized fight-and-flight bid for liberty or death, it also scrutinizes the logic that has produced such a pattern. After all, why does the passage mention Brent's dead mother? Why, in fact, open this scene by commenting that the tree her father had planted to mark her slave-mother's grave had become nothing but a black stump? Might this dead tree be a submerged reference to those father-lacking "genealogical trees [that] do not flourish in slavery"[27] of which Frederick Douglass spoke in his 1855 *My Bondage and My Freedom?* Read in such a way, Brent's black stump insists that the eventual survival of African American family trees will depend on remembering both mother's and father's narratives. Indeed, what this moment foregrounds is just how much the heroism of "give me liberty" owed its density and the desiring urgency of its conceptual power not only to the other half of the cry, "or give me death," but to the culture's dichotomous gendering of the either/or logic that associates liberty with masculinity and death with femininity.[28] Of course, Brent's slave-father has literally died. But his death is figured as heroic and his voice reanimated as the sacred, rebellious, defiantly liberatory paternal. The mother, by contrast, has been silenced. Not mute but muted, her grave bears a blasted and unfertile symbol. Thus does Jacobs's scene subtly question the value of "rising" to a liberty that has been defined through a muting or outright denial of the feminine. The genealogical paternity that Douglass wrote of as vital to "civilization"[29] cannot for Jacobs be fertile if rooted on a feminized and silent grave.

Hazel Carby called Jacobs's graveyard scene a moment of "transition from death as preferable to slavery, to the stark polarity of freedom or death." Further, said Carby, Jacobs's narrative "disrupt[s] conventional expectations of the attributes of a heroine . . . by transforming and transcending the central paradigm of death versus virtue."[30] Indeed, Brent's revision of virtue is marked by her own claim that slave women ought not be judged by standards of morality denied to them as a constituting factor of enslavement (*ILSG*, 56).

Yet isn't it precisely in understanding that her children are not (as Carby says) "the fruits of her shame" but "her links to life"[31] that Brent does not, in fact, choose *any* stark polarity? However much Brent's narrative endorses "freedom or death," it also shows that such an endorsement threatens to debase the "black" motherhood Brent is in the process of making more legitimately valuable than "white" purity. Separating herself from her children by making the classic slave narrative break for freedom may thus put her outside a definition of "mother" she intends to claim. When Aunt Martha warns, "Nobody respects a mother who forsakes her children; and if you leave them, you will never have a happy moment . . . and your sufferings would be dreadful. Remember poor Benjamin" (*ILSG*, 91), Martha's word "nobody" reminds Brent that she risks damaging both her reputation (as she has already done once, in sacrificing her virtue) and the respect her children have for her. Losing her own virtue is one thing; losing her children's respect is quite another. Brent's voluntary desertion treads very shaky narrative ground, given how antislavery rhetoric stressed the immorality of slavery's involuntary separation of mother and child. Risking no one's sanction might mean that her story would become unintelligible, perhaps aphasic.

Moreover, in heeding Aunt Martha's injunction, Brent does remember her uncle – all too well. His "rememory"[32] is always painfully before her, doubly resonant with liberation and loss. And since, unlike Uncle Benjamin, who has no children, and who is remembered with a love that makes the day he was captured "seem as but yesterday" (*ILSG*, 21), Linda might be forgotten by her family if she cannot create for them a story of self-liberation worth remembering. This is loss terribly compounded. As she says, she does not wish to leave her children, and quite particularly her daughter, who is about to go, ironically and tellingly, to the Free North "without a mother's love to shelter her from the storms of life; almost without memory of a mother! . . . I had a great desire that she should look upon me, before she went, that she might take my image with her in her memory" (*ILSG*, 139). Here, Brent shares Aunt Martha's morality: in freedom former slaves such as Linda and her daughter may incur what predominant cultural traditions have prescribed for women as a fate worse than death. But, unlike Martha, Linda Brent also knows, through her experience of Dr. Flint's degradations, that slavery is, in and of itself, a fate worse than death. Escape must remain a risk worth taking, not only for men like her uncle, but also for women like herself and her daughter.

The story-teller's trick that Jacobs must pull off, then, is to tell a tale of freedom for herself and for her children that activates a new narrative economy, one in which what some (say, Aunt Martha) might be able to read as desertion translates into devotion – a narrative where liberty does not require death.[33] However, such a trick inevitably brings back Brent's opening, central dilemma: how to be a Patrick Henry, or how to activate the cultural respect associated with the liberty his story has symbolized for the Uncle Benjamins of Brent's world, without either devaluing Uncle Benjamin's memory or weakening the value of Brent's. How to validate the choice made by Uncle Benjamin and cry, "give me liberty or give me death," without discrediting female experience and maternity? How can she adapt his choice without adopting it? Clearly, Brent is not a white man, nor would she desire to be one. Dr. Flint and Mr. Sands (Samuel Tredwell Sawyer) both illustrate the axis of revulsion Jacobs associates with being a white man. Indeed, she is not male at all, no matter how much her story might be prefigured by Uncle Benjamin's. This means that all the most locatable narrative models for heroic liberty available to Jacobs in 1859 did not fit. Narrative models for "liberation," whether they told of white Revolutionary folk heroes or of the manly, heroic slave escaping North, would exact a price that Jacobs could not pay.

Meanwhile, those narrative patterns that were deemed appropriate to Brent's gender role required frailties Jacobs could not condone. As Yellin and

Carby aptly point out, the pattern of the betrayed, passive white heroine of domestic ideology demanded the woman's death with as much force as the Patrick Henry model would demand death for those men who did not attain liberty. And the tragic mulatta-and-child image of Eliza and Harry Harris in *Uncle Tom's Cabin* made a "black" mother's character just as hysterical as her whiter foster heroine-sister's. These patterns offered little upon which to value the lived stoicism Jacobs saw daily expressed in those around her. As Carby dryly notes, the Cult of True Womanhood did not represent a "lived set of social relations" but rather "a racist, ideological system."[34]

What to do, then, as Carby's analysis asks, with an Aunt Martha who manages to endure enslavement while nurturing a family tree in the very jaws of slavery – a "rememory," as Toni Morrison's Sethe might say, that, as much as Uncle Benjamin's, anticipates Brent's own tale? Despite a cultural mythology that would insist otherwise, Aunt Martha has her freedom without breaking with all her kin. Still, her freedom is severely compromised by racial slavery. She has a potency of sorts; at least she owns her own house, she feeds and protects her starving grandchildren, she can remind Dr. Flint, with visible effect, that he will go to hell (*ILSG*, 82). She may be circumscribed by his economic privilege to sell those grandchildren, his patriarchal power to claim them, and his legal immunity from the consequences of his cruelty, but she is not at his mercy as much as Jacobs is. If such "incidental" female models, circumscribed as they are, still display personal dignity and loyalty, how are they *not* noble? How does one denote a will that has not made the heroic plunge of liberty or death?

This is clearly not an easy task. Even when depicting a woman's potency, Jacobs resorts to paternal, masculinized emblems. As she reports, her grandmother was "a woman of a high spirit. . . . I had been told that she once chased a white gentleman with a loaded pistol, because he insulted one of her daughters" (*ILSG*, 29). Grandmother's pistol-packing does not strictly resemble the heroic liberty for which a Patrick Henry stands, but, then again, it is a culturally approved model of courage – most often for a sentimental father. Doesn't this story rely, in part, on countless depictions of wronged fathers defending the good name of their daughters? In pointing out such an image, I am not disputing that Jacobs sought alternative narratives with which to combat the antebellum Cult of True Womanhood, alternatives that describe an evolving "discourse of black womanhood."[35]

As Frederick Douglass would later show, during the bitter debates within abolitionist–feminist circles over suffrage, the particularity of gender was a vexing issue. Those abstract New England ideals that he had adopted, and which had supported his own right to freedom, could wither in the face of gendered political expediencies and lived animosities separating "Americans." At the 1869 Equal Rights Convention, Douglass, advocating support of the 15th amendment despite its lack of provision for women, said,

"when women, because they are women, are hunted down through
. . . New York and New Orleans . . . when their children are torn from
their arms . . . then they will have an urgency to obtain the ballot"
     A VOICE: "Is that not all true about black women"
     MR. DOUGLASS: "Yes, yes, yes; it is true of the black woman, but
not because she is a woman but because she is black."[36]

Therefore if, as Valerie Smith wrote, Brent's story "is not the classic story of
the triumph of the individual will; rather, it is more a story of a triumphant
self-in-relation,"[37] her tale nevertheless had to work within and out of that
classic language of individuality insofar as she could denounce neither the
validity of Douglass's *Narrative* nor his later pained perception of how racial
identity cross-cuts gender roles in the politics of national identity and citizenship. Jacobs shows how Brent's racial identity has been formed in the masculine context of her uncles and son. She will not deny them. But then again,
such narratives can disavow hers. For of course Douglass's statement reveals
that he was willing, for expediency's sake, to downplay the importance of an
African American woman's experience.

     Thus, although Linda Brent's alterations of classic narratives – whether
the tale of the heroic slave or the tragic heroine – may be specifically aimed at
delineating and revising a black mother's role, *Incidents* does not speak only to
women; these stories must alter the roles for African American men, if not for
the man as well.[38] When her Uncle Benjamin determines to escape, Linda
Brent's first remark to him is a reproach: "Go," she says, "and break your
mother's heart" (*ILSG*, 21). Silently she repents of the statement and yet she
has verbalized it, lending those words the narrative impact of direct quotation. Her reproach does not alter his determination, but it does serve as an
emotional check on the upcoming scene of heroic escape. Then, in recounting Uncle Benjamin's heroism, she tells the story of Phillip, who does not follow the course of the "heroic slave" to freedom. He opts to return home. He
may be returning voluntarily to bondage but he is also going home to his
mother and his family. As he calmly tells Benjamin, "it would kill their
mother if he deserted her in her trouble. She had pledged her house, and with
difficulty, had raised money to buy him" (*ILSG*, 25). Benjamin will not allow
his mother to buy him, and Brent approves of such a decision for, as she says,
"the more my mind had become enlightened, the more difficult it was for me
to consider myself an article of property" (*ILSG*, 199), thus acknowledging the
bravery of a freedom gained through an Enlightenment narrative of individual will.

     Still she validates another story.

     The brave old woman still toiled on, hoping to rescue some of her other
     children. After a while she succeeded in buying Phillip. She paid eight
     hundred dollars, and came home with the precious document that se-

cured his freedom. The happy mother and son sat together by the old hearthstone that night, telling how proud they were of each other, and how they would prove to the world that they could take care of themselves, as they had long taken care of others. We all concluded by saying "He that is *willing* to be a slave, let him be a slave." (*ILSG*, 26)

Without giving up the rhetoric of a self-determination that grants Benjamin his heroic status, she manages to laud Uncle Phillip, whose course might otherwise be described, particularly in antebellum terms, as passive, indeed as feminine. Jacobs's rhetoric suggests as well that Phillip and Martha, in conjunction, constitute an alternative definition of identity that acknowledges, relies on, and is structured through relation and dependence – an intermeshing that makes taking care of oneself mean taking care of others. Pride as well as independence – we can take care of ourselves – emerges from the rhetorical collectivity "we all." And it is out of this translation that an alternative version of national identity begins to emerge.

Strange Words in a Strange Land

Who is this composite being, Phillip/Martha? Can Yellin's term for Linda Brent, "female hero," apply to Phillip as well as to Martha? Phillip's story is not like that of Stowe's Uncle Tom, whose caretaking role leads to his martyrdom. Nor is Uncle Phillip a figure for Mr. Self-Reliance. Besides, as Jacobs has shown, what sort of identity is self-reliance, if those who embody it have been compelled, as Uncle Benjamin has, to deny mother and brother? If being accepted as a freedman means denying family ties, then slave and (freed)man are clearly not the complete metamorphic oppositions identified in Douglass's famous statement, "You have seen how a man was made a slave; you shall see how a slave was made a man" (*N*, 107). Slave and freedman are two sides of the same coin of a patriarchally determined identity. And if the most obvious loss for this coin can be characterized as the absence of the African American woman, what Jacobs makes clear is that Uncle Benjamin loses too. The narrative of heroic manhood as a tale worth telling, that stuff Hawthorne extolled in 1862 as the "pristine value" upon which true poetry "broods" becomes a debased fiction.[39] Only in narratives that stress mutuality, where the many can speak in the same voice, without that "we" cannibalizing the one, will freedom ring clear.

Indeed, younger Benjamin's revision of his namesake's history demonstrates this new logic: "Some of the apprentices were Americans, others American-born Irish; and it was offensive to their dignity to have a 'nigger' among them, after they had been told that he *was* a 'nigger,'" says Jacobs of Benjamin Brent's (Joseph Jacobs's) experiences as a Boston laborer (*ILSG*, 186). This moment underscores the Northern "prejudice against color," recounted in Chapter Thirty-five. It also demonstrates how the noun "nigger" situates a reading of being that, for young Benjamin's fellow apprentices, produces an unquestioned narrative of insult. The insult translates relations of favor into their opposite. Abuse is substituted for praise. Benjamin "was liked by the master, and was a favorite with his fellow-apprentices" until "transformed . . . into a different being" (*ILSG*, 186).

But what sort of a different being is a "nigger"? The searing, restrained irony of Jacobs's tone in this passage is made all the more palpable given just how consistently she has already redefined the racial insult leveled at her son. For instance, much earlier, while Brent hides from her master, Dr. Flint, her friend Betty, who has helped conceal her, would pronounce "anathemas over Dr. Flint and all his tribe, every now and then saying, with a chuckling laugh, 'Dis nigger's too cute for 'em'" (*ILSG*, 103). A process of redefinition based on the speaker's position is evident here: Betty compliments herself for the cleverness that the term "nigger" does not – for some – mean.[40] Young Benjamin's tale takes Betty's compliment further by showing that the force of the supposed insult "nigger" is based on blatant contradictions, since Benjamin could "pass" for a man who had no genealogical connections to an African heritage. His "being" thus is masked not by his history, but rather by the inconsistent views of his fellows and his master, since they had, after all, previously seen his character as a favorite one.[41]

Here, as well as in other works where the light-skinned mulatto/a is placed on the cusp of an imagined racial binary,[42] the cultural racism that has tried to force "nigger" to carry a negative connotation is shown up as a meaningless sham, even in the culture's own system of adjudication, if Benjamin can so easily be judged as "white." The antebellum fantasy that racial characteristics are inherent is quietly scripted as just that. In turn, nigger loses the smack of insult. In fact, Jacobs has made the material content of that insult boomerang back at its source. For if "family" values[43] should truly underwrite the strength of mid-nineteenth-century Northern conceptions of individual merit, a Northerner cannot justify any cultural script of being that would demand a man have, in order to be free, so little regard for his family. Should Benjamin choose to deny the name "nigger," he would be agreeing with his master's reading of that term and would therefore have to deny Linda Brent. Since she is the only one of his acknowledged parents to make the parental tie of any evident positive, material consequence, denying her would be to betray those virtues that so-called Americans had narrated as being of high value. And if Benjamin should deny Linda's maternity by refusing to be identified as a "nigger," he would simply repeat the loss that abolitionist rhetoric situated as Southern slavery's deepest horror, the separation of mother and child.

Thus *Incidents* makes it clear that Benjamin's own self-worth relies on his identification with a heritage that others would try to disparage. His story makes clear how he has learned that his mother's value could not be reduced to a sheer commodity relation; Brent has demonstrated that her "worth" could not be measured two-dimensionally in the terms that slaveholders set down – that is, "by dollars and cents" (*ILSG*, 196). Thus Benjamin knows, through his mother's narrative example, that his own "worth" as an apprentice cannot be reduced either to a commodity relation or by a word whose meaning is, after all, subject to interpretation. Benjamin thus does not deny his being a nigger, despite the insults of "the Americans and American-born Irish" who require such contradictions as props to their own status. His refusal, focusing attention on the repeated terms "American" and "nigger," not only highlights his familial loyalty, but also points to the indissoluable linkage between private family and public or national identity. Jacobs has already posited that link, when she has Brent say of her former lover and the acknowledged father of her children, the United States Congressman Mr. Sands, "is there no justice in the man?" Their son Benjamin's refusal to abjure his mother underscores the link his father has denied.

Which of these "American-born" men, then, Sands or his denied son, truly embodies justice? The choice is clear. Jacobs has made justice, one of the founts of national pride, depend on a refusal to deny family relations. Such refusal will infuse those supposedly private, affectional ties with the political value and legal consequence they should – by virtue of the morality preached in a Christian democracy – already contain.

Of course, Jacobs has proposed such questions about legitimacies earlier in her text, and certainly they are central to most abolitionist work. Still, in outlining such inconsistent logic in this late chapter of her narrative, Jacobs not only reiterates how slaveholding has made for moral, cultural, and political bankruptcies; she also makes young Benjamin's story an emblem of mutuality that defines a way around those losses. His example of a fierce tender feeling (for his mother) translated into a public identity (as proud to be a "nigger" in the face of insult) will explore a semiosis of agency that proposes a new means of signification based on tenderness and dependency, or on the continuities of memory, rather than on false occlusions, silencing mut(e)tations, and self-reliance.

Cannily, Jacobs has used the word "master" in this incident to designate the name of Benjamin's Boston employer. Of course, the word is literally appropriate. Skilled trade apprenticeship in the Free States named employers "masters."[44] But Jacobs's use here cannot help but figure young Benjamin's freedman status as a Northern version of his former Southern condition. Given just how pejorative the word "master" has become over the course of its narrative association with Dr. Flint's public, legally supported and private, sexual perfidy, the word now shudders with negative meaning. Southern hierarchical bankruptcies are imbricated in the language of Northern work-ethic. In these exposures, where the accumulation of associative, experiential meanings behind words like "master" and "nigger" have redefined the way those words signify, especially for her Northern audience, Jacobs's text threatens the narrative surety of tradition. She unseats the anchors of cultural reference that have disallowed value to interracial intercourse (except as a hidden commodity relation) or have allowed a Northern master to see himself as a different being from a Southern slaveholder – any man who was "originally a Yankee peddler" could easily become a slaveholder (*ILSG*, 197).

Moreover, it is precisely in activating this threat to unmoor traditional referentiality that Jacobs's narrative asserts the need for a new value system to underwrite meaning. If it takes a baseless insult to validate "white" worth, then the favor of being white is no favor at all. If it takes death to make freedom ring, then freedom has a tinny sound. One might say here that Jacobs's logic, unlike the cry "give me liberty or give me death," does not see change as suicidally oriented. The logic within Jacobs's *Incidents* shows how the deterministic narrative of mastery has overwritten the vital flux of potential meanings. Prefabricated plot lines that have cut off "American-born" Benjamin will map America as manifestly destined to be exclusive. If such a map – incommensurate with America's own utopian, idealistic sense of itself as inclusive – should stand, then *belonging* to America will mean just that: citizens will be slaves to a system of government that views them as dead things.

Uncle Phillip's obituary is a good case in point. This newspaper item names the deceased Phillip "a good man and a useful citizen." Jacobs has Brent cry, "So they called a colored man a *citizen*! Strange words to be uttered in that region!" (*ILSG*, 201). Yet what *Incidents* has already shown is that those words are as strange as they are familiar. If, as Emerson wrote, America was the "asylum of all nations,"[45] then why was Uncle Phillip denied the name citizen until he was dead? Such idealism scripted American value as based on those "free" associations that would allow for previously unseen or devalued histories.

And yet, as Jacobs says of Linda Brent's stay in New York, "Oppressed Poles and Hungarians could find a safe refuge in that city . . . but there I sat, an oppressed American, not daring to show my face" (*ILSG*, 198). When abolitionist Theodore Parker claimed that America had but "one series of literary productions that could be written by none but Americans and only here – I mean the Lives of the Fugitive Slaves,"[46] Jacobs heard a Mr. Thorne, who justified revealing Brent's whereabouts to Dr. Flint by saying, "I am a patriot, a lover of my country, and I do this as an act of justice to the laws" (*ILSG*, 179). Which one of these stories about Americanness will determine the shape of American citizenship? Is either version adequate? The various "incidents" Jacobs has related all point to a condemnation of any narrative of agency empowered to such an extent as to require the exclusion (death) of others, whether Northern or Southern. Where inferiority and superiority are assigned by narrative fiat so that embodied practices are discounted, ignored, or rendered invisible, there lies violence.

Indeed, for Jacobs, the word "father" – as defined in a system that would empower that role through the systematic disempowering of others – is a word which, more often than not, functions as the very blade that slices off the roots of African American genealogical trees. While Douglass often sought to establish a genealogical (tree)root and so restore a paternity the slavocracy had rendered invisible or legally inconsequential, Jacobs's situation gave her a different view. "What tangled skeins are the genealogies of slavery!" (*ILSG*, 78), says she. Where Douglass sees paternal loss as emblematic of a lost genealogy, Jacobs sees an extant networking of genealogical inheritance. By pulling at these skeins, Jacobs shows how complacent beliefs in the staying logic of (patri)lineal fictions, such as the one that claims paternity is not of consequence across racial lines, are laughable. Jacobs recounts how one slaveholding papa's world was shattered by just such a revelation. Slaveholders like the father of Brent's children could regularly "take" African American women and then sell their (own) children only if they could maintain the fiction that an indissoluble bar of difference existed between black and white, a bar that, among other things, produced differential structures of erotic desire evident in antebellum concepts of sexuality. When Jacobs tells of the wealthy white slaveholder's daughter who "took" a slave lover and subsequently gave him free papers, a story of inherent difference shreds to reveal that what is at issue is not simply "race" or "sex." The issue is authority. As Jacobs has Brent comment, a slaveholder's daughter knows that the inmates of a patriarchal household, including herself, are "subject to their father's authority in all things" (*ILSG*, 52).

As much commentary on Jacobs's famous chapter the "Loophole of Retreat" has shown, using the master's tool of authority may not entirely dismantle the master's house, but it can shake the foundations.[47] These white daughters who "exercise the same authority" (*ILSG*, 52) as their papas may not overthrow the father, but they do replicate the father's behavior in disruptive, "shameful," and revealing ways. So too will Linda Brent, captive in a domestic space, use the (father's) tool of literacy to make Dr. Flint flounder. Indeed, Jacobs's "loophole of retreat," as Smith and Yellin note, is a version of a "madwoman in the attic"[48] trope, and although such a trope cannot entirely succeed in rewriting domestic ideology, it does loop Dr. Flint into a scene that makes him as impotent as that master "whose head was bowed down in shame" (*ILSG*, 52) over his daughter's mimicry.[49] Further, such a doubling-back exemplifies what Northern antislavery politicians feared, that "Slave Power" endangered their own liberties."[50]

Jacobs describes her confinement as a state of a "living grave" (*ILSG*, 147), a description that can double for a description of slavery itself. Yet, by the very act of doubling her condition, Jacobs converts that tomb into a womb. She has found a way to "part with all her kin" without actually departing. She has "died" out of slavery while remaining inside the system, in a sort of suspension between being / not-being that allows the formerly silent grave of the

maternal female to speak out for liberation. And this suspension, while painful, allows Brent to remake "self" and her children into free beings. Manipulating the space of the "feminized," Jacobs engineers the same metamorphosis (brute to man) that Douglass (and Uncle Benjamin) staged with
physical force. But she has done it without fisticuffs and without separation
from the kin, through a strategy of doubling or looping. Indeed, the word
"loop" and the word "loophole" have similar meanings. As Hortense Spillers
notes, a loop is emblematic of "coiling and recoiling and rotation upon rotation"; it indicates both the crack in fortifications from which a cannon pro-
trudes and a closed, magnetic circuitry. It is, as well, a term used for knitting,
thus pulling together, as it were, a number of moments in the narrative –
connecting the fisticuffs in masculinized modes of freedom to feminized
forms, making both say "rebel."[51] For instance, a narrative loop revealing the
closed circuitry of meaning occurs when the slaveholder's daughter takes
what she can get as a white woman. Paternal authority is both replicated and
shot to pieces spectacularly here, by the way this story locates three attributes
in a woman that a woman supposedly could not have: legal power, willful-
ness, and erotic desire. If Jacobs claims this brief story shows how "slavery is a
curse to the whites as well as to the blacks" (*ILSG*, 52), she also locates a potency where none had been thought to exist. And even if this white daughter
was as cruel as Mrs. Flint in brutalizing those "over whom her authority
could be exercised with less fear of exposure" (*ILSG*, 52), the daughter's action
has a curious consequence. She gives her lover the free papers that will end
his brutalization.

It is not, then, a "father" whose name represents "freedom." Jacobs's insistence upon deflating inherent, paternal privilege is evident when she says "I
loved my father, but it mortified me to be obliged to bestow his name on my
children." Such patronymics have been proposed to her by the "mistress of
my father," who later "clasped a gold chain around" her daughter's neck.
Jacobs says, "I thanked her for this kindness; but I did not like the emblem. I
wanted no chain to be fastened on my daughter, not even if its links were of
gold" (*ILSG*, 78–9). Here, Jacobs has Brent connect the abstract power of the
Father – no matter that the father, in this case, is her own, his last name has
been handed down through the patriarchal system of slavery – to the material wealth and self-sustaining fictions of mastery.

In the end, what *Incidents* performs is indeed a very different revision of the
master–slave relationship than the one that the classic slave narrative provided. As Valerie Smith has emphasized, Linda Brent refuses to be robbed of
her maternity, her kinships, or her sexuality.[52] In these refusals, she succeeds
in making "potency," so often attributed to masculinity, signify for a woman.
But she also succeeds in changing how masculinity should be narrated. At
stake here, as I have suggested earlier, is how *Incidents* itself, as a form of private memory, will come to be valued publicly. Will the "feminine" tenderness

of familial dependencies become legal and cultural tender? Her story is involved with cultural disapprovals and shames, yet it must become a sustaining fiction. As Brent says about her loss of the cultural virtue of passive virginity, "I have shed many and bitter tears, to think that when I am gone from my children they cannot remember me with such entire satisfaction as I remembered my mother" (*ILSG*, 90). And yet, as her later interactions with her children show, in the act of remembering this "shame" for them, she will set into motion a new narrative economy of satisfaction. In her tale, if she must recount how her memory might be viewed as debased in an economy underwritten by purity, she manages to trace that devaluation of the pure back to its denied source: patriarchal fictions of mastery. As Brent says of Dr. Flint's death, "The man was odious to me while he lived, and his memory is odious now" (*ILSG*, 196), that "now" being the time of her narrative whose potency has made his memory, not hers, reek.

Still, Jacobs is well aware that the looping circuitry of narrative can loop back at her. So, as Jacobs brings Linda Brent's story to a close, she introduces several documents to prevent a negative loop. The first is a legal bill of sale for Linda Brent, the second a private letter relating Aunt Martha's death, and the third another such black-bordered letter, accompanied by her Uncle Phillip's newspaper obituary. Together, these documents provide a reified recapitulation of the whole narrative, showing the hidden connections between public and private histories. The first document, on record in New York for "future generations," is public, legal evidence "that women were articles of traffic" (*ILSG*, 201); the second and third documents are private letters of grief, but this is a grief that echoes the various familial losses Brent has suffered as a result of the public institution of slavery. Finally, the obituary clipping brings such private loss fully into a public sphere, Phillip's death having been an occasion to contemplate citizenship. For, as Brent notes, she may be as free "as are the white people of the north" but that "is not saying a great deal" (*ILSG*, 201). These documents resonate with legal, social, and cultural connections occluded not just by the "peculiar institution" but by a logic the North shares with the South, a cultural logic that can make the still potentially valuable word "liberty" not say "a great deal."

Notes

My appreciation and thanks, above all, to Sandra Gunning. Thanks also to John Murchek (who pulled me through this work) as well as to Daniel Cottom, David Leverenz, Carolyn Porter, and Rafia Zafar.

1. Harriet Jacobs, *Incidents in the Life of a Slave Girl* (Cambridge: Harvard University Press, 1987), 19. All further references to this work will appear in the body of the text as (*ILSG*).

2. Frederick Douglass, *Narrative of the Life of Frederick Douglass, American Slave, As Written by Himself*, ed. Houston A. Baker, Jr. (New York: Penguin, 1982). All further refer-

ences will appear in the text as (*N*). For selected work on the importance of litera-
cy in Douglass, see also: Houston Baker, Jr., *Blues, Ideology and Afro-American Litera-
ture* (Chicago: University of Chicago Press, 1984); David Leverenz, *Manhood and
The American Renaissance* (Ithaca, NY: Cornell University Press, 1990), 128–32;
Peter Walker, *Moral Choices: Memory, Desire and Imagination in Nineteenth-Century
American Abolition* (Baton Rouge: Louisiana State University Press, 1978), 213–54;
Eric J. Sundquist, "Frederick Douglass: Literacy and Paternalism," *Raritan* 6: 2
(Fall 1986): 108–24.

3. For the purposes of my argument, it is important to maintain an acute awareness,
following Jean Fagan Yellin's approach and her appendixes, that Jacobs chose to
use "characters" to embody the "historical" figures in her autobiographical narrative. See *ILSG*, 223.

4. Jean Fagan Yellin notes, on the basis of arguments such as Robert Stepto's *From
Behind the Veil: A Study of Afro-American Narrative* (Chicago: University of Illinois
Press, 1976); Henry Louis Gates's in *Afro-American Literature: The Reconstruction of
Instruction*, ed. Robert B. Stepto and Dexter Fisher (New York: Modern Language
Association, 1978); Houston Baker, Jr.'s, *The Journey Back: Issues in Black Literature
and Criticism* (Chicago: University of Chicago Press, 1980) and *Blues, Ideology and
Afro-American Literature*, "this genre has been characterized as dramatizing 'the
quest for freedom and literacy'" (*ILSG*, xxvi). See also Valerie Smith, *Self-Discovery
and Authority in Afro-American Narrative* (Cambridge: Harvard University Press,
1987).

5. See Richard Yarborough, "Race, Violence and Manhood: The Masculine Ideal
in Frederick Douglass's 'The Heroic Slave'" in *Frederick Douglass: New Literary and
Historical Essays*, ed. Eric J. Sundquist (Cambridge University Press, 1991), 166–
88.

6. See also Dana Nelson, *The Word in Black and White: Reading "Race" in American Literature 1638–1867* (New York: Oxford University Press, 1992).

7. Rhetoric concerning the 1990 Gulf Crisis – "the liberation of Kuwait" (George
Bush as quoted by Richard Brookhiser), "A Visit with George Bush," *The Atlantic
Monthly* 270: 2 (August 1992) – and the U.S. depiction of Chinese students dying
for a statue of Lady Liberty in Beijing (1988) bear witness to a resurgence of American nationalist idealism wherein a heroic willingness to die is repeatedly juxtaposed with the abstract but transcendent value of democratic freedom.

8. Ronald G. Walters's early essay, "The Erotic South: Civilization and Sexuality in
American Abolitionism," *American Quarterly* 25:2 (May 1973): 179–80, demon-
strates this antislavery claim clearly; for further references, see Peter Walker,
Moral Choices, and Jean Fagan Yellin, *Women & Sisters: The Antislavery Feminists in
American Culture* (New Haven and London: Yale University Press, 1989).

9. Beth Maclay Doriani, "Black Womanhood in Nineteenth-Century America:
Subversion and Self-Construction in Two Women's Autobiographies," *American
Quarterly* 43:2 (June 1991): 203.

10. Doriani, "Black Womanhood," 219.

11. "Mockery" (*ILSG*, 62) is the term that Jacobs uses to describe how slavery, as a
"cage of obscene birds" (*ILSG*, 52), devalues Christian virtue and motherhood. As
Carby notes, "Slave women gave birth to the capital of the South and were there-

fore, in Linda Brent's words, 'considered of no value, unless they continually increase their owner's stock.'" Hazel V. Carby, *Reconstructing Womanhood: The Emergence of the Afro-American Woman Novelist* (New York: Oxford University Press, 1987), 54.

12. As Yellin, Carby, and Andrews discuss, *Incidents* was, for many years, discounted as too melodramatic, most infamously by John Blassingame's assessment in *Slave Testimony: Two Centuries of Letters, Speeches, Interviews and Autobiographies* (Baton Rouge: Louisiana State University Press, 1977), xvii–lxv.

13. Borrowing from Mark Twain's *Puddin' Head Wilson* (New York: Penguin, 1987), 25.

14. This is not to say that the sorts of class distinctions developing during the antebellum years and the concomitant race relations stemming from race slavery operated the same way, but rather that these relations were shaped by similar logic and indeed shaped the dimensions of each other. One cannot speak of how class is constructed in the mid- to late nineteenth century without understanding how racial myths were intertwined with class and vice versa. Jacobs made plain that the racial prejudices she experienced outside of slavery were embedded in that commodity economy which had allowed one class of people to arbitrarily designate others legally as purchasable objects.

15. William L. Andrews, *To Tell a Free Story: The First Century of Afro-American Autobiography, 1760–1865* (Urbana: University of Illinois Press, 1986), 290.

16. Ibid., 289.

17. Ibid., 289.

18. Ibid., 278.

19. Ibid., 279.

20. Jacobs reports that in one of Dr. Flint's elaborate letters of persuasion to Linda Brent, he (writing under a pseudonym) claimed that the "heartfelt tie [that] existed between a master and his servant" was the same as that "between a mother and her child" (*ILSG*, 172); further, Flint repeatedly refers to his desire for Linda as based on such a familial model – "I consider you as yet a child" (*ILSG*, 83) – begging questions concerning incest and pedophilia.

On maternal loss as a widely used emblem in antebellum discourse, see Elizabeth Ammons, "Stowe's Dream of the Mother-Savior: *Uncle Tom's Cabin* and American Women Writers before the 1920s," in *New Essays on Uncle Tom's Cabin*, ed. Eric J. Sundquist (Cambridge University Press, 1986), 155–95; Hazel Carby, *Reconstructing Womanhood*, 20–40; Yellin, *Women & Sisters*, 88–96.

21. Linda Brent's ambivalence about "freedom," given its relation to familial loss and death, is emphasized again when her brother William escapes: "If you had seen the tears, and heard the sobs, you would have thought the messenger had brought tidings of death instead of freedom. Poor old grandmother felt that she should never see her darling boy again. And I was selfish. I thought more of what I had lost, than of what my brother had gained" (*ILSG*, 134).

22. For various claims concerning how Jacobs used "traditional" discursive patterns, with particular regard to her use of sentimental tropes, see Yellin's "Introduction," esp. xxvi–xxxiii; William Andrews, *To Tell a Free Story*; Carby, *Reconstructing Womanhood*, 20–4; Beth Maclay Doriani, "Black Womanhood," 199–221; P. Gabrielle Foreman, "The Spoken and the Silenced in *Incidents in the Life of a Slave Girl*

and *Our Nig*," *Callaloo* 13:2 (Spring 1990): 313–24; Carolyn Karcher, "Rape, Murder and Revenge in 'Slavery's Pleasant Homes': Lydia Maria Child's Antislavery Fiction and the Limits of Genre," *Women's Studies Int. Forum* 9 (1986), 323–32; Bruce Mills, "Lydia Maria Child and the Endings to Harriet Jacobs's *Incidents in the Life of a Slave Girl*," *American Literature* 64:2 (June 1992): 255–271; Laura E. Tanner, "Self-Conscious Representation in the Slave Narrative," in *Black Literature Forum* 21:4 (Winter 1987): 415–25.

23. Borrowing Foreman's title, "The Spoken and the Silenced." For more detailed arguments concerning Jacobs's rhetoric, see Andrews (1986), Carby (1987), or Yellin (1989).

24. Andrews, *To Tell a Free Story*, 278.

25. Although I have argued in "Heart Attacks: Frederick Douglass's Strategic Sentimentality," *Criticism* 34:2 (Spring 1992): 193–216, that the evolution of Douglass's representations demonstrates a changing view of the equation liberty=masculinity, nevertheless his 1845 *Narrative*, as Valerie Smith has demonstrated, turns that equation to his advantage often.

26. See Hortense Spillers, "Mama's Baby, Papa's Maybe: An American Grammar Book," *Diacritics* 17:2 (Summer 1987): 65–81, for a fuller consideration of how the historical condition of patronymic loss in American slavery affects African American representation.

27. Frederick Douglass, *My Bondage and My Freedom*, ed. William L. Andrews (Urbana and Chicago: University of Illinois Press, 1987), 28.

28. The associative links between femininity and maternity, maternity and death, found in a wide range of antebellum narratives are pervasive and well documented. See Sylvia D. Hoffert, *Private Matters: American Attitudes Toward Childbearing and Infant Nurture in the Urban North, 1800–1860* (Urbana and Chicago: University of Illinois Press, 1989), esp. 170–87.

29. On Douglass's lasting belief in the need for paternity, see Frederick Douglass, *The Life and Times of Frederick Douglass* (London: Collier Books, 1962), 27.

30. Carby, *Reconstructing Womanhood*, 59–60.

31. Ibid.

32. In Toni Morrison's *Beloved* (New York: Knopf, 1987), Morrison uses "rememory" to signify the way in which the past comes back despite efforts to keep it "at bay." As Sethe says of Paul D, "Now he added more: new pictures and old rememories that broke her heart" (95).

33. As Carby notes, "In order to save her children, Linda Brent apparently had to desert them" (60). However, Carby's analysis here is concerned with how Jacobs's story of Brent's desertion finds validation in her daughter, Ellen's (Louisa Matilda Jacobs) acceptance. Such narrated mother-to-daughter acceptance, writes Carby, "exclud[es] the need for any approval from the readership. Jacobs bound the meaning and interpretation of her womanhood and motherhood to the internal structure of the text, making external validation unnecessary and unwarranted" (61). I agree with Carby that Jacobs's text does operate in this manner, so that "Judgment was to be passed on the institution of slavery and not on deviations from conventions of true womanhood" (61). Still, Jacobs's awareness that she might speak to future generations of African Americans would make it imperative that she take some account of external (readers') judg-

ments, as influenced by the circulation of cultural narratives, in order to change those narratives' valuation.

34. Carby, *Reconstructing Womanhood*, 49–50.

35. Ibid., 184, n. 14.

36. Douglass at the "Proceedings of the American Equal Rights Association Convention, Steinway Hall, New York City, May 12, 1869," in *Frederick Douglass on Women's Rights,* ed. Philip S. Foner (Westport, CT, and London: Greenwood Press, 1976), 87.

37. Smith, *Self-Discovery and Authority*, 27.

38. Reference to 1960s slang for those in control, particularly white men.

39. Nathaniel Hawthorne, "Chiefly About War Matters," *The Atlantic Monthly* (10 July 1862): 59.

40. With thanks to June Jordan's teaching and her work, most particularly "Problems of Language in a Democratic State," in *On Call: Political Essays* (Boston: South End Press, 1985), 27–36.

41. Stealing from Carolyn Porter, *Seeing and Being* (Middletown, CT: Wesleyan, 1981).

42. On the figure of the mulatto/a, see Judith R. Berzon, *Neither White Nor Black: The Mulatto Character in American Fiction* (New York: New York University Press, 1978); Hortense Spillers, "Notes on an Alternative Model – Neither/Nor," in *The Difference Within: Feminism and Critical Theory,* ed. Elizabeth Meese and Alice Parker (Philadelphia: John Benjamins Publishing, 1989), 165–87.

43. This reference to the rhetoric of the 1992 United States presidential campaign is intentional.

44. Ironically this feudal master–apprentice system was particularly endemic to publishing and printing; Yellin reports that blacks were routinely denied apprenticeship in this trade (*ILSG*, 287, n. 1).

45. Ralph Waldo Emerson, as quoted by Waldo E. Martin, *The Mind of Frederick Douglass* (Chapel Hill and London: University of North Carolina Press, 1984), 223. Martin quotes Emerson from Stuart P. Sherman's collection of Emerson's works, *Essays and Poems.* Emerson went on to write of America as that place where

> . . . the energy of Irish, Germans, Swedes, Poles, and Cossacks, and all the European tribes – of the Africans and the Polynesians, will construct a new race, a new religion, a new literature which will be as vigorous as the new Europe which came out of the melting pot of the Dark Ages.

46. Theodore Parker, as quoted in Houston Baker, Jr., "Introduction" to Frederick Douglass's *Narrative*. Both Parker and Thomas Wentworth Higginson expressed such views (*ILSG*, xxxiii); see also Margaret Fuller, Review of "The Narrative of the Life of Frederick Douglass" in *The New York Tribune,* June 10, 1845, 1.

47. Borrowing from Audre Lorde's "The Master's Tools Will Never Dismantle the Master's House," in *Sister Outsider* (Trumansburg, NY: Crossing Press, 1984), 112.

48. See Smith, *Self-Discovery and Authority*, 33–40, and Yellin, "Introduction," xxxi. Both critics identify this scene as a form of the "madwoman in the attic" scenario that Sandra Gilbert and Susan Gubar traced out for British fiction in their *Madwoman in the Attic* (New Haven: Yale University Press, 1979).

49. My argument is informed by ongoing feminist debates as to the political usefulness and/or effectiveness of linguistic parody and mimicry, particularly as these

debates relate to French philosophy. See Luce Irigaray, *Ce Sexe qui n'en est pas une* (Paris: Editions de Minuit, 1977); Hélène Cixous and Catherine Clément, *La Jeune Nee* (Paris: Union Generale d'Editions 1975); and Judith Butler, *Gender Trouble* (New York: Routledge, 1990).

50. Walters, "The Erotic South," 80.

51. Hortense J. Spillers in "Changing the Letter: The Yokes, the Jokes of Discourse, or Mrs. Stowe, Mr. Reed," as presented to *The English Institute* (August 1987), 40.

52. Smith, *Self-Discovery and Authority,* 33.

CONCLUSION
VEXED ALLIANCES

RACE AND FEMALE COLLABORATIONS IN THE LIFE
OF HARRIET JACOBS

DEBORAH M. GARFIELD

To my dear parents, and to David Levin,
whose unofficial parenting never flags

If autobiographies are selective, so too is our recounting of them. Since the details of Harriet Jacobs's ordeals and coups have been amply rehearsed, especially by Jean Fagan Yellin, Jacobs's principal biographer,[1] I will pursue one important trajectory in Jacobs's life and chart its ramifications for her and for us as scholars. Rafia Zafar, coeditor of this volume, has eloquently suggested in the "Introduction" the tensions *Incidents* has generated in the academy, including those between female African American and female white scholars. Such vexed relations charge not only the recent reception of this book, of course, but also Jacobs's biography itself, with its anxious moments between an African American female and a proliferation of white women guardians and mentors. This productive, if sometimes uneasy, alliance between slave and white woman emerges almost as soon as Jacobs begins the cloistered idyll of her girlhood; and the ambivalent relation between black and white figures lingers as female slaveholders aid in her protracted escape to the North and white women employers shelter her after that flight is precariously achieved. But the chafing bond between the ex-"Slave Girl" and her white helpmates hovers outside the narrative itself, in which Jacobs transcribes private "incidents" into public *Incidents*: in her relationships with the Quaker abolitionist Amy Post, with the sentimental author Lydia Maria Child (who edits, introduces, and claims to christen the narrative into respectability), and with other white authors whom Jacobs solicits to help steer her life's "incidents" into publication.

275

I.   Mourning for the Black Mother: Childhood and White Proxy Maternity

Jacobs is nurtured in the prelapsarian euphoria of 1813 Edenton, North Carolina. Here her grandmother, Molly Horniblow; her father, Daniel Jacobs; and
her mother, Delilah, create a "comfortable home" where "I was so fondly
shielded that I never dreamed I was a piece of merchandise" (5). As with
Olaudah Equiano's autobiography,[2] there is a dual voice here that negotiates
time – the child's, sequestered in illusions of domestic protection, and the
adult's, galled at that protection's dissolution. Jacobs's notion of well-being is
first fractured by her mother's death when the girl is six. When Jacobs's
mother dies, the muffled "talk around" (6) the orphan loudly proclaims her
slave status, which before had been unknown to her. Maternal loss, speech,
and chattelhood seem bound in a funereal nexus. *Incidents* almost immediately
collapses into a rite of mourning, both for the vanished real mother and for an
original personal identity so whole and unfettered it seemed like a dream.

Yet the attentiveness of Jacobs's new mistress, Margaret Horniblow, offers an apparently secure refuge from these two related threats: the tremors of
filial grief and the epiphany of one's servitude. "Almost like a mother" (7),
Horniblow instructs the child in spelling and reading. The mistress thus establishes the sanctity of the word and returns it to a maternal stability, a clean
correspondence between signifier and divine "precepts" which her favors
and assuring Christian utterances to the orphan appear to punctuate. Since
her lessons in reading accompany those in sewing, the mistress also knits literacy into the fabric of domestic belonging. Once again, Jacobs seems buffered
against slavery's afflictions. Though the grandmother slowly crystallizes into
a sacrificing maternal icon, the reader might imagine Mistress Horniblow as
a substitute for Jacobs's lost mother, and literacy a partial tonic for the shocking "talk" earlier advertising the girl's enslavement. Moreover, Horniblow's
privileged place in the matriarchal continuum of grandmother, mother, and
mistress seems further enhanced by the fact that Jacobs arrays more textual
details about her than about mother Delilah Horniblow herself.

The qualified simile "almost like," however, proves a red flag, as we watch
the more seasoned voice intrude upon the child's skewed perception. The
mistress's maternal embrace of a black ward is compromised by the former's
unexpected death when Jacobs is eleven and by a will that, rather than ensure
her slave's freedom, bequeathes Jacobs to the three-year-old Mary Matilda
Norcom ("Miss Emily Flint"), and thus to the child's father, Dr. James Norcom, the narrative's lascivious "Dr. Flint." As Jacobs edges toward puberty,
then, a second mourning has jarred not only the girl's confidence in her own
unpropertied humanity, but also her faith in a white-maternal Logos. Moreover, since Margaret has willed, to her niece Mary, "my negro girl Harriet"
and "my bureau and work table and their contents,"[3] the pronoun "my" lucidly proclaims the slave "daughter's" objectification. Jacobs's "Childhood,"

the period and chapter, devolves into a botched Southern maternalism that entrenches literacy in debased commerce:

> My mistress had taught me the precepts of God's Word: "Thou shalt love thy neighbor as thyself." "Whatsoever ye would that men should do unto you, do ye even unto them." But I was her slave, and I suppose she did not recognize me as her neighbor. (8)

Increasingly attuned to an ironic note, the first chapter frustrates the affinity between slave and "neighbor"; "Childhood" and "hope"; "mistress" and the simile of motherhood; Horniblow's "promise[s]" and "God's Word." Indeed, the enshrinement of Jacobs's mother – "a slave merely in name, but in nature . . . noble and womanly" (7) – now coils retrospectively into a lie. Though the slave child naively imagined the "name" of slave and one's essential "nature" as mutually exclusive, the experienced narrative voice recognizes that the white world forces the slave *name* to imply slave *nature*.

In having nursed a black and a white infant at her breast, the figure of the grandmother ("Aunt Martha") becomes the resonant sign for the racist breach lurking behind Jacobs's early chimera of maternal union. The grandmother, nursing at once her own infant – Jacobs's mother – and the white baby who is Jacobs's mother's mistress, must abandon the slave child in order to succor the only offspring considered legally human. The earlier confusion between slave and neighbor, between the mother's esteemed "nature" and her only nominal role as slave, and between word and practice with the mistress's codicil, is enacted on the grandmother's body. What the text initially conveyed as something akin to a female *gestalten,* with three women cohering on a black daughter's behalf, is now seen as a fallacy so rudimentary that it occurs at the black breast. Nurture gets milked by racist economics. The cherished daughter Harriet, though no field worker, has now been demoted from child to slave, and by implication to the multiple instruments of labor: her dead mistress's "work table" and, soon, Norcom's object. The schisms within Jacobs's own childhood ego widen to embrace the plight of the enslaved aggregate. Slaves are, she asserts in this first chapter's acid retraction of her callow vision, no more than the "God-breathing machines" they push, "the cotton they plant, or the horses they tend" (8). In Jacobs's etiology of persecution, a pseudo-mother's betrayal, supplanting original sin, allows the venal seducer Flint an entrée into the circle of innocence.

The pun latent in Jacobs's disaffection from Mistress Horniblow in Chapter One will surface with less subtlety again in the book, including its final words. After Horniblow's death Jacobs's crises illuminate the ambiguous complicity between two kinds of "bond" – maternal care and physical subordination – as she herself becomes nurse to little Mary Norcom at the same time as she is made the child's property and, in turn, the harassed sexual target of her ward/owner's father. James Norcom not only agilely exploits the

contradictory and incestuous roles of owner, father, and courtly lover in order to seduce Harriet; he also draws from the symbolic mine of motherhood's
tropes. In a pseudonymous note, he writes of the bond between them as one
between mother and child (172). This male "snake" exploits even the hal-
lowed aura of motherhood to mask a rapist's lech, just as he terms himself a
strict father to shield her from the freeman she truly loves and who would
make her the untainted image of her mother's purity. The South's proslavery
familial mythos has given Norcom his parental personae and thus implicated
itself in his villainy. Jacobs's discourse, as many critics in this volume and
other works proclaim, redefines and elevates motherhood. Still, through her
account of her mistress's will and Flint's slippery inscription of himself as
mother, Jacobs is also a vigilant critic of the dubious uses to which the clichés
of a white substitute "motherhood" can be put.

In what we might call the *upright hypocrisy* of slaveowning belles lies the ambivalent relation between white woman and slave-property. In 1835, Jacobs,
in a failed attempt to escape North, takes refuge for a month in the home
of a generous slaveholding matron, probably Martha Hoskins Rombough
Blount, whose husband owns and sells slaves. A friend of Jacobs's grandmother since childhood, Mistress Blount is simultaneously a familiar help-
mate and a domestic intruder in that cadre of figures who, like other rescuers,
risk their lives and reputations to inch Jacobs slowly toward "freedom." Jean
Fagan Yellin is right in suggesting how slaveholding here shades mysteriously
into a femininist simpatico: "But how are we to explain the presence of the
white women who defect from the slaveholders' ranks to help Linda Brent?
. . . One explanation is that these women are responding to Linda Brent's
oppression as a woman exploited sexually and as a mother trying to nurture
her children" ("Introduction," *Incidents*, xxxiii). Yet, as we have seen, white
protection and ownership enter into an unseemly pact from the text's first
chapter, "Childhood," a segment that both commemorates Jacobs's childhood and *buries* it. With the virtuous machinations of this next "kindly" Edenton slaveholder, who risks social censure to hide Jacobs in her house, bond
and bondage again nestle in a peculiar intimacy.

The coexistence of savior and enslaver in Blount's sensibility is signified by
the duality within the mistress's own household. This undeclared skirmish is
played out between the slave-cook Betty, who commits herself to saving
Jacobs, and Jenny, the slave towncrier who might betray Jacobs's whereabouts on her mistress's premises. Language is again decisive. Jacobs artfully
assembles in some detail the shards of Betty's dialect, which, unlike that of the
white rowdies Jacobs confronts after Nat Turner's rebellion, does not square
with amoral blindness. Instead, Betty's vernacular is that of a combatant
whose enterprising caginess, womanly fealty, and urge for freedom will never
be hobbled by enforced illiteracy. Moreover, the sarcasm accentuated by her
colloquialisms lends a spry, almost seriocomic, resolve to Jacobs's escape, a

trickster's condescension. After relocating Jacobs beneath a floor plank in the kitchen, Betty remarks, "If dey *did* know whar you are, dey won't know *now*"; and her kitchen, where black domesticity has already been cursed and distorted by the hearthside's vulnerability to slavery and slave-catchers, echoes with an Africanized incantation of revenge: "When she was alone," Jacobs remembers, "I could hear her pronouncing anathemas over Dr. Flint and all his tribe, every now and then saying with a chuckling laugh, 'Dis nigger's too cute for 'em dis time'" (103). Betty realigns the kitchen's cozy associations with incendiary resolve and unwrites many of those in Stowe's *Uncle Tom's Cabin*. Her anathemas, presented neither simply as "'cute'" Negroisms nor as the dimwitted misfires of insanity, are the bristling signs of a revolution which, as Eric Sundquist notes, is encoded in African American folk vernacular.[4] In the dialogue between Brent and Betty, Jacobs respectfully bequeaths us more of Betty's vernacular than she does of her own literate tongue, which at once sets off the uneducated cook's dialect and is muted by its rebellious pungency. Betty's vernacular momentarily lodges not only Jacobs but also literacy's decorum beneath the floor. And unlike Betty, Jenny is largely denied linguistic representation as surely as the latter forbids the quaking slave girl solace.

Regardless of her protection of Jacobs, Mistress Blount shares at once in Betty's valorous designs for Jacobs's survival and liberation and in Jenny's impediments to them. In Mistress Blount's assent to slavery, her two divergent female slaves are both autonomous entities in Edenton *and* their mistress's warring alter-egos. Thus Jacobs, with an ambivalence resisting wholehearted melodramatic affirmation, writes that "Though [Mistress Blount] was a slaveholder, to this day my heart blesses her!" (111). The mistress's place in a sentimental or feminist hagiography of the heart is slightly marred in a subordinate clause. Maternal gestures like those of Mistresses Horniblow and Blount are as invariably tarnished for the author as that golden chain a white slaveholder offers Jacobs's daughter, Louisa Matilda Jacobs ("Ellen"), at her christening (78–9), a gift reminding Jacobs of slavery's less embellished chains. True, Blount activates Betty's heroics; but Betty is a slave who must perform in secret while her mistress wears the somewhat artificial corsage of law-abiding matron.

II.   Deliver Me from Debt: Northern Service and Servitude

Certainly Jacobs's despair up North rarely compels her to elide the distinction between the more virtuous *slaveholding* matriarchs and the Northern white protectresses whose rescue does not involve assisting those they have institutionally helped to commodify. Even the North to which Jacobs escapes in 1842, however, cannot prevent an inevitable reemergence of the dicey sexual onus attached to black female flesh. Jacobs's unchaste past might disrupt the rapport with those sheltered ladies who have not endured the sexual impasses of bondage. In 1842 Jacobs functions as nursemaid to the infant of Mary Stace Willis (the first "Mrs. Bruce"), who helps her to evade Norcom by resituating her at the homes of friends in Boston. In Mary Willis the stealthy maneuvering of Mistress Blount and Jacobs's own sly geographical dislocations in the garret letters, which gull the doctor into believing she has fled north, bravely coalesce.

For much of Jacobs's tenure with the first Mrs. Willis, however, the relationship between nursemaid and employer maintains its equilibrium through Jacobs's silence about her sexual biographia, especially about her two children and their white father, Samuel Tredwell Sawyer ("Mr. Sands"): "I valued her good opinion, and I was afraid of losing it, if I told her all the particulars of my sad story." As Jacobs strains toward a frail dignity, silence is as vital for the employee as it is for the employer. When Jacobs, unnerved by the indiscretion of leaving the Willis estate once too often without explanation, finally unburdens "my full heart to her," Mrs. Willis listens "with true womanly sympathy" (180) and thus becomes an avatar for what Jacobs would no doubt see as the redeemed delicate female reader of the book. But behind the marriage of true female minds – and races – invariably beats the possibility of impediment. The commingling of a demure white matriarchy and a sexually victimized chattelhood is tremulous at best.[5]

Jacobs's Northern re-experiences of former Southern prejudices about her sexuality foster a shadow-self reminding her of the "slave girl" identity she meant, with her escape from Edenton, to cast firmly aside. The paradigm of fettering alliances continues when Mary Willis dies in 1845 and the stalwart Cornelia Grinnell Willis, Nathaniel's new wife (the second "Mrs. Bruce"), becomes Jacobs's employer in 1850. As Jacobs informs Amy Post, the maidservant "never opend [sic] my lips to Mrs [sic] Willis concerning my Children," and Cornelia's "Charitableness" is evinced by her refusal to ask about "their origins" (235: April 4th [1853]).[6] As Norcom's daughter and her feckless husband, Daniel Messmore ("Mr. Dodge"), attempt to reclaim Jacobs, Mrs. Willis coaxes maternity and freedom into a coherent code of action. Cornelia Willis insists that Jacobs flee with the white mother's own infant so that the pursued servant might appear to travel as nurse and not as escapee.

If Edenton's Mistress Blount clandestinely flouted social decorum and Southern legalities, Cornelia Willis courts, because of the passage of the Fugitive Slave Law of 1850, possible imprisonment. She more unflinchingly positions the cult of female delicacy *outside* the law, not simply within the tame household sanctum. Though hardly the slave-mother's anguished loss of her child through sale and lasting separation, Mrs. Willis's decision to surrender her own infant as a momentary decoy seems a white Northern correlative to the slave-mother's trauma; a replay of Blount's sacrifices; and a throwback to Jacobs's own stratagems for isolating herself from her progeny in order to ensure their liberation. In one sense, such convergences between employer and employee bespeak a transregional and biracial rapport between black and white woman, a revamping of pure womanhood's obedience into a shared maternal hubris – despite the presence of unspeakable sexual issues.

But such is the tenuous balance between white and African American females under the Fugitive Slave Law that Cornelia Willis's sacrifices sometimes amplify the subordination they are meant to squelch. Just as the Northern mother is made a less vulnerable surrogate for the helpless slave-mothers of the South, so another association between North and South ignites. Mrs. Willis, in ultimately buying Jacobs's freedom for $300.00 in 1852, cannot help but recall the spectre of purchaser Jacobs knows too well from Carolinian barter. In place of bondage is Jacobs's inability to release herself from the burden of debt, and indebtedness, to white female "friends" who, out of vaulted aims, remind her how densely she remains enmeshed in the role of "merchandise." Jacobs's assumption that she is already *naturally* liberated causes her to repudiate Mrs. Willis's offer in discordant tones expressing the unavoidable conflict between comrades of different races and redefining white friends into obvious benefactors:

> Dear Mrs. Bruce! I seem to see the expression of her face, as she turned away discouraged by my obstinate mood. . . . I wrote to Mrs. Bruce, thanking her, but saying that being sold from one owner to another seemed too much like slavery; that such a great obligation could not be easily cancelled. (199)

Jacobs's ire at being classified as "an article of property" (199) and oppressed by "obligation" raises a bothersome question: Can any bond between black and white women be sustained when the more privileged companion inadvertently declares the other dependent on white dispensation for an autonomy that is the black friend's by right? Even intimacy, self-sacrifice, motherhood – the resonant lexicon of "womanly sympathy" – run the paradoxical risk of pulling the slave back into the status of Southern ownership and thus of confounding the bonds of the heart with those of property. Jacobs is, of course, relieved by the purchase and her freedom; yet we cannot dismiss the fact that Cornelia Willis's generosity must be dispensed through the paternalistic calculus of buying and selling. Jacobs is again in mourning for her free self.

III.   Publication and Property: Jacobs, White Mentors, and the Auction Block of Authorship

The emotions unsettling even the strong alliance between Jacobs and her white "friends" infiltrate the writing and publication of *Incidents*. Ownership and indebtedness – the burdens of black womanhood we have seen respectively in South and North – invade not merely Jacobs's "auto" but its "graphia" as well. Authorship and publication for an ex-slave rekindle the unresolved conflicts of her roles as Southern chattel and Northern servant and therefore become epiphenomena of a hierarchical friendship whose beginnings we witness as early as her childhood dejection with Mistress Horniblow. Jacobs's position with Cornelia Willis and her husband, the publisher Nathaniel P. Willis, impinges on the very writing of *Incidents*. Jacobs intuits that Nathaniel Willis, pursuing an upward curve in New York society, is not an abolitionist and would object to a slave-author's existing within his estates. As she writes to Amy Post in about 1852, "Mr. W[illis] is too proslavery he would tell me that it was very wrong." Jacobs endeavors, it seems, to avoid alienating not only N. P. Willis, but also the wife, who, whatever her fealty to her servant, might be plagued by the work's strains on her marriage: "Mrs. Willis thinks . . . I could not ask her to take any step" (232: Cornwall, Orange County [New York] [1852?]). Jacobs, keeping even her short "Fugitive" pieces in various newspapers like the *New York Tribune* private, thus writes in the nocturnal secrecy of her attic. There, after laboring a full day, she is beset by fatigue and insects. In the North, not just slavery itself, but writing about slavery, presents another barricade to Jacobs's expression, just as indebtedness replaces ownership in the Willis residences in New York City and Cornwall, New York. One cannot avoid discerning in the Willis attic a less odious double of the garret, where Jacobs was also vulnerable to insects, and in Nathaniel Willis, a social-climbing adversary mirroring Flint.[7] Because of her tenure in the Willis family, Jacobs once more finds herself dizzied by a cycle of repetition and return. Such reinstatements of former traumas are fearful configurings of Jacobs's family history during the Revolution – that of the grandmother's newly freed clan on its retrograde pilgrimage back from St. Augustine to servitude (5).

Jacobs's extended stay with Cornelia Willis, moreover, may constitute a strained affection that the language of the finale images: "I do not sit with my children in a home of my own. . . . But God so orders circumstances as to keep me with my friend Mrs. Bruce. Love, duty, gratitude, also bind me to her side" (201). Orders, keeps, binds, the addendum of "also." This penultimate paragraph suggests the submerged link between unwanted bondage – being *kept* in service, the pull of obligation, and providential decrees – and the deep bonds of female camaraderie. Jacobs longs for a domestic individualism that does not include the service which, as her brother and daughter also appear to sense, reprises slavery's hierarchy in ameliorated form. This longing to flee the dialectic of white and black in the humble but autonomous principality of her own home is incarnated in a graphic trope. Doctors, Jacobs says, maintain "I have a Tumer on my womb and that my womb have become hard as a stone I can never get well while I am at service" (Jacobs to Post: Idlewild, August 7 [1852], Anne Warner #4, 8825). The demands of service disease and calcify the symbol of motherhood.

Subjecting Jacobs's closest friendships with white supporters to the murky lens of suspicion is not meant to undermine the sincerity of such bonds but to suggest the latent racial discomfort and inequity existing even within the tightest of them. Meeting Quaker-abolitionist and feminist Amy Post in 1849 and residing with Post and her husband Isaac for nine months, Jacobs both trusts her dearest white confidante and is persuaded by her to make public her story in order to stoke the abolitionist cause. Although the feat of writing and publication is not the secret attic plot at the Willis household, the letters to Post do show Jacobs fearful and pressured. Exiling herself from the roles of "Heroine" and "Woman" because of her sexual past, Jacobs seems uneasy with her own "persona," Linda Brent. And though a pro forma humility about one's literacy was routine when African American writers addressed a more literate bourgeosie, Jacobs remains acutely conscious of her own un-formed literacy when contrasted with Post's educated prose. Jacobs voices apprehensions that deem her own writing fragmented and secondary, sketchy or nonexistent. Her letters issue from a "poor pen" (234: April 4th [1853]); their "scrawl" is "Hasty" (236: Oct. 9th [1853]). As the "poor Book is in its Chrysalis state," never to become a "butterfly" (238: March [1854]), so too are the letters "poor scrawls," "nothing" (239: March [1857]), or "uncon-nected scrawl" (242: June 21st [1857]). Jacobs's unremitting faith in Post's ear-nestness in correcting her prose – "I cannot ask the favor of any one else without appearing very Ludicrous in their opinion" (June 25 [1853?], IAPFP #1257, BAP 16: 0696–97, as quoted by Yellin, xx) – suggests that Post is dis-tinct from and an extension of the literate female reader. "I have not the Courage," Jacobs admits, "to meet the criticism and ridicule of Educated people" (Dec. 21 IAPFP #82, BAP 16: 0703–04, as quoted by Yellin, xx). Since needlepoint and literacy are intertwined in the female endeavors Jacobs has known both with Mistress Horniblow and in Rochester's aboli-tionist reading circle, the evolving author might well intuit that the commit-ment to domesticity is somewhat continuous with discursive propriety, a flaw in one signifying – even to a sympathetic white audience – an aberration in the other.

IV.   *The White Author as Mistress: Stowe and the Preemption of Black Life*

But Jacobs's desire to own a household corresponds to the gnawing impera-tive of owning her past in print. In the narrative and letters these needs at times seem almost poignantly twinned. And the personal past, Jacobs begins to discover, can be commodified in writing just as the slave's body is bartered in commerce. The "incidents" of a life can be deformed into a shackled nar-rative. The prospect of a white woman mentor's coopting her biography for publication elicits a resentment of the female racial rift second only to that Jacobs has aired against Dixie mistresses like Mrs. Norcom. Jacobs's letters to Amy Post discuss Harriet Beecher Stowe and "my objection" to Stowe's depicting, in the *Key to Uncle Tom's Cabin*, the "romance" of Jacobs's seven-year garret confinement. The letter to Post of April 4th [1853] alternates uneasily between exuberant hostility toward Stowe and a representation of that near-obliteration of selfhood Jacobs risked in the obscurity of the Southern garret and swamp. Though she openly vents her personality against the most noted female abolitionist of her day – "I wished [my book] to be a history of my life" – she also struggles with an epistolary correspondence involving herself, Post, Stowe, and Mrs. Willis that dissipates the "my" of her personality into an almost impersonal spectre. When Post writes to Stowe of, among other issues, Jacobs's "extraordinary event" in her grandmother's garret, Stowe neither consults Jacobs about the veracity of the incarceration nor condenses her inquiry into a brief, nuanced letter to Mrs. Willis. Instead, Stowe forwards Post's entire account to Mrs. Willis for confirmation. As Jacobs laments, Post's letter includes touchy facts about Jacobs's white lover and illegitimate "Children," a sexual past about which Jacobs has kept her employer demurely uninformed.

Stowe's decision to send Post's letter within her own letter to Cornelia Willis resituates Jacobs and her "Children" on the scaffold of exposure. By sending Post's letter, Stowe precipitately unveils the embarrassments of Jacobs's early history to Mrs. Willis and thus purloins Jacobs's own agency to voice its content and explain its rightful context. Moreover, Stowe would reduce the contingencies of slave-experience into one dramatic entry out of numerous other entries in her *Key* and isolate it from the myriad choices and motives of Jacobs's experience. The placement of the spectacle of Jacobs's garret ordeal amid other spectacles simultaneously dilutes the import of Jacobs's trauma and forces it to compete in the *Key* with other entries of factual chattel pain. Jacobs will appease Stowe, she insists, with pertinent biographical "facts," but resents the Gothic narrowing of African American suffering into one seemingly baroque, seven-year "romance."

Despite its frontal attack on an abolitionist diva, however, Jacobs's righteous black aggression succumbs to a tendency to undermine her own centrality as aggrieved party. The letter proceeds nervously through a series of deflections. These displace attention not merely away from Jacobs as a fit witness to Stowe of her own victimization, but also from her role as an acknowledged correspondent of any kind. Stowe first displaces Jacobs's voice by transmitting such incidents, twice-removed, through Post's letter enclosed within her own letter. Next, even when complaining about the betrayal, Jacobs must shade her own ego into that of another's: "we [Mrs. Willis and Jacobs] thought it was wrong in Mrs [*sic*] Stowe to have sent you[r] letter she might have written to enquire if she liked" (235). Jacobs is, of course, keen on preserving Cornelia Willis's sensibilities and her own integrity before her employer. But the "we" also suggests that the female slave cannot express her sense of wrong apart from that of her white employer's; and the black woman's role as direct object is here mystified by the syntactic space after "enquire." Is it, one wonders, Mrs. Willis or Jacobs herself who should have been consulted?

The lacunae in this letter partially account for its confusion. In addition, Jacobs's letter to Post stresses Stowe's refusal to respond to Mrs. Willis's written entreaties – that the novelist not use the "extraordinary" entry – more than to the letters Jacobs herself sends: "she [Mrs. Willis] wrote again and I wrote twice with no better success it was not Lady like to treat Mrs Willis so she would not have done it to any one" (235). While the correspondent disparages the "[un]Lady like" treatment bequeathed her mistress, she seems to exile herself from the prerogatives of "Lady." Ultimately, Jacobs is generalized into the "any one" Mrs. Willis's gentilesse would embrace. Such tactical blocks might well be intended not to offend a prized white champion – Amy Post. Would roundly asserting the depth of her own wound make Jacobs's resentment of the legendary Stowe seem like indecorous black overreaching?

The anger muted and exposed here is also displaced onto Jacobs's daughter, whom Stowe has refused to take to England as a representative slave girl: Stowe "was afraid that if her [Louisa's] situation as a Slave should be known it would subject her to much petting and patronizing which would be more pleasing to a young Girl than useful" (235). Jacobs's allusion to Louisa is certainly a wincing repudiation of the racist politics behind Stowe's rejection of Jacobs's literate and restrained daughter; yet the knot between mother and daughter cannot be severed so tidily. In a letter seemingly written after April 4th that year, Jacobs tightens the association: "think dear Amy that a visit to Stafford House would spoil me as Mrs [*sic*] Stowe thinks petting is more than my race can bear well what a pity we poor blacks cant [*sic*] have the firmness and stability of character that you white people have (Spring [1853?] IAPFP #80, BAP 16: 0707, quoted by Yellin, xix). Stowe, Jacobs surmises in the case of Louisa *and* her mother, cannot shake the darkie stereotype of a child petted, through British attentiveness, into a cooing depravity. And "you white people," if only a playful irony vented to a friend, suggests that the good Post remains one of the "you." Jacobs's sporadic apprehensions about letters that Post leaves unanswered may also highlight a possible sensitivity to the racial inequities in their relationship.

V.   White Certificates of Black Merit

After thwarted endeavors to market her work, the firm Thayer and Eldridge agrees to publish Jacobs's manuscript if it is prefaced by Lydia Maria Child.[8] Abolitionist William Nell introduces Jacobs to this premiere abolitionist in 1860. In order to reinforce Child's validation of *Incidents*, Amy Post and George Lowther are solicited for the "Appendix." The bordering certifications by

two ardent females are eyecatching primarily for a certain deviation from the
ex-slave's assumptions in the main text about the relation between personality and facade. Just as Jacobs's life must be interpreted in terms of the competing perspectives of black and white females, so the text is forced to be as-
sessed according to the official marginalia of these two white supporters.
Post's brief note in the Appendix attests that Jacobs's "deportment indicated
remarkable delicacy of feeling and purity of thought" (203). In her "Introduction," Child promotes a similar equation between a seemly facade and candor. As Child defines it, sentiment is a nexus of comely gestures that are the
extension of the dignified character behind it. Like Post, she thus confirms
Jacobs's virtue by cushioning it in polite forms:

> THE AUTHOR of the following autobiography is personally known
> to me, and her conversation and manners inspire me with confidence.
> During the last seventeen years, she has lived the greater part of the
> time with a distinguished family in New York, and has so deported her-
> self as to be highly esteemed by them. (3)

The fit between decorum and honor here is a chafing one, for this is the identification that Jacobs's narrative repeatedly questions, about slavery's decep-
tions and its racist correlatives in the North. Child situates Jacobs's virtue on
the placid surface – in her restrained bearing, the caste of the white family she
attends, and a fragile conformity to manners that seal her membership in an
"elect" sentimental coterie, the Northern female audience. But in Jacobs's
account of her shock at the benevolent Mistress Horniblow's codicil, her
master Norcom's manipulation of surfaces, his fraudulent role as the community's Christian healer, Mistress Norcom's wistful sadism, or Stowe's silence to Jacobs's letters, the notion of decorum is detached from "candor."
The semblance of virtue Child endorses is made, in Jacobs's narrative and
letters, interchangeable with dissemblance. Child expresses Jacobs's credibility through a lexicon – "conversation," "manners," deportment, esteem –
that fixes character in the estimate of the beholder,[9] yet it is precisely this
histrionic etiquette of beholder and beheld – of seeing, appearing, constru-
ing, "posing" – that Jacobs's *Incidents* takes to task.

This transparent correspondence between essential selfhood and polite
surfaces is a telling one; for it points to the tenuous relation between the sentimental itinerary – of manners and deportment – and personality, and thus
to a *vexed* collaboration between the white reader and the black sexual victim
we have seen throughout. Child suggests this confusion when she first guar-
antees Jacobs's honesty through suggestions of her decorum, but later admits that the lot of the female slave compromises it: "I am well aware that
many will accuse me of indecorum for presenting these pages to the public"
(3). Child alternates between an apprehension that she will alienate her delicate "public" readers and pity for the typical slave girl whose delicacy has

been savagely debased. "I do this," Child notes, "for the sake of my sisters in bondage, who are suffering wrongs so foul, that our ears are too delicate to listen to them" (4). Valerie Smith notes, "Child's sentence rather awkwardly imposes the reader in the precise grammatical location where the slave woman ought to be" (40). Child suggests that the individual white woman – whom Jacobs, to various degrees, has revered and critiqued, bonded with and been bound to – has now expanded into a problematic delicate white readership for the author. Thus, even in publication, the tension between black writer and white reader refigures that of subordinate and mistress. Polemical rhetoric from a female ex-slave entails its own protocol.

V.   African American Authors and Modern Editors

To be sure, Jacobs's drive to appropriate her own text, though edited by Child, is partially fulfilled in her purchase of the book's stereotyped plates for its publication in 1861 and in wresting her narrative from female authors like Stowe, who would filter her own story through their voices. The tension between the dejected Jacobs and Mistress Horniblow or Stowe, however, does not vanish through time. Instead, as my friend and coeditor, Rafia Zafar, suggests in her introduction, the dynamic between African American and white academics continues to haunt the present scholarly revisiting of *Incidents*. As contemporary critics and editors, one African American, the other white, of this volume, Rafia Zafar and I are the hesitant heirs of the collaboration that underwrote Jacobs's life. Especially sensitive to our position as contemporary Lydia Childs, a role that seemed more fitting in its coloration for me, we convened in issues of selection, interpretation, and suppositions about contributors and their audience. As a second issue, however, we also confronted the problem latent in our own racial dynamic – one that characterized the relationship between Jacobs and her female mentors, between the author and her reading public. Like Zafar, I do not imagine a scholarly habitat in which the strain between black and white scholar will not continue with some of the rancor and charged sensitivity it caused in Jacobs's life, in the pain of its inscription, and in her book's rocky reception history. We both agree that this vital text will forever both unite and alienate the black and white academics who promote, interpret, and teach it.

To what degree, however, can such races exchange views, collaborate, and ease the critical vexation shadowing *Incidents*? Many of the African American scholars I have encountered and read understandably maintain that a premiere work arduously produced by a female ex-slave has been overrun and swamped by the sheer number of white academic women analyzing it. As propitious as this event is for Jacobs and the advertisement of African American letters, is our response to Jacobs not somewhat of an appropriation? How can we make it less so? As Jacobs appears on the syllabi of courses ranging from avowedly African American ones to more general classes in women's studies and "world literature," one can only hope for a potentially healthy reversal: The dynamic between privileged white mentor and black supplicant that marked Jacobs's relations might now be replaced by that between African American specialists and the non–African American critics who learn from them. Scholars unfamiliar with Jacobs would thus rely on those intricately versed in the historical milieu *and* in the African American critical tradition, on scholars who can help them to reconstruct a context for understanding an author who is so frequently treated as an isolated identity, apart from the slave community she valued, the abolitionist circle she exuberantly joined, or the welter of academic articles and books about her. The network of scholars Rafia Zafar has compiled in her introduction provides an indispensable sense of just how lush the critical commentary is.

One complaint voiced by some of the prized contributors of this volume was that Jacobs gets too systematically caught in a pedagogical or hermeneutic vacuum. They asked that in the midst of generating essays about Jacobs, scholars in other disciplines take the time to place her in the context which a female, African American autobiography demands, that those not thoroughly schooled in African American letters attend to the accumulating essays on Jacobs: to the customs and pressures dictating her authorial strategy; the works in the abolitionist library she tapped to form her narrative; the political assertions that both make her work unique and place it in dialogue with the voices of male ex-slaves, of other black *female* abolitionists, and of white liberationists appearing in this volume – Lydia Child, Henry Thoreau, Amy Post, and others. Hawthorne's Miles Coverdale seemed to be describing our endeavor when he warned that "if we . . . put a friend under our microscope, we thereby insulate him from many of his true relations, magnify his peculiarities, and inevitably tear him into parts, and, of course, patch him very clumsily together again."[10] In the case of Jacobs – or her pseudonym Linda Brent – we risk making monstrous the woman whose complex humanity we mean to revere.

After perusing numerous syllabi of "Western literature" or "world literature" courses, I found Jacobs often following Voltaire, Goethe, Mary Shelley, and others on the list. Just as the inquiring students in such courses erroneously assumed that Sappho's work appeared in fragments because she was an unpolished female poet, so they also made simply comparative judgments about Jacobs that dislodged her from the complex maneuvers characterizing African American narratives in general and one by a woman in particular. As the name Harriet Jacobs makes its entree into varying academic arenas, we can rely on the rich canon of African American scholarship to save her from being sequestered in an academic garret recalling the crawlspace of her imprisonment.[11]

Working with the coeditor and contributors to this project has convinced me of the imperative of adopting, however imperfectly, an aesthetics of humility and hesitation. As readers perused the coded text and letters, the sense of remaining an alien in the dark orbit of slavery and the ambiguities of its inscription fostered a relation to the narrative that can best be described as eager but respectfully speculative. As almost all the contributors suggest in their work, this is no transparent autobiography, and its very hieroglyphics prevent the ease of closure or even the imperative helmsmanship Child exudes as she issues directions about publication: "I want you to sign the following paper, and send it back to me" (246: Child to Harriet Jacobs; Wayland [Massachusetts], Sep 27th, 1860). This is the same Child who, however revolutionary in her political tracts and in her mulatta tales, fails in her "Introduction" to *Incidents* to clarify the sexual menace she labels heinous. Although she bears "the responsibility of presenting . . . the veil withdrawn" (4), the sexual account is shifted to the ex-slave, who must bear the burden of transmitting servitude's "peculiar" transgressions. Perhaps the reader relatively new to Jacobs scholarship should stop short of proclaiming that she has lifted *the veil*. As we read this extraordinary account, might we couch our readings in a humility acknowledging the precarious hypotheses, the heuristic uncertainty, involved in all literary and historical criticism, particularly when race, gender, and a limitation of biographical knowledge complicate our mission? Facing a confusing text, we must expose our own confusions and let them form our meeting place.

Notes

I would like to extend my lionhearted thanks to colleagues at UCLA – smiling cowboy Blake Allmendinger, Valerie Smith, Richard Yarborough, and Eric Sundquist – for their kind help in suggesting contributors; my coeditor, Rafia Zafar, for bravely agreeing to join the project; the patient contributors themselves, including the emerging dynama Jacqueline Goldsby, a loyal Sandra Gunning, John Ernest (who never betrays his last name), and the sane and self-effacing Anne Warner, all of whom sparked warm and generous discussions about Jacobs and her contemporaries; to dedicated editors Julie Greenblatt and Susie Chang; Jean Yellin and Frances Foster, for remaining with the project in its early and precarious stages and for offering gems of advice from their own profound experience. Thanks, too, to Alan Howard and Deborah McDowell, for eagle-eyed criticism during the awkward genesis of these ideas. Gratitude to Robert E. Bjork, whose Viking fortitude permitted him to wander, unaware but determined, into African American studies with me.

1. Please see the biographical "Introduction" in Jean Fagan Yellin's *Incidents in the Life of a Slave Girl: Written by Herself*, ed. Jean Fagan Yellin (Cambridge: Harvard University Press, 1987), xiii–xxxiv. All quotations from this standard edition will be included in parentheses within the text of this conclusion. Yellin is currently completing a biography on Jacobs that adds new material about Jacobs's earlier life and about her experiences postdating 1861, the publication date of *Incidents*. In it Yellin will deal, among other issues, with the power Jacobs exerted as a

well-known personage in philanthropic endeavors during and after the Civil War.

2. See the adept analysis of the double-voiced Equiano and its enactment of the gulf between childhood and maturity in *The Life of Olaudah Equiano or Gustavus Vassa the African*, intro. Paul Edwards (London: Dawsons of Pall Mall, 1969), lxvii–lxix, and in Henry Louis Gates, Jr., *The Signifying Monkey: A Theory of African-American Literary Criticism* (New York: Oxford University Press, 1988), 154–7.

3. See the explanation of Margaret Horniblow's "Deathbed codicil" in "Illustrations" in *Incidents*.

4. This topic is comprehensively discussed in Eric Sundquist's *To Wake the Nations: Race in the Making of American Literature* (Cambridge and London: Belknap Press of Harvard University Press, 1993).

5. Hazel Carby addresses the diverse conflicts between Jacobs and her white mistresses and benefactresses, and between African American and white female figures in other works. Please see *Reconstructing Womanhood: The Emergence of the Afro-American Woman Novelist* (Oxford: Oxford University Press, 1987). Dana D. Nelson also confronts the paradoxes that Jacobs and other African Americans find in associations with white mentors and readers. See the indispensable *The Word in Black and White: Reading "Race" in American Literature, 1638–1867* (New York and Oxford: Oxford University Press, 1992).

6. Many thanks to Sander L. Gilman and Ann duCille for their canny analyses of "black bodies" and the ways they are articulated in various art forms. Gilman, "Black Bodies, White Bodies: Toward an Iconography of Female Sexuality in Late Nineteenth-Century Art, Medicine, and Literature," in *"Race," Writing and Difference*, ed. Henry Louis Gates, Jr. (Chicago: Chicago University Press, 1986); duCille, "Blue Notes on Black Sexuality: Sex and the Texts of Jessie Fauset and Nella Larsen," *Journal of the History of Sexuality* 3:3 (1993): 418–44. Please see other essays in the *Jacobs* volume, including my own, for a more expansive bibliography about this topic.

7. Foreman's essay in this volume offers a more in-depth speculation about Willis and his role in *Incidents*.

8. After Thayer and Eldridge go bankrupt, Jacobs purchases the stereotyped plates of the narrative and, in a gesture befitting her autonomy, directs a printer in Boston to publish it "for the author." The Introduction and Appendix remain intact, however, as part of the "author['s]" text.

9. The immediate insight into another's moral nature by a "pure" observer is a feature of much sentimental narrative, fictional and biographical. Clara Wieland instantaneously intuits the sinister intentions of the wandering artist Carwin in Charles Brockden Brown's *Wieland*. In Stowe's *Dred*, Nina Gordon detects Jekyl's corruption in his contorted "face," while Stowe herself, exercising Nina's instinct for equating character and physical appearance, connects Dred's heroism to the contours of his herculean body. William Lloyd Garrison does no less for Frederick Douglass in his introduction to the 1845 *Narrative*. He deems Douglass, even in servitude, "godlike," a man whose "physical proportion and stature" was in keeping with an "intellect richly endowed" (4). One might argue that the somewhat unsentimental language of much of Douglass's narrative is an attempt to counter

such notions of godhood, to make himself seem more representative of, not a heroic exception to, the average slave's life.

10. Nathaniel Hawthorne, *The Blithedale Romance,* ed. Arlin Turner (New York: W. W. Norton, 1958), 91.

11. Such African Americanists, needless to say, include distinguished white scholars as well – among them, Jean Fagan Yellin, the most well-known sleuth of Jacobs's life and work. Yet for years, as her generous notes to this volume attest, Yellin has immersed herself in a circle of, among other scholars, female African American cohorts, and in a rigorous study of abolitionism from the vantage points of black, as well as white participants.

CONTRIBUTORS

John Ernest is assistant professor of English at the University of New Hampshire. His essays have appeared in *American Literature, American Literary History, PMLA,* and other journals. His essay in this volume is drawn from a longer study, *Resistance and Reformation in Nineteenth-Century African-American Literature: Brown, Wilson, Jacobs, Delany, Douglass, and Harper* (University Press of Mississippi, 1995).

P. Gabrielle Foreman is an assistant professor at Occidental College. She works on race and sentimentality in the nineteenth century and has published in *Representations, Black American Literature Forum, Feminist Studies,* and other journals. She is currently revising a manuscript entitled *Sentimental Subversions: Reading Race and Nineteenth Century America.*

Frances Smith Foster, Professor of English and Women's Studies at Emory University, has published extensively on African American and women's literature. Her most recent publications include *Written by Herself: Literary Production by African American Women, 1746–1892* (Indiana University Press, 1993) and *Minnie's Sacrifice, Sowing and Reaping, Trial and Triumph: Three Rediscovered Novels by Frances E. W. Harper* (Beacon, 1994).

Deborah M. Garfield, assistant professor in English and American Studies at UCLA, has published articles on Dreiser, Faulkner, Jacobs, and abolitionism in journals such as *Arizona Quarterly* and on melodrama for the volume *A Woman's Conscience* (Sorbonne Press). She is currently working on two books: *Sentimental Rage: Women, Subversion and American Narrative* and *EMPATHY: The Exchange of Souls in American Culture.*

293

Donald B. Gibson is Professor of American Literature at Rutgers University. He has authored and edited several books, among them *The Fiction of Stephen Crane* (1968), *Five Black Writers* (1970), *The Politics of Literary Expression: Essays on Major Black Writers* (1981), and *The Red Badge of Courage: Redefining the Hero* (1988). His articles have appeared in *American Literature, American Quarterly, The African American Review, Yale Review,* and *Literature, Interpretation, Theory.* He is currently at work on a book about Booker T. Washington.

Anita Goldman is an assistant professor of English and African American Studies at the University of Illinois at Chicago. An essay, "Negotiating Claims of Race and Rights: Du Bois, Emerson, and the Critique of Liberal Nationalism" appeared in *The Massachusetts Review,* and another essay on the problematics of exile and political identity appears in *Borders, Boundaries and Frames,* ed. Mae Henderson (New York: Routledge Press, 1994). Professor Goldman's book, *From Emerson to King: Democracy, Race, and the Politics of Protest,* is forthcoming, and she is currently at work on a second book that explores the development of black revolutionary poetry and political philosophy in the Caribbean, the United States, and South Africa.

Jacqueline Goldsby is a doctoral candidate in American Studies at Yale University. She is completing her dissertation, which is a study of lynching and realist representation at the turn of the nineteenth century.

Sandra Gunning is an assistant professor of English at the University of Michigan, at Ann Arbor. She teaches American and African American literature, and her book *Writing a Red Record: Gender, Representation and Racial Violence in American Literature, 1890–1912* is forthcoming from Oxford University Press.

Stephanie A. Smith is assistant professor of English at the University of Florida and author of *Conceived by Liberty: Maternal Figures and Nineteenth-Century American Literature* (Cornell, 1994). Her essays have appeared in *American Literature, Criticism,* and *Genders,* and her work includes three novels, the latest of which, *A Love of Other Nature,* is forthcoming.

Mary Titus is associate professor of English at St. Olaf College. She has published articles on gender and race in Southern literature and is currently engaged in a study of race and material culture in late-nineteenth- and early-twentieth-century American literature.

Anne Bradford Warner is associate professor and Chair of the Department of English at Spelman College. She has published several articles on Jacobs and is currently working on a booklength project: Harriet Jacobs and the Rochester Circle.

Jean Fagan Yellin is a Distinguished Professor of English at Pace University and the editor of the standard edition of Harriet Jacobs's *Incidents in the Life of a*

Slave Girl (Harvard, 1987). Her recent books include *Women and Sisters: The Antislavery Feminists in American Culture* (Yale, 1989) and *The Abolitionist Sisterhood: Women's Political Culture in Antebellum America* (Cornell, 1994), which she coedited. She is currently completing a biography of Harriet Jacobs and editing the Jacobs Papers for publication.

Rafia Zafar is assistant professor of English and faculty associate, Center for Afroamerican and African Studies, University of Michigan. She previously coedited *God Made Man, Man Made the Slave: The Autobiography of George Teamoh* (Mercer University Press, 1992), and has contributed essays to *Frederick Douglass: New Literary and Historical Essays* and MELUS. Her study of antebellum black writers, *We Wear the Mask: Transcending the Text in Early African American Literature,* will be published by Columbia University Press.

INDEX

abolitionist movement, 134; in England, 20, 23, 37n20, 39n35; H. Jacobs and, 18, 47, 61, 62, 107, 122, 133, 200, 283, 288; rhetoric of, 19, 77, 100, 109, 112, 147, 188, 194, 200–1, 203, 208, 211, 212–13, 227, 254, 257, 260, 265; women and, 2, 100, 103–4, 106, 115, 150, 180, 187, 188, 261 (*see also* Anti-Slavery Convention of American Women); *see also* antislavery lectures; Garrisonians
Aggie, Aunt: in *Incidents* (slave), 50
America: History and Life, 4–5
American Anti-Slavery Society, 16, 18, 36n12, 46, 100, 103
Andrews, William L., 5, 35n8, 85, 129n56, 217; on black autobiography, 86, 220; on Douglass, 158–9; on *Incidents,* 14, 93n3, 221, 223, 255, 256
Anti-Slavery Advocate, 23
Anti-Slavery Convention of American Women, 179, 195n1
antislavery lectures: audience response to, 16–17, 30, 37n20, 46, 61, 77, 100–2, 103, 124n9, 125n21, 126n22, 131–2; black speakers for, 16–17, 19, 36n12, 37n18, 45–6, 60, 77, 100, 101, 103, 104, 124n7, 125n21, 126n22, 131, 132; and distinction between "lecturers" and "narrators," 37n18; H. Jacobs and, 18, 122; sexual content of, 101–2,

103, 104, 126n30, 131–2; and use of questionnaires, 17, 19, 36n16, 101, 123n3, 130n61; white speakers for, 16, 36n12, 45, 101, 102, 103–4, 124n12
Antislavery Reporter, 20, 39n35
apprentice system, 265, 273n44
Arendt, Hannah, 238, 242, 243
autobiography, 34, 64, 76, 77, 86, 128n44, 173, 220; *see also* slave narrative

Bacon, Leonard, 102, 125n13
Baker Jr., Houston A., 79, 90, 98n53
Bakhtin, Mikhail, 217, 219, 220
Banta, Martha, 200, 202, 205–6
Benjamin, Uncle: in *Incidents, see* Horniblow, Joseph
Betty: in *Incidents* (slave), 167, 220, 264, 278–9
Bibb, Henry, 53, 101
Bible, 71, 157; as used by H. Jacobs, 72, 110, 116, 186, 220, 221, 226–7
Birney, James Gillespie, 125n13
Blassingame, John, 9n11, 12–13, 15, 17, 271n12
Blount, Martha Hoskins Rombough, 278–9, 280
Braxton, Joanne M., 5, 73n8, 180, 196n8, 221, 223, 224
Brent, Benjamin (Benny): in *Incidents, see* Jacobs, Joseph

297

CAMBRIDGE STUDIES IN AMERICAN LITERATURE AND CULTURE
Continued from the front of the book